Crossing Sexual Boundaries

Crossing Sexual Boundaries

Transgender Journeys, Uncharted Paths

Edited by J. Ari Kane-DeMaios, EdD, and

Vern L. Bullough, PhD, DSci, RN

 **Prometheus Books**

59 John Glenn Drive
Amherst, New York 14228-2197

Published 2006 by Prometheus Books

Inquiries should be addressed to
Prometheus Books
59 John Glenn Drive
Amherst, New York 14228–2197
VOICE: 716–691–0133, ext. 207
FAX: 716–564–2711
WWW.PROMETHEUSBOOKS.COM

10 09 08 07 06   5 4 3 2 1

Library of Congress Cataloging-in-Publication Data

Crossing sexual boundaries : transgender journeys, uncharted paths / edited by
J. Ari Kane-Demaios and Vern L. Bullough.
p. cm.
Includes bibliographical references and index.
ISBN 1–59102–388–2 (pbk. : alk. paper)
1. Transsexuals—Biography. 2. Transsexualism. 3. Gender identity.
I. Kane-Demaios, J. Ari. II. Bullough, Vern L.

HQ77.7.C76 2005
306.76'8'0922—dc22

2005024026

Printed in the United States of America on acid-free paper.

To Bonnie Bullough, Norma M. Baldani-DeMaios,
Gwen Brewer, Sonja M. Smith, Jayne M. Thomas,
and Fannie Joypack

CONTENTS

APPENDIXES:

POEMS

Sonja Marie Smith

Sonja Marie Smith was a transgender pioneer who lived in the southwestern United States. She was an expert in skydiving, a counselor for adult children of alcoholic parents, and a poet. She donated a set of her collected poems to the Outreach Institute before she died. She signed her poems as S. Marie D. The thoughts express in a poetic way much of the same feelings that the autobiographies of the other contributors do.

Skydive at Sunset

Our jumpster calls
O'er the engine's roral,
check your gear
line up in the door.
The earth is distant
two miles below.
My heart quickens and it's
Ready-Set-Go

Like human bombs
we dive into space
We'll all join hands
with speed and
with grace.

Our tribute to sunset
has now begun.
The formation is building,
yet missing just one.

My place is vacant
for I'm far beneath.
I cry to the sky gods
in frustration and grief—
I've fallen and I can't Get UP!

First Session

With apprehension and anticipation
We began.

Humor masked the pain,
glib tongue held forgotten
terror at bay.
My heart newly wounded,
still bleeding.
She took my hands and
listened, just listened.
Her gaze pierced the
facade.

A volcano full of hurt
welled up and hot lava of
rage poured out from
deep within my being.

Her arms embraced my naked
soul, long ago abused and
never nurtured. My body
erupted into weeping.

The tears hiss with
the lava-causing steam
shattering the glass wall
of Phantom fear on
its journey.

The lava, cooled by the
flood of tears, starts
forming an island of
strength in the ocean
of chaos.

Through the steam and
acid smoke a small
child appears—

INTRODUCTION

The crossing of gender and sexual barriers is a staple of mythology as well as history since there have been cross-dressing individuals almost from the beginning of written history (Bullough and Bullough 1993). It was not until the nineteenth century, however, that "experts" began to form a vocabulary to describe such practices. The pioneer was Magnus Hirschfeld, who, using the Latin term for cross-dressing, *transvestism*, wrote the first significant study on the topic (Hirschfeld 1991 [1910]). Unfortunately, it was not until the 1990s that it was translated into English, and many of those who cited the work either did not read it or ignored what he said. More widely read in English was Havelock Ellis (1928), who criticized the term *transvestism* since it tended to put the emphasis simply on clothing rather than psychic elements involved. Ellis used the term *eonism*, but it did not catch on, in part because of the ambiguity associated with the Chevalier d'Eon and in part because of the more comprehensive discussion by Hirschfeld. Moreover, Hirschfeld, in spite of the term, included psychic elements. Even in Hirschfeld's time, a new kind of "transvestite" had appeared on the scene, the *transsexual*—an individual who through medical intervention actually tried to change his sex. The more researchers explored, the greater the number of "varieties" they found. Hirschfeld had started with the male heterosexual cross-dresser, added the transsexual, knew and studied female impersonators, and he himself was a gay queen. Some "transvestites" were simply content to wear women's underclothes or be a closet cross-dresser who never ventured into public. Is this because the underclothes satisfied a fetishistic desire or were they simply fearful to go further and had not the opportunity to do so? Is the occasional cross-dresser who appears at Halloween or Mardi Gras different from those who regularly cross-dress and appear in public? Is it essential to cross-dress to express what Virginia Prince, the American founder of the post–World War II movement of transvestism, called the *woman within*, or can it be expressed in other ways? Is a male homosexual cross-dresser different from a heterosexual one? Is a transvestite simply a cross-dresser wanting to be a transsexual but fearful of such a radical change? Are women who prefer to wear men's style clothing including male flaps on their underpants cross-dressers, or is it only men who cross the gender boundaries? Is such a woman a switch on Virginia Prince's terms, expressing the *male within*? Is a female impersonator a transvestite or simply a person who has found a way to earn a living? The answer to all the above is both yes and no. Since terms like transvestite or transsexual seemed unable to describe the varied forms, a new term, *transgenderism*—coined, I believe, by Virginia Prince and Ariadne Kane—was applied to cover the diverse forms of gender expression. Included in this term in its broadest sense are individuals who identify as "butch" or masculine lesbians, "fairies" or "queens" or effeminate gay men, heterosexual cross-dressers, those who seek surgical options to change sex or enhance their ability *to pass* better but still maintain their original sex, and those who have surgery to change their sex organs and body form and adopt a new sexual identity. Some would also include intersex individuals in this category—that is, those born with ambiguous genitalia who adopt a sexual identity not always congruent with their chromosomal sex. Categories can be fairly fluid. A male cross-dresser who has been juggling a dual identity as a man and part-time woman might decide to live permanently as a woman without any surgery. A male-to-female (MTF) after genital reconstruction surgery might become a lesbian and live with another woman. Some MTFs might become prostitutes. A female-to-male (FTM) might live with another male. The term transgender, in short, has become a convenient umbrella term to cover a collectivity of individuals who do not conform to traditionally accepted norms of gender identity or behavior (see appendix 2B). The very use of the term indicates just how much the field of research into nonconforming gender behavior has exploded. One way to view the complexity of transgender behavior is through personal autobiographies of those who are living a transgendered life—occasionally, permanently, with or without surgical intervention.

In this book we concentrate on two major categories—cross-dressers (CD) and transsexuals (TS). Though, as indicated, cross-dressing and impersonation of the opposite gender have been a staple of myth and even of actual history, achieving a new gender identity for a long period of time was very difficult in the past, particularly for males, in terms of both biology and social acceptance. Most of the historical trans-gendered people we have a lot of information about were women, including a number of Christian saints who were only discovered to be females after their deaths. Women, in fact, had more motive to pass as men since taking on a masculine identity gave them freedom, status, and a variety of other benefits, including somewhat greater security if they ventured into the world of men (Bullough 1974; Bullough and Bullough 1993). Many of those women who passed were found to be females only after they had died.

Women could at first be a beardless youth, and then, when this became more difficult, smudge a five o'clock shadow on their faces or wear false beards. Male impersonators became soldiers, sailors, sometimes lords or nobles, physicians, or what have you. In fact, up to the twentieth century, women fighting as men appeared in almost every army, and it was only when preinduction physicals began to be given in the twentieth century that their numbers declined. Still, even in World War I, a number of women, particularly in Russia, fought as men. On the other hand, beards, at least for most Western males, posed an almost insurmountable difficulty for most males wanting *to pass* as a woman except behind heavy veils. While the young of both sexes could pass rather easily in real life, it was much easier for an adult female to pass as a young man than for an adult male to pass as a woman for any length of time. Even the Abbé de Choisy, who lived at the time of Louis XIV in France and whose memoirs of his life as a woman have survived, found that as he aged he could no longer venture into public as he once did without being read. The actresses in Shakespeare's plays were almost all young men who, as they aged, went on to play male parts. Still, men of almost any age could vent their cross-dressing urges by doing a burlesque presentation of women. Everyone knew, however, that it was a man imitating a woman, and it was how effective in his impersonation he was that mattered, which was judged by others, not that he was a man. A real-life attempt at changing gender roles by men was much less acceptable, probably because the dominant masculine society had difficulty in understanding why a man might want to be a woman.

It was developments in medicine, surgery as well as technology, that really made it possible for persons to do more than pass by anatomically changing or modifying their sex enough to become the opposite sex. Two developments in surgery played a significant role, namely, the development of anesthesia and the introduction of aseptic techniques. Both of these occurred at the end of the nineteenth century, and in the early twentieth century surgeons were busy modifying the human body, including removal of the penis or breasts, without too many complications. What made it realistic, however, was the discovery and isolation of hormones in the 1920s and 1930s and the ability to artificially produce them. Hormones could at least initiate sex changes without surgery as Christine Jorgensen, the headline-grabbing transsexual of the 1950s, found out before she went to Denmark. She was even able to fool the physicians about some of the ambiguities of her own body brought about by her hormone intake (Bullough and Bullough 1993). There was still another development that cannot be overlooked, namely, the development of electrolysis for the removal of unwanted hair. Though depilation by tweezers or similar devices is possible for many peoples whose facial hair is not very thick, for many Indo-European males this was an almost impossible task until electrolysis was developed in the middle of the twentieth century. While the end result of using all these innovations led to transsexualism becoming a reality, selective use of some them made it easier for cross-dressers *to pass*.

There was considerable experimentation with gender enhancing or even sex changes in the first half of the twentieth century. Eugen Steinach (1940), for example, began experimenting with the sexual effects of the removal of the "generative" organs in animals beginning in 1910. He reported the feminizing effect on males and the masculinizing effect on females. One result of this was his belief that male potency could be restored through transplantation of testicular tissue in animals. Though he was unsuccessful in his transplants in humans, he came to believe that one reason for potency decline in males was due to the wasting of their semen. He felt that if semen could be diverted before ejaculation, it could build up and strengthen the individual, and so he advocated the ligation of the male vas (vasectomy) to do so. Though his physiology was wrong, since instead of flowing back into the body the semen is secreted in the urine, he initially reported great success with his surgery, undoubtedly owing to the placebo effect. Though Steinach operated more or less within the accepted boundaries of organized medicine, his American followers, where medical practice was then not as controlled as it was in Europe, saw opportunities to get rich. One of the more "infamous" was John R. Brinkley, popularly know as "Goat Gland Brinkley," who advertised widely on his ability to restore potency by transferring goat testicles into men who felt a need for reinvigorating their aging selves (Carson 1960).

The net effect of this among "respectable" medical practitioners was to make them very cautious in dealing with any sexual issue. Only a handful dared to explore further, including Magnus Hirschfeld and Harry Benjamin—both of whom came to be regarded as out of the medical mainstream. Probably the first person to undergo genital transformation from male to female was Dorchen Richter, who under the supervision of Magnus Hirschfeld was castrated in 1922 and began passing as a woman, although it was not until 1931 that he had his penis removed and a vagina surgically constructed (Meyerowitz 2002). She might well have been an intersex person, but not enough details survive. Probably the best-known early case was that of Lilli Elbe (Einar Wegener), who underwent a series of operations, including castration, penectomy, and ovary transplants, and had her sex officially changed in the late 1920s. She died in 1931 either during or shortly after a final operation in which a vagina was being constructed for her (Hoyer 1933). Though the Elbe case received considerable publicity, it appeared to be forgotten fairly soon, probably because of her death. In any case, the German experiments ended with the destruction of the Hirschfeld Institute in 1933 by the Nazis.

It was the would-be transsexuals about whom we know much more than about cross-dressers, although there were many individuals, primarily females, whose true sex was only discovered after their deaths. Still, cross-dressers of a sort could be found everywhere. Female impersonation was a standard of the Vaudeville circuit, and it carried over into many of the early films. Julian Eltinge, for example, was a major star and had a theater in New York named after him/her. Though female impersonation continued to arouse public interest, there was little scholarly interest in it, and few imagined that there were a lot of secret cross-dressers out there.

The realm of possibilities of changing or modifying gender (secondary sexual) characteristics expanded drastically with the discovery of hormones. In 1929 a female hormone then called estrone was isolated. This was followed by the discovery of estriol, and the two were classed together shortly afterward as estrogen. Progesterone was isolated and described in 1934. Testosterone was isolated by a Dutch team in 1935. It took many years to develop these hormones synthetically, and at first they were very costly to produce. By the 1940s, however, injectable forms of some hormones had been developed. What in a sense was needed was a human guinea pig, and the human experiment that caught the public eye was the case of Christine Jorgensen. Just how confusing the whole situation was at that time is indicated by the fact that the physician involved in the case called Jorgensen a *transvestite* in his official account of the case (Hamburger, Sturup, and Dahl-Iverson 1953). His treatment of Jorgensen was in part surgical—castration and a penectomy—but the important thing was the massive hormonal treatment.

Before going to Denmark, Jorgensen had been injecting herself with estrogen to bring about physiological changes, and after Hamburger and his associates examined her, they decided to treat her with massive injections of estrogen, much larger than she had given herself. The large dosages changed the shape of Jorgensen's body to a more feminine contour, and her behavior, gait, and appearance also became more feminine. As her beard became sparser, electrolysis was used to remove the remaining hair. The one thing they did not do for her was to give her a vagina, a failure that was only later partially resolved—and not particularly satisfactorily. Yet, she looked and acted like a woman, something that took considerable practice, before she was satisfied enough to tell her story.

When she leaked her story to the press in December 1951, she became a media sensation. She looked, talked, and acted like a real woman, not like a man trying to be a woman. She had clearly been a man before and had served in the US Army, so there was no question about her change. Seizing her opportunity, Jorgensen capitalized on her change by selling her story to journalists from the Hearst newspapers, and she used this as a basis for going on the stage. Much later, she also wrote her self-censored autobiography (Jorgensen 1967), and it probably will only be when Richard Docter finishes his biography of her that a much better understanding of her will emerge.

It is hard to underestimate the importance of Jorgensen to the transgender community. The immediate result was an outpouring of pleas of people to Dr. Hamburger to have him change their sex (Hamburger 1953), and so fearful was the Danish government that large numbers of people would flock to Denmark that they enacted a law denying such surgery to non-Danes. Other surgeons, however, saw an opportunity to help a large number of people and began to explore the possibilities of such surgery. Some who did so also saw such surgery as a way of making money.

What the Jorgensen case did, however, was to lead large numbers of people uncomfortable with their gender to see surgery as a means of solving their problems. The only immediate medical response to the *Journal of the American Medical Association* article on Christine was by two psychiatrists. One, G. H. Wiedeman, criticized Hamburger for not doing a more thorough psychological workup and for treating the patient with psychotherapy instead of surgery. He concluded his letter with a statement: "The difficulty of getting the patient into psychiatric treatment should not lead us to compliance with the patient's demands, which are based on his *sexual* perversion." A second psychiatrist, Mortimer Ostow, argued that the only thing that would have helped Jorgensen is not the surgery but "intensive, prolonged, classic psychotherapy" (Bullough and Bullough 1993, p. 256).

The question that the public had to face was not whether we as a society could do castrations and penectomies or ovariectomies and hysterectomies, but whether we should. The answer to such a question was important to all transgender individuals. Cutting off a male's penis and castrating him, or, in simple terms, creating a eunuch, had a long tradition. But the hormones made role reversal possible as well. Spaying or ovariectomies in female animals had been less common than castration but had existed for centuries, although not until the nineteenth century were ovariectomies known to have been performed on human females, originally as a treatment for ovarian cancer. Cancer had also been the motivating factor in initiating early breast removal.

There were two different issues involved in how to respond to transsexualism and transvestism. One was a turf war between the psychiatrists, who through what came to be called the *Diagnostic and Statistical Manual* were regarded as the medical experts in the field of sexology, and the surgical community. It was a surgical challenge and a psychiatric nightmare. Large segments of the psychiatric community still opposed such surgery. It was also a war within medicine itself about whether medical professionals should engage in what many regarded as "deliberate mutilation." Emerging as a leader on the pro-transsexual side in this was Dr. Harry Benjamin, who popularized the term transsexualism, a term he said he began using in the early 1950s, although the earliest use of the term was by Magnus Hirschfeld (Bullough 1993, p. 257). Benjamin regarded transsexuals as a third stage of transvestism (Benjamin 1966). But was it an inevitable stage? I think not, but might it be a possible stage?

One result of the controversy over transsexualism was to put transvestism into the background, and for a time even to ignore it. A disproportionate amount of scholarly and scientific attention was given to transsexuals. The same was true in the popular media. During the last few decades, the number of biographies or autobiographies of transsexuals has been several times that of transvestites. Though many transsexuals tried to escape into the woodwork, it was much harder for them to do so than the cross-dresser community. Transsexuals were totally dependent, for example, on the medical community for their existence. Their changing of sex on the job or elsewhere was a public matter. They could not easily avoid confronting the public with what they were. I think one of the long-term results was to raise confusion and uncertainty in the cross-dresser community about who and what they were.

Transsexuals also had to fight harder to move ahead. For a time, their one advantage was that they had more money available than the cross-dressers. This was because of Reed Erickson and the Erickson Educational Foundation that he established. Erickson, a female-to-male, supported many of those involved in the early phases of transsexual research, including Harry Benjamin, John Money, and myself. There were two major issues that had to be settled. A very serious problem from the point of view of many of the professionals who considered entering the field was the setting of standards, something seen by the would-be transsexuals as a deliberate effort to keep medical dominance in the field. While this had not been seen in quite this way by many of those working to set standards, in reality it was an effort to serve as gatekeepers. In their minds, such standard setting was essential in the United States, where the medical professionals involved could always be threatened by legal suits.

Moreover, the problem was never in reaching the would-be customer for surgical and hormonal transformation but in convincing medicine of the legitimacy of medical intervention. This was not easy, and supporters of transsexualism felt it was essential to get the major medical schools behind them by establishing centers or "clinics" for transsexuals. The first such gender identity clinic was established at Johns Hopkins, largely through the influence of John Money. Others quickly followed at Case Western Reserve University, at the University of Minnesota, at the University of Oregon, and at Stanford University. What in effect happened was the growth of a bureaucracy.

These clinics were important in the development of a better understanding of transsexualism and in putting together interdisciplinary teams of psychiatrists, psychologists, and surgeons to diagnose and treat transsexuals. They developed diagnostic criteria included in the third edition of the *Diagnostic and Statistical Manual* (1987). Unfortunately, the clinics themselves were matters of controversy within their respective universities. Even under the best of conditions, the university-based clinics came under criticism, not only from the medical faculty as at Johns Hopkins, but from their would-be clients. Dallas Denny, a male-to-female critic, claimed:

> The clinics viewed sex reassignment as a last-ditch effort to save those with whom other therapies and interventions had failed. Those who were accepted for treatment were usually prostitutes, those with substance abuse problems, sociopaths, those who were schizophrenics, those who were profoundly depressed or suicidal, and others who were considered "hopeless"— i.e., likely to die anyway. It was a classic misapplication of the triage method, with those most likely to benefit from the intervention being turned away, and the terminal cases receiving treatment. (Bullough 1993, p. 268)

If the medical schools were a problematic home for transsexuality, where were the would-be transsexuals to go? Several private surgeons were willing to do the surgery, but the problem of insurance for an independent practitioner in the United States and the desire to protect oneself from lawsuits by getting psychiatric clearances made it difficult. Inevitably, many of the surgeons willing to perform such surgery operated on the fringe of medicine, and it was often difficult for the anxious patient to distinguish between quacks and those who were legitimate, even those who held testimonials from successful cases. As coeditor of this book (Bullough), I have to confess I got involved in this issue during the 1960s and early 1970s when my wife and I worked closely with Zelda Suplee, the executive director of the Erickson Foundation, in sponsoring conferences on transsexualism and cross-dressing, mostly in the greater Los Angeles area, and in directing would-be transsexuals to those surgeons who might help them. One of the problems we had was in recruiting "qualified" surgeons since the foundation was besieged with requests. The problem was complicated by the fact that many of the would-be transsexuals were hostile to the university centers because so many had been rejected for surgery by them, in part because, as Dallas Denny said, the clinics often had stereotypical ideas of what kind of person the transsexual should be.

Unfortunately, those surgeons willing to charge ahead, in spite of all odds, were not necessarily the best ones to do the surgery. Let me illustrate with the case of John Leonard Brown, who Zelda Suplee, my wife Bonnie, and myself at least halfway encouraged to do transsexual surgery, a recommendation we quickly regretted. It soon became apparent that

Brown would operate on anyone who had money with no questions asked. For those who did not have the money, he offered them a discount for every patient they recruited, and if they recruited enough paying customers, he would operate on them without charging a fee. Since his reputation soon barred him from most hospitals, he turned to operating on kitchen tables under unsanitary, not just unsterile, conditions, often with little anesthetic. Fortunately, by 1977 he had lost his license to practice in California, but this did not stop him since we found he had lost his license in Hawaii before coming to California—and he soon lost licenses in Alaska and even in Santa Lucia. One time he let his business partner, not a physician, perform surgery. He eventually set up in Tijuana, Mexico, where any sexually related surgery a client requested was attempted. In 1998, after the death of a seventy-nine-year-old man who had hired Brown to amputate his leg to satisfy a sexual fetish, Brown was convicted of murder and sent to jail. Still, by his own count he had performed six hundred surgeries (Ciotti 1978; Ciotti 2000; Sondegar 1996), and many of his customers were satisfied with what he did.

Fortunately, other surgeons came forth, usually not in main population centers in the United States and even in third world countries. One of the more noted specialists was Dr. Georges Bourou in Casablanca, Morocco, who developed the technique of using inverted penile skin to form a vagina and the scrotum to form the labia in the male-to-female transsexual. With this development, the male-to-female surgery became doable and very realistic. Other surgeons followed, including Stanley Biber in Trinidad, Colorado, and a number of new ones have succeeded them. I think it is unlikely today that a Brown could do the number of surgeries he did without the transsexual network warning about him.

Despite all the attention given to transsexuals by the professional communities and the press and the booksellers, cross-dressing activity had been growing in numbers. If Christine Jorgensen was the key figure in transsexualism, then Virginia Prince was the queen mother of organized cross-dressing activity. As with transsexualism, this writer was also involved almost from the beginning. Virginia and I met soon after she began publishing *Transvestia*, when she and her wife came to our house for dinner early in 1960. Later we went to her house as well as to the second meeting of the Hose and Heels Club, an informal gathering of cross-dressers in the greater Los Angeles area. Perhaps because there was no need for the kind of medical intervention that the transsexual required, the cross-dresser movement grew by itself with Virginia and others acting as the Johnny Appleseeds, throwing off ideas, organizations, and hoping they would take root. Many of them did. Probably her most important concept was the idea of gender expression of the *girl/woman within*, which gave a somewhat larger picture of transgenderism than simply cross-dressing. She founded a movement where one did not exist before. At first, it was furtive and secretive. People gave only their first names. They received their magazines in plain wrappers sent out by a mailing service so no one would know. Virginia briefly got in trouble with the US Postal Service; the person she was fantasizing with through the mail turned out to be a postal inspector. Sentenced to three years in a federal penitentiary, her sentence was changed to five years' probation instead. She was told that if she was arrested again, the penitentiary would open up for her. Since cross-dressing in public was technically illegal in Los Angeles, at that time, Virginia was severely handicapped. Fortunately, she was allowed to give talks to service clubs, like the Kiwanis, Rotary, and others while cross-dressed, and the movement quickly moved forward. Shortly afterward most of the charges were dropped.

Gradually, cross-dressing came out of the closet, something that the transsexuals had been forced to do from the beginning. Fantasia Fair, which was started in Provincetown, Massachusetts, by Ariadne Kane (coeditor of this book), pioneered this new openness, but the need for security was still the first thought in the minds of most. Part of the difficulty was that most of the cross-dressers lived double lives, and they often had wives and children. They did not want to be exposed to the public. As the movement grew, a few came more into the public eye. Virginia herself, after her second divorce, which led to considerable publicity, started living full time as a woman. She, however, had a separate identity for this woman and never went back to her family name. Cross-dressing for her had become more than an occasional event; it was simply part of her lifestyle. She was now out in the public eye passing as a woman, but she was not out of the closet as a transvestite.

Virginia had a very definite idea of what transvestism was. Transvestites were heterosexuals. But as the movement grew, it soon became evident that there were many varieties. Other publishers of transvestite material and other groups appeared as well with different ideas. Never once in Virginia's publications, for example, did I see the term penis used, although I know it played a prominent part in the cross-dressing activities of many transgendered people. Some transgender groups welcomed both homosexual and heterosexual transvestites, while others, fearful of what their spouses might say or do, insisted on the definition of *heterosexual* transvestites. Some transgendered people went on to have a surgical change of sex. Others, not desiring to change their sex, merely wanted to change genders more or less permanently as Virginia had. In fact, Virginia was a main source of the popularization of gender as applied to cross-dressing. She and Ariadne popularized the term *transgender*, which has been a more encompassing term than cross-dresser. Transgender is more than cross-dressing, and, even among the orthodox transvestites—that is, heterosexual cross-dressers—there is much more involved than cross-dressing.

As gays and lesbians began to come out of the closet in the 1970s by proclaiming their sexual orientation and lifestyle, a few daring transgender people also did so. Actually, it was drag queens and butch lesbians who first rebelled at Stonewall Café in Greenwich Village in New York City. Interestingly, as the history of the gay movement is being written, writers are reluctant to give them credit for this rebellion. They were more willing to fight back with police than the semicloseted gay person because they had very little to lose. Drag queens were regularly being arrested for prostitution by the police who knew them well. The police were also very hostile toward butch lesbians. The cross-dressing movement ignored them as well.

The transvestite and transsexual movements led separate existences for many years without much communication between them. This has changed within the past fifteen years as the concept of transgender has gained ground. This coming together was symbolized in 1995 by the first International Conference on Cross-Dressing, Sex, and Gender, sponsored by the Center for Sex Research of California State University, Northridge, and took place in Southern California (see Bullough, Bullough, and Elias 1997). Here for the first time individuals from a variety of transgender communities met with a large contingent of professionals to share ideas and explore new frontiers—a concept that has become increasingly dominant in the "movement." Many of the presenters spoke of their experiences as transgenders, about the *gender shift* process, genital reconstruction surgery, and alternative lifestyles. There was much discussion about how our society treated the transgender community, socially and politically (Ibid., pp. 374–413).

Another major factor in coalescing the transgender community involved the use of the Internet as a resource for a wide range of sexuality and gender diversity concerns. A plethora of new groups and Web sites came into existence to answer questions about many aspects of the "gender world" as well as to provide basic reliable information about sexual and gender diversity.

One aspect of gender that has emerged during this period is the development and usage of a taxonomy of *gender categories* associated with transgender behaviors and presentations. Terms like *transgendered, shemale,* and *transman* have been added to the more well-known terms like *cross-dresser, transvestite, transsexual, androgyne, intersexual,* and so on. (See the Flowchart for Transgender Phenomenon, appendix 2B, in this book.)

During this period, there was much published new material about many facets of gender diversity both in North America and in other parts of the English-speaking world. Here are just a few of the more significant books and their authors.

- In 1992 M. Garber suggested a third category of gender for the cross-dresser/transsexual population, focusing on social behaviors that are not entirely dependent on binary categories of gender like *male-female* and *masculine-feminine* (Garber 1992).
- Bullough and Bullough also broke away from the use of binary models as categories of gender variance. They relied more on data from social and behavioral sciences (Bullough and Bullough 1993).
- Among some Native American tribes there was a tradition that allowed for awareness and development of individuals who did not conform to the normative binary category of *male-female.* Called *berdache,* many of the Plains and southwestern tribes recognized and supported those males and females who exhibited a *two-spirit persona* within their tribal environment. Walter Williams wrote, "It is interesting how some cultures can accommodate to gender-sexual variations beyond the conventional binary categories and are not threatened by it" (Williams 1986, p. 3).
- Anne Bolin, a noted anthropologist, did important work in understanding the path of a transsexual individual. Working with a transgender group in Denver, Colorado, she saw the *transsexual journey* as one type of *rite of passage* within a society and used a sociological model (Van Gennup) to support her premise (Bolin 1988).
- Sandra Bem, a noted psychologist, made a major contribution with her studies and developed a theory about the *lenses of gender.* She identified three and labeled them gender polarization, androcentricism, and biologic essentialism. Her ideas have had major impact on our understanding about gender diversity. She said, "We need to recognize the existence of these lenses of gender, modify them, and then explore and discover one's honest gender expression" (Bem 1994). Gender should be seen as an intercon-

nected set of variables that allow for a sociocentric model and schema for gender diversity (p. 133).

- Following Dr. Bems suggestion, Kane (coauthor) has developed a schema that connects a trio of interconnected variables that are mediated over time by events and behaviors over the life span (see appendix 2A). Called the *Isostacy Model for Gender Diversity* (*IMGD*), this schema was presented at the twenty-first international meeting of the Society for the Scientific Study of Sexuality in Montreal, in November 2002.

Certainly other groups have acted to recognize transgender individuals and issues without distinguishing between them. One of the first to do so was the American Civil Liberties Union, which established a policy that was written back in the early 1960s recognizing the rights of cross-dressers. The ACLU also established a hotline in Los Angeles to deal with issues of both the gay and the transgender communities. For a time Joanna Clark (a postoperative male-to-female), worked out of the ACLU office as an advocate for transgender people. Even minor changes in public perception or action have major importance in the transgender community. For example, some states allow driver licenses to be issued to transgender people dressed in their adopted gender as either men or women. Courts look more favorably on transgender family disputes involving alimony or child custody or visiting privileges.

The biggest battle the transgender individual has had to face is the battle within her or his own person. In the following pages, you will read about the journeys of people who had the courage of their convictions. They opted for the gender road(s) less traveled. Each contributor has a unique experience to share. Some seem to have an easier time than others, but many of the stories are heart wrenching and the sacrifices that some have made seem almost unbelievable. But the stories are true. As editors, we have sought to include not only stories of the individuals themselves but also in some cases the reactions of their spouses and families. Most, but not all, of the autobiographies are of people born as biologic males. In trying to think of an organizing principle for them, the best way seemed to be simply to alphabetize by first name, since some do not include a last name. Also, we thought it important to relate their stories by decade. Read on and learn, and hopefully you will find them interesting as well.

Vern L. Bullough and J. Ari Kane-DeMaios
February 2006

REFERENCES

American Psychiatric Association. 1987. *Diagnostic and Statistical Manual of Mental Disorders.* Washington, DC: American Psychiatric Association.

Bem, Sandra L. 1993. *The Lenses of Gender.* New Haven, CT: Yale University Press.

Benjamin, Harry. 1966. *The Transsexual Phenomenon.* New York: Julian Press.

Bolin, Anne. 1988. *In Search of Eve.* Hadley, MA: Bergin & Garvey.

Bullough, B., V. L. Bullough, and J. Elias. 1997. *Gender Blending.* Amherst, NY: Prometheus Books.

Bullough, V. L. 1974. "Transvestism in the Middle Ages: A Sociological Analysis." *American Journal of Sociology* 79: 1381–94.

Bullough, V. L., and B. Bullough. 1993. *Cross Dressing, Sex, and Gender.* Philadelphia: University of Pennsylvania Press.

Carson, G. 1960. *The Roguish World of Doctor Brinkley.* New York: Holt, Rinehart, and Winston.

Ciotti, P. 1978. "Doctor's Licence Revoked." *San Francisco Gay Crusader,* January 9.

———. 2000. "Organ Grinder." *San Francisco Metropolitan,* March 21.

Cromwell, J. 2004. *Transmen and FTMs: Identities, Bodies, Genders and Sexualities.* Urbana: University of Illinois Press.

Devor, H. 1997. *FTM: Female to Male Transsexuality.* Bloomington: Indiana University Press.

Dreger, Alice D. 1998. *Hermaphrodites and the Medical Intervention of Sex.* Cambridge, MA: Harvard University Press.

Docter, Richard F. 1988. *Transvestites and Transsexuals.* New York: Plenum Press.

Ellis, Havelock. 1928. *Eonism and Other Supplementary Studies.* Philadelphia: F. A. Davis. It was published as volume 7 in the collected works of Ellis, *Studies in the Psychology of Sex.*

Feinberg, Leslie. 1996. *Transgender Warriors.* Boston, MA: Beacon Press.

Garber, Marjorie. 1992. *Vested Interests, Crossdressing, and Cultural Anxiety.* Boston, MA: Routledge Press.

Hamburger, C. 1953. "Desire for Change of Sex as Shown by Personal Letters from 465 Men and Women." *Acta Endocrinologica* 14: 361–75.

Hamburger, C., G. K. Sturup, and E. Dahl-Iversen. 1953. "Transvestism: Hormonal, Psychiatric, and Surgical Treatment." *Journal of the American Medical Association* 153 (May 30): 391–96.

Hirschfeld, Magnus. 1991. *Transvestism: The Erotic Drive to Cross-Dress.* Translated by Michael Lombardi-Nash. Amherst, NY: Prometheus Books. The German original appeared in 1910.

Jorgensen, C. 1967. *A Personal Autobiography.* New York: Paul S. Erickson.

Meyerwitz, J. 2002. *How Sex Changed: A History of Transsexuality in the United States.* Cambridge, MA: Harvard University Press.

Money J., and A. Ehrhardt. 1982. *Man/Woman, Boy/Girl*. Baltimore, MD: Johns Hopkins University Press.

Rudd, Peggy. 1990. *Cross-Dressing with Dignity: The Case for Transcending Gender Lines*. Katy, TX: PM Publishers.

Sondergard, G. 1996. "Sex Surgery Underground: An Interview with Donna Colvin." *Transsexual News Telegraph* 6: 38–39, 42.

Steinach, E. 1940. *Sex and Life: Forty Years of Biological and Medical Experiments*. New York: Viking Press.

Williams, Walter. 1986. *The Spirit and the Flesh: Sexual Diversity in American Indian Culture*. Boston, MA: Beacon Press.

FINDING MY WAY

Alison Laing

The need to be a woman seems to have been with me since the very beginning of my childhood. I vaguely remember being shocked by the realization that there were any differences between boys and girls. I can also remember tales about how horrified I was at being mistaken for a girl. My mother had kept my hair long and curly. There was a story repeated even into my adulthood by my mother about how pretty I was. Well-meaning folk would smile at me and say to my mother, "What a pretty little girl you have." I would stomp my feet and scream: "I'm not a girl! I'm not a girl!"

Actually, without realizing it, or maybe it was subconscious on my mother's part, she allowed and actually encouraged me to be "mother's little helper." I would help set the table and mix the batter for cakes and the like. Later she bought me a little stove and the implements to bake cookies and cornbread. Joy to me was, on the one hand, getting a hat like my daddy's and, on the other, having a little stove and cooking utensils so I could cook like my mother.

There are many vague recollections as well as stories told about my early days. The most telling event that occurred in early childhood is of an oft-told tale about my wanting a big doll, and I even recalled this later in life, with the aid of hypnosis. It seemed that I had to get a shot from the doctor for some reason and I wouldn't even get out of the car. I kicked and screamed until my mother thought I would pass out. Finally, she tried negotiating with me. I said I wanted a doll. I had asked for one before but had been denied it. She finally gave in and I then went into the doctor's and got the shot; afterward we went down to the "dry goods" store to get the doll. I wanted "The Doll," an almost life-sized Shirley Temple doll. Because I knew I obviously had the upper hand, and to insure not to have me "throw another fit," Mother gave in.

This story always upset me for some reason. Under hypnosis, my therapist was able to help me to remember the rest of the story. When we got home, it was time to take a nap. When I was alone in my youth bed (which still had sides), I crawled out and snuck under the bed with my big doll. I began to undress "Geraldine" (this is the name my mother said I gave her) and tried to put on "her" dress. I sobbed as I related this part of the story to my therapist, and I now remember this event with clarity. As one would expect, the dress did not fit and I was crushed.

My family life was filled with ups and downs as my mother and father argued and fought to the point that I would pull the covers over my ears so as not to hear it. Sometimes it would end with my mother coming into my room, waking me up, and telling me to get dressed while she literally threw some of my clothes into a bag. We would then take off in the car to head for her parents' home. I would sleep in the back seat, sometimes with one of her fur coats over me. I not only remember loving to be under the soft fur, stroking it and the silky lining, but also thinking I did not want to grow up to be like my "daddy" or the other men I had seen.

When I was four or five years old, I began tap-dancing lessons. I could tell by the boy-to-girl ratio that this was a girls' world. I tried to hide my admiration for the pretty dresses that the girls wore, but I remember even more of a deep desire to own a pair of those shiny patent leather "Mary Janes" tap shoes with the little straps.

Around eight or nine years of age, when I knew my mother would be gone for a time, the house cleaner caught me trying on a pair of my mother's stockings and a pair of her shoes, both of which were too big. I do not remember if she told my mother, but, if she did, nothing was ever mentioned to me. Apart from these incidents, I cannot remember any other cross-dressing experience.

GUILT AT AN EARLY AGE: DECADE 2 (YEARS 11–20)

During my prepubertal and pubertal years, I began to realize that I had this desire "to be a girl" and it was going to stay with me. Even then I knew that it was wrong and that I had to overcome this perception. At age ten, there was an event that I will remember until my dying day with regret. The school was to have a pageant with each class representing a different country. Our class was given Holland, and we were to do a little dance dressed as Dutch children. There was an imbalance between the number of boys and girls in the class, and the teacher gave me a pattern for a girl's costume, pointing out that I was the smallest boy in the class. She hoped I would not mind. I threw the pattern down and defiantly stated that I would never want to do such a thing. Another boy said he would have no problem doing it. To this day, I can remember the night of the pageant and how cute he looked with lipstick and a cheap little Dutch girl wig and how he was having a lot of fun hamming it up. For years I regretted giving up what I felt would have been the only opportunity in my lifetime to "be a girl." That was what I wanted to be more than anything else in the world.

I attended a rather fundamentalist "Bible Belt" church at twelve and heard implications that there were some acts that boys did that were sinful. I knew what that meant. While the specifics were never spelled out, I assume one of them must be related to my desire to be a girl. When I became a teenager, I prayed that I would lose this desire. I thought that if I was a good boy, if I went to church and Sunday school, read the Bible, and tried my best to be good, this sinful desire would go away.

In spite of this hidden desire, I grew into a "typical" teenager. Though I was not active or good in the rough-and-tumble sports, I began to date nice girls. I also joined the Boy Scouts and became active in my troop, working my way up the ladder in rank and leadership. I even once cross-dressed, at least partway, at a youth fellowship meeting of my church for a Sadie Hawkins party, a festival based on a comic strip character, *Li'l Abner*, by Al Capp. There was only one other boy who dressed this way, although the minister also did. I had to wonder about them both, but especially the minister since he had done a very good job of dressing as a woman.

Over time, I ran across articles in the newspapers and in magazines like *Confidential* about "transvestites" being caught and exposed. I also heard about the My-Oh-My Club in New Orleans with its fabulous female impersonators as well as the traveling Jewel Box Review. So I knew it was possible to do this sinful thing and not get killed. But certainly not in the South where I lived, except maybe at a nightclub in a big city.

I did well in high school, graduating at sixteen. I started college at a local teachers college mainly because my folks were afraid that I would have a tough time living away from home. I vowed not to let my obsession to cross-dress destroy me. I lied about my age to join the National Guard so I could become a real man. Still the desire to be a girl never went away. Both in the guard as well as at college, I was approached by other young men in such a way that I knew they were "homo," as it was called then. I was polite but fended them off.

I was having the time of my life meeting and dating young women, most of whom were cute and good-looking. I contrived all sorts of circumstances to find ways to be around them, to meet with them and enjoy their company. Church groups were the best place to experience this, so I got deeper into the religious world little by little. I volunteered with them to help sell Girl Scout Cookies and to launch the Senior Girl Scout Mariner's boat.

Eventually, I got the family blessing to go to college "up north" and knew that, besides going to a great university, I was at last felling the South and the "redneck" mentality that might lynch a person like me if they knew my secret. The college up north was demanding, but there were chances to dress for plays twice, as well as at Halloween. However, I was careful not to do it at the same location more than once. I always made sure that everybody knew I did not like it. I did a little dressing in the privacy of my room, being extremely careful with lipstick removal. Some nights I would sleep in an article from my women's clothes cache, which I kept well hidden.

COULD MY DESIRE COME TRUE: DECADE 3

The news of Christine Jorgensen's sex change in 1952 made the yearning of my dream of being a woman stronger. I now knew it was possible. I continued to fight this desire by, among other things, searching for a "real girl" who I thought could make a man of me and save me.

I dated many nice girls, and they all seemed to like me. My personal morality aided me in refraining from being aggressive regarding sexual relationships. We would do a lot of petting, kissing, even intimate caressing, but I abstained from intercourse, waiting for the "right" girl to come along.

During this period of my life, I learned to cross-dress, sneak out of the dormitory, and go to nearby museums, movies, and even shop. All the time, I was frightened to death of the prospects of being cited and "read" by a policeman. Also during this period, I went into a denial about this behavior. I developed a selective memory loss in which I could pretend that what I did never happened. Without knowing it, I was developing an alternative personality. This was good in some ways since I no longer felt the guilt and disgust as much as I had before about this behavior. Superficially, I became a more outgoing and happy person.

Once when everyone was out except for me, I got dressed and went into town. It was a holiday season, and I figured that I would not be noticed in all the crowds. I saw that a policeman seemed to be watching me, so I headed back toward my car. He followed me and I started to run. He started to chase me. Somehow, I outran him even though I was wearing three-inch heels. My heart was still pounding when I realized I had lost him and was able to get back to my car and safely home. I did not go out cross-dressed for a dozen years after that.

Still I was in a position to find magazines, especially in downtown used-book stores, which had articles about transsexuals as well as transvestites. There were many feature stories about beautiful female impersonators as well as the tragic lives of men who had committed suicide under the stress of this need to be a woman. Movies with transgender themes were also available, especially *Some Like It Hot*, but others were not as "nice." I soaked it all in, and the burning desire continued to cause conflict.

By necessity, I was dressing much less and at the same time becoming all the more frustrated and angry with the world. I lost myself in church work, PTA, Scouts, night classes, and anything that kept me busy every night. I could put on a happy face, but deep inside I was hurting and very angry. How long could I keep this up?

IT FINALLY CAME TO A BOIL: DECADE 5

The anxieties of this behavior, along with a stressful career and raising teenage children, played havoc with the relationship with my wife. It is a miracle she stayed with me. It seemed that everyone else in the family was getting what they wanted out of life, and I was only getting a lot of hard work to support their wants. Here I was, in my midforties, and, yes, I was having the typical midlife crisis, but more. Over a period of about ten months, I had several "anxiety" attacks. At first I thought the strongest pains, the tingling sensation, dizziness, and weakness, were symptomatic of a heart attack. Each time the doctors would observe me, then send me home and back to work in a few days. Finally, my doctor concluded that something else was going on. He gave me a card and advised me to see a psychiatrist. I was devastated.

I literally prayed about this situation, and the next week I ran into an old friend who was a psychologist. We had taught Sunday school together and had several interests in common. So I made an appointment with him. After the first hour, where we had sort of talked about a lot of things, he said we needed more time and quickly. He suggested that we meet for lunch and then follow up with another session right after that. He had assured me that he would give me a diagnosis of work-related stress so that there would not be too much of a stigma. I called in to work and said, "They are doing tests," so I will be very late. At lunch, my psychologist friend encouraged me to have two large glasses of wine as we continued to talk. He asked if I would just blurt out my most serious problem. I sank in a chair and said in a whisper, "I think I want to be a girl." His first comment was, "Now that is something that we can deal with."

I had two and half years of weekly sessions, sometimes two per week. At that time, he and others knew little about transgender issues. But after much analysis and many tests, he decided that I was most likely a transsexual. To be sure, we dealt with other issues—my domineering mother, my children who I thought were becoming wild, my stalled career, and many more, including my fear of death.

From my first years in the military to my rise to a top-level manager, I had lived in fear.

I was certain that someday a man in a suit would walk into my office and say, "Put on your coat and come with me." I was certain that someday I would be declared a security risk simply because of my transgendered behavior and that I would lose my job and end my career. Because of my technical training, I had found good work in high-technology research and engineering. This included the two-year tour of duty in the military and several years in government research followed by a long career in the defense business. As fate would have it, the technologies in which I was trained were directly applicable to providing products and services to highly sensitive and classified government work. I had applied for and was granted a "security clearance," and because my specialties became more and more sensitive, higher clearance levels were required.

During these years, I was deeply "closeted," in part because of the security constraint but also because of the fear of social rejection. When two alleged closeted "gay" men working on a similar project were determined to have "sold out" to the Soviets, possibly because of the threat of blackmail, I was given a briefing by my government customer to be on the lookout for such "sexual deviants." I just knew I had to be next.

I decided to carry the card of a very friendly FBI agent who I had come to know while working on some missing classified documents. Then, if I was ever approached by foreign agents, I would immediately contact him and work with him to trap them. I figured that if I was going to go down, I would take one of them with me. Fortunately, nothing of this nature ever came about.

The pressure and frustration of suppressing my transgender tendencies began to affect my health and family life, which, as mentioned above, ultimately led me to seek professional help. I knew that if "they" (either the US government or the Soviets) found out about my cross-dressing behavior, the game would be over. As part of the therapy, leading to self-acceptance, I began telling my dearest friends, my minister, my doctor, and my lawyer about the behavior. They were often surprised, yet no one seemed to reject me. By this time my direct family relations already knew.

This was a great relief to me, for now, I thought, I was not really vulnerable to blackmail. It then dawned on me that I was still vulnerable because of the very conditions being used to help reduce security risks. Eliminating personnel with a so-called deviant behavior who worked on classified projects was a prime reason for dismissal. I could still lose my job if I was "discovered." I did my best to get out of doing classified work to the extent of "losing" the forms for getting a clearance update and telling managers I wanted to travel overseas more often, which would necessitate a lower lever of clearance. Somehow, they signed the papers for me, and they even applied for special permission for me to travel. When I decided to come out of the "closet," I thought, "Well, now they will really find out about me."

BURSTING OUT AT LAST: DECADE 6

How I "came out" is quite a story. The pressure continued to build as I refrained from dressing. It had become almost impossible with three teenage kids in the same house. Work was more competitive, and I was under great pressure to perform. I was very active in community and local social affairs. It all began to take its toll. I had continued my therapy, and eventually the therapist diagnosed me as a transsexual. When we considered the consequences of openly becoming a transsexual, my spouse encouraged me to proceed with plans but would make no promises as to what her relationship would be once I transitioned. In spite of the fact that there was nothing I could do about it at the time, this new knowledge seemed to liberate me.

Eventually, I discovered a local gender-identity clinic. So I went down and talked with the social worker there. The first thing she did was to give me a card that said I was undergoing transition and was required to dress as a woman. I met a few of the other transpersons. They called this experience their "get out of jail free" card. After only a few sessions, the social worker thought I was not really a transsexual since I really wanted to stay with my wife. She asked me to try to find some way to "socialize" with other "transvestites" and see if my gender feelings improved. She furnished me with four contacts. Not one of them responded after I sent out the first letters looking for help. After several tries, one responded. The message said, "Call Eve on Tuesday Night" at such-and-such a number. It was signed Ariadne Kane. I called Eve (who I learned later was Betty Ann Lind), and she told me about a wonderful gathering of cross-dressers and preoperative transsexuals that took place in October in Provincetown on Cape Cod. It was called Fantasia Fair. It was relatively expensive, and I was certain it was a scam and that I might be "taken" or "outed." But I was desperate to find some relief for my pent-up desires. So I decided to "go for it." Eve persuaded me to sign up for the full nine days.

I had some concerns about sending money, and I worked out how to do it under an alias. After I sent in the registration fees, I received mail from the fair administration as well as the parent organization at a postal mailbox, under my femme name. It was thrilling. I was becoming "real." Best of all was the program book: thirty or fifty pages describing the event, its leadership, the speakers, and lots of photographs. I was so excited that for several weeks I read it every night before going to bed. I memorized the names and faces and all the activities. Based on the guidelines in the book, I began to acquire the clothes and all the things that I would need for nine days in Provincetown.

The trip to the end of the Cape was longer than I had thought, so I arrived rather late in Provincetown. I located the Pilgrim House, the place where I was to report, and got there just as they were closing up. I was greeted by a gracious, charming, and lovely lady who I recognized as Sheila Kirk from her photograph in the program book. I was assigned to an inn called the Elephant Walk, which was run by a wonderful innkeeper named Lenny. He told me that most of the "girls" were already at a reception just down the street. I hurried and unloaded the car, walked to the reception area, and entered a most fantastic world—

more wonderful than I had ever dreamed possible. I was among those who were like me and who accepted me. They were all beautiful people. At last, I had found my community, a new family, and my new home.

I could write pages about the memories of my first fair. I called my wife the first night and every night thereafter and cried so much I could barely talk. I begged her to come so she could see this most incredible event: there were engineers, postal workers, professors, seamen, salespersons, people from all walks of life and from all parts of the world. They all had the same interests; they wanted to express themselves in a gender role that was different from that which was expected from their natural birth sex. After I had spent several nights alone at the fair, my wife agreed to fly in for the last three days. To her credit, she was pleased with the event and pleased that it was making me so happy.

There were many, many wonderful highlights of my first fair. I will share only a few that impacted my life to this very day. One was being able to go to the Provincetown Meetinghouse, a Unitarian-Universalist church, to worship in a truly welcoming fellowship. Years later, I actually delivered the sermon there. Another was getting to meet and know Virginia Price, one of the only cross-dressers I had ever heard of and who I once saw (in a silhouette) on television. She spent a lot of time "educating me" about this phenomena. I also heard an inspirational speech by Marissa Sherrill Lynn, who spoke about a new organization on the horizon, the International Foundation for Gender Education (IFGE), located in Waltham, Massachusetts. The end of this most glorious event was punctuated at a grand banquet where I was given the award for "Ms. Congeniality." I knew that I would be hooked on Fantasia Fair for my lifetime. And I still am.

Later on, I learned about other events taking place in different parts of the United States. I went to the first IFGE convention in Chicago that next spring. I flew half-dressed, completing the final change and makeup on the plane. I was thrilled to see even more beautiful people and attended many great seminars and workshops. I went for a weekend in the Poconos and another Provincetown program in the late spring. With all the travel, the convention expenses, the purchase of new wigs, makeup, and clothing, I was racking up a lot of expense. But I was at last happy. On the other hand, my dear, understanding wife was getting very concerned, so I slowed the pace of activity down for the summer. I was still excited about returning to the fair in the fall.

One other thing of serious note occurred. I found out about a group that was meeting some distance away from where I lived and went a few times, but it tended to be a real downer experience. I could see that something better was needed, and a new friend agreed. It turned out that we lived fairly close to one another, so we met, put our heads together, and with the help of three others we created the Renaissance organization. Over the next several years, I got involved in all sorts of local work concerning the transgender community, attended many conferences, and started taking on leadership roles in various organizations. I was enjoying my life even if I was only able to be in my preferred role part time.

With the joy in being able to express my feminine side comfortably, there were more visible signs of change in appearance. These included plucked eyebrows, longer nails, shaved wrists, and pierced ears. A secretary at work noticed some of these changes, so I told her about my feminine side. She loved it. A woman engineer who was working for me also noticed and commented that she was seeing a positive change in my behavior. She asked if I was becoming a woman. I shared my secret with her. Again, no problem. I told a very close male colleague who asked about the nails and earlobe holes, and he did not seem to have a problem. Later on, he told me he always worried about what he would say if he were interviewed on a security update background check. Fortunately, it never happened.

LET'S GIVE IT A SHOT: DECADE 7

As soon as I approached the seventh decade, I hoped to take early retirement. I started a business based on one of my hobbies, and I did quite well at it for several years. I was also able to find time to go to more transgender events. I went to the Texas T-party, the Be All You Want to Be, and California Dreamin', as well as the IFGE Convention and Fantasia Fair. Wow, this was great.

I reconsidered the idea of reassignment surgery, in spite of what the social worker had suggested. However, I also thought that perhaps I did not need to have surgery and considered the option of being transgendered. I was on a low dose of hormones for quite some time, and I asked the doctor to increase it. I asked, "How big will my breasts get?" He replied, "Not as big as you hope, I'm afraid." Well, he was wrong since I became well endowed within a year.

Now I was retired. I still worried that some fanatic security officer would determine that I had lied on my security application and ask me to return past salaries or strip me of my commission.

I continued to participate in the many organizations being quite outspoken about how to do things better. I was on several transgender group boards and involved in lots of activities. In 1995 I was asked if I would be willing to become the executive director of the IFGE. I believed that this was the premier organization of the transgender community, so I was honored and decided to take the job. It would involve moving to the Boston area, but it also would give me a chance to do my own real-life test. In April 1995 I accepted and was brought aboard into that position.

Try as I might, I found it difficult to live full time as a woman for any extended period. I discovered there was always something I had to do in my masculine role. My parents were both ill, and I had to make frequent trips south to be with them. Since the IFGE could not cover the income I expected, I decided to hang on to part of my little business. A few of my clients knew about my alternative lifestyle, but many did not, so I dealt with them in my masculine role. While I have lived in a feminine role over 80 percent of the time for over two years, the longest time I lived en femme was one stretch of forty-one days. This was accomplished while I was traveling extensively in the position as executive director. Under the current role I felt sure of myself and was very happy.

It was during this period, however, that my wife was diagnosed with a chronic illness and given only a few good years before she would be disabled. Also at this time, my father died and my mother was getting very feeble. Mother's illnesses demanded that I take more responsibility of managing her care. Eventually, it became necessary to give up the IFGE position in October 1997. Mother died a few years later. However, medical advances and good care resulted in slowing down my spouse's cancer and allowing her to remain active. I continued to be active on the IFGE board and with other groups as well.

PEACE AT LAST: DECADE 8

As I move into the eighth decade, I am very comfortable in either masculine or feminine gender roles. I still do a "gender shift," and I feel good about both personas. I still work with several transgender organizations. Recently, I spent some weeks of each monthly period living and working as a woman in a large metropolitan city. I was surprised at the acceptance and personal feeling of freedom. I "outed" myself at a local church by participating with a GLBT group. They were truly very accepting.

So here I am. Having decided to live a bi-genderal lifestyle without any major body modifications or facial changes, I am quite satisfied with living part time as a man and part time as a woman. It is not easy, but it has its rewards. I can keep my interests as a man as well as those I have as a woman. I spend a lot more time with the transgendered community activities. My spouse knows that she can always have her husband when she feels the need for male companionship. All the children, now adults, know and accept this arrangement, knowing that their father is there for them, for any reason. Now I enjoy the roles of husband and father more than ever.

It's now forty-plus years since my spouse and I were married, and we have worked out most of the challenges regarding my transformation. We have one of the best relationships as husband and wife, and as friends and partners, that I know. It is built not only on love and caring for one another but also on respect for each other as individuals. I thank God for this relationship and my contentment with a bi-gender lifestyle, both of which have made for this to be truly the best of all possible worlds.

EXPLORATIONS OF AN ANDROGYNE

Ariadne Maria Kane

The firstborn male in my family, I began life in a cold-water brown-stone house in New York City. Apparently there were some serious economic problems at that time, so I was sent to stay with relatives and lived most of my first three and a half years growing up with my dad's parents and his younger sisters and brother. I was the "golden light" of the entire household and was showered with much love and attention by grandparents and aunts. One of the traditions of my family was the Saturday night home party. The entire family, including cousins who lived in the neighborhood, would come to Grandpa's house to eat, play, and dance. There would be platters of homemade traditional Greek specialties made by my grandma and my aunts. In addition to dancing and singing, there was lots of storytelling about life in the remote region of Greece where my grandparents came from. I can remember being carried on the shoulders of my uncle, who led a traditional group folk dance, and receiving wonderful attention. I usually slept in the bed of one of my aunts or uncles. I can remember arguments about whom Ari would sleep with tonight. Once I slept with an aunt, who wrapped me in one of her cotton nighties. It felt warm and was another form of love that this aunt showed me. My grandfather had scenes from his Greek village painted on the walls of the bedrooms: lots of blue sky, a green mountainside, and a shepherd tending his flock of sheep. These years left a deep impression on me. I was bathed with much love, attention, and affection by my dad's parents and siblings.

It was different when I returned to live with my parents and sister.

My parents were always fighting about something or other. My sister, who was about two years younger than me, was always crying. It was a different, less pleasant environment.

At about age five I had my first adventure that I can remember. We were living in a tenement in another borough of New York City. I was given a tricycle for a birthday gift and decided to take a "trip." I rode from my home, past the end of the paved road and sidewalks. I soon found myself in the "countryside" where there were some small farms and no clearly marked sidewalks. It was a pleasant day, and I was totally unaware of where I was or how far from home I had traveled. I stopped at one of the farms and asked the lady of the house if I could have a drink of water. She offered me the water and also gave me a few home-made cookies. She asked where I had come from, and I told her. She said that I had gone about five miles from home. It was getting dark and I began to think about my return home but didn't know my way back. Fortunately, the lady from the farm called the local police station, and they made contact with my parents via a personal visit by a local police vehicle near my home. The police informed my parents that I was okay and that they would return me. When I got home, I was greeted by my parents, a welcome hug from my mom and anger from my dad. They both were very angry about what I had done and, as punishment, they took the tricycle away from me. I also received a thrashing from my dad. Secretly, I was very glad I had this adventure. It opened up new worlds to me. I vowed that when I got older I would travel all over the world.

It was in those early years that I began to wear feminine apparel and accessories. Always curious about why girls and women wore different types of clothing, I decided to secretly try on some of my mother's apparel. I can remember as a prepubertal, putting on a pair of her high-heeled blue suede pumps when no one was home. Her shoes fit my feet, at that time, although they felt funny when I tried to walk in them. Later on, I got bolder and tried on other items of Mother's. Some of them felt silky smooth and comfortable. I liked the feeling and promised myself that one day I would dress completely. I fantasized about what it would be like to be dressed as a woman all the time. My mother was very attractive, with good taste in clothes and choice of accessories. By dressing in her clothes, I felt as though I was emulating her and also spiritually getting close to her. The question was when could I get the opportunity to explore this fantasy without being discovered? We lived in a railroad-style tenement, at that time, and there was not much privacy.

An opportunity came a few years later. My folks announced that they were going to be away all day on a Saturday for some important social event and would be returning home late that evening. My sister was away, staying with a friend for the weekend. I was eleven years old at the time.

When I finished my household chores, I thought about the exciting afternoon I was going to have dressing in Mom's clothes. I selected an outfit from her wardrobe and the appropriate lingerie, consisting of panties, a bra, a garter belt, a full slip, a pair of seamed nylon stockings, and a blue crepe dress and matching pumps. I was meticulous in noting the places where all these items were found so that I could return them, exactly where I had found them.

Remembering the process I had seen when watching my aunts or mother dress, I laid all the chosen items on my bed and in order and began the process of dressing. I recall thinking about what to insert in the bra to give the right shape for the upper part of the dress. I ended up using a pair of heavy socks in each cup. Since I had no experience with makeup, I decided to explore this item of "womanhood" at another time. It took about twenty minutes to dress from the skin out. Once satisfied that I had all the items correctly placed (including the seams of the stockings), I walked up and down the length of the flat. On each pass by the full-length mirror in the master bedroom, I stopped, gazed at the image, smiled, and said aloud that I was a very attractive "woman." After an hour or so of this activity, I made some tea, sat in the living room, and did some reading. It was approaching midafternoon and I thought I would spend a few more hours "dressed" since my parents were not expected to be home until about 8:00 or 9:00 PM. I felt there was enough time to change and return Mom's clothing to their proper places.

Between 4:00 and 4:30 PM, I heard a jingling of keys in the door of the flat. I panicked, not knowing who it could be. I timidly asked who was there and heard Mom's voice. Very quickly, just like Superman, I dashed into my bedroom, latched the door, ripped off all the clothes, stuffed them under my bed, and dove under the bed covers, frightened, sweaty, and stark naked. I waited until I heard my father yelling to unlatch the door or he would break it down. I put on my bathrobe, unhooked the latch, and quickly returned to my bed, pulling the covers up to my neck. My parents entered the room demanding to know why I had latched the door and why I was in bed. I told them that I was feeling chilled and "ill" and wanted a warm place to rest. As my father came closer to examine me, he noticed a piece of blue cloth sticking out from under my bed. "What's this?" he asked in an angry tone of voice as he pulled out the torn pieces of my mother's clothing. I was tongue-tied, but he demanded an answer. Not saying another word, he undid the belt from his trousers, and I knew that I was going to get the beating of my life. My mother, who was equally upset, calmed him down somewhat, and they began to argue whether or not to punish me with a beating. In the meantime, I was crying profusely. After some hesitation he let down his stance for beating me and Mom suggested that I should see our family doctor to get a professional opinion about my strange behavior. Perhaps I needed some medical help. After I agreed to see the doctor, my father calmed down and returned his belt to his pants, still very angry about "his son's crazy behavior." Mom was somewhat relieved that a major family feud had been averted, at the least for the moment.

My appointment with the doctor was arranged for early Monday morning. I stayed in bed all day Sunday, nervous and not wanting to eat. My father did not talk to me at all. I timidly apologized to Mom for destroying one of her dresses. My sister returned home from her weekend later that day and was upset by the events and the current atmosphere at home. They hinted to her about what had occurred but did not dwell on the details.

On that Monday I went by trolley car to the doctor's office alone because both Mom and Dad had to work that day. After he physically examined me, the doctor said that I was fine, physically, but he was less certain about my cross-dressing episode. He said that he had had another case similar to mine several years before and it turned out to be nothing serious. He reminded me of my enviable status as both a bright and a healthy young man and admonished me to "never do that crazy stuff again." He reported to my parents that I had a moment of idle fantasy, common among bright young boys at that age, and not to worry about it returning. I was so relieved about the doctor's report that I vowed never to experiment with wearing women's clothes again. Mom was pleased to hear the doctor's professional opinion about my behavior, but Dad thought the doctor was "favoring me." He perceived my dressing-up experiment as reason enough to be "sent to an insane asylum," although he took no steps to have me committed. The "storm" having passed, it would be more than four years before I considered cross-dressing again.

During adolescence, I got work as a newspaper delivery person in my neighborhood. I continued my schooling, graduating from high school at seventeen years of age, and became a Boy Scout, where I learned about my talents as a hiker, canoeist, and lover of the outdoors.

These were all wonderful adventures and provided little idle time to fantasize about cross-dressing and becoming a stage personality.

I entered college right after high school and soon became involved with nonacademic student activities. The student-body president asked me to organize and manage the all-college prom. This was a first-time event at the college I attended, and I was responsible for all phases of the project. Many of these included negotiating with a major hotel for rental of its ballroom, scheduling Charlie Spivak and his Orchestra as the main attraction, ticket sales, security, and hopefully having a large turnout. It was a major undertaking and proved to be a huge social and financial success. It also was an important personal experience that gave me heightened self-esteem and catapulted me into being elected president of some prestigious campuswide organizations. In short, I discovered that I had strong leadership ability, and this resource would be one of many talents that I would use later in life.

I got married right after college. I met Cindi during my senior year and became infatuated with her. She was attractive and very bright, two qualities I admired in women at that time. While we had our differences, we also had a core of common interests. Cindi had been accepted for a graduate program at a major university in New York City, and I had the prospect of starting my career, as a management trainee, with a major company there. Within two weeks of our marriage and having completed the tedious process of interviewing with officials at several different levels, I was informed by the company that it would delay my training for an indefinite period because of the current economic recession. I decided not to wait until someone from the company called me. I explored the current job market looking for a position commensurate with my academic training (biophysics major, math minor) and proven leadership skills. I found several positions during the next three years, but the jobs did little to challenge my intellectual interest. I decided to seek graduate training in biophysics. Cindi was proceeding well with her graduate program, getting enough scholarship funding to pay for school and also allow us to live, albeit frugally, in New York City.

Our marriage during this three-year period was not doing well. Our differences became greater and our interests less common. I applied and was accepted into a graduate program in biophysics at a major university in Western New York. This meant we had to separate. We agreed that being apart for three months would give us both a chance to review our relationship and decide whether we wanted to stay together or get divorced. Within a month of starting my program, I received divorce papers from Cindi's attorney. Emotionally devastated, I found myself unable to concentrate on my studies. When I returned to New York City to confront her about her decision, I found our apartment empty and she was not around. Eventually I met with her and found out that she was living with a colleague from her graduate school program.

The breakup of our marriage made me realize how emotionally vulnerable I was. It challenged me to rethink about the set of traditional values that I had clung to and thought were immutable. I experienced, for the first time in my life, a deep depression with no immediate relief in sight. I began to cross-dress again, thinking that my femme fantasies would help me to forget the emotional pain of the last three years. It was marginally helpful and gave me the courage to call a friend from the past. Alan had relocated from New York City to Boston and, when I told him about my situation, he offered to come to my apartment in Western New York and stay with me until I could see some light at the end of the "tunnel of despair." Within a week after his visit, the depression subsided and I was able to continue my graduate studies. We became close friends after that, and he invited me to visit him in Boston. I did so, at Easter time that year, and I enjoyed the visit and the ambiance of the city. It also provided an opportunity to examine the values in my life. I looked at my career objective of being a laboratory scientist and decided that it would not work for me. I needed social interactions with other people in a professional setting where I could make a difference. Alan suggested that I give some thought to finding a position as an instructor of science and mathematics and relocate to Boston. I did so and lucked out with an offer of a fine teaching position in a private school that served as a preparatory school for MIT and other major technical colleges and universities. After five years of enjoyable teaching in Boston, I was offered a position at an American school in Italy. My friend Alan accepted an assignment in Africa with the Peace Corps, and I accepted the teaching position in Rome.

Relocating to Europe allowed me time to reassess my value system in a different culture. I spent the next four years teaching math and physical science in Italy, Switzerland, and Greece. In addition to my teaching responsibilities, I was involved with a UNESCO project comparing the mathematics syllabi of four European countries and the United States. I also established a tutorial service for those American students living in Italy who wanted to go to major universities in the United States. I became proficient enough in Italian to do technical translation services for firms wanting to connect and do joint projects with American companies. All these were successful projects. They illustrated that I had some talent and creativity about teaching and the learning process.

During my stay in Europe, there was relatively little interest in cross-dressing or in development of a femme persona. I attribute this to many other activities that occupied much of my time. I did cross-dress for some specific events, like Fastnacht in Munich, Germany, and Mardi Gras in Naples, Italy. These were fun activities and did not create a sense of true "gender shift." For the first time, I had friends who encouraged my androgynous behavior and presentations. I could be who I wanted, when I wanted, without feelings of being stigmatized or living with the anxiety and fear so typically associated with these experiences. There was a sense of a liberated inner spirit that bolstered my self-esteem without having to polarize either roles or presentations about my gender.

Returning to the United States after four years abroad was somewhat of a "culture shock" for me. My parents were getting on in years, and showed it. My beloved grandma had died; my sisters got married; and the political landscape had changed. My good friend Alan had returned from Africa and began a teaching career at a well-known private school in the Midwest. Added to all these changes was a renewed interest in cross-dressing. I was now living alone and started to amass a femme wardrobe and accessories from a variety of sources. My interest was wearing the clothes and using the props of gender to enhance a fantasy about being a "true woman." I remained a closet cross-dresser for two years.

After a serious search for a creative and challenging teaching position in selected parts of the United States failed to find anything that measured up to my ideals, I returned to Boston and decided to try self-employment. With the knowledge and wisdom gained from my European experiences, I founded Educational Dynamics Ltd., a curriculum consulting service.

Our objective was to develop and offer dynamic programs in mathematics and physical sciences that would be fun, challenge students, and please educational establishments, both public and private. I developed several modules for teaching Euclidean geometry to marginal math students, using cityscapes, skylines, and cardboard carpentry as objects for understanding fundamental geometry and its applications. Another project focused on teaching the principles of Einsteinian relativity using some simple experimental techniques and procedures. A third project involved the development of teaching modules for emerging technologies (digital systems and satellite communications). Sponsored and funded by the National Science Foundation, it was called the Man-Made World. This program was piloted in several major school districts throughout the United States. In addition to the research and development aspects of these projects, I was asked to pilot run them in several school settings. All these programs were well received by heads of math and science departments. However, there was much resistance to changing curricula in the public school systems throughout the country. As a result, many of these programs were never incorporated into the core high school course offerings.

Another aspect of my consulting service was the development and implementation of travel education programs in seldom-visited parts of North America, Europe, the Middle East, and Asia. Here, we offered the intrepid traveler a unique experience through involvement with aspects of the local cultures of these countries, quite different from the travel programs organized by major tourist organizations.

In all, though it was an exciting period of creativity and learning in areas of education for me, it failed to bring the needed economic growth that I needed to sustain and continue my work in innovative education. I closed down my company after three years of activity. Finding work in creative educational establishments proved to be tougher than I expected. Still living in Cambridge, Massachusetts, I looked for a combination teacher-administrator position that could use my skills, experiences, and talents. With my background in the sciences, I thought I would enter the field of medical research and healthcare. After a considerable search, I found a position in a major teaching hospital in the Boston area as an assistant hospital administrator. I was given the responsibility of coordinating all aspects of research projects in pulmonary medicine. There were many challenges associated with the position, including grant management, grant writing, purchasing of specialized laboratory equipment, hiring of technical personnel, and so on. One challenge I was unable to resolve had to do with "political intrigues and jealousies" between research associates and higher-level hospital administrators. After two years at this job, I realized that I was not going to make a real difference in the way basic or clinical research was managed. I resigned the position and decided to look into different fields of work.

One of these fields was in the area of real estate appraisals and property management. I took the test to be a real estate broker and started to sell residential property in Boston. I gradually shifted to commercial sales and leasing, and this led to an interest in appraisal of real estate. I became a certified real estate appraiser. In addition, I got involved with property management. I did all this work for a total of five years. It was good, but my mind and spirit continued to search for teaching opportunities.

OUT OF THE CLOSET—
CREATION OF THE CHERRYSTONE CLUB

In the early seventies, I read about a cross-dresser club in Boston. With the article was a picture of the club president and also a telephone number. I was reluctant to make contact for fear that the members might be "sexual perverts." I was interested in the art and practice of cross-dressing from aesthetic and social viewpoints. I was, basically, heterosexual and had no desires to bar hop or look for male sexual partners. After much hesitation, I made telephone contact with the club president. (S)he sounded warm and reassuring about the philosophy of the club, its screening and membership policies, and its emphasis on the importance of feeling secure about the meeting place. She added that many of the members came from middle-class environments, had respectable jobs, and were married in the traditional sense. To be invited to a meeting, I had to have an interview with "her" or one of the members. She interviewed me, found me acceptable, and invited me to attend a meeting in order to get a feeling for the ambiance and social interactions among the members.

After a three-month procrastination on my part, I decided to attend one of their meetings. It was at the duplex apartment of the club president and was an awesome experience. I came early in order to meet some of the veteran club members. I remember guys coming in, dressed in masculine attire and carrying suitcases. They would go upstairs and change clothes—put on makeup, a wig, and accessories—and come downstairs, cross-dressed. It was virtually impossible for me to recognize the person who went upstairs as a guy and returned as an attractive-looking woman. Some chose a casual mode of dressing reflecting the fashion period while others wore elegant dresses as if they were going to a major social event. I was struck by the diversity of the clothing choices of the club members as well as by their friendliness and sincere desire to make me feel comfortable. I chose not to dress at this premier meeting since I was unsure that my limited wardrobe would be suitable. In addition, I never learned the art of using makeup or having an appropriate femme wig for a comfortable presentation. They readily answered many of my questions, both practical and legal. I was alerted by the club coordinators not to ask the legal names of any members and avoid questions about the type of employment they were engaged in. Each always introduced himself with a chosen femme name. It was a memorable evening and served as a prelude to leaving the "closet" of the solitary cross-dresser.

From that first meeting period, I began to get my act together so that I could dress and enjoy a pleasant social evening of conversation and practical tips to improve my image. I purchased my first wig and bought a complete cosmetic kit. I got many tips about using makeup effectively, covering my beard, highlighting my natural features, and so on. I expanded my wardrobe options and learned how to coordinate outfits. I practiced both at home and at the club facility. After a month I became adept at making the transformation, going from two hours in the beginning to forty-five minutes. The discovery and involvement with this cross-dresser club became the catalyst for coming out of the closet and allowing the femme person in my psyche to grow. It also served as a staging area to ask many questions (computers were not available then) about cross-dressing and cross-gender behaviors and helped to clarify many critical personal issues.

One year after my becoming an active member, Maryanne, the club president, announced that (s)he would be having "sex reassignment surgery" and her duplex apartment would no longer be available for weekly meetings. At this point, I was a strong advocate for a cross-dresser club and the enormous positive value it had for many cross-dressers and cross-gender people to learn about and be more comfortable with the behavior. A "house" search committee was created with me as the chair. We looked in many locales both in Boston proper and areas within a fifteen-mile radius of Boston. Within two months, a location was found in Boston and a new cross-dresser/cross-gender club was born. We took the name of the Cherrystone Club. We had many programs at Cherrystone and attracted many new members. We connected with a more vocal lesbian/gay group and did some joint programs together. Members came from all the New England states. Some of us were invited to speak at sociology and psychology classes at many college campuses in the area. I got invites to speak on local public radio and regional talk shows about cross-dressing and cross-gender behaviors and lifestyles. It was from these experiences that Fantasia Fair and the Outreach Institute of Gender Studies were created.

THE OUTREACH INSTITUTE OF GENDER STUDIES (OIGS)

Our purpose was to provide reliable information about gender diversity, make available hard-to-find resources, create educational programs and services for healthcare agencies and regional transgender groups, and network with lawyers and medical professionals to provide them with pertinent data and information that helped in the resolution of legal and medical cases. The *Outreach Newsletter* was created in order to share information on all matters related to gender diversity and transgender concerns. It was published quarterly and had a subscription base of more than one thousand individuals and professional agencies in the United States. It evolved into the *Journal of Gender Studies*. Several original papers were published as well as book and movie reviews, conference announcements, and selected useful resources.

Fantasia Fair was a program created by the Outreach Institute to provide an interwoven set of educational, social, and practical programs for adult cross-dressers and cross-gender people throughout North America. It took place in Provincetown on the tip of Cape Cod, Massachusetts, every October and lasted for seven to nine days. We invited interested and well-known healthcare professionals to contribute to the several symposia that were organized and also to give a seminar on their specialty to the participants. We introduced the idea of having a fashion show and also a talent show (known as the Fan/Fair Follies) for participants and invited townspeople to these programs as our guest audience. In all, the Fair was the most innovative program for transgender people in the entire world. The Fair served as a template for many other conferences and living/learning gender vacations both in the United States and Europe and Japan.

We launched a program for couples specifically to address the conflict issues about gender roles and presentations. These outings took place on weekends, in country settings and were designed to clarify and help the couples to be more positive about this unique aspect of their relationship. Known as Project Hopeful, these were given in the spring of the year, for several years, and were much appreciated by the couples who came as participants.

Another innovative program was known as the New Woman Conference. Here, the focus was on concerns and issues of postoperative transsexuals. Topics included medical and legal issues for the new woman (discrimination in the workplace, custody and visitations rights to see their children, etc.) and several social and spiritual issues. It was the first time that more than twenty postoperative transwomen met in a comfortable setting to discuss their problems interactively. This program continued for about five years and was extremely helpful in clarifications and realizable strategies for new women and their issues.

By 1995 there were several new groups that were ready to assume responsibility for many of the innovative OIGS programs and services. This factor coupled with the emergence of a large number of transgender chat rooms and Web sites on sexual and gender diversity on the Internet made some of our activities superfluous. In 2000 the Outreach Institute of Gender Studies closed its doors.

In terms of my personal life, my first marriage and subsequent divorce made me very cautious about entering into any long-term relationships with other women. For a time, I became a champion of the semicommitted coupling idea without establishing a bond of matrimony. I had several such relationships over these decades, until I met Nina. We met on one of the many hiking trips I led for my Outing Club. She was a lover of all things outdoors, of teaching music, and of kids. We courted each other for more than nine years before I felt comfortable enough to propose marriage. We tied the knot in the early seventies and have been together for over thirty years. I feel it was one of the better decisions I made in my life.

COMING OUT TO NINA

I wanted to share with Nina my involvement in the Cherrystone Club and its many activities. After much thinking about it, I developed a How-When-Where strategy. We would have dinner at an intimate restaurant in Cambridge. I wore a dinner jacket and tie for the occasion. As we had cocktails and appetizers, I began my saga with a general introduction of the subjects, and during each course I related more, until dessert time, when I told her my own connection with the story. She seemed intrigued and wanted to meet Ariadne that night. I suggested that it would be better to do this later on, since it was getting late. As positive and supportive as she said she was, I was a little apprehensive about a face-to-face meeting so soon. In fact, I delayed the meeting date by one month. When Nina did finally meet "her," it was truly a moment of truth. I was fearful that, upon seeing me cross-dressed, she might end our relationship. The rendezvous finally took place at my apartment, with me in femme mode. As we got comfortable with being together, the conversation turned to the practical, aesthetic side of my presentation. We laughed about the funny combination of items and accessories I wore, and she offered some suggestions for improvement. I opened a bottle of champagne to celebrate the moment. In general, it was a very positive introduction and led to her getting involved with Cherrystone programs and other transgender activities over the next decades. An important result of this experience was to let my potential partner know about my femme side and behavior before any marriage commitment was made. This approach allowed for options in developing a positive long-term relationship together. This was a wise decision. Over the next twenty-five years, Nina provided much support to and for many aspects of my transgender/androgynous lifestyle.

RADIO AND VIDEO APPEARANCES (DONAHUE, SUSSKIND, AND OTHERS)

Almost from the beginning, I served as a spokesperson on the subject of cross-dressing and cross-gender behaviors and lifestyles, and my reputation spread. I was a guest lecturer on many local and regional college campuses. I appeared on several radio and television shows in Boston and other major cities in New England. In 1979 I received an invitation to be a guest on the *Phil Donahue Show*. This was the most popular TV talk show in America at that time, and the opportunity to reach millions of people and share my experiences and ideas about cross-dressing and cross-gender lifestyles was appealing. It also meant possible exposure to members of my family and friends who didn't know about this side of my life and might recognize me. This presented a serious dilemma for me. I talked it over with Nina and, after much deliberation, decided to accept the invitation. The format was a one-hour program before a live audience with a professional sex educator, Mr. Donahue, and myself. It was a challenging and exciting one hour, answering questions from both Donahue and the audience, explaining some of the knotty issues, in lay terms, and remaining calm and coherent. This was a first for the transgender community and was well received by viewing audiences in many parts of the world. I found out later that this particular show was rerun many times over the next two years, even in Europe. After the initial show, I received more than eight thousand letters, most of which were very positive and complimentary. It was truly a highlight in the "coming out" series of personal events in my journey through life.

In 1983 I was invited to be a guest on the *David Susskind Show* on PBS. The format here consisted of three other cross-dressers and myself in dialogue with Susskind. The significance of this appearance was that it was viewed by a more informed audience and allowed for good, in-depth discussion of the issues.

One important by-product of these national video appearances was an awareness that we had reached many cross-dressers and cross-gender folks who were very much in the closet. I was able to talk about the Fantasia Fair and its value as a program of personal growth. By now, the Fair was about five years old and had been successful in providing an interwoven program of educational, social, and practical activities and events. It was the model from which several other transgender conferences developed. Now, in its thirty-fourth year of operation, it continues to educate and inform participants about gender diversity. It is still held every October in Provincetown.

PROFESSIONAL ASSOCIATIONS (SSSS, AHP, AASECT, AHP, WCS)

Within two years of my emergence from the closet, I became a member of several important professional organizations. These included the Society for the Scientific Study of Sexuality (SSSS), the Association for Humanistic Psychology (AHP), and the American Association of Sex Educators, Counselors, and Therapists (AASECT). I gave many presentations on a myriad of topics related to sexuality and gender diversity. We introduced an important workshop at these meetings. Known as the Gender Attitude Reassessment Program (GARP), this gave healthcare professionals a broad pallet for understanding and insight into the world of gender. I met and became friendly with many of the leading therapists, educators, counselors, endocrinologists, and behavioral psychologists in both North and South America. In 1981 I was invited to be a presenter at the First International Conference on Androgyny, held in San Diego, California. In 1989 I gave a major workshop on gender issues at the ninth World Congress of Sexology (WCS) in Caracas, Venezuela.

COUNSELING, COACHING, AND CONSULTING

With all this professional activity, I became known as a gender specialist and became affiliated with the Sexual Health Centers of New England. It was here I developed my counseling and coaching skills, providing counseling services for clients who presented with gender conflicts and issues. I also served as a consultant to a number of clinical professionals around the nation who had transgendered clients with special problems (intersex, erratic social behaviors, etc.) and who sought help in developing an appropriate counseling strategy with them.

I returned to graduate school and received a doctorate in human sexuality education.

Gradually, I developed a private practice and provided professional services in sexuality and gender education and clinical counseling. In 1976 we created the Outreach Institute of Gender Studies (OIGS), which provided a basis for much of the information and data to give several academic papers and numerous public and national presentations on the subject. The OIGS became a major resource for sexologists, clinical counselors, therapists, nurses, physicians, and educators and lawyers.

DECADE 7 (YEARS 61–70)

Currently, I'm in the seventh decade of the life span. New and exciting challenges have come my way. I have gotten involved with learning about the aging process specifically over the last three decades of the life span. The focus has been on both gerontological and geriatric concerns.

In geriatrics, I have become familiar with many aspects of body health. In addition to personal assessment of my own body health, I have become aware of some body ailments as well as some specific disease states that affect one's health. These would include skeletomuscular changes, gastrointestinal problems, cardiovascular issues, and brain-neurologic concerns. Just learning about the basics associated with each of these has been mind-boggling. To share some important aspects about body health, I have developed several learning modules and created a workshop entitled the Health Awareness and Action Program (HAAP). It is designed for all people interested in the changing health perspective as we get older. A unique feature of this workshop is to share some new and non-Western treatments and strategies for coping with potential health issues associated with the aging process.

Associated with physical health are the psychological and sociological changes for the individual, as she/he approaches the seventh decade of life. Issues of time management (going from a working lifestyle to a leisure lifestyle), relationships with significant others, children, personal recreational needs, and attitude shifts are some of the many changes that happen. These gerontological concerns become the substrate for building and maintaining a healthy balance among body, mind, and spirit. Here, I have created several learning modules for learning what they are, how to adjust and adapt to change, and how to construct a positive mental attitude about getting older and still enjoying an active lifestyle. I have developed a workshop that introduces these issues and teaches some coping strategies for enhancement of the aging person. Called Aging Issues, Coping Strategies (AICS), it is designed for all individuals, including many trans folks entering into and becoming aware of the aging process.

As an androgyne of six-plus decades of life, I am constantly in awe of the process of change and the importance of time in the management of aging. It has bearing with regard to my gender role and presentation issues. Combining the current role and presentation with some of my past experiences in creating a new image is a challenge, especially in the face of megachanges in American society. I still enjoy a healthy loving relationship with my partner. I am amazed at the changes that have occurred in the transgender movement and take some pride in the effects that have resulted from the innovative programs and ideas I introduced thirty years ago. I have done some of these new workshops for the gay-lesbian-bisexual-transgender (GLBT) community. I have reentered the teaching world as an adjunct professor, teaching programs on aging for positive learning and lifestyle enjoyment.

In closing, I would like to share three pillars of a personal value system with the reader. These are:

- Do unto others, as you would have others do unto you. (Golden Rule)
- Know thyself and love thyself. (Plato)
- An unexamined life has little meaning. (Socrates)

These have been instrumental in exploring my lifestyle as an androgyne.

MY WONDERFUL ASKEWNESS

Bet Power

Even though I was born a female, I always imagined myself as a boy/man. I even made up a story.

Herohito is the masculine name I've given to the slim Japanese American woman scientist who I was in the incarnation right before this one. Herohito was born in 1900. I do not know his real name. Perhaps one day I will discover it, in a search for my male ancestral roots. In the early 1940s, Herohito—a good, sensitive, intelligent man—gave 100 percent of his creativity and genius as a physicist to an American corporation he thought was using his groundbreaking work to help the world. In actuality, his scientific brilliance was perverted without his knowledge or consent—and his hard work and research was used to build the atomic bomb that was dropped on Nagasaki and Hiroshima. Some months after this devastation in the land of his father and grandfathers, an American woman revealed Herohito's unwitting participation in the covert military program to Japanese authorities. Betrayed by this woman he loved, Herohito was forcibly removed from his lab, flown to Japan, the land of his birth, tried and convicted of treason, and, soon after, brutally raped and murdered in prison by Japanese guards. In early 1947 Herohito bled to death from castration on the floor of his cell. His/my spirit roamed the universe disembodied and traumatized, from 1947 to early 1950. Then the consciousness that was Herohito's took refuge within a female form, for the first time ever in a nobleman's long centuries of male history.

DECADE 1 (1950–1960):
BORN INTO A SNOWSTORM

On March 10, 1950, I was born in Chicago, Illinois. Outside, a blizzard raged and the sound of the hawk's icy blasts punctuated the dawn. Poverty, violence, alcohol, and addiction would not make it easy for my parents to care for a third child. Prejudice against all people different would not make it possible for them to love him. In the background of my newborn awareness, along with ever-present big-city white noise, the Blues and Chicago's endless wind formed the soundtrack for the life of a tough little boy who peered out from within the body of a girl.

But a higher power had wisely chosen it so—to give Herohito time to rest for a while—my female form was a protective shell in which to hide and heal, a mere container to safely camouflage his masculine creativity and power. Generations of male wisdom would not now be spotted so easily by enemies, nor ever again be twisted to their own destructive ends. Bet Power is a new life in which to piece together Herohito's devastated manhood, indeed the warring shattered manhood of all men alive. Such is the breadth of Herohito's influence and, now, of my opportunity. Such is the depth of my loving trans-gentle-manliness.

The earliest thought of myself was that I was a boy. Memories from ages four and five do not include any confusion or self-scrutiny of my gender at all. I was a boy, and that was that. Rather, my early images revolve around Belmont Beach at Lake Michigan; my dad, home from the navy, swimming miles out into the water; and my mother—a non-swimmer—sitting pretty in her bathing suit safely on a blanket on the shore. My dad would carry me into the water as I stared at the tall ship tattoo sailing on his muscular right arm just below his gold-bronze shoulder. He'd swing me in the air over his head, my arms clasped tightly around his neck, then swim in strong forward strokes with me lying thrilled and happy on his broad back. Dad and son did the breaststroke and dog paddle as one. A few years later, he taught me to swim by throwing me into the deep end of a public Chicago park system swimming pool. He also let me apprentice to him when he did carpentry and taught me baseball, bowling, billiards, five-card stud poker, and how to smoke a pipe. He tried to teach me to fish, but my heart wouldn't agree with bait on a hook. He raised me like a boy; he taught me as his son. I learned about drinking and violent tempers, too. I learned to be wise and deep, watch baseball on TV and at Wrigley Field, never hit a woman, and not talk a whole lot.

I was a small, tough, and wiry kid. From the start I was athletic and cross-dressed in my older brother's hand-me-downs. Winter photos of me (the few that I have) at ages four, five, and six show me in flannel-lined corduroy pants and a little wool boy's jacket or sweater, sitting and standing just as I do today, in masculine poses. We had an inflatable swimming pool that had blow-up horse heads around the rim. One summer photo shows me bare-chested in swim trunks and a cowboy hat, straddling the pool like I was riding the plains. I dreamed of having a pony like the rich kids in the suburbs or in Wisconsin, or even like wranglers out West did.

I played league ball with my older brother's friends, catching hard baseballs in my bare hands (although sometimes I had a mitt) in the "vacant lots" near our inner-city home. I'd race across broken bricks and shards of glass and itchy weeds to be the guy who outhit, outran, and outcaught them all. Stealing bases and leaping to make saves in deep left field were my signature moves. My knees remained scraped at all times, and I would never wear Band-Aids. I had to overdo any physical activity. I had to out-race, outbike, and outclimb all the boys. From these early days on, I have always experienced myself as way bigger than my body. None of my brother's friends suspected I was female. If they had, they would never have cheered for me or accepted it when I beat them at sports.

I played tag, hide-and-seek, and wrestled with my brother and his gang, too. We hung out in the summer months, ate tulip squeezes, and traded bubble-gum pack baseball cards in the "clubhouse" my father built adjacent to the basement. We roller-skated in the empty garage when my dad went out bowling or to the bar for a beer. We marveled at his collection of car license plates from the thirties and forties nailed to the garage walls. We never allowed girls into the clubhouse and kept them out of our games. My two sisters—one older, one younger than I—were merely permitted to watch.

Those were the days—the days of my boyish innocence. The sun shone bright, the clouds formed animal shapes, and the grass in the backyard next to my mother's rose-and-phlox garden felt soft and high. I lay spread-eagled on the lawn in dreamy peace, looked up, and tried to decide if it was the sky ceiling that was rotating ever so slowly. Or was it the earth floor moving dizzily below my back?

One day when I was six, my mother sent me to the corner grocery store alone, to pick up ground round at the butcher's. She put groceries more and more frequently on the tab and started using me as a buffer between her and creditors. As I walked toward the store, I could see a woman my mother's age walking toward me, about a block away. I heard a car screech and saw it veer off the street and onto the sidewalk, crushing the woman into a plate-glass basement store window. She was killed instantly. All I recall was a cloud of blood rising before me high into the air. I ran back home in shock, wanting my mother to console me. Instead, she dragged me back to the scene of the accident, clutched my hand as I squirmed to get away, and forced me to look at it again. She stood there and repeated, "Just pretend it didn't happen."

That was the day I lost my own mother. From that day on, this woman who stopped being a mother to me, attacked me physically and abused me sexually. There were nights when she came home angry at 1:00 AM from her factory job that she rubbed her hands all over my body—outside what would become my shell but not me, and inside my genitals—telling me she hated men, hated sleeping with my dad, and calling me her little husband. Sometimes, she would pull me out of bed by my feet to the floor, punch me mercilessly, then make me rewash the dishes from the family dinner because she noticed some bit of dried food I had missed on a fork. The incest and night-raid physical beatings went on for thirteen years, until I got strong enough to fend them off. She did not cause my transsexualism. She took advantage of the young man who was already there.

Toward the end of the 1950s, I escaped the violence escalating between my father and mother (they fought about his drinking and not having money; she derided him for earning less than she) by twice a week walking a mile to the local public library branch and reading all the books there in a row. First, I sat there for hours reading the children's and adolescent-age stories. Then I asked the librarian for permission to start on the adult books, and I read them alphabetically from the shelves—one, two, three, even five, at a time. Stories about horses and Alfred Hitchcock murder mysteries were my favorites, although I also liked Madeleine L'Engle's *A Wrinkle in Time*.

Whenever I returned to the house, the incest pattern repeated. Since there was no lock on my bedroom door, the woman who was supposed to be my mother—undoubtedly under the influence of god knows how many pills—entered with a tray of booze and rubbing alcohol, and told me I was very sick and couldn't go to school. She fed me the booze and rubbed me sexually with the alcohol. This routine got played out over and over again.

Even so, I loved my mother. Dad faded away more and more into a drunken, absent silence. I loved him so much that I reinvented him in my mind as a perfect, all-wise, and all-loving father. He seldom spoke and, to my eyes, made an especially handsome Buddha. I wrote an essay about my dad for school and won a classroom award, a medal to wear around my neck.

Then, I stopped being athletic and no longer played physical games. I didn't want to know that my body had turned into a painful magnet for mommy dearest. I experienced myself as a devotee of literature, music, and art. I began to write and form myself into a male poet, but I became aware, when the woman who was supposed to be my mother touched me and plied me with booze, that my body was female. When I lay profoundly alone in my bed looking out the window up into the sky, I knew I was horribly vulnerable and I knew I was trapped. The days of my outdoor freedom were over. I was a target. Like my father, I was emptiness and silence itself.

With my outrage turned in, I stop speaking to anyone for a period of six months. I did it to survive, to keep myself alive inside. Both boy and girl—I was a genius! Still, I was a one-of-a-kind alien on this planet—no, in the entire cosmos. That was a wonderful, special thing—but scary, painful, and very lonely, too.

DECADE 2 (1961–1970)

Both my father and my mother were fine with my cross-dressing when I was young. It saved them money on new clothes. It didn't become an issue until my confirmation. In their Polish Roman Catholic parish at the age of thirteen, I was expected to wear a lacy white dress for my confirmation and first communion. It was the first time such an outfit was imposed on me. I threw a tantrum. I kicked and screamed and fought my mother on the floor. I wouldn't stop until she let me wear my corduroy pants underneath the blasted dress. I went up to the altar and took a female confirmation name (the first name of the choir's soprano and organist I was crushed-out on), wearing both a dress and pants. Now, I was a problem child. My mother allowed me to wear boy's clothes in the house, but she began to want me to dress and look like a girl when I went out in public to church or school.

Deep-voiced, I sang alto in the children's choir, performing four-part harmony Latin classical masses. I loved to sing because I heard my own male voice then. I also learned to read sheet music.

In 1964 I taped a black-light poster of a sailboat on the wall above my bed. I told myself that when I turned eighteen, I would leave my parents' house and head for the sea where I would travel freely, adventuring around the world in *Blue*. I read a book to teach myself how to handle a schooner. In reality, I merely managed to take my brother's old ten-speed racer bike and use it to escape my parents' house, living partially on the streets. The cement walkways along Chicago's lakefront and metropolitan downtown felt safer to me than the bed in my mother's house. When I was in the house, the incest intensified. At times, my mother manipulated my father into participating in sexual scenes with us kids. The woman who was supposed to be my mother, that is. She controlled me when I fought her off by telling me I was sick and crazy. She said she loved me and it was her right to touch me that way. I began to know that not only did I not have a mother but I was losing my dad to his betrayal as well. I often thought of myself as an orphan in those days. The one who was actually ill and grew sicker was my mother. She self-mutilated as the family sat on the sofa watching TV in the evenings. Blood dripped down her forearms, and no one said a thing. Her pathological behavior was not discussed at all. We never, ever talked about our feelings, with words. She howled with her hot flashes for twenty minutes nonstop and threatened to kill herself by running from the house in her nightdress and slippers, hoping to slide in the snow. We kids were the fault she said, and my father.

What was happening to my boy body? Where did it go? One day, I sat on the toilet and wiped blood from between my legs. I thought I was injured or dying, and I called for my mother to help me. She came into the bathroom and said to me, "Now you're a woman—your older sister will tell you what to do," and left. This was serious and shocking news. What the hell was going on? Boys don't bleed like this, do they?

Already accustomed to childhood malnutrition, I ate very little to keep myself from developing curves. Some days, I did not eat at all. I rode my bike and drank some water. I slept overnight on the grass in front of the Art Institute or on a bench in Union Station. I hung out in Lincoln Park listening to black and Latino conga players. I learned how to street dance, to pop-and-lock. I wanted to be a breaker boy, but I never felt free enough in my body to pull it off. I loved to race my bike at full speed till I was exhausted, then lie on my back under a tree hearing street music and watching how flat my chest looked as I stretched my arms out behind my head. My breathing raised my chest up and down a little, but I reassured myself that I was still a boy—I was determined to keep the front of me as small as possible, nice and level. I thought often that the worst thing to be in this life was a woman or a girl. My masculinity was ever present in my consciousness, my mind, despite my physical body. Because everyone called me "she," I sometimes thought of myself in the neutral, as a "person" rather than a boy. No one in the world anywhere knew or understood this fact—that despite my body, I was becoming a young man.

When I was fifteen, Dad taught me to drive in a snowstorm. He took me in his big Buick Roadmaster to the parking lot at Lane Tech High School and said if I learned to drive a car in such hazardous conditions, I would always be able to drive safely through anything. My grandmother and mother didn't know how to drive. My older sister never wanted to learn. Though I was scarcely tall enough to see out over the dashboard, I was the first female in the family to get behind the wheel and go.

I made sure I did very well in high school and college. I knew education would give me my only chance in life. I loved school because while studying I could be entirely cerebral. School was also a great place to escape my parents. My boy self shifted its location entirely out of the trunk of my body and into my brain. I was an A student, an impeccable scholar. From the captain's wheel located in the area from my eyebrows up, I would steer my life successfully around all obstacles, as a man.

One man who helped me grow up was my uncle—my father's older brother who lived in our house, up in the attic. He was a sober alcoholic who my mother had taken in after he lost his wife, sons, executive position, life savings, and parts of his internal organs—everything—to booze and racetrack gambling. By the time I was in early adolescence, he provided the spiritual and emotional fathering to me that my dad became incapable of. Uncle was calm and serene even in a battlefield household. He surrounded himself with Agatha Christie novels in his tiny attic bedroom, and he never failed to intercede for me when my mother or older siblings tried to target me. It is because of my uncle that I am a voracious reader, queer archivist, and book collector today. It is also because of him that I, too, eventually joined AA.

In the Catholic all-girls high school, I coped with uniforms by rolling my skirt up at the waist and adding a pair of white suspenders underneath the blazer. I liked the blazer's masculine cut, and below it I wore a white button-down men's shirt. I often paid for these improvisations with detentions given me at inspection time, until I learned how to quickly remove my suspenders while waiting in line for the nuns to look us over.

I developed a romantic friendship with a senior named Teresa. She was a writer and a year ahead of me in high school. We wrote to each other during the summers when she was away with her parents in rural Wisconsin. We kept up our passionate letters for years after we graduated. I still have them all—the ones she sent to me. I also had a serious crush on my chemistry teacher, Sister Sebastian. I knew it was mutual when she hugged me tight and long after class and told me she wished she could see who I was behind my eyes. A few years ago, I heard she left the convent with Sister Rita. They came out as lesbians, proclaimed their love for each other, and had a commitment ceremony.

I began to have sexual dreams about girls and women. In them, I was always a rescuing male. Sister Sebastian lied about my age and told Polk Brothers department store I was eighteen when I wasn't yet sixteen years old. She did it to help get me out of my parents' house by making a little money. She got me my first after-school job checking credit applications for customers who wanted to buy stoves and refrigerators. I brought every small paycheck home to my mother. I felt like a provider, a breadwinner boy. If only my hard-earned money would stop my mother from ripping Dad's T-shirts off his back in rage when he failed to help her make ends meet. When the red trail of her fingernail scratches on his shoulders someday faded, only then would I regard myself as successful. Somehow this was all my fault. The fact that my dad earned very little to start off with, and spent part of his paycheck on bowling and beer, never entered into my mind. My mother told us she only wanted two kids—and I was the burdensome third of five.

I wore the same pair of blue denim overalls—with a peace-sign patch and a women's liberation fist sewn onto the front—throughout my teen years. I used the narrow pockets on the bib to carry my pens, money, toothpicks, and one of my father's pipes, to be cool. I liked the bib because it flattened my slightly rounding front and served as a kind of armor—a breastplate for a 105-pound street warrior. I drank and smoked dope; dropped acid or mescaline whenever I could; and I wore my hair long like the hippie boys. I was a famous poet in my mind. If a volume of my poetry didn't get published by the time I turned thirty, I would kill myself on that very day.

My mother pressured me to date boys, even tried to get me to marry one. I went out with her favorite, George, but only once. To get through the awful ordeal, I chugged a whole bottle of gin in the back seat of his car, and I punched him in the face when he tried to fuck me outside my parents' basement door. In my late teens, I had sexual relations with a white male poet and a black combat veteran. I never allowed them to penetrate me though, so I controlled the sexual action, allowing only oral. I think I was curious to see a penis up close and how it worked, that's all. Sexuality with men didn't do a thing more for me. What was I missing and how could I get it? I certainly didn't enjoy myself. Both relationships with these men were difficult and brief. Both came out a few years later as gay.

By age sixteen, I had figured out how to pass well enough to gain entry into male leather bars and drag-show clubs. I wore a broad-shouldered leather jacket or a tight denim one, and put on a cap and high leather boots (with a six-inch blade tucked down the side for my safety, at all times). I passed everywhere, even though I was under the legal drinking age. Everywhere, that is, except at Man's Country. They always read me there and sent me away from the door. I remember walking the streets of New Town (the gay area of Chicago that is now called Boys' Town) and thinking about the leather men and transvestites. I clearly knew I was like them and could be one of them someday. But I couldn't tell how, since my body was female—and females weren't a part of those groups.

I marched in black civil rights demonstrations and shut down expressways and the University of Illinois campus buildings in massive student sit-in protests against the Vietnam War. I ran from tear gas and the sound of billy clubs cracking protesters' skulls at the 1968 Democratic National Convention. I felt myself to be a radical male antiwar, antiracist revolutionary, and a visionary poet. I went to Workers World Party meetings and learned about the Haymarket Riots. I helped an anarcho-feminist friend of mine silkscreen protest posters at a secret press and bookstore in a dark, abandoned southside warehouse. In the coffeehouses and storefronts, I listened to Imiri Baraka, Allen Ginsberg, Muddy Waters, Bonnie Raitt, and B. B. King. Still physically fighting off my mother's advances at times, I'd lay in my bed and sink the earplug of my transistor radio into my ear, turning up the volume when Janis Joplin wailed—now there was a dynamo female living her life like a guy.

By 1969, the year of Stonewall, I knew I was stunningly different. I knew I was queer in some way. I had hot sex with myself, fantasizing in elaborate detail about women. When I wasn't trying to come down from an endless bad drug trip, I felt my male power rising toward wonderful release. Sometimes it dawned on me that I was a straight guy. I vowed that my bedroom would always be for me a place of total freedom. This one place in the world—the realm of my own bed—would be my kingdom, ever and always free from any limits or rules. I vowed this. I promised myself.

Around that time, my mother's incestuous game stopped working on me anymore. I was twenty and finally able to keep her off my body—no longer a child and much stronger now. She retaliated by telling me I was crazy and that, unless I let her caress me, she would call a doctor or a shrink. I volunteered to find a shrink, and I started to go to psychotherapy.

Still continuing to emerge sexually, I fell madly in love with my first therapist, a woman named Ota. But she was homophobic, I later learned the hard way, for when I came out to her about my euphoric dreams of bouncing on her breasts, she told me I was getting worse. She called in a doctor who prescribed a stunning array of powerful antidepressants and antipsychotics.

DECADE 3 (1971–1980)

Hooked and weakened by the pills and almost always high, I heard my mother take a phone call from Ota, the therapist, one day. Ota had called my mother to urge her to have me committed.

I'll never forget the sad bus ride with my mother when she took me to a mental prison and signed me in. How much betrayal from women could one guy take? My heart was broken, and I had no sense of place for myself anywhere in this world. Being a young man in a female body attracted sexually to women wasn't lesbian and it wasn't gay. It wasn't quite heterosexual, either. It couldn't be transsexual because that was only for Christine Jorgensen. What was I, then? Nobody around me was like me. Nobody around me knew. I was the most exotic creature walking the planet. And now I was bagged. A cage in a zoo or a regular prison would have been better than the mental prison.

My problem was that I was narcissistic, the shrinks said. "Narcissistic personality disturbance with anxiety and recurring panic attacks" was how I was diagnosed. That gave the hospital guards license to feed me seven psychiatric prescriptions at a time, put me behind bars in isolation whenever I talked about my sexual desire for women, and try to somehow mold me into a straight woman. I went very far away from my inner self there, just a thin thread holding on. I had out-of-body experiences. I felt like I had died. I looked around me at the people on the ward and saw that they were all either black, Latino, butch dykes, or poor whites. And then there was me, a minority somehow, too.

One day, in the isolation room, after intrusive questioning from an attendant to tell her why I wouldn't let men fuck me, I got it. My being behind bars, doped up on pills to the point of being nonfunctional, was political. This was all a social control game. It was intense pressure to make me a straight woman. The mental prison was a holding pen for racial and sexual minorities. The drugs, more than the bars on the windows and the alarms on the doors, were the glue holding me in that place.

I secretly stopped taking all pills and made up a story about having a boyfriend on the outside I just had to visit. After six weeks of telling a story about dating this fictional man, I was released.

Then I went cold turkey off all the drugs. I joined the radical antipsychiatry movement and became a grassroots leader in the Chicago area, giving workshops and talks to lesbians about the side effects of prescription drugs. I raised consciousness through offering reading-and-discussion circles; on our study list I put books like the *Physician's Desk Reference (PDR)*, Thomas Szasz's *The Myth of Mental Illness*, and Phyllis Chessler's *Women and Madness*. I found unbelievable strength somehow while standing in my truth. I moved out of my parents' house and shared my first apartment with a straight woman receptionist I had met at the mental hospital. I finished my last year of undergraduate college, although, since I was struggling through drug withdrawal, I barely got by. In 1972 I located a butch lesbian psychologist and went to her for help. I told her that I felt like a man inside and wanted to be sexual with women. I told her that, of all kinds of people on the planet, I felt most like a straight guy inside. I thought like one. I acted like one. Sure, I was sensitive, politically and socially progressive, and an artist-writer, but underneath I was a straight guy and I was wearing a female body. What did this mean? I knew by now that I wasn't nuts and that "going crazy" wasn't a place I could go. I deeply believed—and still do—that madness is manufactured through the social control mechanism of drugs (both illegal and prescribed) and alcohol. I asked her what I was.

She said I was a butch lesbian and I did not need therapy. I should go down to the Lesbian Feminist Center and get involved there. She thought that was my rightful community. She was close, but she was wrong. In the early 1970s she had not yet heard about female-to-males.

I detoxed within the Chicago lesbian community, where women taught me to eat vegetarian and use herbs for my healing. I lost the unnatural fifty pounds I had gained as a side effect of the pills—and I started looking like my man self again. I am grateful that I regained my health and strength through the support and examples of dykes, but I never really felt like I fit in with them there. I didn't think of myself as a lesbian. I liked the words "butch" and "stone" and tolerated "dyke" when applied to myself. Still, I always felt myself to be the butchest of the butch; my stride was longer and my attitude much cockier than any woman—and scarcely any man—around.

I volunteered in the Lesbian Feminist Center selling dyke books in its bookstore. In the back of the storefront center was a collection of books, periodicals, and subject files—the New Alexandria Lesbian Library (NALL). The butch who had founded it had her master's in library science; she showed me how to preserve and process lesbian and feminist community archival holdings. Soon I shifted my volunteer work away from the bookstore and completely into the library. I was becoming a queer archivist in one of the earliest lesbian collections in this country. It kept me around books, a place of safety for me. It also kept me around women, not nearly as safe. In 1972, while taking a tae kwon do karate class, I met a lesbian who soon became my first woman lover. The feeling of "coming out" into my rightful sexuality with females was one of indescribable freedom to me. The relationship lasted maybe two years. I immediately took another lover—a woman who came to volunteer in the NALL. During this relationship, in 1977, I completed my master's degree in comparative literature and sociocultural processes. I was the first person in my Polish American working-class family to achieve a master's degree.

I wanted a man's career that would use my writing talent and love of words and pictures. I took a position proofreading page layouts and editing ad copy for a magazine publisher on Michigan Avenue. In 1978 an art director at this company whom I had befriended took me to her apartment and gave me my first very short haircut. Sue was a straight woman and she explained to me that showing my ears for the first time might be a little bit of a shock, but she was certain I would feel and look much better that way. My first guy's haircut! I was blown away with Sue's boldness and a sense of my own daring and happiness. I was now a genius male poet in my mind. I wrote nonstop and planned a male career in writing. I adopted a professional motto, a mantra that I still chant today, "I am writing, I am fighting for my life."

In 1977 the Lesbian Feminist Center closed. I rescued the books and magazines from the NALL and moved the collection into a Rogers Park apartment I shared with my second woman lover. We took vacations every summer in Boston, the north shore, and Cape Cod to visit the woman who had founded the library. She had moved from Chicago to Cambridge, Massachusetts. When I saw the ocean at Gloucester for the very first time, I dove in with all my clothes on—I knew I was months away from somehow moving down east.

I broke with my bio-family entirely in 1979. I did it to survive and to cut off any further abuse, repression, and psychological destruction from them. The family party line was that they had done nothing wrong—no incest, no physical beatings, no emotional abuse had ever occurred. Rather, I was the crazy one because I made it all up when I talked about what my parents had done to me—and now I was queer, as well. I decided I could no longer have my reality crushed in that way and live through it, much less have a chance to grow. The only answer was to run away, leave Chicago, and never look back. In the fall of 1979, I rescued the NALL collection from an uncertain future, packed it up in a truckful of boxes, and moved with my second woman lover to ten acres of pristine wooded land in Huntington, Massachusetts.

I found a job as a proofreader in an ad agency near Hartford, Connecticut. A senior vice president there quickly gave me a break and promoted me to copy chief. This executive was an impeccable advertising designer, a daily wearer of Italian haute couture, and a warm, perceptive gay man. I lusted after his beard, his jewelry, and his suits and ties. From Sam I learned to add art direction to my professional skills set, as well as writing for print and radio advertising. I've never had a better mentor or a more caring one. He recognized my *transgenderism* before I myself had words for it. While working in the agency, I kept a glass jar of nuts on my desk to nibble on as I wrote. One day, Sam swished through the agency, as was his wont, dropping queenly sarcasms in his wake. I heard him say at the top of his voice, "Oh look out, Bet has his nuts on the table today!"

DECADE 4 (1981–1990)

I had trouble with my women lovers, time and time again. They abused me verbally or even physically, and then left me for women who weren't masculine like me. I responded to this pattern by choosing prettier and prettier women—they had to be gorgeous high femme and they had to be bi or straight. My pattern then changed only in one way: when they abused me and left me, they left me for men. Another thing was always the same in these relationships: the women drank alcoholically, though I could not see it back then. And I spent most of my social time dancing and drinking myself into blackouts with them in queer discos and backroom bars.

I drank heavily for years myself in dyke, gay, and trannie bars.

Looking back on that period, booze was a substance I used to keep myself from feeling my masculine feelings inside. I was the proverbial "man inside the bottle," pushed down, repressed, and corked up inside a glass pen. I could feel like maybe I was a butch lesbian when I drank in the bars. I thought I had a chance at fitting in somewhere. But in 1982 I decided to quit drinking entirely. Booze no longer fit in with my increasingly vegan and chemical-free diet. I didn't think I had a problem with addiction or booze. After all, I hadn't had a drug of any kind for nearly ten years; it was just my lovers who repeatedly hurt me who had the problem. I knew there was a destructive pattern that I was caught up in with the women in my life. To stop drinking, I told myself, would somehow fix the recurring problem of betrayal from my lovers. I went to Al-Anon, where I focused on the connection between booze, pills, and women in my intimate life. However, without a program of recovery for myself and with no admission of my own alcoholism and addiction, I was just a dry drunk walking around powerless—a powder keg waiting to explode.

I hit a serious second bottom in 1983. When a third woman lover left me for a baby dyke, I lost control in a fit of rage, kicked in her bedroom window to find them there, and was arrested and jailed for breaking and entering, and trespassing. Behind bars again briefly—this time in prison but reminiscent of the mental hospital—I came to the awareness that my problem must somehow be alcohol. Perhaps, it dawned on me it was *my* alcoholism and not just my lovers'. I went to an alcoholism counselor to discuss this. And I asked a powerful psychic to do a past-life regression with me. Not knowing me at all, she told me about Herohito and gave me information that I had always, in every past life, been a man. This current incarnation had tucked me protectively into a female form. It didn't matter; I was still Herohito evolving and going through my betrayals from women in order to learn how to heal.

In late 1983 I admitted I was an alcoholic and addict, and I starting going to AA. I've been clean and sober, one day at a time, ever since. In AA, I have found a practical spirituality, a philosophy, and a way of life that works in profoundly wonderful ways for me. What's most important is that, in 1983, I came out as both trans and an S/Mer. I had an easier time finding community and support for the latter identity than I did for the former. I knew there were transsexuals out there, but I still hadn't heard of even one who was in a female body to begin with, like me.

I took a break from love relationships for a couple of years. One day in October 1986, a booklet and a note arrived at the NALL collection that I house in my Northampton, Massachusetts, home. The note said perhaps some visitors to the lesbian library would be interested to read the booklet. The note was from Louis Graydon Sullivan. Lou authored the booklet and it was a planetary first: *Information for the Female-to-Male Crossdresser and Transsexual.*

In utter amazement and joy, I finished reading it in two hours from cover to cover. Most of the passing, binding, and packing techniques Lou wrote about I had been doing on my own, instinctively, for years. There was a tip about trimming sideburns at a masculine angle that was new to me. But more important, this booklet brought Lou into my life. At that moment I felt a huge liberation and relief—there was at least one other man on the earth living in a female form, like me. Though *Lou was gay and I was straight, that didn't matter.* What mattered enormously was another human being was like myself and that he gave me, at long last, the language to describe myself. I wasn't a woman. I wasn't a genetic man. I wasn't a dyke or a lesbian, or even gay. I wasn't crazy, and I was no longer alone. I was a *female-to-male transsexual. I was an FTM.* I was *transgender.* I was a heterosexual *transman.* Just weeks after reading Lou's booklet, I flew out to San Francisco to meet him. In the middle of our conversation at his kitchen table, Lou got up and told me he had to take his AZT. He was HIV-positive and dying of AIDS. Lou was the most important and, to this day, dearest friend of my life—but I didn't have him with me for long.

DECADE 5 (1991–2000)

I corresponded with Lou and had frequent phone conversations with him from 1986 until he died in 1991. During that time, in 1989, I met and fell in love with a woman I came to consider my wife. I'll never forget how happy Lou was for me when I sent him a photo of Lonnie dressed in her red dress, sun hat, and high heels. He had been trying to fix me up with women since he first met me, hoping to cure my perennial loneliness.

Before Lou died, he asked me if I would take over leadership of his group and newsletter, *FTM*, and come live in San Francisco. He had a roll of stamps and a long list of names on the *FTM* mailing list that he would turn over to me. I wanted very much to continue Lou's work and to have an FTM community of my own, but I had a successful career and a wife going to school in the Boston area. I just couldn't leave my whole East Coast life behind.

When Lou died, I felt utterly alone again. I only knew one FTM cross-dresser in all of New England, and there were no FTM groups yet anywhere on the East Coast—not even in New York City. So, to find other men like myself—and to carry on Lou's work but on the right-hand coast of this country, on my forty-second birthday weekend, I founded the East Coast Female-to-Male Group (ECFTMG). Lonnie and I held the first meeting of ECFTMG on March 8, 1992, in her apartment in Watertown, Massachusetts. The meetings alternated for the first few months between Watertown and Northampton. Eventually—and ever since then until today—the group has met monthly in my home in Northampton.

I had a community at long last! Carved out with monthly mailings and meetings of just a few at first, then tens and even twenties and—one meeting—forty men and partners who came to ECFTMG, a pioneering FTM community began to grow and spread in Northampton and eventually throughout western Massachusetts. Boston followed suit within a few years, with FTM support groups cropping up everywhere. Ten years after ECFTMG began, there were four separate FTM support groups meeting monthly in Northampton alone. In addition, the Sunshine Club in Hadley, Massachusetts, and the Twenty Club in Hartford, Connecticut, were mainly MTF groups.

I gradually left the lesbian community entirely, no longer going to lesbian events or keeping up with the social goings on, local gossip, and news. It was a community that had nudged me out, anyway, and sometimes quite rudely. My maleness and my sadomasochism were both unwanted. By 1990 I was a *transman* directing not only ECFTMG but also SHELIX, a monthly support group for lesbian, bi, and trans S/Mers, and the curator of a national queer archive, as well. I decided that the holdings in the collection were, in reality, not just lesbian but overlapped in their documentation the lives of gays, bisexuals, and transpeople as well. Thus, in late 1991, I renamed the New Alexandria Lesbian Library the Sexual Minorities Archives. I began a period of intense collecting of the literature, history, and art of transpeople, bisexuals, gay men, and S/Mers as well as continued to collect the herstory of lesbians. Meanwhile, I was sorting out internally my own FTM transition path. I gave myself visits to a gender counselor and time to figure out whether or not I wanted to medically transition. My wife Lonnie and I had the best sex of our lives, but she still wanted me to change my body to be more male. It would have been simpler and easier for her to introduce me to her social and religious circle at Harvard if I looked and sounded like a man instead of a transman and if she could pass for a traditional heterosexual woman.

But I always felt negative about testosterone for myself. I was an addict in recovery and I never wanted to be dependent on a chemical ever again. Besides, no one yet knew the long-term effects of this sex hormone on the body—and I wanted to live to be 105! And the pain of being surgically cut across my private parts—forget it! Okay, call me a coward, I told my wife and the whole FTM community I had helped form and which I lead, but don't call me anything less than a transsexual or a man, because that's who I am.

Gradually, I came to define the right space for myself—sometimes meeting with rejection from some within my own transgender community—as *a female-to-male, nonhormone, nonoperative transsexual man.* Damn anyone who can't or won't understand my delicious complexity and my rebellious resistance to all things medical and psychiatric, I said. This is *MY TRANSGENDER JOURNEY* and I have good reasons for letting my body be. I was already a man—and had ever been so. I didn't need or want testosterone and TS surgery to make me into me.

As Thich Nhat Hahn says, "I am not my body." In his wisdom, I found new meaning to describe the truth of me. I am a heterosexual man wearing a female form on top of which is another "skin" of male clothes. *I'm a nonoperative FTM transsexual.* We do exist. Get used to it. Throughout my life, I've instinctively shaped my body to appear manly through alternative but natural means—clothing, haircut, weight control, masculine mannerisms and movements, binding, packing, lowering the pitch of my voice, and investigating plant-based androgens that are natural testosterone boosters. I emerged in these ways and continued to look more like my true self, first as a younger man and then more mature as I reached middle age. Though using nonchemical, nonsurgical means, I've changed my body over time to look fully male. I pass as a man 80 to 90 percent of the time. The only people who still use female pronouns about me are some at my office. Others use no pronouns at all and simply repeat my first name in carefully constructed sentences. With anyone I want to be close with, I soon tell them about who I am: I am a man wearing a female body. What you see is not necessarily what you get. Discrimination in employment, based on my gender identity, gender expression, or sexual orientation, has been a reoccurring battle. Sometimes I have won lawsuits, and sometimes I have lost. Yet I have managed to push my career up the proverbial corporate ladder a step at a time, achieving creative director–vice president positions in advertising and marketing that are scarce even for genetic men. The difference for me is that I daily wear thick armor when I go to work. Still, I have the right to be the best professional man I can be.

The darkest months, which turned into years, of my life was when Lonnie—the love of my life—left me for a genetic man. That was in 1995, and I've chosen not to try again—rather, to remain her husband in my heart anyway—ever since. Through everything, I've remained clean and sober. My response to curve balls life throws me is always to deepen my spiritual program and move even closer to my higher source.

DECADE 6 (2001–NOW)

The Sexual Minorities Archives, the East Coast FTM Group, my sponsorship of gay men and transmen getting sober in AA, my antiracism and antiwar work—all keep going strong. I have that new freedom and new happiness that AA's promises guarantee. I am settled and serene about my decision to remain *nonhormonal, non-op.* I feel deeply it is an important statement from me to my *trans community* and to all people who cross my path in this world. Isamu Noguchi, born in the United States in 1904 to a Japanese father and an American mother, became an international art figure in the 1930s and 1940s. He was known for creating breakthrough abstract sculpture and public plazas, including the Garden of Peace in Paris. For Noguchi, creating ceramics in Japan was "a seeking after identity." He put aside the traditional potter's wheel and broke away from traditional forms and traditional methods. By breaking almost every rule (for example, by taking clay off the wheel and hand-building most of his pieces instead of throwing them, and by using the "wrong" glazes), the modern artist set himself—and Japanese ceramics—free. His works of art combine his Asian and American heritages and reflect obliquely his life-long struggle to reconcile both backgrounds. Museum director Julian Raby coined a new word to describe a showing of Noguchi's amazing ceramics at the Freer and Sackler galleries in spring of 2002: "askewness."

If Noguchi threw pottery askew, then I have done it with my self, modern transsexuality, humanity, and manhood. Break the rules. Set yourself free.

COPING

Charlene Day

In any discussion of coping with cross-dressing or any other thing in a person's life, it is important to understand the background and formative years of that person. I have included some of the things that I think affected my life.

When I was of preschool age, I had a dream that I could climb up under a woman's skirt and walk around in her body. You can see that the dream had quite an effect on me since I still remember it today. Later, perhaps in college, I read that small children often think that women are hollow because they see up under their skirts, so apparently I was not the only one who thought so. Of course, with women wearing pants and long skirts, that may not be true today.

In my elementary school years I saw an article in the newspaper about men in the Hasty Pudding Club at Harvard University who played women's parts in plays. There were pictures of some of them in glamorous outfits. I remember I was very envious of them, but I only dreamed about wearing such glamorous clothes. In those same years, I remember playing a game with a couple of girls in my neighborhood, the purpose of which I have forgotten, but somehow it put me into girls' clothes. I could barely restrain the pleasure I had in doing something that would be considered so "sissified." It was from this experience that I developed a game I played with myself called "Detective" where I could wear feminine clothes as a disguise. I even made a wig.

The next major event I remember is my parents suddenly uprooting me and sending me off to military boarding school in Southern California. I thought, when summer vacation would come, I could go back to my old home, but that did not happen since, when they came to get me, they told me that we now lived in Southern California. I asked them about my dog, Spot, and they told me they had left him behind with some "nice people." I did not believe them and felt totally betrayed by my own parents. I never really trusted them again. Without warning, I was living in a new city and had lost all my childhood friends and my pet dog without any real explanation. For some reason, my parents seemed to have been ashamed of where we had lived previously, and they made me lie about it. I was afraid to go against their wishes because my mother in the past had often beat me with a switch for any supposed infractions of her rules, which I did not always understand.

That fall, as puberty set in, I entered a new school with no acquaintances or friends at hand. My mother was very dominating and neurotic about having her house in pristine order. I never felt I could invite anyone to our house because they would not feel comfortable. In those days, most everyone I knew smoked, including my mother, but so determined was she to keep her house clean that as soon as anyone put out a cigarette in an ash tray, including her own, she would empty it right away.

It was during my high school years, when I knew my parents would be out for a night and late in coming home, that I sneaked into their bedroom and tried on my Mom's nightgown and some of her clothes, careful to put them back just right. Any thoughts of dressing up, however, were pushed to the back of my mind by World War II when I joined the navy and left home. They came to the fore again late in the war when I got a chance to dress up in a USO show. The aunt of one of my girlfriends whom I had met at the USO made the costumes. The old desires returned, and I kept the outfit to wear as a costume at a Halloween party also put on by the USO.

After the war, I married a woman named Louise and returned to California. The lure of being around those feminine garments proved too much for me, and when she was away I surreptitiously tried on her clothes, although most of them did not fit. Somehow I began to wear a nightgown to bed—first as a sort of joke, but it later turned into a regular thing. After all, it is easier to pull up a skirt than pull down pajama pants if the urge comes upon you. Through all of this I knew that I was not a homosexual, but I did not know what I was. I took advantage of every Mardi Gras or Halloween party to dress as a woman. One of the groups I belonged to decided to put on some stage plays and variety shows. One of the plays, titled *A Womanless Wedding*, had all the women's parts played by men. I was in seventh heaven, particularly since so many rehearsals were required. It was almost a given that in the various shows where there was any opportunity for a man to play a woman I would get the part. I often made the costumes myself. One that I had made for a play and took on a Caribbean cruise won the first prize in the costume category. I am fairly certain that many of my fellow actors recognized there was more than "play-acting" in my desire to wear women's clothes.

By this time I had heard about transsexuals such as Christine Jorgensen, and I knew about drag queens, but I was sure neither of these descriptors fit me. Still I dressed at every opportunity. In the 1950s and 1960s I did a lot of traveling for my company, and I took along a nightgown and other items of women's clothing to wear in the hotel rooms. On one trip I made a costume for one of our shows. I had to sew it all by hand, but it was a labor of love. It was not until the 1960s, when I read a book titled *A Year among the Girls*, that I was clued in to the fact that there was an organization for heterosexual transvestites.

I quickly began to investigate, met Virginia Prince, and joined what was then known as the Foundation for Personality Expression (FPE). I have been a member of it and the succeeding organization, the Society for the Second Self (Tri-Ess) ever since. Shortly after I joined the FPE, I met a TV named Betty Jo who was retired on disability because of failing eyesight and took the opportunity to live full time as a woman. She became a mentor to me as well as a good friend. I could visit her anytime with the proviso that I came dressed as Charlene. With her encouragement, I began to go out in public, including having dinners at local restaurants. When she died, I attended her funeral as Charlene. By that time her secret life had become known, but no one cared. I am fairly certain that most of the mourners suspected my true gender, but no one gave any hint to the fact.

One of my dreams was to be able to "pass," and I took care to try to do so. I had little hair on my legs and hardly any on my body or arms, but I did have a lot of facial hair. The obvious solution was electrolysis, and I spent a few years getting it removed. I had to do it in small stages so as not to raise suspicions. Often I went dressed as Charlene. I became increasingly daring.

I went to a beauty shop that gave lessons on makeup. I told the proprietress about my desire to dress as a woman and my need to learn how to apply makeup more effectively. She agreed to give me lessons, which I attended as a woman.

Because of these preparations, I have been able to go almost anywhere as a woman. One thing that I have observed over the years is that young TVs (in their twenties) seem to pass without much trouble, providing they do not dress flamboyantly. They have a fresh, youthful appearance. Those men who try to pass in middle age are more likely to be read. Us older broads get by because people don't expect us to have nice skin or be beauty queens. I do have a clothes sense that my wife appreciates. She asks my advice about clothes for herself or presents for others. We often go shopping together, but she will not accompany me when I am dressed up.

She is not interested in becoming involved in any transvestite group or going anywhere with me dressed. She has a fear of being recognized and anguishes over what people might think when that happens. About once a week I do dress up completely at home. Unlike some transvestites, I do not wear any woman's underclothing under my man's attire. I either dress one way or the other completely.

Over the years I have revealed my secret to several friends. One is a widow who I have known for several years. She had seen me in several plays in which I played the woman's role, and one day I showed up en femme at her house and explained how I liked to dress as a woman on any occasion I could. She was very accepting. So were Agnes and her husband Buck who moved into our area. Agnes was told that I liked to dress up, but Buck did not know this. When Agnes left on a trip, I went to their house en femme and told him about my cross-dressing. We had a long conversation and, as the evening arrived, he suggested that we go out to dinner together, something we did several times before he died. Occasionally, I still go out to dinner, dressed as Charlene, with Agnes.

One Saturday, Agnes asked me if I could take her to her doctor's office for an appointment. I had already gotten dressed for a meeting and saw no reason to change. I picked her up, took her to the office, and brought her home. On the way back, while I was stopped at an intersection, my neighbor pulled up alongside me. He recognized my vehicle, and then he recognized me. He just honked and waved, and, though he later kidded me a little bit, it never affected our relationship. As my life progresses more friends know, both men and women, and they realize that my cross-dressing was more than taking parts in shows and wearing women's costumes at Halloween. They have accepted it, and it hasn't changed our relationships. Only one friend was not accepting, although no further mention was ever made of it and we remain good friends. I do not cross-dress around him. In general, women have been more accepting than men. When my son and I were on a camping trip when he was in his teens, I explained about my cross-dressing, and he had no problem accepting it.

I do still enjoy shopping for clothes. When I feel low, getting a new blouse or skirt is a pick-me-up. After all these years, I still get some kind of thrill when I zip up that skirt or the back of my dress. Now, even though I have long been retired, I still continue to dress. It is part of my coping mechanism.

IT'S BEEN
A HELL OF A RIDE

Michael/Christine Hochberg

Where to start? When it all came together I really do not know, but I can state very simply that it has been one hell of a ride. The early days of my life were spent as an only son of an upper-middle-class family in the San Fernando Valley in Los Angeles. My parents, Alex and Renee Hochberg, provided me with anything and everything a spoiled child could want. Both were raised in East Los Angeles by truly unique and positive reinforcing parents. Their union has now lasted fifty-three years, and I have been with them for forty-eight of them—through thick and thin.

Yes, I did play baseball, basketball, and all other team sports at my local park. At the same time, I collected baseball cards that are still part of my existence today. All along, however, I knew something was different about me. My first recollection of this difference was wanting stuffed animals and dolls. Of course, you could never tell your parents about these desires. From a distance I observed what girls were wearing and doing. Girls were pretty, and I could not be pretty. Girls were soft, and I must admit I was softer than most boys. Boys were dirty, and I didn't like that. Finally, as I approached my bar mitzvah, I began the trans journey. To this day, the journey has been a complete high except when my mother pointed out that things were missing from her drawers. I did everything I could to convince myself that being a girl was okay. Of course my parents did not feel the same way, and skipping two grades in school put me at an extreme disadvantage in my social life. There I was in high school—with kids two or three years old than I was—doing my best to find myself in their circle. Rough obviously, difficult also, but holding back my secret was impossible. Growing up after my bar mitzvah, I started taking risks in every aspect of my life by cross-dressing. I would not drive, but taking the bus to Hollywood and other places was a very normal part of my cross-dressing life. As my risk taking increased, I decided to remove my arm and leg hair. This action was greeted with discomfort as well as questions from several people. What can one say?

My mother and father did agree on one thing. It was my life and my decision to make, but if I were to pursue this any further it would be regarded negatively by them. My parents provided a tremendous amount of love but were never very physical about their affection. They knew I often was not very happy. At Halloween I wanted to be the *girl* who was inside of me. I knew and realized I was reaching for something. When I dressed as a girl/woman, I received far more attention than I did when I dressed as a boy/man. My outlook and costuming was extreme —I stood out and loved it.

Prostitutes and club girls were people I identified with since they were risk takers and used their looks as a form of rebellion. During my college years at the University of Southern California, I lived my life around the varsity football players as their student manager. As a manager, you take care of everyone else first before you enter the picture. The players knew something about me was rather different, but they never put me through any form of embarrassment.

I started going to clubs with people who felt as I did at an early age. And thirty years later, I still consider myself a club girl most of the time. I know for certain that I enjoy the nightlife and all the social and physically risky situations one could find oneself in. I still dress in an extreme fashion while in the club environment. It is a part of me that will never change. My parents never see this part of my life. In my twenties, I would dance in after-hours clubs for money, attention, and fame. Here I was— a clean-cut, clean-image male by day and a workingwoman by night. In terms of working, I would dress and present for the attraction and compulsion to be what some could term a slut. Such a life had its ups and downs, but I never felt any danger taking my clothes off so others could see my working attitude.

Over the years, I grew to know that there were other people like me. The support group scene in Southern California offered me an opportunity to breathe, adapt, and converse with other "women" of similar feelings. I played a major role in giving newcomers to the movement a chance to be who they are, and for a long time this seemed to be my destiny. As the groups grew in a positive way, I was starting to get bored.

When I needed an outlet, I would throw myself into new situations giving me an excuse to cross-dress. For the most part, these adventures were safe and fun for everyone who attended. I still needed more exposure. What was this Jewish American Princess to do? I had heard through various people that there were conventions and retreats for cross-dressers, but I was not certain this was the answer. Finally I attended and hooked up with a few individuals, never dreaming that his safe haven would replace my involvement on the Southern California scene. At such conventions, I would dress out of control and be told so by those in attendance, but somehow things clicked for me. I liked people. People liked me, and I pretty much found where I was going next. Yes, I did my share to raise an adopted son and provide a caretaker for my wife. Being "Girlie," however, was always in the mix.

If one is to seek attention and overall controversy in the trans world as I did, I know and realize many of my peers would like me to disappear. At the professional conferences, many people view my presentation as over the top. Too much makeup, eyeliner, bright eye shadows, and even glitter draws me into controversy. Why is it I continue to be on every event's *most wanted list*? Funny as it may seem, I bring a ton of energy and positive focus to everyone I encounter. I do realize that not everyone is the same and that my high level of visibility can be very detracting. In this era, where trans people are working hard for civil rights and justice, I find myself in a minority of those who are criticized for being so outlandish. I do not possess any fear of hurting the movement, but I am certain that those who criticize me mean well. Although, I must admit, I have been thrown out of conventions and local trans meetings because of my somewhat outrageous appearance, I still believe in the groups and their programs. I feel that these events are more successful with me being present.

If one wants to get into a discussion with me about my appearance, I have learned to be a good listener. I may not believe in everything others say, but I will bend if it is warranted. In setting an example for other trans people, some might say that I definitely fail the course. Yet my responsibilities with the various groups have grown since my initial appearance in 1993.

As I approach the *half-century* mark, I know one thing is certain. I am not going to change. Take it or leave it. The colors of my outfits will be bright, the glitter will shine, and the ever-present hats will not go away. I am having a great time with cross-dressing and know there are very few replacements for the enjoyment this brings me.

It may sound silly and weird, but I truly believe I work harder in my femme role than in my masculine one. I push people to the maximum. Others find me interesting, and I have found myself very much at home with sociologists, psychologists, psychiatrists, social workers, and college professors. They may see me as somewhat excessive, but I love to assist them. I find these professional people to be very sensitive and appealing to my needs.

I have been out to trans groups for the past sixteen years, and I have attended every transgender convention in the United States. I have won numerous awards and have acquired a wide variety of friends. I still dress a bit funky, with a hat, body glitter, and "costumes" that leave little to the imagination. When appropriate, I dress down to meet the particular requirements of a conference or a meeting. Overall, I am having the time of my life assisting at every conference program. I have never grown tired and probably never will of being *on display*. My life as a cross-dresser is exciting and challenging, for certain. I have an ability to make others feel at ease. I have set many goals for my *feminine* life, and I achieve some of these every day. I know that I am not going away. I feel that songs like "The Lady Is a Tramp" and "You've Got a Friend" typify what I am trying to do with my life.

A COMMITTED JOURNEY

Christopher Barrett

I was a product of the post-WWII and Korean War baby boom, born
in the mid-1950s, and grew up in an average (whatever that is),
suburban, *Leave It to Beaver*– and *The Lone Ranger*– watching household.
Cowboy shows were a big hit back then, which influenced the toy
industry quite a bit. I had God-only-knows how many guns, a Bat Mas-
terson cane, my Rifleman rifle, and my favorite: my derringer. The derringer had a white handle and mounted on a silver belt buckle—what a
beauty! It came complete with bullets that you stuck Greenie Stick-em
Caps onto, for providing the appropriate BANG, and (the best part) gray,
plastic bullet nosepieces, which would shoot out of the gun barrel when
the trigger was pulled. Those were the days! And my cowboy outfits: I
got my favorite one for Christmas when I was five or six years old. Since
my mother liked aqua, the shirt was a black and aqua beauty with a
shiny, silver, star-shaped badge pinned to it; the pants were jet black; and
the boots were black with swirly white stitching; and, although I was of
course a "good guy," I wore a big, black hat. And my niece, who lived
with us and was more like my two-years' younger sister, had her red and
white cowgirl outfit with white fringes and a white cowgirl hat and
boots. We thought we were so cool—I guess you can only really understand my ramblings if you grew up *way* back then!

Anyway, my childhood seemed pretty normal for those days—that is,
of course, if I had been born a boy. Unfortunately, this was not the case.
My poor mother tried to nudge me in the direction of all those frilly
things, but I was just not buying any of it. I guess I was pretty indepen-

dent and determined to do things my way, even at an early age. Since I was the last of six kids (I have three sisters and two brothers) and an after-thought at that (there are eight years between my brother, the youngest of the first five offspring, and myself), I guess my parents were resigned if not thrilled with my "quirks." After all, I was sure to grow out of it.

I remember an incident when I was about four or five years old that, in retrospect, is rather telling. I was with my sister, who was in her late teens, on the walkway beside our house. She was pushing a baby car-riage with one of my nephews in it. I was old enough to know the phys-ical difference between boys and girls, yet I asked her what exactly *is* the difference. She chuckled at me and said, "What do you think?" The problem I remember having is that the physical difference seemed to me more of a side issue; the way boys and girls, men and women, act and are treated so differently *had* to mean that there was more to it than just that! This was an insight that, for some reason, most of the world just doesn't seem to think much about. To tell you the truth, I believe that if I had fit very comfortably into that world on this issue, I probably would not question the concept myself, either.

Things got a bit more complicated when I was about to start kinder-garten. I didn't like getting up early, and I certainly didn't like having to get into any "stinky old dress"! And I couldn't see going into a classroom to play games and (God forbid!) take a nap at some teacher's discretion. I could do any of those things just fine on my own and in my own good time. Well, the kindergarten program had a morning and an afternoon session, so after the first week when things didn't seem to be going too smoothly, they decided that I might adjust better to the afternoon session. Ha! By the end of a couple of weeks, I'd had enough and locked myself in my parents' office, refusing to come out until they promised no more kindergarten. You could look on all of this and say I was pretty much a brat, yet I prefer to think of it as my learning to set my life on my own track, regardless of the cultural/social expectations of the rest of the world—good training for what I was to face later in my life.

In spite of my kindergarten-dropout status, by the time first grade was upon me, I was ready to buckle down and accept my role as a school student and adjusted quite well. Yet that entailed implementing and enforcing a name change for myself. For, you see, I was always known by my nickname, "Honey," and that's all I had ever gone by. I couldn't very well go on to first-grade status with a name like that! So I insisted that, from that point on, everyone would call me by my given name. It took quite a bit of stick-to-itiveness on my part to get my family to adjust, but they survived. Needless to say, looking back, it was another valuable social lesson that I would draw on many years later, when I would finally drop my given name and adopt a new moniker that I had chosen for myself.

Fortunately for me, for the most part, socially, the girl-versus-boy thing hadn't been too much of a hindrance for a good part of my younger days. Throughout my grammar school years, I always played more with the boys than with the girls. I liked playing sports and did well, especially given that I was usually one of the biggest kids there. I usually didn't feel the effects of discrimination against me, just because I was a girl. Whether it was kickball in third grade or softball in fourth and fifth grades, I was usually one of the "captains" who contributed to the fate of so many kids who, probably to this day, still shudder at the times when teams were being picked and their names were saved till the end of the list. Survival of the fittest didn't seem so bad to me back then, for it was only right (wasn't it?) for the best kids to excel. In other words, it didn't affect me adversely back then, so I hadn't a clue how awful and cruel it must have felt.

There was one day, though, in third grade that I'll never forget. During recess, a bunch of us would go out and play football in the far field. I was usually the only girl, but once in a while another girl would join us. Then that fateful moment came when I was hit right between the eyes with the fact that I was a girl and that the rules applied differently to me than to the rest of the guys. The principal came in and announced that she had seen some girls playing football with the boys out in the field at recess and that she did not think that it was a good idea because it was too rough a thing for girls to be doing. Although she mentioned it as relating to girls across the board, I felt it directed at me, since I was primarily the one to whom it applied. To this day, my face gets red and my ears burn when I think about it; I was embarrassed and indignant at the same time, especially since her reason was because it was too rough for such delicate creatures as little girls and I could pretty much pulverize most of the boys who were playing.

In fourth grade, we read a story about a girl who was being teased about being a "tomboy." She was embarrassed and hated the tormenting. My reaction to that story was more of bewilderment. After all, what was there to be embarrassed about? I saw it as something to be proud of. Sometime within the next year or so, one of the girls who had been pretty active playing some of the sports with the boys thought it important to have a conversation with me about a subject her older sister had discussed with her: now that we were getting older, we really should think about growing out of the tomboy mode and start acting more like the girls we were. Well! That might be fine for her, but I couldn't see how that could be a good thing for me! Again, so many things could be in keeping with just growing up, just like everyone else, nothing that I wouldn't eventually grow out of. But, in retrospect, it was just so much more than that for me. The tough part is that, at the time, there was just no sure way of telling whether it was just a phase or a deeper indication of what was to come.

I must admit that puberty was a difficult time for me. And yet, it's a tough time for just about everyone. I really struggled with feelings of being more of an odd duck, of not fitting in. I stopped growing at about twelve years old and just continued to grow heavier rather than taller. Finally, at five feet six and over 200 pounds at the age of thirteen, I crash dieted until I got back down to 165. I tried to adjust and accept who and what I was, physically and culturally. Yet, now that I have the information from later chapters of my life, I know why the pieces just never seemed to fit.

Throughout high school I spent a good deal of my time on the sports teams. I believe that those opportunities helped get me through: the camaraderie, the discipline that they taught me, and the energies that they allowed me to get out rather than bottle everything inside were all invaluable. It wasn't until years later that I realized how many of the girls on the teams were dealing with their own sexuality issues. I know now that there were a few occasions where someone was not quite sure which side of the fence I was on, yet I was clueless and probably confused the individual because I wasn't sending or receiving the signals either as straight or gay. I didn't belong in either world as they were defined for me in that female body.

I wanted to be "normal," yet I just didn't know how to fit that norm. I kept telling myself I was normal, although that never really was the case. I had no other frame of reference at the time to know how to judge. I assured myself that I was attracted to boys, yet in retrospect I know I was subconsciously keeping myself more asexual rather than letting that demon out in the open, whatever it was. I can recall friendships with girls that, if I am truthful with myself, I know felt, in some ways, more than just friendships—cases where feelings of jealousy concerning their boyfriends came across as just wise-crack comments. In one instance, I had a good friend who I hung around with quite a bit just after high school graduation. After an argument, she refused to hang around with me anymore. She never really said exactly why; it wasn't until a year later when her sister made some wise comment implying I had homosexual leanings that I finally caught on—I had no idea and, to this day, I don't know exactly what I said to give her that idea; yet, I know she must have picked up on some feelings and signals that I had no idea at the time that I was sending out.

COLLEGE

So it was time to go off to college. It was only a little over an hour's drive from home, so I drove home most of the weekends that first semester. Then, in the second semester, I struck up a really close friendship with a new resident of my dorm. After a short time, I stopped heading home for the weekends. We were just friends, and after a while, very good friends. She was a few years older than I and a lot of fun. She was straight and, I was so sure, so was I. After all, one is straight until proven otherwise, right? I had been with neither a man nor a woman, so I was normal, just slow and careful. Well, it sounded okay to me, anyway. I did decide it was time to prove to myself that I was okay, so during a party (which was not a common occasion) at the dorm one night, I set my sights on one of the few guys who showed up. It was my only interlude with anyone of the male persuasion, and it included no more than making out while fully dressed. Although he suggested we go to my room, I can honestly say I had no feelings about wanting to do any such thing; I was going through the mechanics, yet there was no spark or excitement about the whole process. A few days later, a friend at the dorm admitted that she had questioned my "leanings" and was surprised that she was wrong. I was pleased that her mind was set to rest and even implied that my trips home during the first semester were full of such busy opportunities.

My good friend was one of only a few others who found a guy to spend some time with that night. I didn't admit to myself how it had bothered me that she had been with someone. As time went on, our friendship grew stronger and we agreed to sign up to room together the following year. As the semester was winding to a close, we decided to hang around the area in an apartment with her roommate during the coming summer rather than head for home. On one of our last few nights at the dorm, most everyone had moved out and the three of us decided to go to the drive-in. Ironically, the movie was *The Poseidon*

Adventure, and just like the ship in the movie, my life was about to be turned upside down! We brought drinks with us and we got pretty drunk. The roommate passed out in the back seat while my friend and I were in the front seat. Somehow, we found ourselves touching tenderly. Nothing happened that night that I would call sex, for we never touched each other in a sexual way. We drove home to the dorm from the drive-in and pretended to be too sleepy to go into the building. The room-mate eventually woke up and dragged herself into the dorm. We stayed in the car, scared and yet not wanting to get out of the car. We eventually wound up making out until almost dawn. When we went into the dorm in the morning, we didn't talk about what had happened; we were both just too embarrassed. It was later that afternoon that we did discuss what had transpired. We both were sure we were "straight" and somehow just found ourselves in a "special situation." We were both confused about whatever it was that was happening to us; things just didn't fit either of our expectations of our lives. You see, I still didn't grasp what was "me" deep in my soul.

One big clue came to me very unexpectedly the next semester. I joined my new "roommate" in a class she was attending. The class subject was Biology: Human Sexuality. Given the overwhelming interest in such a subject, the class was actually held simultaneously in four large auditoriums, with the instructor being video-broadcast to the alternate campus sites. There was a shortage of seats, so I was seated on the steps looking straight ahead at the instructor on the video screen. He was talking about a subject that I hadn't the faintest idea could apply to "real-life" people: transsexuality. My first reaction was to chuckle, for this subject was only something you read about in the trashy tabloids or laughed at in Hollywood movies; and at that, the stories were always of men who transformed themselves into women: stories of someone named Christine Jorgensen or a movie character named Myra Breckenridge. But then something "snapped" inside of me and I had a bit of a sick feeling come over me. Could such a thing really apply to me? I have to admit that the thought scared the hell out of me over the next several months. I tried very hard to reject it for about six months, but, eventually, I came to accept that it fit "me."

I can't explain it any better than to say that it's something that I just came to accept, something that I just "knew" was right for me. It certainly isn't something I wanted to be true, especially since following through on such a thing was too incredible to think of. My mom was a nurse, and I just never went to doctors. I couldn't imagine submitting myself to doctors for what would be needed if I were to follow through with this dream someday.

Over the next several years, I found it interesting that there were a number of women who, although they were heterosexual, had felt some unexplainable attraction to someone such as myself, as if I had been a male. I know it sounds like a lot of BS, and all I can tell you is that it happened to my life. You can take it or leave it; I know what happened to me. What I *can* tell you is that it is a very uncomfortable thing for everyone involved. As an example: a young woman I worked with while I was still in college had become a good friend of mine. If I had been a young man, I might even call some of our interactions flirtatious. I found myself one evening admitting to my friend that I felt myself more as a young man rather than as a woman; as you can imagine, it was a very serious and awkward conversation. She was struggling and eventually shared with me that she had had dreams of her being with a young man whom she knew to be me, although she knew it could not be so; and this information I had just shared with her fit too strangely with those dreams. We continued to see each other as friends for a short time, but then she moved away and I never saw her again. She wrote some poetry that I found very pertinent; I would like to share one of her poems here and to include a message for her (A., if you are out there and read your words included here, it would be nice to talk with you again).

QUESTION

You stepped on my eggshell;
Why did you have to
open my mind to
all the beauty in life
and to all the ugliness in that beauty?

Couldn't you leave me unchanged?
Why did you have to open my mind to
all the ugliness in life
and to all the beauty in that ugliness?

Now I sit in my half-opened shell
looking at the grass,
the white crumbling
under the heavy weight

in the ideas you let me see.
How I wish I were blind to life
and to your love,
for now I am caught
between my old world
and the new world of your presence.

Why did you step on my eggshell?
Eggshells should not be broken.

ANSWER

I broke your eggshell
Because . . . I loved you.
I left you sitting in
the half, broken part
so that I could share the world
with you.

I broke your eggshell
because I chose to call you friend.
And now you see the
ugliness and all the beauty
in that ugliness because you accepted.

I broke your eggshell because
I wanted to walk into the world with you.
You're not crushed by my ideas,
but you do fear them
and as long as you fear them and me
you'll have to stay in the broken, half-shell
alone, lost in the misty grass.

Don't be afraid . . . I'm here . . .
I broke the shell and I won't leave you
but together we'll see the ugly-loveliness
within each other
and not from a shell.

THE SECRET

I lived my life for a long time in secret, telling only a few about myself and what, someday, I intended to do. When just out of college, I told my fifteen-year-old nephew that someday I would go away and just disappear; I couldn't tell him why nor when, yet for some reason I wanted him to know and to expect it. My mom was in poor health with heart problems, had been since I was in junior high school, and I couldn't risk telling her for I feared it would kill her. So I knew I would not act on anything while she was still living.

My first love and I continued our relationship, although we portrayed to the outside world that we were just very good friends. Throughout that relationship, I was continually feeling guilty for putting her through such a clandestine situation. Although when we were alone together we treated each other as man and woman, to the outside world we were nothing of the sort; we struggled through living a double life. To this day, I consider that relationship as a marriage without the benefit (nor hindrance) of the "piece of paper."

There wasn't really a lot of information back then in the 1970s on the subject of transsexuality, at least not that I could find. (I use the term "transsexual," rather than the term "transgendered," which seems more accepted today, because that is the term used at that time and it is how I came to identify myself.) Libraries listed a limited number of books, articles, and so on, and most of those were missing from the shelves. Occasionally, TV talk shows would come through with an interview that I was lucky enough to have run across. On one such show, a woman named Jan Morris discussed her book, *Conundrum*, which described her life and transition from her childhood as a little boy. I ran right out and found that book, hoping to find more insight into this curious thing that was happening to me. I must admit I couldn't relate to "knowing" at the young age of three or four years old about being born into the wrong body. Then again, it was a lot easier for a little girl in the 1950s to just act like a little tomboy and get away with it for the better part of life than it was for a young boy to act like the girl inside. The book at least gave reinforcement to me that this sort of thing really happened to people.

Then there was a show I happened to find syndicated on late-night television. It must have been a lot easier to discuss this sort of thing on TV after most folks were fast asleep. I would guess that this was in the mid-1970s on a show with a host I had never heard of: a young man named Geraldo Rivera. I believe that the show was something like *Good*

Night America, with a theme song of "The City of New Orleans." The guests that night were Christine Jorgensen and a young man in his thirties. They discussed this man's transition in his early thirties from his life as a female. My first view of a real, honest to goodness FTM! I remember feeling horrified, at the ripe young age of twenty-two or so, at the thought of ten more years being a female; I felt such sympathy for the man who had waited so long. God knows I had no intention of doing so! The interview included a mention of an Erickson Educational Foundation, complete with an address for contacting them. I couldn't believe my luck in catching such a program. I wrote a letter asking for information—and kept it in my drawer for almost ten years.

A few years later, the issue of transsexuality moved to daytime TV: I viewed a Phil Donahue show that included a panel of transsexuals. I can't remember at this point whether or not they were all FTMs, but I do know that one of the panelists was a gentleman named Jude Patton. He was a burly guy with a nice, bushy beard and balding; I remember his quip about the hair migrating from the top of his head to the bottom of his chin. Mr. Donahue was very gracious and handled the subject in a very respectful manner—not the norm, especially in those days. I sent away for a transcript of the show, which also helped me emotionally to have one more link to those who had "been there" before me. The transcript became one more treasured document that I hid away and prayed no one would ever find. Many years later I was lucky enough to meet Mr. Patton and thank him for all the work and the sacrifice he endured in his endeavor to pave the way for so many others.

My mother's health was not good, and I lived with her so that she was not alone. She took in my "friend" and treated her like an adopted member of the family. My mom never questioned me about the relationship, yet at one point she asked my "friend" to take care of me after she (my mom) was gone. My mother died, after a long period of painful illness, when I was twenty-five years old and it was devastating to me. I had never lost someone close to me up to that point. It was a very emotional time for both myself and my partner, both during my mom's illness and at the end.

Soon we purchased a new place and finally could live our relationship without hiding, at least when we were at home. I became friends with a man I worked with, and, after some time and with the influence of a mutual friend, we each owned up to the fact that we did not fit the definition of "norm" to the outside world. We each felt incognito at work; to say the least, we helped to break each other's bubble of perceived anonymity. The mutual friend was instrumental in getting me "out" into the world, for until then my partner and I had never been out and about in the gay scene. We didn't feel that we actually fit there, yet we were easily accepted there, which was certainly not the case in the straight world. It was at a gay bar one night, with Donna Summer's "Our Love (Will Last Forever)" blasting in the background, that I clarified to my work buddy that I felt myself a transsexual, not a homosexual, and his reaction showed immediately his understanding: he pointed to my partner and myself and exclaimed, "Oh, my God! That means you're really a straight couple!" I was so happy that someone actually understood and I was so sure that the song was right: that my relationship with her would last forever.

The truth is that I never really felt quite good enough. I couldn't be the man in the outside world that I felt myself inside to be. I knew it was difficult for my love to live this kind of hidden, double life, and I hated myself for putting her through it. I hated my body and I rejected being touched intimately, so our physical relationship was very one-sided. I realize now how emotionally important it is for each partner to be able both to give and to receive. We loved each other very much, yet we had to restrain ourselves and keep our love a secret from the world. We had been in a loving, committed relationship, yet we did not know the feeling of expressing our closeness out in society without feeling something was "dirty" about it. After being together for six to seven years, we took a trip to Provincetown and actually held hands at a restaurant while we had breakfast—something that may seem like "no big deal" in the scheme of life, yet it was one of the most memorable moments of my life. I remember that moment whenever I see the repression of so many good people living a gay lifestyle in this culture.

As I moved through my late twenties, I knew that I had to do something about my ever-present dilemma. I knew I would persevere and find a way to become on the outside the man I felt myself to be on the inside. I had no idea how I was going to do it; I just knew that somehow I would.

I became more daring in sharing my intentions with some of my friends and family. I can't say that they really understood; yet, for the most part, the people I shared my secret with did not let it ruin our relationship. In retrospect and in discussing the matter with some of them since my transition, it appears that it just isn't "real" to someone in its "being talked about" phase. It's a little freaky or maybe I'd grow out of it—just like being a tomboy. It's just not something many people have any experience with, so they don't quite know how to react. Many people afterward expressed that they didn't really think I'd do it. Some folks reacted negatively, saying it was going against God's plan. I have a lot of gay friends, and seeing me as their gay friend was more easily acceptable than what I had divulged to them—after all, what was so wrong with my just accepting that I was gay? One very good friend insisted that I was not a transsexual, as I had defined myself, because I hadn't had any operations to that point; she went so far as to prove it to me by getting out the dictionary to show me the definition, only to find that the dictionary supported my position that a transsexual is someone who feels that they were born into the body of the wrong sex, even though they may still be living in the social role of the birth sex.

TRANSITIONING

In the early 1980s, I stepped up my efforts to position myself for doing something more than just talking about being a man. I had pursued a career that would provide me a bit more freedom to do so (I knew that my hopes in high school of becoming a teacher would not be wise) and moved toward smaller companies, which might have a more open-minded leadership. I tried to find literature on the subject, but at that time it was still not easy to find much. I did find a relatively new book in my local library called *The Transsexual Empire: The Making of the She-Male* by someone named Janice Raymond. I was thrilled—until I got into reading it. I feel compelled here to warn anyone reading this that Ms. Raymond has no understanding of transsexual issues and uses the transsexual dilemma as a platform to espouse her own feelings of female inadequacy in a male-dominated world. Her feelings of female oppression from a male-dominated culture are well founded; yet I find her attack on the validity of transsexuals (citing MTFs as males using the transition to the female world as a way to dominate in a more perverse way the female community and citing FTMs as victims of the male community being physically butchered by the medical community and emotionally battered and cajoled into believing that they could possibly be happy being males) as insulting and berating—she knows naught of which she speaks. I must admit that I was so concerned that the book might be found by someone who had nothing else available to offset her absurd concepts that I might have lost the book before returning it to the library.

I never lost awareness of the letter I had written so many years ago after seeing the Christine Jorgensen interview by Geraldo Rivera. I carefully removed it from its hiding place, placed a stamp on it, and dropped it in the mailbox. How simply mailing a letter can cause one's heart to pound so heavily, I can't explain. Yet here I was, thirty years old, experiencing just that.

In any event, the internal strife was taking its toll on my relationship with my partner. The irony was that I was getting closer to finally doing something about addressing my transsexuality, yet the woman I so wanted to share my life with as a man was drifting further away. Over the years, life's struggles had started wearing on our closeness. I knew that I could not see myself living that lie much longer. I know she wanted this as much as I did. We were both scared of the unknowns that transition represented. And our bond was just not strong enough at that point to see us through this together. We split up and she moved out.

After a good deal of time passed (months, I think), I finally received a response from my letter to the Erickson Foundation. Apparently, the climate of the times was very difficult and the foundation had closed; yet, thanks to the dedication of many anonymous people who unselfishly gave of themselves to follow through, the letter was passed on many times until it reached someone who could provide some information. To all of those people, whoever you are, thank you so very much for your help. I received a packet consisting of a collection of pamphlets from various agencies and individuals on the subject of transsexuality. It included some information from a man named Lou Sullivan, other information from various groups around the country on transsexuality and transvestitism, business contacts for various counseling opportunities, and so on. A man name Rupert Raj, I believe from Canada, was writing a newsletter for FTMs, and I subscribed to that. I couldn't believe it: I was excited and overwhelmed at the same time.

There really wasn't a lot of support for transsexuality in and of itself, especially the FTM variety. Most was as an add-on to the transvestite community. I must admit that I was a bit uncomfortable with the association. Yet without that support through that much more organized subculture, the transsexual would have had little group support back then. I had learned enough to know that any hopes I had for transition required counseling in order to open the door to the medical community. I have to admit that I resented that, feeling I didn't need any "shrink" to try to talk me out of what I knew was right for me. I resigned myself to go through the motions and do whatever I had to do to move ahead toward my goal, in spite of the fact that I was sure I didn't need any type of counseling.

I was lucky to find a counselor listed in the packet I had received who was only an hour away from where I lived. I called, left a message, and waited impatiently for a call back. I didn't have to wait long. I received a call at work from a Mr. Ari Kane (now Dr. Kane), and when I realized who was calling, I ran to find an empty office while Mr. Kane was kind enough to wait. Out of breath and not knowing exactly what to say, I lifted the phone and finally began a conversation that was to be a great turning point in my life.

The voice on the other end was polite, yet very abrupt, no nonsense; I'm sure he was not interested in wasting his time. I explained how I had received his name and number and asked to set up a session. We scheduled an appointment, I believe, for the following week; I believe it was the beginning of December 1984, when we first met face-to-face; I was thirty years old. I don't remember a lot about that first meeting. We discussed the process, Harry Benjamin's "Standards of Care," and he explained that counseling can last sometimes for several years. I got the feeling that my new counselor had mellowed a bit with me and I felt comfortable enough to trust him—then again, there weren't too many other choices, were there?

We embarked on an intensive schedule of appointments, two to three times per week. We discussed my personal history, how and why I had come to the conclusion that I felt I was a man, what does being a man in this society really mean to me, what are the options and alternatives, issues relative to hormones and surgeries, and many other things. At one point he gave me an assignment to go to the combat zone to visit an adult bookstore; when we discussed the experience afterward, he told me that one of the reasons was to test my resolve in going through difficult experiences to accomplish my goal. He was supportive yet tough and challenging. He led me through discussions of life scenarios, and we discussed many potential experiences of transition and beyond.

I was very masculine looking anyway, and for years I had pretty much dressed "casually" (interpretation: in men's clothing). I guess you could say I tried to present more of a neutral image, for appearing more like a man presented other problems when living as a woman. It's all so very complicated, isn't it? After a few months, I decided it was time to bind my chest and experiment with what that was like out in the world. I was nervous that everyone would notice and ask me about it. To my surprise, not one person said a word.

I experimented with strangers to see how they perceived me, and I paid close attention to the subtle feedback I got from them. We discussed how most people accept what they are presented with; if it walks like a duck, talks like a duck, acts like a duck ... it must be a duck! My face and softer features were tough to get away with, yet I worked to minimize their effect and present more and more of a masculine image. I was surprised to find how people seek out signals to categorize us as male or female. I could literally look the same and go into two different places and in one instance be greeted as "sir," yet at the next place it was "ma'am." It was interesting to me to find out how I was sending signals that I didn't even know I was sending; depending on the "reader" of those subtle signals, I was addressed one way or the other. For example: I had been wearing what today would be considered a "sports watch"—masculine, only the smaller, women's variety so that in the years prior to my transition it was more acceptable (actually, when digital watches first came out, they were large and only came in men's sizes; I was given a bit of grief about wearing a man's watch, so when the smaller ones came out for women, I switched so I could fit in better). At a dark pub, I thought I would be successful at passing myself off as a man; however, the waitress lost no time in asking my friends and myself what we "ladies" would like. I was confused and finally settled on the watch. I stopped wearing it that night and was amazed at what a difference it made.

My counselor introduced me to a book called *Emergence* by Mario Martino, an FTM who had transitioned and had been living as a man for over ten years at the time; I remember being so envious and could only imagine what that would be like. We discussed the strain of going through this sort of thing alone, and my counselor was concerned that my partner was not going to be there to help me through. I called her and we talked about it; she even agreed to come to a couple of counseling sessions. It didn't work out, but our love and support of one another is something I will always be grateful for. We are good friends, like family, to this day.

At the time I endured this treatment for two purposes only: to get it over with and to use it as my ticket to the surgical community. I have to admit that now I see it as an invaluable learning experience, and I am forever grateful for the training and support I received from this person who has come to be someone I consider a very dedicated and sincere friend. In recent years I have observed others going through their own transitions; however, today it seems that the careful counseling is an option, not a necessity, in order to travel this path, and most seem to think that it is just not necessary (and too expensive) and forego it. I know I would have done the same thing if I'd had the chance. Yet, having gone that route, I see the value in the counseling I received and how it prepared me for what I had to go through. And it also helped me to understand a bit better how others were affected by what I put them through.

After six months of intensive sessions, my counselor informed me that he agreed that I was indeed a candidate for transition. The tough part was just beginning. He suggested a doctor (I told you I didn't do doctors, didn't I?), and I actually survived that appointment and got my first prescription for testosterone. Testosterone options at that time were by injection or pill form; my understanding was that the pill form was not as effective and the doctor had concerns of internal organ damage (liver?), so the shots were the way to go (did I mention I *really* didn't do needles?!). I got the prescription filled and a good friend of mine who was a nurse agreed to come to my house and give me my first shot; I was so nervous I got a bit queasy, but I lived through it!

I had decided that the time to fess up at work as to what was going on would depend on how soon the changes took effect, since that varies greatly with each individual. In a matter of weeks, my voice began to lower; a friend at work asked if I was getting a cold, because I sounded hoarse. The clitoris reacts to the hormones and begins to grow longer and thicker. Facial hair starts to sprout, although, in my case, it took a good six months to start forming in any reasonable fashion. Muscle structure starts to shift. The skin roughens and the texture of the hair changes.

Now all that counseling was about to be put to the test. I found out firsthand what I was told in the counseling sessions: that people see what they expect to see. So, as I gradually changed my appearance, my friends' perception of me remained as the "old" me; we seldom "revalidate" what we already know. Yet people who did not know me wasted little time on settling on "sir." I worked for a small company with good people, some of whom had come to be very good friends of mine. I discussed what I was going through with a couple of them prior to divulging my situation to the company; they were shocked yet very supportive. It's not every day that someone you know comes up to you and informs you that he is in the process of a sex change! Hell, I had never met a transsexual myself at that point (at least, that I knew of!).

Soon it was time to go into the front office and explain what I was going through. I was lucky to be in a position whereby the president of the company was also a friend. That helped me on a personal level, yet, because of our friendship, I felt bad for putting him through this situation on a professional level. I explained to him what I was planning and made it clear that, although I would love to continue working with him, I would understand completely if he felt that the professional relationship needed to change and I would look for another job; I just asked that he help me out by giving me a good recommendation. He handled it all very well, assured me that he would be supportive, and said he needed some time to discuss this with my manager (who was also a good friend of mine) in order to figure out how to handle this. I can't tell you how lucky I feel to have been in such a supportive environment. These two people led the way for me to transition on the job; not that everyone in the company was understanding, yet with the leadership of the company behind me, I was able to keep my job and be productive. We dealt quite a bit with outside clients, and there were some dicey times when I'd have to handle phone calls from people requesting to speak to my "old" name as we attempted to wean the clients who had been dealing with me. It's actually comical to look back on some of it now; yet, at the time, believe me, it wasn't all that funny. And men's room/ladies' room issues can get really complicated. After some time it became necessary for a couple of clients to be informed of my new status, for they had been insisting that I be involved in their projects and could not understand why my company was not making me available to them. To my surprise, everyone handled themselves very professionally and in a supportive way. I have to give a lot of credit to a lot of people who somehow rose to the occasion when faced with this very out-of-the-ordinary situation.

Friends and family also had to be informed. Little by little, during the same time frame that the work situation was occurring, I made my way to many of my friends to let them know what I was doing. In a supportive way, many helped me out by passing the word on to others. I tried to handle this whole thing in as unobtrusive a way as I possibly could. I felt it was not my right to impose this on anyone. I put it out there and let everyone know that I was interested in maintaining relationships, yet if they could not do that at that point (or ever), I would understand. It takes people time to digest all of this. I can't tell you what position my transition put others through; those are stories that are just as important as the ones from the point of view of the transsexual. Maybe someday their impressions will be captured in print and presented to the world. Nevertheless, little by little, people came to address my transition in their own ways and, tentatively, we reestablished our relationships. Some people never could get past it—that's okay, too. I feel that it's important to allow them their space, as long as they just leave me alone and move on. How can I expect someone to respect what I need to do for me if I can't give him or her the same courtesy?

In the counseling I learned to just state my case, not defiantly or apologetically, just matter-of-factly. It's amazing how people seem to accept that much more easily than other options. For example, I played volleyball every week, and I had to go up to people, some of whom I didn't know all that well, and say "I'm going through a sex change process and would appreciate it if you would call me Christopher now. . . ." Hmmm, somehow it just worked! As more and more people accepted it, it made it easier for others to follow along. As I had learned before, people hold on to images that they know, so it was easier in some ways for people who did not know me that well, since it really didn't affect them. And new acquaintances related to me as a man, even though they might have thought it was a bit freaky if/when they found out.

My friends were supportive, yet in some ways they did not yet relate to the fact that I looked more like a man; they struggled to "humor me" yet felt awkward in public because they felt sure that it appeared odd to others, sure that they all "knew." And as a culture we are really entrenched in the pronoun thing, to a level that we oftentimes don't realize until something like this stirs things up. A few instances to illustrate this: At one point relatively early in my new role, a group of my work associates and I were at a client site having dinner at the end of the day. We were in a fun mood and joking with the waitress. As we were ordering, the gentleman to my right pointed to me and said, "I'll have what she's having"—which caused everyone at the table to twitch as time stood still for a nanosecond. The waitress just laughed and thought he was just joking around, not thinking a thing of it. It took the rest of us at the table a second to remember to continue breathing.

I had entered a restaurant with a group of my longtime friends. As the waitress was seating us, I asked where the bathrooms were (leaving it generic). She pointed, and I headed off. When I got back, one of my friends was so excited she couldn't wait to tell me. I had no sooner headed away from the table than the waitress said she'd wait till I got back from the men's room to tell us the specials. I told my friend, "I told you people have been seeing me this way for some time now," to which she responded that she knew, but it really didn't sink in as real to her until things like this reinforce it.

The friend who I had mentioned earlier (who had gotten out the dictionary a few years earlier to try and convince me that I was not a transsexual) had invited me over to dinner. She had another friend over whom I had never met yet who had been informed of my rather unique situation. My friend was very candid and the discussion led to her discomfort in knowing how to handle this, for surely everyone must be able to tell. Her friend assured her that she in no way saw me as anything but a man, something my friend needed to hear in order to begin understanding and accepting that I did indeed appear to be a different person than the women she still related to in her mind.

I didn't interact closely with a lot of people in that time frame. It took time for people to adjust. I had friends who were supportive yet were honest enough to share with me that they were confused about some things and needed to talk things out, if I would oblige them. I felt honored that they were interested enough to want to work through their issues about this. One friend shared that she can kind of understand how someone would want to go through something like this so they could fit into the world and be part of a man and woman relationship. But she'd heard that some people believe themselves to be transsexuals yet change their sex just to be involved in homosexual relationships, and that just didn't seem to make sense to her. Although I had never met anyone in such a situation, I responded to her that it made perfect sense to me, and I proceeded to tell her why; it wasn't until quite some time later that I actually met someone in that situation who substantiated my response to her. I think it's an important concept that many people just don't understand about being a transsexual. I felt myself to be a transsexual because I felt in my heart and soul to be male, regardless of the sex that I had been born into. I wanted to be related to as a man, physically and culturally. I was not comfortable being touched and treated as a woman. This had nothing to do with whom I was attracted to; it had everything to do with whom I wanted someone else to be attracted to. As it turned out, I was born a female, attracted to women, yet did not want to be with a woman who wanted me as a woman. So it made sense to me that someone could be born a female, want to be touched and thought of as a man, yet be attracted to men—the attraction is separate from the sense of self. That distinction is not obvious to those in the majority who happen to fit sense of self and attraction to others as a single entity. Yet it may help to clarify why the majority of people living a homosexual lifestyle have no inclination to consider themselves a transsexual, as many uninformed heterosexuals might think, because they are quite comfortable that their sense of self matches the sex they were born into.

And I learned that my interpretation of how people were reacting to my transition was not always accurate. In one situation, my two brothers and a sister were meeting at the younger brother's house. My sister needed a ride home from there and I agreed to give her a ride, since I would be in the area. My brother, whose house it was, preferred that I not show up at the house, since it might be awkward. So I agreed to meet at a convenient spot, and someone would drop my sister off. The older brother, although it was on his way home, said that he did not feel comfortable and preferred not to be put in that position, so the younger brother agreed to drop my sister off. He hugged me when we met in the parking lot, and I felt at the time that he was the more accepting brother, the more willing to deal with the situation. I know now that I had it completely backward! As it turned out, the older brother was trying to come to terms with the situation, but just wasn't quite ready yet to meet face-to-face. The younger brother, on the other hand, was actually refusing to accept the situation, so he just still considered me his little sister; therefore, there was nothing really to deal with. The younger brother has taken many years to adjust to this; it wasn't until a good ten years later that he started coming around, with the help and support of his second wife (whom he married five years after that incident), who's only known me as Christopher. I know of stories of some folks who resent their family's lack of support of their transition; yet I prefer to look on it with sadness rather than hatred—as their right, just as I look on it as my right to choose who I am and how I feel.

In due time, my older brother invited me to his house; he and his family, including his three teenage kids, welcomed and accepted who I am. Although it was a bit awkward at first and I'm sure everyone was nervous, we made it through. I got a call from my oldest sister a short time after that, asking if we could possibly have lunch together. We've talked about that day in recent years, and she shared with me how nervous she had been. She also shared that she found what my older brother had told her about it to be true: that my comfort and confidence within myself and what I was doing helped her to be more at ease with it herself. My niece, whom I considered more like a sister (the one I had grown up with who is two years younger than I) called to set up a visit, bringing her two sons, who were about eight and nine years old at the time. She told me that, on the ride to my house, the younger one said he was confused about this, to which the older one replied, "What's to be confused about? She was our aunt and now he's our uncle . . . it's that simple." I remember my middle sister calling me on the phone and letting me know that she had told my dad. I felt a bit sick at that information. However, it opened the door for getting together with him and we had a good discussion about it. He told me I was a son he could be proud of—that meant a lot to me.

Well, things were going pretty well from a cultural transition point of view. But then there is the legal world. A legal name change was next on my agenda. I filled out a petition and was scheduled for a court date. I dressed semicasually, with a tie, dress shirt and pants, and sweater vest. Others were there changing their names, too. I remember two teenage sisters who looked sort of like a Buffy and a Tina type who were there to change their middle names. The judge asked them why they were doing this, and they giggled and said they liked these new names better than their given names and that their parents were supportive of their choices; he wasted no time in granting their requests. Soon it was my turn. For some reason, he didn't feel as comfortable with a thirty-year-old choosing a different name as he did with some teenagers. He made it clear that this was just a name change and not a sex change document, to which I said I understood and, for that same reason, I felt it was appropriate that he grant my desire to be called by whichever name I chose. He hesitated and said I would have to reschedule for a hearing on the matter and that I should bring further evidence and, if possible, my counselor. So, although legally a person can call himself by any name he chooses as long as it is not for fraudulent reasons, this judge deferred granting my name change. Not sure if I could convince my counselor to travel outside the city to another state, I made the call to request just that. Although not an easy request to honor, my counselor jumped through hoops to accommodate. We coordinated an appointment time that was agreeable to my counselor and to the court. The day finally came and my counselor met me outside the courthouse. He asked me why I hadn't worn a sportscoat, something that had never occurred to me. I didn't have one and I just didn't know any better. I know better now. The judge saw us in closed session. He explained how he was uncomfortable with this whole sex change issue and did not have experience with its legal implications. Yet, at the same time, he impressed upon us that this was just a name change issue and in no way implied any legal confirmation of a sex change. He listened to my counselor present documentation from the medical and mental health communities. I could tell by the way the judge was wincing and how he was shifting uncomfortably in his chair that this just wasn't going well. As he was about to speak his position, I asked to be able to say my piece. I explained again that I was asking for his signature to grant a name change and no more. I guessed that he was concerned that I could use this for fraudulent reasons, and I assured him that I knew full well that I could legally call myself by any name I wished, whether or not he signed that petition. Quite to the contrary of any question of fraud, for the very reason of continuity, I wanted to be able to document who I was and not use my sex change as a way to hide. By doing so legally through the courts, this would make it easier for the law to track who I was. I told him I knew that this was an unusual situation that he found himself in, and yet my own father had come to grips with my situation and accepted me as his son. I have to give the man a lot of credit as he struggled with his conscience that day. Yet, finally, with one more affirmation that this was "just a name change," he did indeed sign the petition. Hurray! I'd made a giant leap forward! With several certified copies in hand, we left the courthouse that day and I was finally, legally, Christopher E. Barrett.

With my new name change certificate, I set out to change my name on all my financial and legal documentation. I was surprised to find that I could not change my name on the deed to my house; I was told by the clerk that the name on the deed was accurate as of the date of the purchase and that the deed would not be changed. So, as long as I owned my property, my old name would still be around to haunt me. I submitted for a name change on my license, which was granted; yet the box under "Sex" still read "F." I resolved myself to ignore it, and, at times when people noticed, I just shrugged my shoulders and laughed, saying something about it being hard to get the computers to get it right, at which they just laughed. I found that some things were just easier to let go at the time. Change of sex documentation on my license required a notarized birth certificate, which did me no good at that point. I found that birth certificate changes in the state in which I was born required a letter from a doctor confirming the sex reassignment had been medically performed. I was shocked to find out that some states will not change the birth certificate even with the doctor's note. I was lucky enough to have been born in a state where it was legally possible, but it would just have to wait for a while.

Although the heavy, intensive counseling was behind me, the sessions continued on a less frequent basis to address my experiences and how I was coping with all of this. The counselor was working with a few other FTMs and set up a little Christmas gathering at the beginning of December. I considered it also like my first anniversary party of my first counseling session. I had bought my first real suit by then and showed up to meet, for the first time, another transsexual. It was an interesting experience, to say the least. I think there were six of us there that night, comparing notes and experiences. Only three of us were currently living as men. That night I met someone who was to become a very good friend of mine, and although he has moved away, we still keep in contact and get to see each other every year or two when we can.

After about a year or so living as a man, the guidelines said it was time I could start looking into surgeries. The first step was for chest reduction. In order to be accepted by the doctors for transsexual-related surgery, the guidelines stipulated that two signatures were needed from the mental health community, at least one from a psychiatrist or a PhD clinical psychologist. So my counselor provided me with the name of a PhD who fit the bill. I must say that he was not too far from being a nutcake himself, but I paid him for his time and he gave me the signature I needed. My counselor provided me with the names of a couple of doctors, so I made appointments with each to discuss the options. Most doctors did a procedure whereby they would cut a line horizontally across the middle of each breast, remove the breast tissue, cut the excess skin, sew up the opening, and graft the areola (the darkened skin around the nipple) and the nipple back onto the chest. I didn't want chest scars, and I had heard of a Dr. Gilbert in Virginia who had come up with a procedure whereby the incision is done around the areola, the tissue is removed through that opened circle, the skin may be tightened in a drawstring-like method, and the areola and nipple are sewn back into place. I presented that option to one of the doctors and, although he stressed that he hadn't done that procedure before, he was willing to try it. There weren't a lot of doctors willing to work on transsexuals, especially since there had been some legal battles (I think in the late 1970s) giving the medical community quite a scare. The doctor presented my condition as gynecomastia, which is a condition in men suffering from flabby, femalelike breasts. So I signed up for the big day and headed for my first day in the hospital since the time I was born. I was scared yet thrilled to be getting it "all off my chest," so to speak. I woke up with draining tubes coming out of my body under my armpits, draining blood from the fresh wounds, and bandages around my chest. I was in great spirits the next morning and was sitting at the table in my hospital room reading a book when the nurse came to the door to give out the medications. She looked at me, looked at the number on the door, did another double take, and asked me if I had just had surgery. She couldn't believe that I looked so good having just gone through surgery. It just goes to show what the power of the mind and spirit can do.

The surgery had gone well, and I returned to the doctor's office almost a week later for him to remove the draining tubes. The body takes time to "settle" after the surgery. I've a muscular chest; when I lay down, my chest was flat, but when I stood up, it became clear that my chest area was too caved in. The doctor suggested a follow-up surgery. This time it was day surgery; he propped me up at an angle so he could get a better idea of the muscle structure, and I was awake (drugged, of course) through the whole thing. I kept complaining that I could still feel it, and at one point he offered to stop the procedure. Wanting to get it all over with, I told him to keep going. The results were better, but still sunken in—and at least I didn't have any scars.

By this time the counseling sessions had dwindled to few and far between. We kept in touch, but not on a regular basis. I found out about a transsexual group that had been meeting once a month for several years in Hartford, Connecticut, about two hours from where I lived. I found my way there and joined in the circle of chairs as the meeting began. I think there were between fifteen and twenty people, and they were all polite and welcoming. They showed a film and then opened the meeting for discussion. I got up the nerve to add my two cents about something in the film and was shocked when someone thanked me for my input and then proceeded to ask me why I was there. Although most of the group were MTFs, here I was in a group of transsexuals thinking that they would all just assume I was one of them, and it hadn't occurred to me that they had just assumed that I was just some guy coming in off the street to do some educational studies. When I recovered from my shock, I explained that I was a transsexual FTM and received a flurry of surprised looks and gasps. I befriended one of the women in the group, and a year or two later, after she had begun living full time in her female role and moved to California, she helped me out by letting me stay at her apartment while I checked out a doctor in the area. I've lost touch with her since and hope she is doing well (L., if you read this, I'd love to hear from you).

By 1988 I started looking for doctors to perform the genital surgery. I wrote letters to doctors from all parts of the country: Virginia, Minnesota, Oklahoma, Utah, Washington, California, Hawaii. To my surprise, they all returned my letters. Some felt they could offer some help; others suggested additional contacts. There really wasn't a lot of choices back then and there were primarily two options: phalloplasty—a neophallus constructed of abdominal tissue vertically in a "handle"-like form and then released at the top in a subsequent operation so that it hangs from the pubic area, a process that resulted in no genital sensitivity nor erectile possibilities; or metaoidioplasty—use of the enlarged clitoris to form a small, but fully sensate and erectile-capable, penis. I eventually narrowed down my list to two doctors to start with: Dr. Laub in California and Dr. Gilbert in Virginia. I then met up with a gentleman (FTM) in Connecticut who had the phallosplasty procedure done. Although he had originally gone to Dr. Laub, he had complications and had follow-up surgery with Dr. Gilbert's group in Virginia. He was not happy with the way he had been treated in California and warned me to go to Virginia instead. I thanked him for his time, and I scheduled appointments to visit each of them.

As it turned out, I had a work trip scheduled in California, which facilitated my visit to Dr. Laub in the Palo Alto area. I called and got the okay from my friend who had moved to San Francisco from Connecticut that I could stay with her while I was in the area. My counselor knew a gentleman named Lou Sullivan in the San Francisco area, and he suggested that I give him a call. We set up to meet for dinner the night before I was to head to Palo Alto. He had just had some problems with his surgery that had been done by, I believe, a Dr. Brownstein. Not to say that that was a reflection of the doctor's procedure; it's just that each of our bodies react differently and sometimes complications need to be addressed. In any event, Lou's scrotum had split a bit on the seam where it had been sewn and he had to have it stitched up. I had a great visit with Lou, and we went out to a bar afterward for a few beers. I can't say that I knew at the time what an important contribution Lou had made to the FTM cause. All I knew was that I had spent an evening with a nice guy who I was meeting because we were both FTMs. (On a subsequent trip in 1989, I called to meet up with Lou again, but he had been having a rough time, weakened by AIDS, and apologized that he was just not up to our getting together; maybe next time. I never saw him again, as he died in 1991 at the age of thirty-nine.)

I was extremely impressed with the way I was treated by everyone at the Palo Alto facility, especially by Dr. Laub and the Gender Program coordinator, Judy van Maasdam. She had scheduled a psychological appointment for me with Dr. Paul Walker, who I found to be a very sincere, likeable man. As it turned out, he was winding down his consultative services with that program, yet I was lucky enough to meet with him before he left; it was not until years later that I realized his contributions to the transgender community. Everyone was supportive and very professional, which was wonderful because I did not know quite what to expect and did not really know if I was asking the right questions. Dr. Laub showed me pictures of his surgeries and discussed successes and potential risks as well as problems he had encountered along the way. I was really struggling as to the option of size (phalloplasty) versus feeling (metaoidioplasty). He was very professional and would not offer an opinion to sway me either way; then he offered that it was his observation that people who tended to feel that sexual pleasure is high on their list of importance tended to choose the metaoidioplasty, whereas those who were less interested in sex tended to opt for the phalloplasty. That did it for me, and I resolved myself that size is not all there is in life. Based on that visit, I decided to cancel my trip to Dr. Gilbert's clinic in Virginia and signed up for surgery with Dr. Laub. We scheduled it for the spring of 1989.

Most of the counseling and the surgeries I required were not covered by insurance. I was fortunate to have a good job and good credit to afford this opportunity. Spring came and I headed to California with my sister in tow to help me out, for when I left the hospital, I needed to stay in the area for four to six weeks after the surgery. We got there a couple of days before the actual surgery so we could go down the list of options for a place to stay and so I could make the presurgery doctor's appointments that had been scheduled. It was an interesting visit to the gynecologist's office—the first and last time I'd ever been to one. Not too many other guys were there. It appeared to be a low-income clinic, and the waiting room was full of women with their children running all about. I was dressed in a business suit, so I did my best to give the impression that I was some kind of salesman there on business. I can safely say that I'm glad I never have to go through something like that again.

The day of the surgery arrived and I was being prepped for surgery. I can't say enough for all of the people who handled this type of situation with professionalism and class. It is more than a bit odd to think back on what it must have been like for the young nurse explaining and presenting me with papers to sign that indicated my understanding that this surgery would involve procedures that would preclude my ability to become pregnant. I assured her I understood and that it would not be a problem. The surgery involved the removal of the uterus and the ovaries, the insertion of expanders in the labia majora area (which provide for expanding the skin for the scrotum to accept testicular implants at a future time), and the formation of a small penis with urethral passage from the tissues of the enlarged clitoris. The removal of the expanders, the insertion of the permanent testicular implants, the removal of the vagina, and the connection of the urethra to the base of the new penis would be done in a follow-up surgery. I had discussed with Dr. Laub about fixing my chest also, yet decided I would need my upper body strength following this surgery and decided to have that done later.

The surgery went very well, and, although not all my experiences were painless, the end result was very good and very worthwhile. After five days in the hospital, I returned to the motel where my sister had been staying. I was shocked, two days later—on a Sunday, no less—to find Dr. Laub at the door with his black bag, there to check on me to be sure I was okay. Who knew that doctors did this sort of thing anymore? To say the least, they took very good care of me, and I owe the good doctor and all those at his office (and my sister, too!) a great deal of gratitude. While I was in the area recuperating, I met another surgery patient who had come from Japan and opted for the phalloplasty (and had gone through the surgery without drugs—now that's mind control!). It was sad to hear what a tough time he was having socially because of all this. Apparently, Japan does not (or least did not as of those days) recognize sex changes, and there was no legal way for my friend to change his name or to change his cultural existence from being female. And his family was not supportive in any way. He was there all alone, and my sister and I provided company and rides for him when we could. I marvel at how easy I've had it compared to what some people have had to endure.

When I was getting ready to return home, Dr. Laub again went above and beyond the call of duty to open his office on a Sunday to see me one more time before I left the area. He put me on a schedule of biweekly visits to my doctor over a three- to four-month period to inject fluid into the testicular expanders so that, little by little, the skin in my scrotum would stretch. My doctor didn't have prior experience with this, but he helped out in any way he could.

The doctor I was going to was the same one who had given me my first prescription for testosterone. A couple of years after I had started going to him (I had been keeping appointments every six months so that he could verify that everything was going okay and could renew my testosterone prescription), he had stopped accepting more clients in the transsexual community, maintaining existing clients only; he no longer kept such close tabs on the medical issues related to transsexuality. In keeping with accepted practices of the early 1980s, which for the most part had been developed from MTF studies, he soon reduced my testosterone intake by 50 percent. It wasn't until years later that I learned that it had been found that the FTM needs to maintain the same schedule of testosterone intake as was needed before the removal of the sex glands. I believe that, over time, that issue had a profound effect on my ability to maintain muscle mass and possibly affected my emotional state.

In the summer of 1989, a few months after my surgery, I was introduced to my friend's second cousin on a visit out of state. Although I had had a few relationships over the years up to that time, I was not expecting someone to come along and blow me away like this lady did. We clicked almost immediately (I say almost, because when she met me that first morning she thought I was a real wise-guy jerk). I didn't realize at first that she was available, but soon it became clear that she had separated from her husband and was just waiting for him to sign the divorce papers, which he had already agreed to. She had a six-year-old son, who I met and really clicked with. He actually embarrassed the both of us by saying, within an hour of meeting me, "Hey, why don't you come down here and live with my mom and me." We didn't really come out and admit to one another that we were interested. Yet we each had asked my friend for the other's home address and phone number. He was not happy with the situation, because, although we were good friends, that didn't make me good enough to go out with his cousin. After all, he had known me "when." We sent each other a card without knowing the interest level of the other. A few days later we talked on the phone, then every night after that. This was a long-distance situation and we both knew it was unlikely that a relationship would be feasible, yet, for some reason, we didn't give up. A special bond had been growing between us, and I would have to let her in on my little secret. Yet I could not see doing such a thing over the phone.

About two weeks after we had met, I got a call from her cousin, my friend, saying he had told her of my "situation," feeling that she needed to know. I agreed with him that at some point she needed to know, yet there's a catch-22 to this thing: by the time someone has gotten to the point of being close enough to have a right to know (I just don't go around announcing to everyone that I'm a transsexual), they should already have been told—but not before that! I assured him that I certainly wouldn't have touched her without having told her of my history first. I had never done so with anyone before and I certainly wouldn't have done so with her. I asked him how she had taken it and whether or not she was okay. He said she had been crying and I should give her some space for a while. I indicated that I felt strongly that I should call and explain it to her. He just suggested over and over again that I wait and, in a few days, call her "one last time." Needless to say, I called her as soon as he hung up the phone. Her son answered and I asked to speak with her, hoping she didn't hang up on me. I could tell she had been crying. I told her I had gotten the call from her cousin and, although I knew she never wanted to talk with me again, I felt obligated to call and at least explain to her, telling her I'm sorry if I'd hurt her. She asked why I said she never wanted to speak to me again, and I explained that that is the impression her cousin had given me. She told me she had never indicated that to him and that it was all just such a shock. If I had listened to him and not called, she would have felt that I didn't care. Suffice it to say we worked things out. We got married two years after that. We have been married now for over eleven years. I found myself a very special lady.

To get back to the surgeries: I decided to schedule follow-up surgery with Dr. Gilbert in Virginia, because it was on the East Coast and closer to my new love. I didn't want to be three thousand miles away for four to eight weeks. So in June of 1990 I readied myself for round two of the lower surgery. The culture in Virginia was much different from California. They seemed to have no problem with making patients wait for inordinate amounts of time during a visit. On a presurgery visit to the urologist, I had been waiting quite some time in a full waiting room and asked the receptionist if it was going to be awhile because I would like to go out and get some lunch rather than just wait around. She assured me that I should wait. The doctor had been called away, and I waited more than an hour more; when I finally was called back to an examining room, I waited another fifteen to twenty minutes before the doctor showed up. He discussed a procedure that they were doing as part of the urinary hook up that involved taking the gracilis muscle from my leg and rerouting it to the groin area to help provide better blood flow to the region of the surgery. I was concerned about side effects of taking a muscle away from its intended function; he assured me that moving the muscle would have little effect, unless I were a world-class soccer player or something similar. So, in my ignorance, I agreed. I have since found out from a chiropractor that the gracilis muscle is a stabilizer of the hips.

During an interview in Dr. Gilbert's clinic, I was asked how I got along with the urologist and if I thought he was okay. I was surprised and didn't have any experience with his abilities to know of any problems I would have with him. In retrospect, this should have been a wake-up signal. But I had been in such good hands in California for the previous surgery that I had total trust in the system at that point.

Also, I had discussed options with Dr. Gilbert about repairing my sunken chest area at the same time. The morning of the surgery he came up with an option to take muscle from my back and bring it to the front to fill in the area. I told him that the whole reason I had gotten to the present state was because I did not want to have any scars, so his suggestion was out of the question and I was not interested in his doing the chest surgery after all. He indicated that the chest surgery was his real interest, and he agreed not to take the muscle from my back. I left it that; as long as he felt he could do something without leaving scars, I would agree to his attempting to fix my chest as part of the surgery. He also mentioned about taking skin grafted from my behind for the urethra linkage, and I reminded him that he had agreed to use skin from the vagina that they were going to be removing.

After surgery, I woke up and waited an inordinate amount of time in the recovery room. My fiancée was waiting upstairs for me on the floor I was assigned to, and it was well over an hour after they expected me up there that I finally arrived. Apparently they were shorthanded. (You can imagine my anger when I got the bill and saw that they had charged several dollars per minute for recovery room time!) Although Dr. Laub had been very concerned about digestive issues and wouldn't let me eat solids for several days after surgery, these folks had me eating solid food that very night. If the experts say it's okay, it must be okay, right? Would you be surprised to find out that I ended up (no pun intended) with a blocked system?

A few days later my chest was unwrapped and I looked down in horror. Although the sunken area might have been slightly improved, they had cut four- to five-inch smiley-face scars across both sides of my chest. And, to top it off, they had left only the top half of each areola/nipple area. When I asked why they had done such a thing, Dr. Gilbert explained that they felt it was the right thing to do at the time and the areola area could be fixed at a subsequent surgery—sure, at whose expense? And soon I realized that the plugs that had been implanted into my groin area during the first surgery to facilitate injecting fluid into the testicular expanders had not been removed as they were supposed to have been during this latest surgery. No wonder they make you sign a piece of paper prior to surgery giving them carte blanche—otherwise they'd have a whole series of lawsuits on their hands!

I got out of the hospital and stayed at a motel in the area, as I had done when I had had the California surgeries. They had to leave a tube in my penis to keep the urethra from closing up, and they had put a tube through my abdomen so I could void the fluids. I was in a lot of pain. No wonder: instead of anchoring the tube in my penis inside at the bladder, like a catheter (and like the tube in my abdomen), they anchored it by poking a hole in the head of my penis, threading a line through it, and tying the other end to the tube. So the whole mechanism pulled on a very sensitive part of my body, namely, the head of my penis, constantly. My poor fiancée was with me at the time. It was about 2 AM. I was yelling that I had to get that tube out of there. I called the hospital to ask if I could take it out, but they indicated that the tube had to stay in for an extended period of time. I ended up (don't laugh) jury-rigging some dental floss anchored to some collar stays, which I taped to my body in an attempt to relieve the pull of the tube on the string through the head of my penis. God, I never want to go through something like that again!

As it turned out, about four to six weeks after surgery, the tube was removed, and I stood in the doctor's office to see if I could urinate out of my penis. But nothing happened. Then the doctor suggested I go into the bathroom and voilà—success! Apparently, we can become so conditioned to "hold it" that we cannot let it flow just anywhere, even when we want it to. Everything with the urethra looked like it was going well, and I returned home.

Before returning to work, I needed to remove the tube from my abdomen; it had been left there as a precaution to ensure I could void if something had gone wrong with the urethra. I was sitting in my living room and prepared to release the tube. When I attempted to pull it out of my abdomen, it would not "give." I called the hospital and asked what I was doing wrong. The intern explained that any number of things could be causing the problem and that I would have to come in to the hospital for them to x-ray it to see what the blockage was. Another phone call with the hospital—another reason to scream! I called my sister-in-law, who is a nurse, and asked her what types of things can cause this. I didn't know if it was just that I was too afraid to tug harder and that it would just come out if I gave it a good pull. But she told me that it should easily fall out, so a tug could be damaging. She said that air inside a balloon inside the bladder keeps the tube in place and that the air had to escape in order to release the tube. And sometimes the air hose gets pinched and doesn't allow the air to escape. Well, I had had the thing in for about two months and it had had plenty of time to get pinched, so she suggested I try to massage the tube to release the pinched area. It worked! So much for the intern. The tube was finally out of my body!

Unfortunately, within a short period of time, it became evident that there was a problem. Soon, the urethra was closing up and the urine was

barely getting through. I was in a lot of pain and could not get enough
fluid out of my bladder. I called the doctor and asked what was going
on; could the gracilis muscle that they had redirected be wrapped around
and strangling the urine flow through the urethra? He calmly said that
such a thing couldn't be happening. So I asked him what the hell could
be happening to cause a rock-hard mass the size of a golf ball behind my
testicles. He didn't know, and he acted like it really wasn't happening at
all, since he couldn't explain it. So the next thing I know I was on a
plane, heading back to Virginia. The doctor attempted to perform a cys-
toscopy (where he puts a scope through the urethra) in his examining
room, but I couldn't stay still because of the pain. I tried to discuss the
options with him, but he abruptly told me that this was his decision, he
was the doctor, and I was not part of the decision process. I didn't know
what options I might have had, so it was off to the hospital for a cys-
toscopy while I was under anesthesia. When I awoke, I had a tube
looped through the urethra and out through a hole they had cut behind
my testicles where the "golf ball" had been. I asked him how this was to
solve the long-term problem of providing a continuous urethra between
my bladder and the tip of my penis, and he said that they could attempt
to hook it up again at a later time. Did you ever go to one of those
mechanics to have your car fixed and after the nth time and more problems, you just give up to keep it from getting screwed up any more?

In spite of all that medical mess I had gotten myself into, I decided
to call it quits with the doctors in Virginia and just try to heal as best as
I could. At least I could function. I was very weak and had been unable
to exercise for a long period of time. I believe that the combination of
that and the lower levels of testosterone took a toll on my body and my
mind. One good thing that came out of the Virginia clinic was the cer-
tification saying that I had gone through sex reassignment surgery. With
that letter, it was a snap to get my new birth certificate.

The following year, my fiancée and I got married. What a triumph
of perseverance and dedication from both of us. A small ceremony was
held before family and friends, many of whom "knew me when." Yet
others, including most of her family, don't have a clue. I really didn't have
a lot to do with the FTM community at that point. I transitioned from
"transitioning" to husband and family man. Soon afterward my wife and
I attended my twentieth high school reunion; it was amazing how supportive so many people really were. Of course, there were whispers and
side-glances from a few, but we just kept our heads high and looked
straight ahead. Did I mention that I married a helluva lady?

My counselor and I have become friends over the years. He gave me a call in the mid-1990s to tell me about an FTM conference being held in Boston. Since we had no other plans for that weekend, my wife and I decided to attend. It's a good thing we did because we met a few guys who we still think of as good friends to this day. We get together maybe once or twice a year, but we feel like we've known each other forever. We gathered again at the Los Angeles FTM conference a year or two after the Boston conference. We're the ones who don't really stand out in the crowd; we're just ordinary guys. If anyone wants to listen, we'll tell them, but no black armbands trying to force someone to accept us or to listen to what we have to say. And we're a bit older than a lot of the FTM crowd these days, though there are a lot of guys who never made it to manhood until their sixties.

I went back to Dr. Laub in 1999, and he straightened out the mess with my chest. I still have scars, but at least they're straightened out, the areola/nipple area is round and reasonable looking, and the contours are really pretty good considering what he had to work with. I have been back on full-strength dosages of testosterone again for more than five years, and I take better care of myself. I'm going to the gym regularly and am the guy in the showers with the small penis.

I've now been living as a man for over seventeen years. The memories of the first thirty years of my life were as if it all happened to someone else. I was there, but in my mind, I was there as a male. Life looks pretty much the same from my eyes outward to the world; the toughest switch was for those looking back at me who had to adjust to a totally new picture. I have to give them all a lot of credit for bearing with me and for what I put them through. It's hard for me to explain why I am what I am. I'm not sure I know why. But I agree with the words of the song: "what I am needs no excuses."

I found a description on the Internet, written by someone named Diane, who I think described very well what it means to be a transsexual. I'd like to close with her explanation:

> Imagine never being able to fully enjoy any aspect of your life no matter how joyous because you are not really there. Imagine having to edit your thoughts, feelings, gestures and interests due to fear of discovery and rejection. Imagine hating who you are so much that looking in the mirror makes you feel ashamed. Imagine having to constantly lie to your family, friends, children, and every person you meet, always. Imagine never feeling worthy of anyone's love because no one can ever know the real you. That was my life before, every

moment, every day, and no breaks. Those are the reasons why I have changed my physical gender and that's why I feel that being a transsexual is not a matter of choice.

(Web site: Diane1962 [http://members.aol.com/diane1962/diane.html])

MY TRANSSEXUAL AUTOBIOGRAPHY

Dallas Denny

Most book-length transsexual autobiographies—and I have read more than one hundred—conclude shortly after the completion of the authors' gender transition, and in the case of male-to-female transsexuals, just after their genital surgery. In the last chapters, the authors assure us their problems and tribulations—which have cast gloom over their hundreds of previous pages—are now behind them, and their lives are wonderful, marvelous, glorious, fabulous. Everything is fine now. Really.

I've no doubt these authors are telling their stories as they recall and interpret them, but a book that on page 352 has the author sulking in the winter woods, contemplating suicide with a shotgun and on page 356 has her lying abed after surgery in a Snow White landscape, with sunbeams streaming through the window, flowers blooming, and songbirds twittering—well, that just sets off my *bullshit detector.*

I don't wish to diminish the pain these and other transsexuals have reported or the positive effects of their transformations via hormones and genital surgery, but I somehow seem to have escaped both the crushing dysphoria and the magical relief reported by many of these authors. This is not to say that transition and surgery weren't just as good for me—they certainly were—but I suspect most of the autobiographies have suffered from the ideologies of their authors. To me, the authors have seemed to be selling the pain of their early lives and the relief afforded them by transition and surgery. Many seem to be, more or less, infomercials to justify their decisions to transition.

Most transsexuals seem to suffer greatly from feelings of gender dysphoria. People I know—and I believe them—tell me they made the decision to transition with the barrel of a pistol between their teeth. I've seen transsexuals in great psychic agony, torn between their desire to achieve a gender presentation that is consistent with their self-image and their sense of responsibility toward their families, their fears of rejection or the unknown, or the knowledge that it's unlikely they will ever be able to pass undetected as a member of their new sex. Whether or not they choose to transition, I sympathize with, respect, and admire them for having the courage to do what they have to do. But their stories are not my story. This is my story.

First, let me say I could have made it more or less successfully through life without gender transition. It's not likely that I would have killed myself or even thought seriously about doing so. I would have been a productive member of society, and I would have had no major malfunctions. At worst, I might have suffered, like many and maybe even most adult Americans, from depression—which sometimes affects me anyway.

Does this mean I wish I had remained in my sex of original biology? No, it most certainly doesn't. I have absolutely no regrets about what I've done to my body or my life. I sometimes have one of those "what if" moments, when I think wistfully about the children I might have had, or the relationship that didn't endure because of my transsexualism, or about not being rejected for more than a decade by my parents, but everyone has these moments of melancholy speculation. I sometimes wonder, in the same way, what would have become of me if I had studied folklore instead of psychology, or how it would have been to have been raised in some small town instead of being dragged all over the world as an army brat. It's what if—not regret.

For me, gender dysphoria was rather less like a knife in my gut than like a pebble in my shoe. It was always there, always uncomfortable, usually irritating, and occasionally agonizing, making its presence known many times every day. I could ignore it for short or even long periods of time, but it never went away, never got any better. It made me frustrated at times, sad at other times, and furious at yet other times. Sometimes I could repress my feelings by becoming so involved with my life that they had little chance to assert themselves, but they were always there, ready to make me feel bad at even the happiest of times—when I would see a movie and wish I were the heroine instead of the hero, when I would be given male insignia like ties and wingtip shoes at Christmas, when I would be expected to "be the guy" and bring in the groceries, when I would be reminded in a thousand ways of my biology. It hurt—not at every moment, and never more than I could endure, but constantly, without remittance. One can live with, but one never forgets, the pebble in one's shoe.

MY EARLY TRANSGENDER EXPERIENCE

I didn't want to be a girl from my earliest memory. I didn't play with dolls. In fact, I was a fairly unremarkable boy. My transgender feelings did rise, however, at an early age, a year or two before puberty. As a child, I was fairly dense about matters relating to sex and gender; being a boy or girl seemed more a matter of haircut and dress than biology. It was only when I was confronted with impending manhood that I was struck with the immensity of what being a male human would mean. I remember discovering the first hair on my face. I was appalled. I wanted to pluck it out, but I didn't because I knew it would only be replaced by two more. I had no sense that I could declare independence from my biology. I didn't want a male puberty, but I didn't see how I could avoid one, other than by rubbing my chest with my mother's hormone cream in quantities calculated to be too small for her to notice. It didn't work; adolescence came, right on schedule.

When I was in my teens, cross-dressing gave me some relief—and not sexual relief; I didn't begin to masturbate until I was in my twenties. No, it was psychic relief; it just felt right. I was able to manifest the femininity I was otherwise keeping secret from the world. When I looked in the mirror I would see not a cross-dressed boy, but a young woman.

The cross-dressing was of necessity brief and episodic, for I had duties and obligations as a male to which I would inevitably have to return. Still, for a short time, I could experience another sort of "what if"—what if I had been born female. Cross-dressing gave me a compelling—if fragmentary—sense of what life would be like if I had been born with two X chromosomes, and it was infinitely more to my liking than the life I was having and would have as a male.

I was fortunate enough, with my baby face, to make a presentable, passable, and even attractive girl. It was frightening to go into public cross-dressed—it was the 1960s, after all, and I would have been in danger if were read—but I did it anyway. When I would dress and go out in public, I would be treated as best I could tell as if I had been born female—both by women, who would give me little woman-to-woman smiles and talk to me in ways they used only with other women, and by men, who would treat me with great kindness and condescension and sometimes hit on me. This gave me a girlhood of sorts—a limited girl-hood, certainly; I would never presume to claim the same sort of girl-hood nontranssexual women have, but I do believe I had a taste, just a one-day-at-a-time taste, of being a young woman.

Paradoxically, cross-dressing reminded me I wasn't really female. Putting on female garb meant that sooner or later I had to take it off. That was jarring, so much so that I soon found myself passing up oppor-tunities to cross-dress. It was a too-painful reminder that all was not right with my world.

I desperately wanted to live full time as a woman, but it was a scary proposition. My body was continuing to masculinize, making an author-itarian statement that I was in fact male, and I had no documentation, no legal identity, as a female. I had no idea how to make the biology or identity problems go away, or even that it was *possible* to make them go away. Alas, I never realized that my birth name, Dallas, is one of those gender-ambiguous names that can work as well for a woman as it does for a man. Had that come to my awareness when I was fourteen instead of forty, and had I known hormones would have given me control over my biology, I rather think it would have given me the information I needed to transition at age fourteen instead of age forty.

Unfortunately, I have no physical mementos of this girlhood. I have only a strip of photo booth pictures taken in 1976, when I was twenty-seven years old—ten years after I began going out in public cross-dressed, and after testosterone had been masculinizing my body for some fifteen years. Still, when I look at these pictures, I see, as I did then, a young woman and not the young man I was the rest of the time.

Since both biology and social responsibilities dictated that I play the part of a man, I did, and I was good at it. I was never teased, never ridiculed, never questioned. Never. In adulthood, as in childhood, I felt safe, loved, and respected. I never felt threatened or in danger in my cunning masquerade as a man, nor did I ever feel I was endangered or significantly affected by discrimination at any time during or after my transition. I have no idea how or why I've been lucky enough not to experience the crushing discrimination, harassment, and violence reported by so many other transsexuals, but I have, and I am grateful for it. Life was pleasant. My body was for the most part to my liking, too. I was by no means in the "wrong" one—it was just that I lacked the means to mold it in ways I deemed critical.

Unlike many male-to-female transsexuals, I never overcompensated for my feelings by trying to be hypermasculine; I performed manhood just enough to give a credible presentation. I never went one step beyond what I thought was needed to keep me safe, and I never valued either the performance or manhood itself. Not once.

Nor did I, like many other transsexuals, try to defeat my transsexualism. This, I believe, saved me from a great deal of psychic damage. I remember, at age thirteen, finding myself, without having made a conscious decision to do so, riffling through my mother's clothing drawers. The immensity of what I was doing, the terrible repercussions if I were to be caught, and the stigma that would be visited upon me—all of these things flashed through my mind. I knew my parents and society would consider what I was doing shameful and would react harshly. I considered for an instant—the thought arose, was debated, and was resolved in less than fifteen seconds—fighting this feeling that had come from nowhere and driven me into my parents' empty bedroom, but somehow, at my innermost level, I realized that whatever was driving me *would not* be curbed. It was too strong, rooted too deep. If I tried to deny it, to defeat it, to rid myself of it, it would destroy me. But I could hide it. It would stand for that.

And so I made the decision not to repress my transsexualism. This was a fortunate choice, I now know, for many transsexuals damage themselves and those around them by their attempts at denial. They overcompensate, becoming caricatures of their biological sex; they abuse alcohol and other substances; they enter dangerous occupations and take needless risks; they misuse others; they marry and have children not because they want to marry and have children, but because they hope it will kill this thing deep inside them that they hate and fear. Often, in their middle age, they implode. No longer able to fight themselves, they either kill themselves or tear their lives and families apart by declaring their intention to transition.

This was not to be my way, this denial. Instead, I would hide my feelings from the world. I would indulge them in secret, telling no one, or at least being circumspect. It was, I say again, a fortunate choice. Perhaps it was a wise one as well.

My early and midtwenties were a blur of work and college and graduate school and matrimony. I was married in 1971, at age twenty-two, separated in 1976, and divorced in 1977. I had little time or opportunity to cross-dress, and besides, it was not an activity my spouse found particularly comfortable.

After the breakup of the marriage, I began cross-dressing again, but under the influence of testosterone, my body had changed. I still passed in public, but not all the time as before. I knew things would only grow worse as my body continued to masculinize. I was beginning to lose my hair on my head and sprout hair on my torso; both were abhorrent.

In 1979 I took myself to the gender identity clinic at Vanderbilt University in Nashville. After paying two hundred dollars for screening and three hundred dollars to take a battery of psychological tests that I myself was trained to administer, I was told by clinic director Dr. Embry McKee that the program would not offer me hormones or surgery or otherwise help me to feminize myself. Why? Because I was too functional in the male role. I had managed to earn an advanced degree, after all. I had a professional position as a child services protective worker, after all. I had functioned in a marriage for five years, after all.

I took myself to Vanderbilt's medical library, where I rounded up and read everything I could find on transsexualism. The literature indicated Dr. McKee had been right in diagnosing me as nontranssexual. Transsexuals were profoundly dysfunctional persons with histories of sexual promiscuity, narcissistic and histrionic personalities, character disorder, sex work and substance abuse, and suicide attempts. Sex reassignment, or so the clinical wisdom dictated, was for only the worst cases, to be used as a last resort.

For the first time since the onset of my transgender feelings more than fifteen years earlier, I found myself wondering if it was possible I wasn't transsexual after all. I concluded I must not be—at least so far as the medical literature was concerned—but then what about that always uncomfortable, usually irritating, and occasionally "agonizing pebble" in my shoe?

Sensing that I was at a junction in my life—one of those future "what if" jumping-off points—I made a decision that placed me at some legal risk but which would profoundly affect my life (for the better). Dr. McKee had told me Vanderbilt would not give me hormones; perhaps, then, hormones were a missing piece to the puzzle. At the Vanderbilt library I researched hormone regimens and, using a prescription blank I filched from the office of a doctor who had refused to give me estrogen, I wrote a prescription for Diethylstilbestrol (DES), a synthetic estrogen that is now off the market but was not then considered particularly dangerous. I popped my first illegal hormone pill in January 1980, when I was thirty years old. I took DES for ten years, eventually replacing it with Premarin in 1990.

Hormones were indeed a missing piece of the puzzle. Within six months my thinning hair had grown back in—this isn't supposed to happen; I can only guess that the follicles were dormant, but not yet dead. Within two years I had grown breasts, and my appearance was distinctly more feminine. Still, however, I continued to function socially as a male. I was still missing some pieces to the puzzle; I had no idea how to move forward.

Throughout the 1980s I was looking for a transgender community—I knew there had to be others like me—but found no sign of it. I knew only of gay bars with drag shows and the Society for the Second Self, an organization for heterosexual cross-dressers. I knew I didn't fit their exclusionary (no transsexuals, no gays) membership policy, but I knew that through Tri-Ess I might find the larger community, if one even existed.

That community did, in fact, exist. I joined Tri-Ess in September 1988, lying, of necessity, about my transsexualism. In early 1989 I made contact with a transsexual support group in Atlanta. From the group I learned about the Standards of Care of the Harry Benjamin International Gender Dysphoria Association (HBIGDA).

The HBIGDA Standards provide guidelines for hormonal and surgical interventions in transsexualism. Here, for the first time in my life, was the game plan. Now I could see just what I needed to do.

In February 1989 I made the decision to do whatever was necessary to compete my transition. My body, feminized by ten years of estrogen, was as prepared as it was going to get. I began electrolysis. By the fall, my facial hair was mostly gone. In December I resigned from my position as a psychological examiner, loaded everything I owned into a U-Haul truck, and moved from Tennessee to Atlanta.

I should say that, despite my lifelong desire to live as a woman, I didn't make the decision to transition lightly. I had no desire to back out of any responsibilities I had incurred as a man—but I had somehow managed to avoid most such obligations. I had no children, I wasn't married, and the relationship that had consumed most of my thirties had failed. I had three siblings to comfort and look after my parents. I didn't have a career I couldn't bear to give up (I worked for the state of Tennessee as a psychological examiner; I would miss the position, but was willing to endure financial privations in pursuit of my transition). I still had much to lose—family, friends, employment—but I was free of obligations to spouse, or children, or society. The only person who would be singularly affected would be me—and although I was frightened at the prospect of joblessness, poverty, even homelessness, and even more frightened at the thought that I would be likely to be mistreated by society, I went for it. Against these odds, after all, I had myself to gain.

After all that, transition was about as socially and physically challenging as falling off a log. I paid my price, certainly, in the loss of relationships. I had lost my soul mate, a woman I loved deeply and who loved me perhaps even more deeply. (Our relationship, which lasted throughout the 1990s, wasn't able to endure the fact of my transsexualism. It didn't matter that I chose not to act upon my feelings; the very fact that I felt as I did was enough to poison the well.)

I had already lost the most important person in my life. Now I lost my parents and two of my three siblings. I never spoke with my father again. I wasn't allowed to visit or talk to my mother for thirteen years, until she called me some six months after my father's death in 2001. I lost my friends. Only one was outright rejecting; the others wished me well but just drifted away, as friends sometimes do when life situations change.

I paid the price by losing everyone who was important to me—but otherwise, my new womanhood was a no-brainer. I didn't have to disguise myself or "try to be" a woman in any way—I could wear greasy coveralls and no makeup and people would call me ma'am. I didn't have to remove hair from my body, I didn't have to resort to artifice, and I didn't have to practice how to walk or talk or move. I was just myself, dropping all pretense at masculinity, and it somehow worked. I had no difficulties passing in public. I had no problem in finding a job equivalent to the one I had left. People treated me nicely—in fact, better than they had when I was doing my clever impersonation of manhood. I had gone immediately and perfectly from a comfortable and unambiguous life as a man to a comfortable and unambiguous life as a woman.

This was wonderful, of course, for I had never set out to make myself into a freak. I had feared ridicule, harassment, being viewed as a walking sex toy—all the usual things a transsexual woman can expect. Instead, I found myself living, as best I could determine, much like any other forty-year-old woman. It was—literally—my dream come true! I had achieved exactly what I had set out to achieve, yet it surpassed my grandest expectations. Life was simple, comfortable, and easy, and all this came to me organically. I had no psychic scars, no fears, no apprehensions, no areas of discomfort. I was just me, same as before, albeit without that annoying pebble in my shoe.

Many male-to-female transsexuals are shocked by the difference in the way they are treated after transition. Truth to tell, I saw little difference. Both men and women held doors open for me—but then, they had always done that. Women gave me that woman-to-woman smile—that was different—and men sometimes seemed not to hear me when I spoke—that was different—and passengers in my car no longer trusted my driving skills—that was different—but those were small things. For the most part, I was treated pretty much the same as before.

In hindsight, I attribute this to my respective presentations as a man and a woman. As a man, I had a bohemian appearance. I wore jeans and pullover shirts, and my hair was long. Sometimes, I wore a beard. As the son of one of my posttransition friends said, when looking at a "before" picture, "Wow! You looked like a biker dude!" As a biker dude, people were a bit uncertain about me. They didn't defer to me as they do to men in suits. (I wore a suit in public on only one occasion and was astonished at the way people behaved toward me; it startled and upset me so much I went home and took it off and never wore a suit or tie again.)

As a woman, I was more mainstream in my presentation, but just overweight enough and just old enough not to be viewed as a sex object. Somehow, things just seemed to even out, and people treated me as they had always treated me. That was just fine by me.

Let me reiterate that, unlike my putative manhood, my womanhood hasn't been about performance. I simply stopped performing as a man. I allowed myself to use gestures and vocal mannerisms I had always consciously blocked. I dressed more or less like women my age. In my early forties I took time to apply makeup and jewelry. As I passed my fiftieth birthday, like many other women, I stopped bothering. Nowadays I wear only a little lipstick, and I've not worn a dress in years. Lately I've lost some weight, and now, fifteen years after my gender transition and thirteen years after my genital sex reassignment surgery, I've found myself starting to bother again, at least on occasion.

I look, talk, and behave rather like other women my age, without having to work at presenting as a woman. I refuse, in fact, to work at it; people can think about me what they will. I'm just myself.

At five feet eight, I'm a bit on the tall side, but my appearance and demeanor, even without makeup or "women's" clothes (I generally wear Birkenstocks, a pullover top, and slacks), result in others seeing me as a woman. I don't "perform" femininity, at least not any more than any woman does; certainly I perform femininity much less and with less self-consciousness than I formerly performed masculinity. To the best of my knowledge, I'm my natural self, albeit with externally visible changes caused by hormones and electrolysis. I've had genital surgery, of course, but that doesn't show and has nothing whatsoever to do with my social performance as a woman. People read me as female.

Many people view transsexuals as freaks, and most see them as artificial creatures. Admittedly, some are. Others are unlucky enough to have secondary sex characteristics that make it difficult for them to pass as members of their new sex. I was—let me be clear here—lucky not to have those characteristic, and I attribute no particular virtue to myself for not having them.

For me, it's not about cosmetics and cloth, but about who I have become. The changes caused by hormones feel organic—*are* organic, as their influence on my body parallels those of nontranssexual women. My facial hair is gone, thanks to electrolysis. The last time I had a razor to my face was 1990. My face was hairless for more than ten years, when I developed—I imagine for the same reason other women my age get them—a single black chin whisker. I don't shave my body, or need to. I have no Adam's apple, no receding hairline. My hands and feet aren't particularly big. I don't own a wig. Long ago, I threw away my false eyelashes; even my mascara is long out of date and dried up. I've become me.

About six months after my surgery, I did acid for the last time. As I was peaking, I stood naked before a full-length mirror beside another transsexual woman, pre-op, who was also tripping. I knew that if we were freaks, if we were unnatural in any way, if we were artificial creatures, we would know it, for LSD disables the ego. We would see ourselves as we actually were, with our psychological defense mechanisms shorted out by lysergic acid. We looked, and we saw two beautiful, natural human beings, and we knew that all those critics of transsexualism—the religious hypocrites (I say hypocrites because they selectively interpret the scriptures to attack us), the feminist hypocrites (I say hypocrites because they circumvent the most fundamental tenet of feminist philosophy to claim our biology is our destiny), the psychiatric hypocrites (I say hypocrites because they rage against our viewing ourselves as whole creatures because it affects their bottom line), the gay and lesbian hypocrites (I say hypocrites because they refuse to allow us our fundamental freedoms, while demanding theirs)—have their heads up their respective asses when they claim transsexualism is, respectively, immoral, unnatural, unhealthy, and untrue. The LSD spoke and it spoke true, and it told us they were wrong.

As I write this, I'm in my fourteenth year at my job as a behavior specialist, working with adults with developmental disabilities in a county position. I own my own home in a funky little lake community in the middle of Atlanta; if all goes according to schedule, it looks as if it will be paid for in another five years. After fourteen years, my family has reestablished relations with me. I'm a prolific writer, and most of what I produce manages to find its way into print. I'm in my fifth year as editor of *Transgender Tapestry*, the house magazine of the International Foundation for Gender Education. I'm on the board of two nonprofits and, after ten years of transgender activism that threatened to consume me (it was a burning the candle on both ends thing), I continue to do activism on a moderate level. I no longer work at it every waking minute, as I did throughout most of the 1990s.

After five and a half decades of eating whatever I've wanted, I recently had a health scare—an infected leg that resulted in a diagnosis of diabetes. I've turned much of my energy to getting my body back into proper shape. It's a new challenge and one I'm starting to relish, as six months of effort have begun to translate into a difference in the way I look and feel.

My life is comfortable and safe and pleasant. I'm not wealthy—that was never my goal—but the bills are being paid. I'm beginning to plan for retirement, which will come between five and ten years from now.

I have no gender dysphoria these days. None. I don't long to menstruate or become pregnant, or otherwise prove I'm a "real" woman. I'm happy with being a transsexual woman; in fact, I wouldn't have it any other way. I'm content with my no-longer-new gender role, and with my body, and with the changes I was able to bring about through hormones, electrolysis, and surgery. I'm proud of the changes my activism, and that of others, has brought to our society.

Even though I still do daily work on gender issues, I rarely think about and never dwell on my own transsexualism. For me, gender and sexual reassignment were good and fulfilling things. They removed the pebble from my shoe. Life is good.

A RELATIONSHIP WITHOUT A TEMPLATE

Some Historical Highlights

Esben Esther Pirelli Benestad and Elsa Almaas

E *sben Esther:* "From what source did the fear derive?" I often pondered this question. For years I kept my feminine aspect a secret. When my former wife, Liv, caught me "red-handed" in her attire, none of us told anybody about it. I promised never to do "it" again. The "it" became something that we tried to hide from everybody but ourselves, ourselves including my mother, with whom Liv had spoken on the subject, without asking me for permission. I did realize, however, that I could not and should not stop her if she needed to share this shocking reality with someone else.

The "never-more bubble" burst, however. After a couple years, I took up the dressing activity again, and we kept the secret, until the loneliness became unbearable for me. I was alone in my femaleness. Liv would not see me dressed as a woman. The guilt and shame I felt slowly transformed into realization and anger—realization that there was nothing wrong with me and anger because there were people who would find my actions wrong in some senses of the word.

Liv and I divorced in 1986. Before that I had been in love with another woman. That relationship was brought to an end after it was disclosed to Liv. Nevertheless, I learned it was possible to be loved the way I am. I soon met another woman and fell in love with her. My insight told me that to stay with Liv would be wrong and hurtful to everybody. At the same time, I had really looked into the haven of being loved and accepted with all my talents.

Elsa Almaas came into my life on October 16, 1986. Our hands met behind a column in a hallway. Neither of us has ever been able to figure out from where derived the force that made our hands meet and merge. What we do see, however, is that they still hold on after seventeen years, as these words are written, and they still believe in their mutual goal: a continuous, fruitful life together. Our relationship became one that embraces the spiritual, professional, and erotic dimensions, within a context of mutual love and understanding.

It was love at first sight, love even before our minds clearly conceived it. The hands were the first to move. It was a love that has been challenged and has survived in our relationship—*a relationship without a template.*

SECRECY?

Elsa: I met Esben Benestad in 1986 and fell in love with him. I was organizing a Nordic conference in sexology, and I had invited him to give a presentation on some research he had done on heterosexual transvestites. Before he came, he told me that he was a cross-dresser himself. I asked him whether this was a problem, and he assured me that it was not. At the conference I introduced him to a group of friends, and one of them burst out when they met, "Oh so you must be the transvestite!" Esben was struck with surprise; I do not think he had ever been in a setting where his cross-dressing behavior could be talked about so openly.

Esben Esther: The culture crucified my wife, my mother, and me on the cross of secrecy. My father was spared on the grounds that all this might be harmful to him! He was a medical doctor, a general practitioner who in his time assisted births in the rural areas around Grimstad, with his bare hands and quite primitive instruments. I did not tell him about my femme gender expression before I divorced Liv. He began blaming her for the failure of our marriage, one that lasted for sixteen years and had brought forth two children: Elisabeth, my daughter, in 1971 and Evan, my son, in 1974.

By the time I met Elsa, I was an openly trans person with friends and family. My mother stayed away when I expressed my feminine side. She did so in solidarity with my father, who felt that he would not like to see me in feminine attire, even though he eagerly read all the papers I published and all the interviews about me that appeared in newspapers, magazines, and on television.

Elsa: I did not realize how painful it had been to keep this secret. I do not believe I ever accepted the shame that had been the reason for the secrecy. I realized, however, that Esben was vulnerable to gossip and talking behind his back. I thought it would be strategic for Esben to be, publicly, well known and respected as a doctor and sexologist, before he disclosed his *cross-dressing behavior* to the world. It would be good for people to know the masculine side first, as I did.

THE END OF FEAR AND SECRECY?

Esben Esther: I had lived my femme life in secret and had been discovered "red-handed." I had disclosed myself to friends and family. I had met a partner who I had often dreamed about but had never actually encountered. My secret now became public. When journalists came to interview the sexologist couple in Grimstad, they would ask: "And now, Esben, will your own *cross-dressing behavior* be a subject for this interview?" I would answer: "No," and Elsa would support me. Gradually, we both knew that the time to go public was imminent.

I harbored many fears. What about my patients? I was a highly respected general practitioner in our little town. There were still some catastrophic thoughts in my mind telling me of bolts of lightning that would strike me, windows that would pop out from their frames, and the angry voice of the universe that would sound: "Be damned and condemned!" I did not listen to my fears. Anger and insight had by far outlived the power of those fantasies. With Elsa as a master of strategy, we moved toward public disclosure. To find the *right* journalist, who would not cause any problem, was a major challenge for us.

Elsa: Years went by, and his femme persona was no secret to the children and their friends. Our own friends got to know both his masculine and his feminine sides. Like ripples in water, the femme side of Esben became known to the world. The first public appearance was in Sweden, where he was interviewed by a newspaper. Later, we both appeared in a Norwegian TV program, together with my son, Tomas, who proudly declared: "They love each other very much!"

The final barrier was to present himself, as a woman, in the town where we live. It is the masculine side that works as a general practitioner, although, for special occasions, his femme side may appear.

Esben Esther: There are many aspects of the coping process. Many people challenged the state of secrecy. Secrecy is a heavy and sticky burden. It weighs on the shoulders of whomever is carrying it, and it sticks to those who may come in contact with it. My secret had stuck to Liv and became a burden for her, too. We had informed our children and our friends; this burden is not easy for those you are close to. This typically includes most family and friends with no *muzzle* on anyone. With Elsa, this process went on like ripples spreading in a pond hit by a stone in the middle. Soon all our friends were involved, no longer in a sticky secret, but in the *gender diversity* of Elsa, me, and our relationship. We are well aware that some matters of privacy are normal. Basically, one could say that all personal matters into which we had searched intensively and found common insights could also be brought up in any conversation with friends or family.

The absence of secrecy allows us to be free to play and to shop wherever we are—for Elsa, for my femme self, or for my masculine side. In the spring of 2005, I bought a nice pair of shoes for my masculine side while dressed as my femme self. Shoes have always been a special problem for me since my foot is size 13. Elsa was there when I made the purchase, and there was a beautiful exchange of smiles between us. Sometimes we present a kind of *show* for shopkeepers and sales assistants.

DIAGNOSES

Esben Esther: Everything I had read on the subject of *transvestism, transgenderism,* and *transsexualism* was recognizable from the point of view that the subjective experiences were linked to the "patients" described. However, these materials did not provide a plausible explanation about their etiology. The medical/psychological literature did not describe me. It described someone diagnosed as sick as a result of being trans—someone who I had yet to meet. I had met transgender people who had become sick because of the hardships of being a trans person in a nonaccepting world. The idea of being *trans,* however, could not be a disease by itself. This insight made me angry, for having to suffer the guilt and the shame from a society that, in the subtlest of ways, taught me that I was *no good.*

Elsa: I thought I knew everything about the trans phenomenon, because I had read the medical, psychological, and sexological literature on *transvestism* and *transsexuality.* I soon learned that this was not so easy.

In my psychological training, I was convinced that it was, if the behavior was not pathological, at least, very inconvenient to host more than one persona of an individual. I thought integration was a must, but Esben argued against my conviction. He was a living example of a well-functioning, healthy, confident, intelligent person, without any neuroses or unhealthy closeness to his mother or distance from his father, as far as I could judge. My textbooks obviously talked about neurotic and suffering people, but my new love was not one of them. We had to have many conversations to get some mutual understanding of who we were. I finally realized that it was impossible for me to fully understand Esben and how he felt. We also realized that it was equally impossible for him to understand me, or for anyone to understand another person. Yet we were able to write a book on *gender in transition!*

LANGUAGE

Elsa: In 1986 I met a man who was a cross-dresser. This meant that he dressed as a woman about once a week. I soon learned that he really would like to live in his feminine expression more often than that. Gradually, I saw what forces were behind his wish to express himself as a woman, and I felt afraid—I was afraid of losing the man I loved; I was afraid that he would become a *transsexual woman.* We attended a conference some years ago where Dr. Richard Docter was presenting on this subject. I asked him what usually happens to *cross-dressers* as they grow older. He assured me that most of them gradually become more feminine. Many end up living full time as women. I was not calmed by this information!

We developed a continuing process on what to call the baby and find good words for our experience. I felt like I was living in a real-life experiment. The first thing I learned was that my husband had a dual personality; as a man his name was Esben Benestad, and as a woman "her" name was Esther Pirelli. Most of our friends and family learned to respect this. This was also a dual experience for me, but in a different way. For some years he said that through his eyes, the world was the same. However, some experiences convinced him that this was not always true. On one occasion, we were at a conference where Esben had a beer with a friend the first night. The next day we met for a glass of wine, and Esther made her entrée. Our friend jumped up to find a chair for *the lady,* and in the middle of his move, he realized that he had almost responded to *Esben*

Esther as a woman. This has also been my own experience. When Esben Esther is in "her" femme expression, I can see the man, but he comes out as a woman to me, and it becomes impossible for me to respond as I would to the masculine expression. It is therefore most natural to use the femme name. At the same time, it has felt like I am participating in some kind of a game, calling my husband by a femme name.

As years went by, Esben and Esther felt more and more uncomfortable being a dual personality, and when the Norwegian name law was changed, making it possible to have both a male and a female name, Esben and Esther became Esben Esther. This seems to be a right decision, and many have come to use his *double* name quite easily. However, many of our old friends and some of our family just say that they have learned to use the different names and that should be sufficient!

The development of names also represents a change in self-experience, I think. It has become important for Esben Esther to be allowed to be a bi-gendered person, without having to present as two individuals. This has challenged traditional theories even more, and during the last few years we have met several people who are challenging the world in a similar way: not being a man, nor being a woman, but representing both personas in one body.

Esben Esther: Over the years we have met a great many trans people of all ages and backgrounds as well as some intersex individuals. I have come to believe that for some individuals gender identity is somewhat rigid, while for others it seems to be more flexible. Schwaab and others have demonstrated "dimorphic structures in the bed of the hypothalamus." Zhou and colleagues have demonstrated that transsexual brains inherit neurological traits that appear typical for the gender identity experienced by the individual in question. This makes sense to me, and it helps with my coping strategies. While not positively proven, it does confirm much of my personal and clinical experience. Transsexualism is not a mental disorder; it is a neurobiological condition. I believe this region of the hypothalamus to be like the groin. Most people would prefer to be either one sex or the other, but some are genitally intersexed. It is my belief some may be intersexed at the hypothalamic level, while others represent many different combinations of the major options. I call myself bi-gendered, since language at this time does not offer me better options. Personally, I have been unable to apply a better term to communicate my own mind-set to the society in which I live.

FAMILY

Esben Esther: As they grew older, my parents expressed a desire to come with us as we toured Europe in our family car. One year we went to Verona, Italy, to hear the opera *Aida* performed in the ancient outdoor Colosseum.

My father was more than interested: "Are you really going?" "Is it a long drive?" "Are you bringing friends?" We answered to the best of our conscience. Afterward I would say to Elsa: "He wants to come with us." "Yes, she answered, "but then he would have to meet you as a woman, wouldn't he?" We agreed to wait for a direct request from him. It came some weeks later: "Would you take us old ones with you in the back seat?" "Sure!" we said, "but then you must meet Esben as Esther." "No problem!" was his smiling response. As Paris once was worth a mass, Verona was worth a son in feminine attire.

At the age of eighty-three, my father, my mother, Elsa, and myself, in my feminine expression, entered a hotel in southern Germany. "This should have been made into a movie!" my father exclaimed. We sat down at the dinner table, and the waiter addressed my father as the *Pater familias* with his wife and daughters!

My mother had already met me. By accident she came in one day when we were planning a big party. There were many people present who were unfamiliar to her, including a tall lady in casual wear. She introduced herself to the guests, and soon it was the turn of the "tall lady." My mother is correct and polite: "We have not met before I believe," she said with her hand stretched out. "Oh yes we have!" I replied in the best of my male voice capacity. A tremble ran through her before she said, "You look a lot like your daughter, Elisabeth!" Then she turned to greet someone else.

Elsa: In a later conversation with my mother-in-law, she said that she had to use all her power to collect herself in the situation Esben Esther just described.

Esben Esther: Elisabeth was the one who at the age of thirteen wanted to fight for her father's right to be a woman. Since then, she has expressed worry to the point that the man might "die" or disappear. She supported my right to make real whoever I am. She often talks with me about girls' concerns like clothing, makeup, and so on. We do talk on the telephone every so often. I sense a positive affirmation from her. The ease with which my family interacts with me is growing.

My father mentioned a movie directed by my son but did not live to see it. My father died in 1998 at the age of eighty-eight. To the end, he was a good friend of both Esben and Esther. The last thing we did to each other was to hug.

My son, Even, did a documentary titled *All about My Father*, which had its premiere in 2001. It has been shown at eighty-eight film festivals all over the world, earning many prizes. Many years ago, a well-known Norwegian TV team wanted to make a documentary about my bi-gender lifestyle. Even, who was eighteen years old at the time, asked if I could wait until he had learned the skills to make that movie. I certainly wanted him to do the project. Thus, we waited eight years for Even to complete his studies to be a film director. In this seventy-two-minute movie, Even discusses his doubts and worries concerning his bi-gendered father. I am portrayed through my son's eyes. It is a beautiful demonstration not only of the particular problems of a family with a trans person but it is also a view of some existential issues inherent in a father-son relationship. Without deep love and trust between Even and me, that movie could never have been made.

With the public presentation of this movie, Elsa and I had to look deeper into our relationship. In its own way, the movie became an expensive form of family therapy.

Tomas has been a great support and a critic, too. He is the one who tells me what I can and cannot do. Mind you, his instruction does not concern my right to womanhood, but rather how that womanhood should be presented.

Elsa: When I met Esben, my son, Tomas, was ten years old. He immediately accepted Esben. One of his comments while he was holding our hands walking down the street was: "No, I can be current!" Tomas is now twenty-seven and one of Esben Esther's most fearless critics. When Esben Esther let his hair grow to avoid using a wig, Tomas said, "Oh, I really hate a balding woman!" Esben Esther has met quite a few members of my big family, in both modes of expression. My mother's first reaction was to take a picture, which she is keeping in her album. We asked how she would explain the picture to various people. Her response, "That this is my son-in-law, of course!" One of our little nieces was studying "Auntie Esther" with a pondering look on her face, and then she said: "I think it must be Uncle Esben behind all that mess!"

After the film *All about My Father* was shown, my mother said that it was an important film. "You know," she said, "people really want to be accepting, but they dare not ask questions. Now, by viewing the film they can get the information they need. Our friends are much more comfortable now."

THE MISSION

Esben Esther: I see my *bi-gender* lifestyle as a mission. I know that Elsa is not particularly happy living with a dedicated missionary. Nevertheless, this lifestyle has given us a better understanding of gender issues and of human life. It has been a great comfort in helping us to cope with our special relationship.

PUBLICITY

Esben Esther: If you have genitals pointing outward, the option of fame is imminent. You just have to appear in a dress once or twice, and you are the talk of the town. If this talk spreads to the media, you are soon to be the talk of the country. I have not as yet been the talk of the world. However, by the showing of my son's movie, *All about My Father*, I have come very close.

If you have your genitals pointing inward and you live with someone like me, your options of fame are accessible. The difference between Elsa's and my fame, in this regard, is that people have a tendency to feel sorry for Elsa, while they seem more in awe of me. Added to this fame is that we are both official faculty members teaching the first university course in sexology in Norway. Being popular mailbox-answering professionals on the Internet as well as in other media, we communicate this unique expression of our commitment to each other.

Some people may see me as a disturbed person, and some may see Elsa as suffering from some kind of disturbance, as well. However, I think that we have disturbed a whole nation's view on gender roles and relationships. It has earned us respect from many and admiration from some to the extent that people I don't know stop me on the streets to hug me.

THE RISE OF CHALLENGES

Esben Esther: It dawned on Elsa that living with a trans person is more than living with a man who has some whimsical peculiarity. It actually means living with a woman, not a full-time one, but nevertheless a woman. After about one year of living together, I went away for a trans meeting in Sweden. Elsa stayed home to finish her first book. Not long after my arrival in Sweden, she called me and said that she missed me and that she planned to come and "kidnap" me! I was flabbergasted. Elsa had just gotten her driver's license, recently, Sweden is far away from our home in Norway, and I was to be kidnapped. Frankly, I was flattered. These two events were to dominate the hours to come. She arrived very late, after having gotten lost on the crossing from Norway to Sweden. In a span of about four hours my joyful anticipation of being captured had been replaced by great fear and images of Elsa off the road, in a ditch, in a lake, or trapped bleeding in a car wreck. This was before our days of mobile telephones, and Elsa did not have the phone number of the hotel where I was staying.

The *kidnapping* took place in the early evening. I deserted my duties as "Queen of Scandinavian Transvestites." Elsa and I left for Oslo and the day after for Grimstad. I had every intention to stay in my feminine mode, when trouble arose. Elsa had not set out to kidnap a *woman*; she was after her *man*! We talked the issues through, and resolved some, including how we were to return home. We continuously invented and reinvented our lives. We both knew that there was room to explore.

DECEPTION

Esben Esther: For many years I was taking hormones behind Elsa's back. I knew she could feel it. I knew she could not cope with it. When she asked me directly "Are you taking hormones?" I answered "No" and added that some men grow breasts as they grow older. I knew I was deceiving her, but, in fear of losing her, I dared not tell her the truth. I felt terrible. At the same time I was trying to cope with my own feelings and longings. I had long experienced the benefits of estrogens and antiandrogens, not only on my body, but also through the ease of mind that emerged with the advent of this treatment.

I was stuck between two of the dearest forces of my life: my love for Elsa and my desire for womanhood. Could I be a self-denying transsexual desperately trying to stick to heterosexual commitments in order to keep my spouse? I do not think so. It is possible, it seems to me, to stay male enough to satisfy both Elsa's concern for masculine presence and my inner need for femme gender expression.

THE NEED FOR HELP

Esben Esther: Where do people go when they are in trouble? In whom can they confide concerning their life crises, their subjective and mutual relational pain and sufferings? Family therapists? Yes. Psychologists? Yes. Other skilled therapists? Yes. But where do you go with a relationship that lacks a template? Most therapists operate by templates—templates based on their own conceptions and beliefs and templates of diagnostic manuals. For the times I have felt that a therapist would have been helpful, I knew there was no therapist within reach who could be of any help. Those with experience in trans issues were themselves in trouble and in search of advice—those therapists were mainly ourselves. We had the insights and the experience, but in this case we were incapacitated. The few others I knew of were very far away.

LOSS AND GRIEF

Elsa: Many have asked me how I can cope with this gender duality of my husband. I can assure anyone that it is not easy! The difficulties have expressed themselves in both obvious and not so obvious ways. The obvious is that Esben Esther has removed all his beard and body hair. This gives me a different person to touch. I would be lying if I said that this has been okay all the time. As I have gotten used to it, I do not think so much about it. It is also obvious that I am sharing my life with a woman much of the time. This, I must say, is in itself an exquisite pleasure! What is not so pleasant is to be without male company and in certain situations to not be the feminine focus in our relationship. When we, for example, are window-shopping for jewelry, he is more interested in finding something for himself than in considering what could be a nice present for me.

What was not so obvious was the strange way Esben Esther behaved when I wanted him to understand how I felt about *him* or *her*. For many years, it was my experience that, when I tried to talk about the difficulties in my life, of being the wife of a trans person, he just withdrew into something that seemed very lonely and dark. Ultimately, it felt like we were always talking about *him/her* and about the pain of not being accepted, of not having a place in the world, of not even having words to express oneself, but having to make up one's entire existence. I understood these feelings despite my frustrations! There was an anger inside

Esben Esther that he did not want to share with me. I think it was beyond words, beyond what could be shared and talked about. It was something not of this world. It needed the goddess of the Hawaiian volcanoes, Pele, to deal with this anger.

PELE

Esben Esther: Some years ago I met with the volcano goddess Pele on the Big Island of Hawaii. She sensed my inner struggle and said:

> *I see your pain, your great turmoil.*
> *I know it by my link to soil.*
> *I hand you clarity if you desire,*
> *I am the Deity of heat and fire.*

Sensing this as a true divine offer, I smiled and said:

> *I must confess:*
> *I ask no more, I pray no less!*

She told me to tell my story and shed some light to the well of loneliness that I had described to her.

> *It takes, I said, that I can tell,*
> *a lot to face that deep, dark well!*
> *She answered smilingly: To cope,*
> *just see it as kaleidoscope.*
> *A fertile, twinkling treasure bin,*
> *your deep and sacred womb within.*
> *I tell you here and now, tonight:*
> *It can but be conceived by light.*

> *And then, I asked, how shall I act,*
> *when light has rendered its impact?*

> *Then day by day you have to rise*
> *and face the scrutiny of eyes.*
> *There is a troubled lot to do,*
> *before they see the same as you.*
> *You must reveal, you must declare*
> *to gain a sense of being there.*

I had given her some insights to the forces I felt fighting within me. She responded:

> From every pit, each glowing hole,
> through manly spirits I control.
> I must, myself, burst out in fire.
> My yearn for being does require
> that I express my gleaming heat.
> Secluded powers spell defeat.
> By fire's aid, I rise up high,
> from heat alone, I fade and die
>
> You must give birth to be alive,
> from whatever source your births derive.
> Birth is by any way of seeing,
> the ground for all array of being!

How then can birth be given to something not heard and talked of? Likewise, I wondered how I could communicate my own insights and hers to the loved ones around me. I could also feel that some of my emotions were those of rage, a rage furnacing deep within me, a rage that but seldom had exploded into any kind of outward wrath.

Pele said:

> From heat grows rage, from wrath rise fire,
> you choose your ways as you desire.
> But will you take a kind advice,
> you choose the warmth and melt the ice.
> Lead rage to heat, leave wrath for fire,
> and you shall meet what you admire.

Her words became an ethical guidance for me: "Lead rage to heat, leave wrath for fire." They brought me close to happiness.

> I sensed through trembling well so steep
> the shift of magma in my deep.
> It was alive my very soul,
> I heaved in yearn for being whole.
> I could erupt at any time—
> in hot cascades or more sublime.
>
> I saw myself in smoke and flame
> give rise to wild, to fierce to tame.

I felt as ripe as budding spring
and ready for most anything.

Though
before eruption came to be,
The Goddess, Pele, spoke to me:
We have encountered sweet as brothers,
like we did meet as heated mothers.
We have both sensed the inner urge,
to let our powers meet and merge.
It takes a motherhood of soul
to merge such forces to a whole.
It takes some qualities of male,
to let erupt such forceful tale.

As we inhale, as we expire,
we must for light and tale inquire.
We own a well of some extremes,
that can make living Hell it seems.

To seat a wholesome rest require:
To mother heat and father fire.

Elsa had traveled with me to the Big Island of Hawaii; she was by me as this epic unfolded, and she gave me all the space and support that I needed.

Elsa: After Esben Esther's meeting with Pele, everything became much calmer—for a while. The next unexpected challenge for me was that Esben Esther seemed to be getting more and more feminine. He took speech lessons and learned to modulate his voice into a feminine mode. His body changed, and I thought that this was because he had a biological femininity inside that could not be held back. As Even says in his movie, "Everything changes, even your voice." It came to a point where I had enough, and I told Esben Esther that I wanted to separate. This was a painful decision. It was even more painful for Esben Esther, and he finally confided one of his painful secrets.

Esben Esther: One more year went by before I told her my secret about taking hormones. I told her in desperation, because she was to leave a spouse who had become too feminine in body for her. After much discussion laced with tears and final honesty, we decided to stay together.

Elsa: I was shocked to learn that he had been taking hormones for many years. When I thought that his breasts developed by my caresses, it was hormones that did the job! I had been asked by one of our students what made me so different from many wives of other cross-dressers, who divorced their husbands. I assured him that it was because they felt cheated. I did not, because I had known all the time. Suddenly, I knew I was cheated, too!

What made me stay at that moment was the assurance that he would stop taking the hormones. I thought that he might become more masculine again. What also happened was that we had a meeting at a very deep level, and it felt like we were bonding through sharing the same fate, a body of knowledge that we could talk about but that no one would understand without experiencing it.

Esben Esther: I tried living without hormonal support and found myself in increasing distress. After some months I had to talk to Elsa. This time I did not covet these feelings as I had done before. Elsa saw my pain, I think, and we agreed on antiandrogens in combination with a 5-alpha reductase inhibitor (Proscar). In but a few short weeks, even though I may have had some disappointments about my body changes, I felt much better and our relationship improved.

BELONGING

Esben Esther: For years I did not feel comfortable with the world. Believing that I had to keep a major part of myself secret from everybody, I deprived myself of the option of positive *belonging*. Pele told me that I had to "give birth" to be alive from whatever source that birth derived. To carry a quality inside you that has the power of changing not only you but also others deprives you of any *belonging* linked to that quality. Furthermore, it deprives those around you of some major components of your resources. This quality must be presented to the world. That was my challenge. The challenge to the world was to receive the special gifts I had. Elsa came to see me as a woman. It was scary for her. It added to my sense of *belonging* as a woman. It was joyful and sad—joyful because I was affirmed as woman; sad because it threatened our continued life together. *Belonging* arises when others perceive you the same way as you perceive yourself. *Belonging* is positive when that which is being perceived is given a positive value both by yourself and by others. For me it is positive to experience a woman's *belonging*. By itself, this is not negative for Elsa. But being a woman as a partner does threaten our relationship with regard to the more basic elements of living in society; that is, of being considered as a bi-gender person in a relationship with a genetic woman. Friends, family, shopkeepers, assistants, bartenders, receptionists, and many others—they are there to affirm one's gender roles and presentations through daily interactions.

The absence of secrecy allows for the freedom of living. A major contributor to our continuous love, understanding, and coping is our freedom to move and to present ourselves as an apparent heterosexual couple. Often we are offered queen- or kings-size beds when entering a hotel somewhere in the world. If we are traveling as two women, then we are offered the option of the hotel staff pulling the queen- or kings-size beds apart. To observe some of these changes from our position is a rare privilege. There will be some who see us, possibly, as lesbians. Some will, as the waiter in a San Francisco restaurant did, ask Elsa if she thinks that her *husband* was satisfied with the meal.

The absence of secrecy also allows for ease in disclosure. We never accept any offer of bed division; we smilingly respond that we prefer to sleep together. We do not get embarrassed if somebody sees me as a "man." What is this disclosure anyway? If people see me as a man when I am in feminine mode, I think that they see me as a *transsexual* or a *transvestite*. I could also be perceived by more "informed" people as a *trans person*. This is not a shameful disclosure, but a truthful observation—bless them all for being observant. For those people I fear, who read a "male" body under my womanish appearance, this comes from remnants of personal shame still present. I know that I can never become a woman like those who were born with a body to match that gender identity, but I have learned it is an option to find pride and belonging within my special edition of being human.

The absence of secrecy allows for freedom of movement. We have traveled in many parts of the world. Some trips were done as two women only, while for others, as a combination of bi-gender and two women. In the early years we traveled only as an apparently "normal" couple. Elsa would love to do such a tour again, but she will not do so unless it would be joyful for me, too. We have given workshops and presentations in many European countries, Australia, Cuba, and the United States. We have gone on boat tours in England and sightseeing in many of the major cities in Europe, the United States, and Australia.

We love to dance, and we dance best when we are both in heels. I am a woman leading like a man on the dance floor. Elsa's *space* is not always responsive to my dancing cues. However, I am the person who is attentive in watching out for others on the dance floor. At times, it feels like we are one two-sided organism. When we dance, we enter into a state of trance, together.

We often flirt with the world. I know that we both enjoy it. We have our favorite shop for ladies' wear, and we both receive letters from the manager, Solveig, when she has special offers. In addition, other interactions with people around me have given me a sense of belonging as a woman.

Some years ago Elsa and I had lunch at a restaurant in Valencia, Spain, and I was in my femme mode. After the meal I needed to use the bathroom. These were located on the floor below. I still remember the red carpet in the staircase. I turned left for the ladies' room, and there was a lady at a table collecting the equivalent of a quarter from each user. She pointed to the ladies' room. I replied with a "thank you" that contained more gratitude than she would ever know. This little event demonstrated better than words what it takes to accomplish *gender belonging* as a woman. To achieve this in a gender role not congruent with my body is a basis for my coping strategy. This includes coping in my relationship with Elsa, in the world, and in life. *Gender belonging*, for me, is earned by learning the social and psychological aspects of femininity and for establishing my womanhood.

TIME SLIDING AND THE *TRAUMA OF RETENTION*

Esben Esther: Perhaps the most challenging issue that influences our relationship is that I suffer from the *consequences* of a special *trauma of retention*. This is similar to the problem of overcoming early gender and/or sexual trauma, like many queer people. When we were small, we could tell our mothers that we needed to pee, and they would smilingly come to our rescue. Likewise we could express our hunger, thirst, or sleepiness, and our parents would tend to us. What we could not express, however, was possibly tingling sensations in our genitalia. If we did any experimenting that involved sex games with the kids next door, we knew to keep silent about it. In subtle and obscure ways, we learn that society around us made us realize that these were not matters of open expression. However, these feelings and experiences were stored in our subconscious. This is what I mean by the general *trauma of retention*. It most surely affects the ways that we as adults are able to express sexual and erotic feelings. Often these feelings are played out, clumsily. This *trauma of retention* strikes people like me who didn't have the permission to talk about sexuality in general, and definitely not the permission to express a gender choice or desire—that is, "Mama, I would much rather be a girl!" Similarly, it is almost out of the question for little Tina to express her love for Doris or for little Peter his enchantment with Tom. Nor is it permitted for Richard and Sue to say that their grandfather has put his penis into their mouths. These special *traumas of retention* influence the way we cope with challenges in adult life and relationships.

During childhood, adolescence, and young adulthood, I stayed hidden in secrecy. Gradually, I came to realize that there was basically nothing wrong with me. I had no illusion that the rest of the world would perceive it the same way. Within my own inner world I did not harbor much shame; I was happy during childhood and adolescence staying home alone. In those *sacred* moments, I really enjoyed the exploration of my femininity with the help of my mother's clothes and makeup. I had learned that if the outside world knew and saw my secret femininity, it would be a catastrophe. In my emotional life, I viewed the world as my opponent—a force that would damn and dismiss me. My images of this dismissal and damnation were vivid and fearful.

Over the years I have been blessed with a relationship that offers the quality of mutual affirmation. I have overcome many obstacles in a world that I firmly believe would have destroyed my *affective* self. Elsa and I have contributed toward changing much of the hostility experienced in public. Yet when Elsa opposes my femme side, she counts the days of manhood to the days of womanhood. She feels (and fears?) that I actually enjoy being feminine only and that I see the masculine side as something necessary to keep her. I have trouble seeing her perspective. Like many traumatized people, I tend to slide in time, away from the here and now, to the days when I imagined the world as a fierce opponent. Elsa ceases to be Elsa, my much-loved partner and wise advisor, and she becomes a representative of the evil world that I so long have hated. For those times, I find peace and shelter within my own mind. Even to this day, I can slide into the same sheltered realms and become inaccessible for those who most want and need to reach me. It has been a great challenge for me to find holds in the days that are current, instead of sliding back to times of the past.

I remember one time in Guadaloupe. We were traveling with a

group of predominantly gay men. They were our guides and promised to take us to a restaurant run by a woman and her husband, if he was sober. I was in white shorts and blouse, and Elsa was dressed likewise. We both wore sandals and bikini tops under our outer garments. It was a beautiful night, the food was delicious, and the male part of the restaurant-running couple was absent. Music started to play, and we danced—man with man, woman with woman, woman with man. I was even invited to dance with some of the other people in the restaurant. Soon the husband arrived. He was handsome and apparently sober, with a *glimpse of eroticism* in his eyes. The husband asked Elsa to dance. He was a good dancer, and clearly his hands held her buttocks very tightly. They both enjoyed the rhythm of the music, while our gay friends enjoyed some more food and sipping champagne. After having danced several numbers with Elsa, the husband turned to me. I had been watching with eager anticipation and was asked to dance, by him. Strong hands seized my buttocks, and I was led on the dance floor as never before. The husband's eyes shone with joy and I sensed a totally innocent eroticism. The gay men at the table nearby became silent. They were no longer sipping their champagne; they were drinking it, as though it were water. Through a corner of my eye, I read fear in their otherwise calm and confident faces. After three lovely dances, I thanked my dance partner and came back to the table with the others. I wanted to know what had happened to them, and they said they had to guzzle the champagne to calm their fear that my dance partner would have killed me if he had known about me.

RESOLUTION

Elsa: We went to Bali, and stayed at Ananda Cottages in Ubud. We lived next to the rice fields, in an open cottage, with the family temple and the family workshops situated between our cottage and the dining room. When the birds stopped singing, the rain started, and we had to stay inside. While it rained, we talked and talked.

One may wonder from where their fearful fantasies of the Balinese were derived. After all, we were all healthy and strong human beings. We both understand what the *trauma of retention* does to a person when he is alone with a painful secret. It says that you do not exist; that you are not accepted in the way you experience yourself. One feels the whole world is against you; that you are the whole world in many situations.

We learned that when I saw the *black* anger—when Esben Esther withdrew into himself—we needed power to cope. We could not use all our energy to deal with the rest of the world. We needed that energy for ourselves. I told Esben Esther that we would never survive as a couple if his, or her, main focus in life was to be a missionary for all trans people. Without having a life for yourself, you cannot be a good representative for other people. The birds started to sing, the rain stopped, the sun shone again, and we went out to find ourselves a Hindu god to protect "the little things in life," a god to remind us to stay home and take care of every little thing that helps us build up energy: the plants in our living room, the garden, keeping the kitchen organized, reading books, being with friends and family, sailing, picking mushrooms in the forest, and going skiing in the mountains. I am not used to seeing myself as a religious person, but it seems like I am being protected, and it appears as if there is a blessing in my life. I am challenged to go deeper in understanding what other people are dealing with in their lives. I have become deeply interested in the mysteries of human beings. I am being "queered" by my husband, and thus being welcomed in gay and trans communities; I am included in a world that I otherwise would not know. In addition, I feel very grateful, from personal experience, in knowing that few people are actually "straight" and that the world really is much more fun than imagined from *conventional* lifestyes.

Esben Esther: Our relationship has gone from better to excellent over the past twenty months since the hormone revelation. We are awed by mutual condition of love. As we sat in our living room again contemplating our relationship over a glass of red wine, Elsa said, "I am sure that 'this condition of love,' is the basis of our ability to cope with all our challenges, which have no templates." There are many individuals involved in this process of coping. As individuals, we represent a very complex system of interactive elements. This system of interactive elements is in perpetual motion with other systems that are both long and short term, in duration.

Elsa and I have learned to cope with our own interacting systems and how they conflate to form a resultant system, representing our relationship. We see our relationship as synergistic. Together, we have accomplished more than just the sum of our added powers. The conflict between my need for hormonal support and Elsa's need for a manly man lies mainly in our relationship as a loving couple. If we were we living separately, no conflict would have arisen.

MORE BLESSINGS!

Elsa: It is a lot of fun living with Esben Esther. First of all, he is a good person! He or she is kind, intelligent, good humored, likes to play, have a good time, and enjoy life. He or she is also serious, hardworking, sincere, faithful, and loyal! He or she can be very egoistic, stubborn, and is almost always right. However, I am careful not to leave all decisions to him or her because a small percentage of the time he or she is absolutely wrong!

Esben Esther: We have a beautiful life with the qualities of love, openness, playfulness, innovation, and absence of secrecy. We have access to good fellowship and mutuality, partly because we represent a variety of gender roles and presentations. Seldom are either of us bored when we go out shopping. There is almost always opportunity for mutual interest. These are qualities, I think, that really strengthen our relationship.

Elsa: We are a good team; we can work, play, and travel together. We both enjoy the company of friends that we have met all over the world. We share three children and their partners. They give us a lot of pleasure and a few sound frustrations from time to time. We have a house on a street where there must be about seventeen guardian angels who are out of work after the primary school moved to a safer place. In all the years that the school was situated on the Main Street of our little town, no child was ever injured by the traffic! These angels are now taking care of everybody else in our town. A strangely comfortable atmosphere has developed, which among other things has resulted in the annual Festival of Pleasure.

My son says that our backyard is a focus of energy. It is a place to dwell, it is a place of peace and calm, and it is a wonderful place to live. It is obvious that, whether it is true or not, the god for the *little things* has dominion here.

I do not think that we can judge big issues like sexuality and gender expression. They are just ways to organize lives—lives that often seem too complex to fit into the understandings we have developed. I feel like the Greek philosopher Protagoras when he said, "About the Gods, I know nothing, partly because of their nature, partly because of my limited time on Earth!"

I could say the same about sexuality and gender expression.

Esben Esther: I can certainly subscribe to that!

A PART-TIME WOMAN

Elaine Lerner

I. JUST TWO WOMEN

It was blustery outside, but my friend Ann and I were warm and cozy in the small restaurant. The place was packed, yuppies reading the *Times*, elderly couples perusing the menu, college students talking excitedly, young families on their way home after church. I caught our reflection in a mirror, two attractive forty-something women having Sunday brunch. No one was paying much attention to us. But I couldn't help wondering if people would have been more interested if they had known more about me. I am transgendered; I was born a man, but now I openly and successfully live part of my life as a woman. No one else knew what we knew, but I am sure that if the others had known about me and how I live my life, many probably would have been quite curious, others fascinated, some repulsed. If TV shows and movies are any indication, being transgendered is like being cloned, or tattooed from head to toe, or frozen and revived. It's one of those topics that everyone wants to know about, and just about everybody has an opinion about. But being a man sometimes and a woman at other times, a part-time woman, is no big deal to me. It's just the way I am, just the way I live my life. Almost always, my transgenderism goes unnoticed unless I bring it up. Most of the time I don't even think about it. Nobody in the restaurant noticed that day. Why should they? We were just two women having brunch. But it was not without a sense of irony that I looked around us and wondered what the others would have thought, had they known my story.

What is my story? I suppose others might expect some dramatic tale: Misidentified at birth? Kidnapped as a toddler and forced to grow up as a girl? Dodging the law in a skirt and heels? Actually, the story starts quite unremarkably.

II. CHILDHOOD

Many of the transgenders I have talked with have similar early childhood memories—clomping around in mother's high heels, hiding in her closet, and feeling the soft fabric of her dresses. These are usually among their earliest recollections—from three or four years of age. I can remember incidents even before that—a favorite teddy bear, a visit from Santa, the wood-fired kitchen stove in my great-grandmother's kitchen—but none of these very early memories are in any way "unusual" or connected to cross-dressing or transgendersim. Why? Maybe my story is not quite like the others. Maybe I liked high heels, too, but I can't remember it. I might have even suppressed it. Perhaps many little boys hide in Mom's closet and put on girls' clothes sometimes; this just subsequently seems more significant to transgenders. In any event, my recollections of crossing gender lines simply do not go back that far.

I have plenty of transgender memories from adolescence, which I recall with a mixture of wonder, delight, and guilt, but until recently this facet of my life seemed to begin with the first stirrings of puberty, perhaps when I was ten or eleven. Then, not long ago, I suddenly remembered an event that reflects an earlier interest in gender-swapping. It was in second or third grade, which would make me seven or eight years old. For the school Halloween party, I was dressed as a pirate, and my friend Jack was a ghost. Jack's mother came to pick us up from school that day. As she opened the car door, a little girl dressed as a princess came bouncing out of the school and jumped into the front seat. We squeezed past her into the back. The princess turned around and flashed us a smile and a lilting "Hi, Jack." Jack simply groaned and said, "My cousin." He had plenty of cousins.

As the car pulled away from the school, I wondered who this fascinating creature was, with her ruby lips and silken gown. Jack's mother said, "You sure are a pretty little girl." I agreed. Jack started chanting "Jimmy's a girl. Jimmy's a girl." At first, I didn't get it. But as the little princess reached back to punch Jack on the arm, I recognized her. The cute little "girl" was Jimmy, a boy I had played with a dozen times. In that instant of recognition, it was clear to me that although there is but little difference between a boy and a girl, for me that tiny difference makes all the difference in the world. I knew that I wanted to try being a little girl, more than flying on an airplane or having my own puppy. I had never felt such a strong pull; I was terrified by the enormity of my yearning. In the instant that the little girl became Jimmy, I first felt a secret ache that has been with me ever since.

Another early memory goes back to when I was nine or ten. My friend Wayne and I were into reading superhero comics—Superman, Batman, the Flash, and all the rest. Shuffling home from school one day, we tried to imagine ourselves in the place of a chameleon-like creature that could alter its appearance to resemble any object. Wayne wanted to wreak havoc in the form of various ferocious animals. I thought it would be more interesting to be taken for a different person, specifically a girl. "What would you want to do that for?" he asked critically. Why something as weak and wimpy as a girl? Exploring the female mysteries seemed to me the most interesting and exotic use of my morphing powers. But it was clear he thought this was pretty crazy, so I dropped the subject. But comics continued to feed my fantasies. In one *Superboy* episode, a teenage Clark Kent wakes up to find that some interstellar virus has changed him into a girl. Of course, even his super powers have not prepared Clark to deal with a variety of awkward female situations—how to walk and talk and smile and deflect male attention (the kinds of things I have to do every time I go out as a woman). In "Miss Jimmy Olsen," the cub reporter goes way undercover. In the opening panel, "she" is strutting past a knot of whistling construction workers, her long red hair swaying and her skirt revealing a pair of shapely legs. She is thinking "Those wolves would die if they knew that, under this feminine disguise, beats the very masculine heart of Jimmy Olsen, cub reporter." I wanted to do that. I looked at that story again and again, until I had practically every panel memorized.

On the threshold of puberty, I tentatively started acting on my desire to dress as a girl. I can remember many times, alone in the bathroom after taking a bath, wrapping a towel around me like a sarong, and stuffing washcloths in the top to form a pair of breasts. In front of the bathroom mirror, I posed and pirouetted, examining my feminine shape from every angle. If suddenly disturbed, I simply let the towels fall to the floor, leaving me exposed but unincriminated.

Right from the start, it was clear to me that no matter how good this flirtation with the feminine made me feel, it was a forbidden pleasure. From a very early age I knew what kinds of behaviors are acceptable and appropriate for a little boy. It was okay to climb trees and play sports and cowboys and Indians, to drive toy trucks around the sandbox and build towers from Tinkertoys. But little boys don't play with dolls, stage imaginary tea parties, or play house. A boy wears jeans, a T-shirt, and a baseball cap. A pink party dress? Long hair with a bow? Patent leather Mary Janes? What? You would have to be crazy. Or some kind of sissy.

The only "sissy" activity I remember at all was a preschool fascination with paper dolls. I suppose this presaged my interest in dressing up. My mother helped me cut out the dolls and clothes, but warned, "We will put these away before Daddy gets home, okay?" She and my father, my peers, and the rest of the culture were sending pointed signals about the acceptable kinds of behavior for a boy in our culture—"You are a boy. Be a boy. Act like a boy." I was picking up the signals loud and clear, and that really was no problem. I wanted to be a boy and act like a boy. I didn't want to be a sissy, and there was nothing wrong with being a boy. I just wanted to dress up like a girl sometimes and see what it was like. This was very clear and very strong, but it contradicted all the rules I was getting from the people around me. I didn't fit in. I was confused, uncomfortable, and guilty about it. It was only part of my life, but gender identity is a very fundamental part. So I kept my desire a guilty little secret, a secret that has affected my life for more than forty years.

III. ADOLESCENCE

I must have been around twelve years old when I first donned an article of women's clothing—one of my mother's old nurse's uniforms. Succumbing to an excited impulse, I tugged off my T-shirt and pulled the white dress down over my jeans. I stuffed in some socks to fill out the bosom, and then examined myself in the cracked mirror over the laundry tub. I squinted and tried to imagine myself with long auburn hair, a silky dress clinging to my feminine figure. At this moment, more than three decades later, the feeling I remember most is not excitement or relief, or even shame, but rather a feeling of warmth and security. It was as if in the dress I was finally safe.

But safe from what? I subscribe to the idea that transgenderism is inborn, not a consequence of upbringing. That said, I think my desire to dress as a girl was reinforced by my need to hide—from my father. He was a big, boisterous, physical man—a merchant seaman who acquired a wife and family and suddenly found himself permanently dry-docked. I think he resented being tied down and took his resentment and frustration out on my younger brother and me. My father was a big man—about six feet tall and well over two hundred pounds, with a barrel of a body and huge hands. He had a violent temper, and a whimper could throw him into a rage. Many times he slapped me across the back of the head, or pushed me between the shoulders, or swatted at my arms as I reached out to protect myself. He acted unpredictably, on impulse; there was never time for an organized spanking. When he got mad, he reminded me of Jackie Gleason doing his "To the moon, Alice" routine. But it wasn't funny. He never gave me any physical bruises or broken bones. But I lived in constant fear of his unpredictable outbursts.

My brother tried to fight back, but I took a different tack with the old sailor. I resolved to be a good boy, bide my time, and get away to college as soon as I could. I participated in football, basketball, and track. I wrote for the school newspaper and yearbook, and I played trombone in the band. I was elected president of my senior class and was voted most likely to succeed. I got interested in science and took all the science and math courses I could fit into my schedule, and I eventually majored in biology in college. Talk about an overachiever. How much of this was motivated by the guilty secret that I wanted to cover up? And how much of my guilty secret stemmed from my desire to be a different person, hiding in a role as different as I could imagine from the role handed to me at birth? Surely my father wouldn't beat me up if I were a girl. How did my early life shape my desire to cross-dress? How did my desire to cross-dress shape my early life? It is interesting to speculate, but as much as my life might be explained by the answers to these questions, I cannot answer them, and probably never will.

Once I had tasted of the forbidden fruit, I wanted more and more. Both of my parents worked, so if I was home and my brother was not around, I could explore my mother's dresser and closet and try things on. I stuffed one of her bras with rolled-up socks, wriggled into a panty girdle, and zipped myself into a dress. I tried on earrings and necklaces, gloves and scarves, hose and heels. Every so often, I needed to stay home from school "sick," and I would deck myself out as a woman from head to toe. I would lock all the doors, pull all the drapes, and pose in front of a full-length mirror. I felt really sexy, and sometimes the sight of my reflection in female clothing and the touch of the garments on my skin would give me an erection.

I can remember three favorite outfits. One was a silky black party dress that hung straight down from the shoulders—what used to be called a "sack" dress. Another was a greenish brocade suit with a straight skirt. This was in the early sixties; in the suit, with white gloves and a pillbox hat, I imagined that I looked like Jackie Kennedy. (My mother even had a bouffant wig that she wore when she needed a quick hair-style fix. I probably wore that wig more than she did.) But it is the red dress that I remember best. No longer in style, the dress was stashed in a garment bag in the basement. It was wool, with long sleeves, a fitted bodice, a dropped waist, and a long, full skirt. It had a modestly high neckline, but a keyhole cutout accented by rhinestones revealed a sug-gestion of cleavage. I looked great in that red dress. It just now occurs to me that the first dress I bought when I decided to embrace my trans-genderism in my forties was a burgundy clone of that red wool dress.

During the long stretches when I couldn't dress up, my fantasies would flower. In one scenario, I was a spy who could only escape across the border as a woman. In another, my boss needed my help in impor-tant business negotiations, but I could only participate disguised as his secretary. Or I was a federal agent, disguised to foil skyjackers. My fan-tasies were bolstered by visual aids. I returned, after a fashion, to my paper doll days, cutting the faces out of the women's clothing section of an old Sears catalog and inserting my school pictures. This was tricky, because the model had to be just the right size and turned at just the right angle. I also retouched my school pictures, turning a dress shirt into an angora sweater and a buzz cut into a puffy hairdo with bangs. One day as I lay on the floor working on one of these retouching jobs, I felt the prickling and swelling of my penis that I often felt when I was wearing women's clothing. I kept drawing, and dreaming, and rubbing my crotch against the floor, and suddenly there was an explosion. It was my first orgasm, outside a wet dream. I must have been maybe thirteen years old. Even before the free fall was over, my ecstasy was tinged with shame. I knew I wasn't supposed to be masturbating, and surely not accompanied by perverse fantasies. I played dress-up even in my wet dreams, which had been disturbing me for a year or two preceding this first daytime ejaculation. I couldn't tell anybody about them, and I surely couldn't talk to anybody about this. So I locked this pleasure inside, along with the ache and the shame. Subsequently, I sometimes got turned on enough by women's clothing to orgasm, and many times fooling around with girls. But I really did not masturbate until I was in college. How could I have had that much self-control?

For the next twenty years, the fantasies that accompanied solo sex often involved dressing as a woman. My early sexual feelings were definitely tangled up with my transgenderism. This was confusing, but I was a bright kid, and I knew how to use a library. Soon I stumbled across the term *transvestite* and realized that was me. From very early on I knew I liked girls, so I was not a homosexual. And I certainly did not want to be without my penis, which gave me so much pleasure, so I did not want to do what Christine Jorgensen had so bravely done. But the fact that *transvestitism* was most often found in books and articles dealing with human sexual perversions did no great wonders for my self-esteem. My need, and the dreams and rituals that assuaged it, remained my guilty secrets. Throughout my teenage years, I continued to dress up and dream of dressing up. As I put the clothes on, the sexual tension and excitement would increase, often to the point of orgasm. Then I would feel guilty and unclean, and I would try to get the clothes and makeup off as fast as possible. I tried to put it out of my mind, but soon the need to dress would return. The excitement and orgasm felt so good, and afterward I felt so bad, so ashamed.

Most of the time, however, I felt and acted pretty much like a normal teenager. I even got interested in girls. After a slow and awkward start, I began dating Gail, who was the brightest girl in my class, if no great beauty. To everyone, we had seemed destined for one another from grade school onward. I was never one to confound others' expectations, so before long I gave her my class ring—we were "going steady." Ours was a typical teenage romance. There were chaste kisses, a bit of back-seat groping accompanied by pro forma protests, some picnics by the river, working on the school yearbook together, a couple of hayrides, a couple of proms, lots of after-game dances, lots of laughter, and some tears as high school came to an end and we departed for different colleges. I do not recall an overt connection between our relationship and my cross-dressing. Unlike one of my cross-dresser friends, I don't think I wanted to wear Gail's dress to the prom. It could be that for the two years we dated, I was just too busy to think about cross-dressing much, let alone indulge in it.

In high school I channeled my artistic tendencies into an interest in photography. My uncle gave me an old enlarger, and I commenced to make enlargements in a darkroom set up in the basement laundry room. I soon realized that I could use my skills to make some pictures of myself in my female guise. But I had to figure out how to trip the shutter of my cheap camera by remote control. I rigged up a sort of deadfall, like a cardboard box rabbit trap. I put the camera on a table, and then placed a heavy book on it against the shutter. The book was propped up by a stick, to which I had tied a long string. I got all dressed up, posed prettily, and then pulled on the string. This process was nerve racking, because I was scared of getting caught. Even if I managed to escape to the bathroom, it would have been difficult to explain why I had set up such an elaborate picture-taking apparatus. Fortunately, I never got caught. (In fact, according to my mother, nobody ever suspected anything about my secret life until I told them as an adult. Maybe I would have made a good spy.)

In all my favorite outfits, I posed like the models in magazine ads, with my shoulders back and my breasts held high. The pictures were always full-length shots; I wanted to see my whole body. I sneaked the photos out and looked at them often, feeling some of the same excitement I felt when they had been snapped. Of course, I had to hide the pictures. My solutions were not exactly James Bond, but as far as I know, nobody ever stumbled upon my stash. I hid the photos (and some pilfered clothes) in an opening where some plumbing went up through the basement ceiling. I destroyed the photos during a fit of paranoia when I was in college—the first of several "purges." I wish I had them now—the only vestiges of that exciting era of experimentation and self-discovery.

IV. COLLEGE INTERLUDE

In college I didn't get much of a chance to express my feminine side. At home during the summer I continued my occasional dress-up days. But there wasn't much privacy in a dorm. I do remember buying some stick-on false nails, which I painted and kept hidden at the bottom of my sock drawer—and once ripping them off, somewhat painfully, when my roommate walked in unexpectedly. As a college senior, I worked up the courage to see the film *The Queen*, a documentary about a drag beauty pageant. I was envious of the contestants' beauty, but appalled by their marginalized lives. Also during college, I reconnected with Anthony, a gay friend from my high school days. I liked hanging out with Anthony because of his witty, urbane take on life and his appreciation for art and music. Then, as now, I was pretty clear about my sexual orientation, so I laughed off his overtures. I know it drove my father crazy to see me with an obviously gay friend, but, to his credit, he never said anything. Anthony took me to a gay bar in Detroit. I remember some very sexy statuary, ordering a black Russian (the only drink I could think of at the time), and getting groped by a couple of guys. The male attention didn't turn me on, but neither was I repelled; mostly, I felt flattered. In subsequent years, I found that several of my college friends were gay, but at the time we didn't act on it, or even talk about it. One became a minister, another a high school teacher. Anthony went on to play in a symphony orchestra, but died in the AIDS holocaust of the eighties.

I had my first real sexual experiences when I was a college sophomore. These early trysts were unremarkable; their relevance to this story is that they distracted me from my transgender tendencies, while at the same time evoking a feeling of duplicity. Until very recently (when I started sharing my transgendered side with my partner), I always felt as though my lovers were not getting the whole me, that I couldn't fully share myself or risk being "found out." They didn't have specific complaints; I probably didn't seem much more distant than a lot of men. But I felt like I was shielded from genuine affection and emotion, behind bulletproof glass. I suspect that the biggest price that I have had to pay for being transgendered is this feeling of being cut off from others, not just sexual partners, but spouses, family, and friends.

V. THE WILDERNESS YEARS

I went on to attend graduate school, met a woman and married, and set out on a career as a biologist and college professor. Sharon and I enjoyed a modestly conventional, successful, and happy life. But with regard to my transgendered side, my twenties and thirties were the wilderness years. Getting started in my career and marriage absorbed a lot of energy. But I also felt that I needed to leave my youthful feminine dreams behind and live up to the expectations imposed by my parents, my in-laws, my wife, my job. Besides, what kind of outlet could I look forward to? More guilty dress-up behind shuttered windows and locked doors? So I suppressed—mostly successfully—my desire to cross-dress and settled into a routine of work and family life. Like many idealistic couples in the seventies, Sharon and I went back to the land. We grew some of our own food, she sewed some of our clothes, we rode bikes to work, and we went on backpacking trips for recreation. I even grew a beard. Pushing down my transgendered side became such a habit that I didn't even think about it for months at a time.

That's not to say that I didn't have my moments of relapse. Sharon was a rather tall, big-boned woman, and her loose peasant dresses fit me. Every few months, when she was away, I would slip into her clothes. She didn't use much makeup, so I bought some of my own, and even my first wig, a long pageboy style. Every year or two, my guilt would get the best of me, and I would throw out all my female attire, or even burn it all. (Many of my transgendered friends went though similar periodic periods of guilt and "purging.") But I can remember one exquisite summer night when Sharon was away, and everything—the dress, the hair, the makeup—came together perfectly. I looked into the mirror, and for the first time in my life, dream and reality intersected—I had become a woman. Looking at the woman in the mirror, I felt excited and somehow whole, but also guilty and scared. The shame and fear won out, and I purged once again. But my dream was nurtured. The woman in the mirror was a premonition of a more balanced life to come. But at that time I just wasn't ready for it.

Sharon and I were close, but we never really had a satisfying sex life. It didn't bother me much at the time, perhaps because I didn't feel I deserved it. Looking back on it, I think I married Sharon partly because I thought no one else would have me, as if somehow people could plainly see that I was damaged goods. As time went by, Sharon became more and more withdrawn, and I withdrew from her. Finally, after nine years together, we parted. After a period of healing and self-exploration, we resumed contact, and now we are friends, though we live far from one another. In her forties, Sharon recovered memories of the childhood sexual abuse (at the hands of a family friend) that had shut her down sexually. Her self-examination actually helped motivate me to get in touch with my own gender identity issues, but that is getting ahead of the story.

VI. MIDLIFE—DANGER AND OPPORTUNITY

After the divorce, my cross-dressing increased. I had a lot more privacy, free time on my hands, and (like many transgenders) I found cross-gender behavior comforting during times of stress. But I was also lonely, and before long I met a woman, Paula, who was fun to be with. After a year of dating and a year of living together, we tied the knot. I was thirty-eight years old. Paula was good for me; she encouraged me in my work and writing, and accompanied me on foreign travels and a Fulbright in Europe. She was also much more inclined than anyone in my life to take on the inner journey, "peeling the onion" of the psyche, through counseling, meditation, reading, self-help, and yoga. Once she even dragged me through an Erhard Seminars Training (est) seminar. I participated—with varying degrees of reluctance and enthusiasm—in some of these journeys. But mostly I was an envious observer, drawn to explore and express my true self, and at the same time afraid of where that might take me—and what others might find out about me. (In fact, I was also afraid of what I might reveal about myself under the influence of anesthesia or drugs, so I was afraid of surgery, and I missed the best part of the sixties. I really didn't inhale then, and I remain rather inexperienced in that area.)

But inevitably, at midlife, I was drawn, like Dante, into "that dark wood." I guess you could call it a midlife crisis, but that sounds too negative, unless one looks to the Chinese character for *crisis*—a combination of *danger* and *opportunity*. It took ten years of introspection, therapy, learning, and hard work, but so far at least I have managed to dodge most of the danger and seize the opportunity. What has emerged from my midlife crisis is a bi-gendered life that is my dream made real—a conjunction of male and female, a balance of yin and yang.

A combination of circumstances led me into and through my midlife confrontation with—and ultimate transformation via—my transgenderism. One was Paula prodding me to participate in life more fully. Global travel and career success are okay on the outside, but what about the inside? I was in a rut—not unhappy, but not happy, either. Because of her own inclinations (funny how we are drawn to the people from whom we can learn), Paula was more aware than most that I failed to really engage with life, to connect with other people. She suggested that I get some counseling. Then, of all people, Sharon called, out of the blue, and told me of uncovering her childhood abuse. Unnecessarily, she apologized for some of the fits and starts in our marriage and extolled the therapy she had undergone to get at the truth. Somebody was trying to tell me something. All right already—I'll get some counseling.

Eventually, I found the right therapist, but it wasn't easy. Actually, I had consulted with a psychiatrist several years before. While I was going through my first divorce, I had become alarmed about how crossdressing might impact my life. I picked him out of the phone book essentially at random, because I thought his name sounded promising—Dr. Newman. He turned out to be a grandfatherly man with beard stubble and suspenders. I spilled the beans to him right away. He assured me that I was not the only one with this "problem" and that my difficulty wasn't so much the cross-dressing, but rather my worrying about it. I heard his words, but I didn't feel anything—I just didn't get it. I gave up on Dr. Newman after two visits. I just wasn't convinced, and nothing about my behavior changed.

This time—starting to fall apart and more motivated to find real help—I wanted to choose more wisely, to find somebody a little more "with it." Paula and other friends suggested Dr. Garfield, a young psychiatrist with some rather woo-woo New Age ideas. Some of the stuff I had heard about him spooked me (Crystals? Channeling an ancient warrior?), but I was desperate enough to want to try something really different. It turned out that some of Dr. Garfield's ideas were pretty far-out, but he was willing to use techniques I could accept—meditation, dream work, reading, journaling, hypnosis.

Weekly, for the better part of a year, the good doctor held my hand as we rummaged around my psyche and I got used to the shadows and scary noises in there. Essentially, he got me to understand and accept the idea that there are reasons for what we do that do not involve thinking and logic, but rather emotions and feelings. Sometimes we have these feelings and emotions for good reasons (fatherly abuse) or bad reasons (peer pressure). Often the feelings are just there, for no reason at all. But it is important to recognize that the emotions and feelings are real, and they will express themselves if we don't find a way to express them. Of course, we all know this on some level, but up until then I just didn't know that I knew it. Very little of my work with Dr. Garfield had anything to do with gender or being transgendered per se, but he did encourage me to cross-dress if I felt like it, and to use the cross-dressing as a way of finding out more about my inner world.

So, for the umpteenth time, I assembled a small wardrobe and started experimenting anew with clothes and hair and makeup. But this time it felt a lot safer. This time I had permission—if not from the culture at large, at least from my shrink. Paula knew I was in therapy, but I was not yet ready to tell her about the gender issue. Luckily, she was out of town taking a class for a long weekend once a month. So I was free to dig out my hidden stash and dress as a woman for an extended period while she was gone. I journaled, meditated, tried drawing pictures, and took pictures of myself (a cross-dresser's obsession) that I could look at during the long stretches when I couldn't dress.

Dr. Garfield helped me immensely, but he was pushing me toward the wrong goal. Although he did not disapprove of my experimentation with cross-dressing, he wasn't entirely comfortable with it either. Looking back on it, his ultimate objective was to get past the transgender issue—to put it back in the closet, out of sight, by getting me to integrate my masculine and feminine sides. I was not opposed to the idea. I tried to feel and express some sort of integration. Cross-dressing whenever my wife was out of town didn't seem like any kind of long-term solution, and I yearned for a way to express all my facets as normal men and women do, without dressing up. But he was pushing me too fast. My "integration" did not feel like a genuine change, but rather something I felt forced upon me, to please him. Then I found out why he was rushing things. The state medical board was after his license. He was just a little too far-out. We had a couple of wrap-up appointments, and then he left the state. Now I really felt lost. I couldn't integrate, but I couldn't go back into the closet, either. Nor could I see a way to express my transgenderedness more openly. Not even my wife knew about it. Quite a fix.

I made it to the end of the school term, and then I cried every day for the entire Christmas vacation. Paula and my friends could see that I was in pain and offered comfort, but I was not yet ready to tell them what was really going on. What really pushed me over the edge was a talk show—the Maury Povich Show, to be exact—that featured a couple who had volunteered to change roles for two weeks. He appeared on the show as an attractive woman, and she appeared as a man. They both looked great, thanks to the help of professional makeup and wardrobing. The audience was rapt and respectful as the gender-bending couple described two weeks of walking in the others' shoes. "She" had gone shopping and out to lunch with women friends. Women accepted her, and men flirted with her. I was fascinated, envious, and agitated. The ache to be a woman returned, stronger than ever, and my crying jag got worse. Finally, I dragged myself to the home of a counselor acquaintance, Lisa, who was kind enough to see me that first time at her home on a Saturday. For two tearful hours, I poured out my story, and she offered to help me.

Over the next four years, we continued much the same kind of work as I had done with Dr. Garfield—journaling, guided meditation, dream work. But Lisa, as a woman, was much more accepting of my feminine side and my desire to express it. Her approach was eclectic—whatever seemed to work. Carl Jung really resonated with me. Without getting into a long (and probably erroneous) discourse on Jungian psychology, let's just say that we worked to break through the masks, reclaim some of the parts that I had relegated to the scrap heap, and get to the real me. I realized that everybody is a mix of traits we call masculine and feminine; they are just human—nothing to be ashamed of. I had always come across to people as a gentle, communicative, feminine (but not effeminate) man. But for some reason (call me crazy), I need to express some of these characteristics by dressing and seeing myself as a woman. Lisa let me follow my own desires, without judging me. As she pointed out, who was it going to hurt? She even came to my house once and we went through my closet, discussing various "looks" and trying on clothes like a couple of teenagers. I think it helped that Lisa didn't really have any experience with transgenders, so she didn't try to "diagnose" me and put me into a box. And because I had no contact with other transgenders for a couple of years (not even on the rudimentary Internet), my transgendered identity grew and became stronger, without being forced into some preconceived stereotype—cross-dresser, transsexual, whatever. (Actually, it turns out I'm more of a "whatever.")

This makes it sound easy—but it was anything but. There were a lot of tears, and one time I became so angry—not at Lisa—I smashed a radio. But she never questioned that my feminine side was real and deserved respect. More than any other person, Lisa helped give birth to the present-day Elaine.

VII. COME OUT, COME OUT!

As I started feeling stronger and less ashamed about my feminine side, I felt dishonest about not sharing that part of me with Paula. I think I also needed validation that being transgendered was okay. I wasn't really afraid that Paula would reject me over being transgendered—after all, she was the one who suggested the therapy—but I was concerned that she might feel rather blindsided about it. Plus, I couldn't figure out how to break it to her. Then we went to see *The Crying Game.* As we walked home after the film, Paula expressed sympathy for the transsexual character, and that was all the opening I needed. The conversation went like this:

"You know, I have always wondered what it would be like to be a woman. It's one of the issues that has come up in my therapy."

"Really?"

"I'd like to try dressing as a woman. It has always been kind of a fantasy of mine."

"Hmmm. It's kinda weird, but what's the problem? Have you ever tried it? Why don't you?"

"Would you be okay with that? Would you—help me?"

"I think I could. We'll have to get you some clothes and stuff—but I'm afraid you are not going to make a very good-looking woman."

Paula was wrong about that, but she really came through for me. We ordered a book titled *My Husband Wears My Clothes* and did a little research on transgenderism at the university library (funny, how I knew right where to look). Paula accompanied me on a nerve-racking shopping trip to Nordstrom, where "she" picked out a couple of dresses, a black wool skirt, and some conservative black high heels. Right from the start, I was into classic, mainstream clothes. In fact, I still wear the skirt. A few weeks after the shopping trip, she helped me with hair and makeup, and we shared a nervous candlelight dinner—my "coming out." But now that I was interacting with other people, I needed a name. In my typical thorough fashion, I checked out books on *Naming Your Baby*, but of course, Tiffany and Brittany did not seem appropriate for a woman my age. For a few months, I was Helen for Helen of Troy. (One could do worse than launch a thousand ships.) A short time later, after a vacation in France, I decided to Frenchify it into Elaine, and Elaine it has been ever since.

Life for me continued much as before, but at least I no longer had to hide the evidence of my cross-dressing, and could talk with Paula about the subject. In fact I talked about it so much that she got sick of hearing about it. "Don't you ever think about anything else?" That was the start of a rocky period for us. So I turned to the Internet. There was no World Wide Web as yet, and therefore no transgender Web sites, so there were no online clothing suppliers or makeup lessons, much less pictures of transsexuals' vaginas or information on hormone dosage. But there were transgender e-mail newsgroups, and I listened in. It was comforting to know there were others—many others—like me, but I often projected myself into others' transgender obsessions and it disturbed me. I thought about it a lot—my therapy was rocky, I wasn't sleeping well, and I started losing weight and looking haggard. My department secretary eventually noticed and asked me if I was ill. She wasn't the only one who was concerned. This was in the mid-1990s, as the AIDS scare was peaking. I'm sure some people thought I had HIV. This idea probably was reinforced by a vague feeling that a lot of people—gay and straight—pick up from me that I must be gay. I really throw off the "gaydar." (Just recently I came out to a longtime colleague, and she said, "I always knew there was something about you, but I could never figure out what it was.")

I was still obsessed with the couple who had changed places, and there was no shortage of other talk shows with cross-dressers and drag queens on parade. It seemed like the pressure was building toward a major change. I decided that I wanted to get out into the world as a woman. I got my chance the next Halloween. One of my friends suggested that "the gang"—three couples, all close friends—get together for a special Halloween party. She was getting counseling that involved acting out the various "personas" that made up her personality, so she thought it would be fun for each of us to come in costume as one of our hidden personas. I tried to act only mildly interested, but my heart leaped. Perfect!

The night of the party I was so out of my mind with excitement that all I could see was myself in the mirror. It was the first time that I had ever left the house as Elaine. My best friend, Nathan, showed up as a crotchety old man, Allison was a sullen teenage boy, and so on. But from the moment I walked in the door, the night was mine. Nathan was speechless for about half an hour; the others were full of incredulous compliments. I couldn't stop grinning. Interacting with other people for the first time hinted that there was a bit of a personality split between my masculine and feminine. As a male, I would have brought a bag of chips, not an elaborate Italian dish. I even flirted a bit with Nathan and Tim, but unlike my male side, I didn't have much of a sense of humor. Marci said, "Let's go out—I want to see if people can figure out you are a guy." I asked her if she was nuts, but it didn't take much for them to talk me into it (it was Halloween). In no time I was walking though a supermarket in a party dress and heels. I can remember how scared I was as a guy approached, looked right through me, and said, "pardon me" as he reached for a jar of applesauce. I did it! My first outing! "One small step for man!"

After that, my course was set. I went back into the closet for a few months, but I was comforted by the certainty—well, at least the wish—that I was going to have some kind of real life as a woman, out there in the real world. Paula was losing patience, but she accompanied me on my first real foray, a "shopping" trip to a mall. (For transgenders, it's always a mall.) To make sure we weren't spotted, I did this in Palo Alto, California, about five hundred miles from home. I also enlisted a couple of California friends as spotters. The tall woman in the only picture taken that day is dressed in a black blazer, a black skirt, and flats. She looks excited and nervous, her jaw set with grim determination. I remember being so flustered I couldn't focus on anything enough to shop, like a bank robber must feel as he walks in to make a "withdrawal." It was as though my entire brain was occupied with how to walk, how to hold my hands, what to say if someone spoke to me. I found out from my friends later that my excursion was almost cut short by a couple of obnoxious gals with baby strollers who clocked me as soon as I walked into Neiman-Marcus. They tried to cut across the store to intercept me and get a closer look, but my spotters cut them off. I did hear somebody in a bookstore whisper "Is that a guy?" but soldiered on nonetheless. The high point was catching the reflection of a long-legged woman in a store window, then realizing it was me! That trip to the mall was such a blur that I needed something real to hold on to, so I managed to gather the courage to buy a gold necklace at Macy's. I still have that necklace. My friends were floored when I paid for it on Elaine's Visa card.

Back into the closet, but a few months later, I opened the morning paper to find an article headed "Cross-dressers Convene for Conference." The annual IFGE (International Foundation for Gender Education) conference was being held about a hundred miles away—and it was starting that evening. I had heard of such gatherings, but I had mixed feelings: The notion of a cross-dressers' convention struck me as mildly ridiculous and a bit pathetic; I wasn't sure I was ready to declare my affiliation to such a marginalized group. And I was scared—afraid of being drawn into some kind of dangerous transgender subculture. (I had seen "shemales" in porn magazines, and recoiled at the thought those exotic hybrids might be like me. Neither was the kind of stuff I read on the trans newsgroups very reassuring.) Paula was scared, too, for much the same reasons, and she asked me not to go. There were tears; I hated to make such a difficult choice. But ultimately, I needed to be with my people. With a mix of anticipation and dread, I packed two sets of clothes and drove up that day to check things out.

Disguised in borrowed glasses and a coat and tie (a real disguise for me), I checked out the scene in the hotel lobby. Nothing seemed out of the ordinary at first, but then a knot of rather overdressed, very large-boned women walked by. I was in the right place. My nervousness dissipated as I watched the double takes of the other hotel guests. I found my way down to the conference room where registration and information tables were set up and spotted the table of the WCGA—the West Coast Gender Alliance. An older gal in a flowered dress beckoned me over with a smile. I was very nervous—before that moment, I had never met another transgendered person—but for some reason I sensed that the gals staffing the table had seen my kind before. Soon I was filling out an information form and showing them a picture of me as a woman. A gal butted in, looked at the picture, looked at me, and clucked, "Hmmm. You're in big trouble." I never did register for the conference, but I booked a room, slipped into a bubble bath, and then changed into a short violet cocktail dress. Soon I found myself at a reception, balancing a plate of appetizers and trading beauty secrets. My most vivid image from that night is a gal asking me to help zip her hairy back into a too-small chiffon prom dress. I also remember wondering what the waitstaff was thinking, but after a very short time, the scene didn't seem so strange to me, and it probably didn't to them, either. Later in the evening, a gang of us went out to a jazz club for drinks. I hid in the throng, but the next morning I was feeling energized and free. I donned a sweater and skirt, walked several blocks over to Nordstrom, and bought a pair of earrings, just to prove to myself that I could do it. I can remember thinking, "I'm *worth* it!"

After the conference, I started attending monthly WCGA socials and occasional dinners and parties. My transgender life shifted into high gear, and I learned a lot. There were workshops on makeup and clothes, and gossip about where to safely shop and go out to dinner. Mostly, I just found a place where I could go out in (semi-) public and feel comfortable, practicing being a woman. I also made some friends. When I joined the WCGA, I thought I would find a group of people with whom I had a lot in common, people "just like me." Indeed, I did click with a few of the gals I met at the IFGE conference and in my early days at the WCGA, and some are still close friends. But I soon realized that, aside from one big issue, overall this group of gals (and some guys) had no more in common than the people in the Democratic Party, the Rotary Club, or the PTA. I found that, in fact, the WCGA is *more* varied than most of the groups I belong to, because being transgendered cuts across all social, political, and economic lines. I met doctors, engineers, businesspeople, teachers, factory workers, salespeople, police officers, computer geeks, a cabdriver, even a grave digger. But although I now know hundreds of transgendered individuals, I have only found a few transgendered people whom I can really call my friends. My closest trans friends are a systems analyst, a lawyer, a railroad worker, a banker, and a government official. Two of them have divorced, transitioned, and are now women full time. The other three are married "weekend warriors." Go figure. I'm still active with the WCGA, having put in my stint as president and perennial emcee of the annual awards banquet. And I write a monthly advice column (a combination of Dear Abby and Martha Stewart) for the club newsletter.

Transgender conferences have also been a good training ground for me, providing opportunities to be a woman for a weekend or a week. Some of the conferences, like the venerable Fantasia Fair on Cape Cod, are warm and fuzzy gatherings of the transgender tribe, with a big self-help component. Others, like the annual IFGE convention, take on political issues like transgender rights; and others, such as the International Congress on Sex and Gender, are more like scientific conferences, featuring papers and presentations with a medical or psychological slant. My favorite has always been Esprit, a down-home gathering in a small resort town in Washington State. I have had my moments at conferences, hosting and singing in cabaret shows, walking the fashion show runway, presenting seminars on "The Biology of Sex and Gender" (the only thing on this list I really know anything about), and even winning the coveted Miss Femininity award at Fantasia Fair—the only such recipient, I am told, who has failed to subsequently get sex-reassignment surgery and become a full-time woman. Oh well.

As I started going out more often as a woman, it became difficult to explain the absences engendered by my double life, so I decided to come out to my friends—one at a time, starting with Nathan. We went for a walk, and I hemmed and hawed, but finally fessed up. I can't say he was surprised. In fact, he admitted that it explained a lot about my Halloween "performance." My friends are not judgmental about my transgenderism, but they don't really understand it. How can I expect them to get it, when I don't understand it myself? The best I could do for Nathan was to ask him to compare my transgenderism to his love of music: "Suppose you wanted to play your piano, but people thought piano playing was perverted, and they wouldn't let you do it. How would you feel?" It was a lot easier with a lesbian coworker and her daughter. After they met me as Elaine, the daughter turned to her mother and said, "Cool, Mom—He's queer."

It was surprisingly easy to come out to my mother. She came to visit, and on the way home from the airport I knew that it would be okay when she told me that a close friend of hers had confided in her that he was gay and HIV-positive. It took me a couple of days to get around to telling her about me, though. I started by saying I was getting counseling, circled the real topic for what seemed like half an hour, and finally got to the point: "You have heard of the inner child, right? Well, I'm kind of finding out about the inner woman. I need to see things, so I have been dressing up as a woman." She said, "Makeup and everything? Go on! Really?" Then I told her I had been doing it for a long time, and had always wanted to do it, but it was my darkest secret, and I had always been ashamed of it. I was starting to cry, but she smiled gently: "Is that it? I knew something was up. You were so nervous. Actually, I am relieved—you were having such a hard time, I thought you might have some sort of terminal illness or something." I could feel it was going to be okay, but I asked her, half jokingly, if she still loved me. She said, "Of course I do—and I feel blessed that you would share this with me." Not too bad for a seventy-five-year-old!

Unfortunately, Elaine was starting to come between Paula and me.

It wasn't that Paula disapproved of my transgenderism per se. She saw how it energized me and didn't want me to give up my newfound zest for life. But the downside was that I had become very self-involved—absorbed by my new "hobby," often talking to my trans friends on the phone, modeling clothes, experimenting with makeup, even admiring my new (pinched and padded) body, a lot like a teenage girl. In fact, I have often seen transgenders go through this teenage phase, and even though it usually lasts only a year or two, that is still enough to alienate their friends and loved ones. In addition to my distraction, my life as Elaine took a lot of time—and even though Paula tried to do some things with Elaine, most of the time I was in Elaine mode we were not together. It was as if I had suddenly taken up mountain climbing, or become obsessed with golf. Not surprisingly, Paula was not happy that my focus was this "other woman." Spending a lot of time together was always more important to Paula than to me, and my distraction exacerbated this difference. Over a period of several years, during which time we made several halfhearted efforts to rescue the marriage, we drifted apart, and finally divorced. As at the end of my first marriage, I had mixed feelings. The divorce left me much more free to explore my developing life as a part-time woman, but I was lonely for a long time. Over the last couple of years, Paula and I have rekindled our friendship. Sometimes I imagine that if we had been able to weather my "adolescence," we might still be married. But we have moved on. Fortunately, she is once again my friend—and Elaine's, too. Every once in a while I'll get a call from Paula: "Hi—I'm at Nordstrom. Elaine better get right down here—there are some great sweaters on sale."

VIII. MATCHMAKER, MATCHMAKER

The breakup of my marriage left a void. At first I thought maybe I was better off without an intimate relationship. My lifestyle did not enhance my marriages, and I did stay busy doing things with my friends. But at the end of the day most of them went home to their partners, and I was alone. Gradually, I got back into circulation, and in the five years after Paula and I split, I dated a number of women. With most of them, I kept my double life under wraps. But I was uncomfortable with that, they could sense that I was hiding something, and it always seemed like there was a lack of "chemistry." So I placed a personal ad on an Internet dating site that mentioned that "sometimes I like to cross-dress" (no point in scaring people), and I did meet a couple of women who were not fazed by it, at least in principle. But then somebody in my hometown responded, and I realized that my picture and ad were on the Web for the whole world to see—including the neighbors—so I changed the ad immediately.

I started to wonder whether I should be open to a different kind of relationship. I have always thought of myself as a heterosexual male, attracted to straight women. But as a woman, could I be with a lesbian? They like buff gals, and often flirt with me. (Once out dancing, one said to me, "I would give anything to have a woman as tall as you." I replied, "So would I.") As a guy, I sometimes feel like a "male lesbian" anyway. But with a lesbian, there is the problem of what happens "the morning after." I didn't want to face that. A cross-dresser acquaintance was in a relationship with a lesbian for a while, and she was never satisfied with him as a guy.

What about a man? I do enjoy male attention and flirting with men as much as the next gal, and having a man be attracted to me is validating and flattering. Straight men have come on to me and bought me drinks, but they didn't know what they were getting into. I'm polite, and I don't want to embarrass them, but that is playing with fire. The fact is, even if I were interested, most straight men would run like hell if they thought they were coming on to "a guy in a dress." And male homophobia is dangerous. For some transgenders, getting involved with a man has been fatal. That said, I have been out with a couple of straight (?) men who knew about my lifestyle. It was all very polite and didn't go anywhere. Then there are the "trans fans," men who are attracted to women with "a little something extra." In my experience—another lesson I share with genetic women—these guys are only interested in one thing. I never had to face it, but with men there is again the question of what happens the morning after. Enough said.

What about gay men? That never seemed like a realistic possibility because most gay men are attracted to men who *look like men*. And, quite honestly, I am not. In my interactions with men, I have realized that I am not attracted to them *as men*; any interest I have in them is mostly a response to their interest *in me*. Even if a man were interested, I don't want to use a relationship just to boost my own feminine ego. But I do value and enjoy my gay male friends, and it is a kick to go out with a man and be taken for a normal het couple. (A transsexual I know took this idea to the brink when a closeted gay male friend who needed to project a "normal" life took her along to a business conference as his "wife." Yikes!)

I was attracted to a couple of gals I met at transgender conferences. One was a tall, attractive transsexual, and I would have been smitten with her trans or not. She was interested in me, and we carried on a long-distance relationship for about a year. One would think that a match between too trannies would be the ideal situation. I thought so, but it didn't work out that way. She was slightly younger than I, but had only been a woman for a couple of years. We were out of synch. She wanted to pour herself into her new job, try new things, play the field, while I needed to settle down. And she fretted over my transgendered lifestyle! Because she was stealth in her new life, she was afraid that I would blow her cover. More seriously, she projected her own situation onto me. She wanted a man, saw a lot of herself and her story in me, and worried that I would transition as she had and leave her flat.

At another trans conference, I met a genetic woman with lots of professional ties to the trans community. Much of her lifestyle revolved around transgender, and she had collected many friends on the trans fringe—a dominatrix, a porn actress, sex workers, and so on. This was very interesting for a while—like hanging out with Andy Warhol. But my life is interesting enough already—I needed a more normal relationship.

A couple more years went by, and I was starting to wonder whether a relationship was a realistic possibility. The odds just didn't seem in my favor: Most women in my age range are already in relationships, and many who aren't taken are set in their ways, with lives dominated by jobs, their exes, their adult children and grandchildren. On top of that there is the indefinable chemistry, and on top of that the concern that maybe one woman in a hundred would accept my lifestyle. A friend and I calculated the overall odds at one in ten thousand. Would I need to go out on ten thousand dates? A bleak prospect. By and large I stopped even responding to inquiries from women about my personal ad. I was about to drop the ad altogether when I got a different kind of e-mail, from a woman named Laura. Her letter was intelligent and witty, and piqued my curiosity. We met, and she turned out to be just what I said I was looking for in the ad—tall, smart, and funny. From that moment we have been spending a lot of time together.

Laura works as a computer systems analyst in a city about an hour away. She has a biology degree and is almost exactly my age, so we have a lot in common. She is very outgoing and self-confident, a bit eccentric in her demeanor and dress. We were spending so much time together that I had to tell her about my double life soon after we met ("Please don't look in that closet!"). I wanted to tell her; I knew she wouldn't judge me or feel threatened, but I was nervous about it. Her reaction: "Well, nobody's perfect." And then she laughed. Before long she met Elaine, and soon after we tried it out at dinner in a nice restaurant. Since then, we have gone out a lot both ways. It didn't take Laura long to adjust to treating me like a woman friend, although we sometimes have a hard time keeping our hands off each other. She says it helps that she sees me as two different people who happen to share the same knowledge and experiences. That helps keep things clear for us when I am in masculine mode as well, because most of the time we basically interact as a "normal" heterosexual couple. Laura enjoys my feminine side along with the masculine, she appreciates how some important parts of my personality are informed by my experiences as a woman, and she actually gets the same kick out of reexperiencing the world from a slightly different perspective. She is quite stylish, and even enjoys playing "dress-up" along with me. The best part about it is that I love her for who she is (not just because she is willing to put up with my peccadilloes), and she loves all of me (and doesn't just tolerate the gal so she can have the guy). We have a lot of fun together. Recently we vacationed for a week in New York City—half the time as the handsome urban couple, and half the time as gal pals. I never thought I would be visiting the Metropolitan Museum, going designer resale shopping (Versace, Chanel, Armani) with my best girlfriend, and sharing afternoon cocktails at the Plaza—as a woman. The two of us looked like taller versions of the gals in *Sex and the City*. We had a wonderful time. I am so lucky!

IX. SOMETHING ELSE

During my Sunday brunch with Ann, we were laughing over something and she grabbed my hand affectionately and said, "Elaine, you are something else." I'll say! Of course, each of us is unique, but I am truly one of a kind. I know a lot of closeted or semicloseted cross-dressers. I know many transsexuals who now live—openly or in stealth mode—full time as women. (In fact, several of my former "cross-dresser" friends have transitioned from male to female in the last few years.) But I know of very few transgenders who are trying to openly live their lives as I do— as both a man and a woman, just at different times. I don't really think of myself as transgendered, but rather "bi-gendered." Most of the time, especially at work, I am a man. People who know me as a male never suspect there is anything unusual about me unless I tell them. Two or three times a week, I change clothes, hairstyle (and even my eye color), and spend some time as Elaine. Most of the time, people don't find anything unusual about me as Elaine, either. I have two wardrobes, two e-mail addresses, two sets of credit cards, and even two cars. (The sporty Acura never leaves the Bat Cave unless Elaine is behind the wheel. My town is too small; people know my other car.) I have two sets of friends (although there is starting to be a lot of crossover), two social lives, and two sets of activities. A double life can be exhausting, but it is also exciting. I feel like some kind of "gendernaut," able to go places and have experiences that most people can only imagine.

I feel really lucky to be blessed with the physical and psychological characteristics that make a bi-gendered life even possible. Basically, my face and body can go either way. I look masculine enough as a guy, but I am slender, with narrow shoulders, and have relatively small facial features. I wear a size 12 or 14 dress, but because of my height, I have the proportions of a size 8 or so. I do have big feet—women's size 13—but thin ankles and wrists, and slender fingers. My legs, eyes, and smile are my best features. I stand out in a crowd mainly because I am tall—six feet two, which makes me taller than 90 percent of the *men* in the United States. But with a little help from padding and cosmetics, except for my height, I can blend in pretty successfully as a woman. I don't like the phrase "passing as a woman"—or the idea. It implies that I am trying to be something I am not. I may have been born biologically male, but if one accepts the idea that gender is a social role, I am a woman when dressed as a woman. Much of the time, transgenders are maligned because we do not cleave to the gender stereotype that is supposed to go with our biological sex. But, in this instance, the stereotype works in my favor, and I turn people's preconceptions back on them. People expect a woman to look and behave a certain way, and I can do that, so they accept me as a woman. Does that make me a woman? It depends on whether one thinks that I "am" a woman if I am treated and accepted as one. I am okay with it. I do suffer from a bit of "survivor guilt," though. It bothers me that there are transgendered gals who want to be full-time women in the worst way, but have a difficult time because physically they are very masculine looking. I thank my lucky stars.

My personality also suits me fairly well for a bi-gendered lifestyle. As a teacher, I spend most of my time helping young people, unlike friends who have to butt heads all day in the business world. Many of my colleagues are women; biology is the most egalitarian of the sciences. Kindness, gentleness, and approachability are assets in my profession. I smile and laugh a lot. I have to be very verbal, and I'm a good listener. In fact, some of the skills that I have cultivated as Elaine are helpful to me as a teacher. For example, the opportunity to "walk a mile in another's heels" has helped me to be more empathetic. I understand how women can be pushed around in a classroom setting, especially in male-dominated science classes. Sometimes I feel like a woman in male drag. With my friends, there is no need to be macho. We talk, laugh, and hug a lot. Most of my male friends are more interested in art, literature, and current affairs than in "guy stuff" like sports or cars. I am comfortable with my women friends, and they feel safe with me, so it's easy for us to talk. I don't have to shift gears much when Elaine is around.

Luckily, I'm pretty well equipped when it comes to gender bending. But that's not to say that I don't need a little help when I go out as a woman. It generally takes me an hour or more to get ready. I have to shave very close, but most of my beard has gone gray, so it doesn't show. I use more makeup than most women my age require when they are just popping out to the supermarket, but not more than a professional woman might wear to work or for an evening out. I wear contacts to change my eye color. (It's a small town!) My hair is thinning, so I have to wear a (stylishly short) wig, but this actually works in my favor because it changes my appearance drastically. My breasts are silicone, and I pad my hips and butt, but other than that, all my clothing is standard feminine issue. I have been at this long enough to have an extensive wardrobe: T-shirts and shorts, business suits, evening gowns, little black dresses, sweaters and jeans, purses, jewelry, shoes. It's an expensive hobby! My favorite "look" is a dark tank top or sweater and a long dark skirt—stylishly casual.

Of course, there is more to being a woman than just the clothes. Women have their own language; they walk, sit, smile, eat, laugh, talk, and even sneeze differently than men do. Many transgenders have a hard time mastering all these details. Some take a left-brain approach—they observe, dissect, and practice the feminine "moves," and perfect them step by step. I was blessed with a sort of right-brained feminine gestalt—fortunately, I could walk the walk and talk the talk right from the start, like some kids who just know how to swim or sing. That's not to say that high heels are easy! The most difficult challenge for me (and many transgenders) is speaking like a woman. It is not so much a matter of pitch (many women, like actresses Bea Arthur and Lauren Bacall, have lower voices than many men), but rather intonation, timbre, rhythm, and variations in pitch. Luckily, I had some help. Early in my journey, I spent a month in the San Francisco area and consulted some local experts. I got some basic tips from a transgendered voice coach. I also spent an afternoon with a genetic woman who is a "feminine image consultant" for the transgendered. She admitted that she didn't find the guy who first came to her door very promising. But after spending an afternoon working with me as Elaine—sitting, standing, walking, picking up a teacup, talking ("Just whisper, but loud.")—she insisted that I borrow her bag and trench coat (I was short on accessories) and spend the rest of the day "out on the town." I'll never forget her confidence and generosity, and my trepidation on my first real trip out alone. It was quite a day. That night, in a restaurant on Union Street, a guy tried to pick me up. After I dodged him, the evening went further downhill when I locked my keys in the car.

In addition to the voice coach and image consultant, over the years I have had a bit of electrolysis to get rid of my remaining dark whiskers (for many transgenders, getting rid of the beard entails tremendous pain and expense), a couple of laser treatments to thin the hair on my legs and arms, a few consultations with a speech pathologist who helps transsexuals, and some singing lessons to help increase my vocal range. And then there are the makeup lessons and makeovers, the wig stylist, the helpful gals at the breast form shop, the Nordstrom personal shopper who moonlights as a transgender fashion consultant, the seamstress who made my hips, the other seamstress who lengthens my sleeves, and several other women in my life who have given me help and advice.

I know lots of genetic women who are not all that thrilled with PMS, sexual harassment, the threat of breast cancer, and making less money than a man. So why should I go through all this trouble to be a woman? I think partly I want to break the rules, to subvert people's prejudices and expectations via my own private bit of "street theater." It is also a matter of self-expression; I love the art of makeup and dressing in women's clothing. We have so many options in style and color and mood that are not available to men. (In male mode recently I walked into the Gap, saw all the pastel women's clothing on one side of the store, and the men's in green and brown on the other, and asked the salesperson if I was required to enlist in the Special Forces if I bought a sweater.)

Ultimately, I think, I want to be a woman because I want to discover what it *feels like* to be a woman, to look at things around me through a woman's eyes (as much as that is possible for someone born male). It's like going into the post office in France. Everything is familiar, but a little different, and therefore much more interesting. That's what it's like for me when I am a woman. Traveling, getting my car serviced, shopping at the supermarket, interacting with project teammates, dining out, even driving—they all feel a bit different. As a woman I have to smile a little more to disarm people. I have to defer to men and get out of the way of teenagers; I try to take up less space. Men open doors for me and cut me some slack in traffic. But they also ogle me at times, and sometimes I don't feel safe in a dark parking lot, or when a man approaches on the street. Sometimes I'll exchange a little smile with a woman who is tending to a child, or a woman will confide in me about her family or her husband. Then I get a glimpse of a world that is inaccessible to men.

If my forays into womanhood are so wonderful, why don't I transition, as some of my friends have, and live as a woman full time? Maybe even take female hormones and have sex-reassignment surgery? I have looked into the possibility and thought about this long and hard, from various angles. A couple of times, I even "decided" to transition, and even worked out a timetable for coming out to my coworkers and having surgery. It would be much easier for me to transition than it is for most transgendered individuals I know. I am single and have no children, so it would not disrupt my family. My profession and workplace are quite accepting of women, with open-minded, well-educated people who would accept the change, if not celebrate it. I could afford the financial hit, and I could pull it off physically—able to blend in fairly well without being hassled. Transitioning would be exciting in many ways, and as a transsexual I would be somehow legitimized, perhaps taken more seriously. (My nontrans friends would say, "He must have been serious about it to do something this drastic." And my trans friends would comment, "She's full time, not just playing at it.")

But I can do what I need to do without being a woman 24/7. Transitioning would be tremendously disruptive to my life. Relationships with family, friends, and coworkers would be tested. I wonder how distracting it would be to my students; would I be able to teach effectively? There are a lot of negatives. More fundamentally, however, if I were to become a full-time woman, I would be conforming to society's roles, expectations, and stereotypes, not being true to my own path. I don't want to transition just to follow the rules—not after finally coming to terms with a life that flouts the conventions. Why take all the man/woman, male/female insight and wisdom that being transgendered gives you, and then squeeze it surgically and socially into the conventional category of either man or woman? Out of all the people on his planet, transgenders should be blowing those categories wide open, not reinforcing them. In some ways, going both ways is more difficult, more transgressive than transitioning, and I find that appealing. But unfortunately, I don't really have many role models; in our culture it is pretty clear that one is expected to be a man or a woman—not both—so not many people do what I am trying to do. Still, what I want to learn is so important to me that I am willing to break the rules—to be a woman for a while and then come back and compare it to being a man, to journey to France and have new experiences, then return home and see how the landscape of my own country has changed. For me, going both ways just makes life richer (if a bit tiring, and definitely more complicated). Friends ask me if I plan to transition, and I reply, "Why move to France if you can go there, speak the language, eat the food, and enjoy the art whenever you want? And then come home and sleep in your own bed?" I didn't choose to be transgendered. (Why couldn't I instead be compelled to write a novel, climb mountains, or work for peace in the Middle East?) But I can choose to be bi-gendered. It works for me.

Although I still occasionally participate in transgender meetings and social activities, and occasionally go out to eat or shop with transgendered friends, I can't really learn about what it is like to be a woman if I only go to trans conferences, socialize in gay bars, and hang out with other transgendered individuals. That isn't what women do; to me it's just building a bigger closet. From the start I have been relentless in busting out of the closet and going mainstream. So I lead a busy, "normal" (as normal as possible) life. A couple of times a week, I go out to eat, to a movie, shopping, or to a concert, lecture, or play. A favorite treat is going to the opera. Once in a while I take a vacation somewhere and spend a week en femme. As a woman, I have flown all over the country, taught classes, ridden a cable car, visited the Smithsonian, participated in a wedding, attended an art auction, sung in a choir concert, taken my car into the shop, gone dancing, even worn a bikini at a public pool (we have the technology)—pretty much the same kinds of things any woman does. Once, I even saw President Bush in drag. (Ah, let me reword that!)

I lead a full life—more than a full life—and spend a lot of time with my friends. There are several long-term close friendships in my male life, but it has only been in the last few years that I have developed friends as a woman. All my friends know about my lifestyle, but there is not a lot of crossover between the two groups. As a woman, I am not entirely free to go out with the people in my male life—at least not close to home. These friends are comfortable with me as a woman, but we are well known around our small community, and people might figure out what I am up to by seeing me with "the usual suspects." There is no such risk in being seen with the friends in my female life, so I am comfortable going out with them. The main reason I cannot be entirely open about being bi-gendered is my work. Many trusted individuals at work know about my lifestyle, but my closest colleagues in my department do not. Neither do my students—hundreds of them, past and present. I am concerned that if word got out, my effectiveness as a teacher would be compromised. I'm not worried about the reaction of people who actually meet me as a woman. Even if they are wary of the idea, they usually get used to it very fast if they spend some time with me. I'm mainly concerned about colleagues and students hearing about my "aberration" second- and thirdhand. There is a lot of misunderstanding, apprehension, and prejudice around transgenderism, and it would just not be possible to meet with and reassure everybody who hears about it. That is just too complicated. In a couple of years I plan to take early retirement, and then I will feel freer to live as I please. For now it is simpler to be discreet.

Will I ever feel comfortable being openly transgendered? The answer to that depends partly on changing my own attitudes, and partly on changing the attitudes of society. Here I look to my gay and lesbian friends as role models. Unfortunately, transgenders are now where gays and lesbians were back in the 1970s. We have a long way to go. But as a woman, I am doing my part to hasten the acceptance of transgenderism. Whenever I get the chance, I speak about transgender to college classes (not on my campus)—mostly sociology, psychology, and women's studies. I have worked to have gender expression included (along with ethnicity, sexual orientation, etc.) in local antidiscrimination laws. Recently, I was asked to serve on the board of the state's largest human rights organization. A couple of years ago, I participated in launching the Conversations Project, a series of discussions aimed at fostering communication and understanding among transgenders and the gay and lesbian community. The project culminated in us acting out our stories in the form of a play—*Transparencies*. For the last two years, I have sung in a GALA (Gay and Lesbian Association) chorus, performing and meeting people all over the state. Most important, when I am out and about, I don't try to hide that I am transgendered. I don't advertise it, either, but if someone figures out what I am about, and is curious, I am open about it. If transgenders successfully blend in, people don't know how many of us are around, they don't have a chance to get used to us, and this slows our acceptance and assimilation. I am not entirely comfortable with this paradox. Nor do I have any desire to be the Rosa Parks of transgenders, but I am open with people when I recognize a "teachable moment." For every outgoing transgender like me, there are many who are closeted and scared. I like to think that if more of us get out into the world, other individuals—trans and nontrans alike—will feel freer to express themselves and follow their true paths.

THE WIFE

Helen Boyd

My husband was watching football one night when the announcer pointed out a woman in the crowds, the wife of an assistant coach whose father had also been a coach. "She better like football," I said, and he laughed. Women's lives are almost always marked by what I've started calling "identity by association." Throughout history, women have gained their identities through their husbands: the woman who married a farmer becomes a farmer herself; the lawyer's wife hosts dinners full of lawyers and other lawyers' wives; even the First Lady's reputation can stand or fall depending on her husband's. There are exceptions, and there are starting to be more. It may be more likely that the lawyer is now the woman herself, and her career good enough evidence of her own identity.

But the partner of a transgendered person ends up in a kind of atavistic relationship where her identity is very much influenced by the transgenderedness of her partner. Wives of cross-dressers worry about secrecy; partners of transsexual women become publicly identified as lesbians if they stay through transition.

The question I've been asking myself a lot recently is whether or not I'm transgendered because my husband is. The wife of the assistant coach is going to get used to the lingo, used to her husband's coach friends; she might start forming her own opinions about salary caps and whether or not that linebacker should be traded. But she doesn't actually become a coach herself, does she? The lesbian who wears the T-shirt printed "I'm not a lesbian but my girlfriend is" is a lesbian herself despite the sarcasm of her T-shirt: it takes two gay people for a gay relationship to exist. But it only takes one transgendered person to create a trans-gendered relationship. Even if I hadn't written a book on the subject, being the wife of a transgendered person meant, in a way, that I had become transgendered, too.

I'm still not sure exactly how that happened. As an independent woman, I never expected to be judged by my husband's behavior. I cer-tainly didn't expect to have his identity determine mine. Even if we had chosen to stay in the closet, I would have been a cross-dresser's wife, and my struggles would have revolved around privacy, secrecy, and keeping the patina of "normal" in our lives. But the closet was never an option for us.

Most of the time, it's the cross-dresser/cross-gender person who wants out, and his wife tries to hold on for dear life. For me, staying in the closet was never an option. I had seen too many gay and lesbian friends come out. The thing is, I'd told friends and family about my boyfriend's cross-dressing when I was under the illusion that my future husband was a transvestite: someone who dressed for sexual pleasure, for fun, drag. It was such a revelation to me that my tomboy self had found a man who understood how to play with gender, who knew what it meant to not fit in the preassigned box, that I was happy to tell friends (and had been given the directive, from him, that I only tell those I could trust with the information, which turned out to be far more people than he ever expected). I had never been a girly-girl, and anyone who knew me for more than a day knew it. I had struggled most of my life with a way to make peace with how feminine I was and wasn't. I'd learned to accept the fact that I didn't wear high heels but did love makeup; I avoided formfitting clothes but loved having long hair and stopped at every jewelry vendor I passed. That is, I'd figured out a way to be "a woman" even though I knew that me and the box marked *F* weren't a perfect fit. I read the kind of gender theory that the feminist commu-nity has been discussing for years, and I had accepted my not-by-the-book womanness as a kind of thesis: gender, the feminists said, was a construction. Being female may have been "natural," but being "a woman" never was. I freed myself as much as I could from the cultural constructs of what was expected of me and went on with my life. I com-promised my self-expression for the sake of my social life, but under-neath it all, the tomboy was alive and well. I had begun to live by what RuPaul would later neatly sum up: "Either you're naked, or it's drag." Simply put, I just stopped taking gender so seriously, and if I wanted to date, I didn't feel I was compromising my feminist identity in order to attract a guy. When I was happier being single, I could cut my hair as short as I wanted and order a beer in a bar alone without getting hit on. I worked gender to my own ends.

When I met my husband, I figured his being a transvestite had led him to similar conclusions. It was a miracle to me that he wasn't comfortable with his box, either—and that he thought I was sexy in trousers. I thought he was sexy in a corset and black stockings. It was the kind of match made in heaven that I couldn't help telling my friends about, and each of them, in turn, was amazed. No one thought he was weird, though they did think the likeliness of our having met was uncannily slim. "If we could find each other," I remember saying to others, "then anything is possible."

As our relationship grew more serious, and after we started living together, the problems started to creep in. As we went out more, he was turned on less by cross-dressing at home, which threw a bit of a wrench into our sex life. His desire to dress more and more like a "regular girl" revealed to me that there was more to his cross-dressing than I'd initially thought. When his unhappy ex threatened to send photos of him en femme to his parents and I said, "So let her—you can always tell them it was Halloween," he blanched.

I started asking questions; he gave me a copy of Mariette Pathy Allen's *Transformations*. When I bought him presents, I started picking denim skirts instead of vinyl ones. He showed me TG Forum, but when I didn't find much partner support there, I started searching the Web. I started to worry. Dating a transvestite was fun; being in a committed relationship with a transgendered person was an entirely different matter. But it was too late for him to remain a closeted cross-dresser, and I would have never wanted a partner who felt so deeply repressed and afraid. The threat from his ex acted like a subconscious suggestion. Both of us knew we didn't want to face anything like that again—and besides, most of my friends already knew.

I knew it wouldn't be easy living as an out transgendered couple, just as it isn't easy for my gay and lesbian friends. But I knew, too, that as a legally hetero couple, we didn't have the worst of society's prejudice to face: we could get married without objections from the Religious Right, and did. We could share health insurance. We got all the privileges of being straight, despite the fact that we didn't feel we had much in common with most straight people. As long as my husband's ID was still marked *M*, we were legally heterosexual, and we would have a whole raft of cultural and civic protections that others don't have. Legally, I like to joke, we "pass" as a straight couple, even if I can't talk to most about our sex life.

But what about the rest of it? The cultural judgment? The ostracism by friends and family? None of that ever happened. Yet somehow his being transgendered made me transgendered, too.

A relationship is always a search for balance. All couples try to find the right amounts of disparate elements: commitment and freedom; togetherness and independence; responsibility and indulgence; solitude and sociability; excitement and security; stability and growth. In a transgendered relationship, all those types of balance are needed, but the strains an emerging transgender identity can put on a couple can cause greater stress for both partners. Will my femininity decrease as his increases? Does his need to implement change threaten our stability? Will his urge to be free of his male role upset my sense of our roles within the relationship? Can keeping such a big part of himself private negatively affect our social life? If I can't connect with, or am not also in love with, his feminine self, will my independence from that part of him lead to estrangement? All these questions—and many others like them—are ones we have had to answer for ourselves. Some balances occur naturally and others are always a little off. I found, however, that what kind of balance—if any—occurs, it is usually a result of long, honest conversation, difficult stare-at-your-feet-while-you-spit-it-out admissions. Some of the things we have to say to each other bring us back to the tension that most people feel at the beginning of a relationship. He worries that his self-expression will finally cause me to say "Enough." I worry that the changes he needs to make to his body and/or personality will change him too drastically from the man I fell in love with and find attractive. For most people, there is a sigh of relief when someone gets to know you very well and isn't going to leave when you tell that dumb joke or admit some lifelong weird habit. My brother is fond of saying "The honeymoon's over when you fart in bed," but, for most, the end of the honeymoon period leads to one of stability and the mundane that is appreciated by both partners. We never seem to arrive there, because his transgenderedness makes that kind of easy acceptance of the other an impossibility. He doesn't know who he is yet, and neither do I. We have first dates all the time. First dates are fun when you don't have anything to lose, but when you're on a first date after five years of commitment, shared experiences, love, and lovemaking, it's like coming home every day hoping your house hasn't burned down.

Let me put it plainly: I can't abide the hooey about my husband being "gender gifted." Luckily, neither can he. I know there is an urge within the community to find the positive about the transgender experience, and I'm absolutely in favor of not sitting around feeling sorry for ourselves. I don't know what "gender gifted" means, but it stinks of euphemism to me. My husband's transgenderedness is not a present, or if it is, it's a present I'd return if I had the receipt. So would he. Not because we don't like it—we both do, to an extent—but because there's nowhere to put it. We can't put it in the closet because that makes him unhappy, and we can't put it out in public because that makes everyone else unhappy. It's not particularly ugly, just cumbersome, and there isn't much room in our lives for it. We really just don't know what to do with it, so every day we hand it back and forth and try a new shelf. Right now we've decided to hang the thing out the window for everyone to see, because otherwise we can't move around our own living room.

To me, transgenderedness is more like a job than anything else; no one really wants to work to pay the rent, but if you don't you can't shower or have a clean bed to sleep in. You find a job you can live with, a boss you like, coworkers you can talk to. When you need to pay the rent, you don't purposely go out and find the worst possible job, the job you hate the most. You make decisions about living with transgendered-ness in similar ways. You try to find ways to be functional about it; otherwise you're both miserable, and where's the fun in that? If you could not have a job, you wouldn't. If you could choose not to be transgen-dered, you wouldn't be, and everyone who tells me otherwise I surmise must be doing some really special drugs, or they are trying to convince themselves and everyone else of something that isn't true. At least it isn't for us. That said, there is lemonade to be made from lemons, after all.

One of the most important aspects of living with transgenderedness is the level of honesty I previously mentioned, but in that it's not unlike other kinds of crises that—if you survive them—can make you a better person. Near-death experiences make a lot of people more generous and helpful, and they destroy others with anxiety and depression. Living with a child who has greater needs than your average child can cause a kind of strain that tears couples apart or brings them together. Some people do come around to realizing that the crisis caused by transgenderism in their lives has, over time, made them better people: I've met a lot of cross-dressers for whom this is true. The reality is, any crisis that requires the kind of time, money, and honesty that transgenderism requires is a trial by fire: you don't expect it, you don't ask for it, but you either live through it or you don't. Any crisis, I've come to realize, that you can handle with your head on and your heart open is one that is bound to lead to growth. Transgenderedness does no less for some people's lives and relationships, but for others, it's a death knell.

The conversations we've had about gender and identity have been the reason that we've found growth instead of destruction. I understood my own gender identity as a kind of gigantic cultural myth, and understood how little of what is meant by "woman" actually represents me. How could I fault a man who didn't jive 100 percent with how the word "man" is defined, or who couldn't manage the energy and attention it took to pretend to be that all the time? I know I couldn't. I couldn't imagine living with a man who fulfilled society's expectations of what a man is supposed to be, either: I wanted a husband who could be tender and self-expressive, and who wouldn't grunt at me for the next forty years. Maybe who I was somehow guaranteed I would marry a transgendered man, but I doubt it. Plenty of tomboys marry guys who are butcher than they are, and others grow up and marry other women. I kind of ended up somewhere in the middle, with a man who is more feminine than most men and less feminine than most women.

Which is kind of funny since I see myself as more feminine than most men and less feminine than most women, too. We are sometimes painfully similar. The only difference, as far as I can tell, is that some of my masculine traits were encouraged when I was growing up. In a large working-class family, getting a job and getting the hell out of the house were strongly encouraged—and both goals require independence and the ability to pay the rent. Had I lived alone and supported myself in 1920, I would have been called a suffragette; in the 1990s, I was only a young woman starting her life as an individual.

For my husband, there was nothing about his feminine feelings that could be encouraged. Childhood intuition or some other very strong signals encouraged him not to tell his mother how much he enjoyed putting on his sister's tights. Maybe he didn't tell his mother because he'd taken something of his sister's without permission, but then why didn't he just ask to try them on? Because he knew he was a boy, and boys don't wear tights. Psychologists say kids work out the gender rules around the age of three. But no matter why, he didn't tell anyone he sometimes wished he were a girl. When he watched *Charlie's Angels*, he wanted to be Sabrina. So did I.

Some days that's what being the partner of a transgendered person is like: you both want to be Sabrina, who was, after all, the least girly of the three of them, and certainly the sexiest, even in her turtleneck sweaters and pants. Sabrina was pretty and confident, aggressive and sexy, smart and graceful. A liberated woman, you could say.

I could say I wanted to be Sabrina and maybe my brother would roll his eyes, but mostly no one cared. If my husband had declared he wanted to be Sabrina, all hell would have broken loose. For my husband, half of her traits were verboten. Confident was good, but pretty was out; aggression was strongly encouraged and sexy was—for women. Smart was good as long as it didn't interfere with him being good at sports, and graceful . . . well, we all know graceful young men end up hairdressers.

So the deeply homophobic tic in this culture permeated his nine-year-old brain. He couldn't be graceful because that meant he was a faggot, and there is nothing worse than being a faggot. Even homosexual boys know that, and many of them have spent lifetimes pretending to be otherwise, and still do. There are few femmes in gay culture, because even faggots hate faggots. Remember: there is nothing worse than being a faggot.

Which is what was, unconsciously and consciously, drilled into my husband's head. Something—he didn't know what—would happen if he told his mother he liked to wear his sister's tights. Something terrible. So he didn't. She never knew. She still doesn't. His whole family breathed a sigh of relief when he met me. When he proudly introduced me first as his girlfriend and then as his wife, they thought, "phew." He wasn't a homosexual after all, his father might have thought, and his mother tried to forget that time she found several pairs of girls' panties in his sock drawer. They tried not to see any signs of his femininity, because they wanted him to be happy.

(We have such a deep wish that people be happy that we ask them to hide huge chunks of themselves, pretty much guaranteeing they will not be happy. *Girls don't give other girls flowers*, we tell the little girl who brings one of the girls a rose on Valentine's Day, too young to know better. *You have to wait for him to ask you out*, we tell the girl who asks the boy out on a date. *Take that off this instant, young man*, we tell the boy who comes downstairs in his sister's pink nightie to announce he wants to be a princess for Halloween.)

But his family must have seen it. Why on earth would they be so relieved that he wasn't gay if they hadn't? I keep telling him his mother knows even if she doesn't know the words for it. She knows her son like most good moms do. But she's not talking. What mother wants her son to grow up and be feminine? She'd never mentioned catching him in one of his sister's dresses because she figured it was a stage he was going through, an older brother's jealousy of the attention his pretty kid sister got. But does she know her son is feminine? Of course she does. No mother who is breathing wouldn't notice femininity in her boy. She just encouraged him to play ball and hoped he'd "toughen up." He did. As a result, he's spent a lifetime lying to her and everyone he knows about who he is. His family has only ever known half of him, and they have missed out on the half, which he, willingly and mostly unconsciously, kept hidden. He may have learned to play the boy, but when he goes to a bachelor party, all the strippers want to lap dance for him exactly because he's "not like the other guys."

He's not like the other guys; that's why I asked him on our first date. He was quiet and thoughtful and good-looking and confident and sexy. He had something more than thoughts of baseball and beer behind his eyes. I thought he was just an emotive type, being an actor, a dreamy bookish guy. But it was more than that, which I'd find out later. He says if I had known what he was wearing when I called to ask him out I wouldn't have asked him out. I'd already been told he wasn't gay and that he was single. For me, there were no other questions to ask. "So does he wear dresses?" had never occurred to me, but now that I'm married to someone who is transgendered, I think it's the kind of question women need to ask about prospective dates a lot more. This is not the kind of thing you want sprung on you after twenty years of marriage, or even five. It's really not the kind of thing you want sprung on you at all, not even after a half dozen dates.

I had no idea what being transgender meant; I'm not sure I understand what it means now. Feminine men are not all transgendered. Transgendered men aren't even necessarily feminine. I don't know why a gay, feminine friend of mine isn't "classified" as transgendered but my husband is. I don't know what makes me not transgendered, either. I don't know why other couples—where the guy is small-boned, delicate, sensitive, and gentle, and who stays home to take care of the kids while his wife runs the marketing division of EnormoMart, Inc.—aren't considered transgendered.

Apparently we are a transgendered couple because my husband wears a dress sometimes. He prefers his nails painted, his underwear silky. He prefers to feel pretty over feeling handsome; he married me, I think, because I asked him on a date. He likes to feel like a girl, and despite how much gender theory I have read, I have no idea what that means. The idea of saying "gentleness is feminine" or "aggression is masculine" is completely beyond me. As a feminist, I just can't accept that my husband is feminine because he's passive, or delicate, or pretty. I think trees are passive and delicate and pretty, and I don't think of trees as feminine, either. When he talks about his own femininity, I don't rightly know what he's talking about. His behavior, on the other hand, I understand.

If he wants to paint his nails because they look nice, then he can paint them any color he likes. If he wants to make his eyelashes longer because they make his eyes look bigger, I'm all for it (not that he doesn't have the biggest, most gorgeous eyes in the world in the first place). If he wants to wear a dress because it makes him feel sensual, or powerful, or sexy, then who am I to stop him? I wear jeans nearly every day because I feel comfortable and confident in them.

So honestly, I don't know what he's talking about most of the time when he refers to his "inner feminine." I don't know what transsexual women mean when they say they have "a woman's heart" or "a woman's mind." I've always thought of my mind as genderless, my heart—well, my heart pumps blood, it has nothing to do with sex or reproduction or even romance. When Jennifer Finney Boylan said recently that she knew she was transsexual because she thought about gender every day, I thought, "Well, so do I." I think a lot of people who aren't transsexual think about gender every day.

These are the kinds of things I thought about gender years before I met my husband: *I thought about how fashion designers make clothes that don't fit women's bodies, and I had no idea why. I wondered how many people thought I was having sex with my former boss simply because he was male and I was female and because I worked out of his home. I asked other women if their feet screamed in pain when they wore high heels and couldn't figure out why they wore them anyway. I pondered how it is that being "submissive" is supposed to be a feminine trait when all the dommes I've talked to tell me more men want to be bound and gagged than women. I couldn't work out why it is that "cooking" is a feminine chore when most of the chefs are men. I wanted to know why boys don't cry.*

I finally decided I just don't know what Jennifer Finney Boylan is talking about, but I'm worried, too, my husband is going to decide he's transsexual because of how she defined it. If what Jennifer Finney Boylan meant when she said she thought about gender every day was really that she thought about gender every single day personally and deeply, that those thoughts daily caused her deep distress and emotional pain, and that thinking about her own gender made her feel impossibly overwhelmed by what it might take for her not to think about gender every day, then she should have said that. I'm pretty sure that is what she meant.

Maybe women who don't have transgendered husbands know what masculine and feminine are. Maybe transsexual women do, too. Maybe cross-dressers do. All I know is the more I think about gender, the less I know about it. I couldn't lay a dollar bet on any one human character-istic being "feminine" or "masculine" anymore. You name it; I'll name the exception. There is no gendered human trait. Not one that stands up to scrutiny. And yet at the same time there are only ever these two categories, male/female, man/woman, boy/girl. Two big groups, whether it's sex or gender or chromosomes. And yet no human thing—characteristic, habit, even item of clothing—fits exclusively and without caveat into either one of those damned two boxes.

But I still haven't figured out if I'm transgendered because my husband is. It's pretty obvious to me that others see me differently than they used to, but I'm not sure exactly what they see. When I'm on the subway by myself, they see a woman in her thirties, a bookish Brooklyn hipster/artist, a former punk rocker, a married woman (if they notice my left hand). But they can't tell, just from looking at me as I read *The Madman and the Professor*, that I am married to someone who is transgendered. Some days, some might guess I'm a lesbian, but that has more to do with my short hair and "comfortable shoes" than who I'm married to.

But once my husband is with me, all that changes.

When he's fully en femme, we're often just assumed to be lesbians.

When his presentation is more effeminate than feminine, I'm sure others come to some pretty interesting conclusions. Part-time drag queen (him) and fag hag (me)? Sissy boy and tomboy? Siblings? Roommates? Friends?

One time, in a small boutique in Park Slope, my husband wanted to try on a pair of pumps, and he asked if he could see the pair in a size 10. The woman who owned the place was thrilled with her own open-mindedness and hurried off to find his size. He took off the shoes he was wearing, slid a foot into one of the shoes, and they chatted away about the make of the shoes. "Everyone says they're very comfortable," she explained. He looked at his foot in the mirror. They didn't exactly make his feet look small, but he didn't look as if he'd cut off his toes to fit into them, either. That's when I made my fatal mistake.

"I don't see how heels are ever comfortable," I piped in, and both my husband and the saleslady looked up at me as if I'd just arrived by spaceship. I had interrupted their pithy chatter. My husband, recovering himself and remembering exactly who I was, said, "But you don't like heels."

"I like them okay," I clarified, "I just can't wear them. But at least one of us can."

The saleslady looked first at him and then at me. She'd figured out I hadn't just dropped in from Mars, and that I was with him. But who was I?

After we left I had a hollow feeling in my stomach. I realized that if people assume my husband is a drag queen, as this woman had, then they would also assume he was gay. This means, of course, that I am either one of two things: if they read me as straight, I'd become his fag hag, but if they read me as a lesbian, I was his friend. How the average saleslady might read me that day probably depends more on my own presentation at that point (sundress or jeans, sandals or sneakers), but there is no instance in which our relationship hasn't been "disappeared." There is no room in today's cultural context for a drag queen with a wife, which means, of course, that when we are out together, and my husband tries on pumps, we are delegated "friends" instead of husband and wife.

And that hurts. People wear rings for a reason after all—not just as a private symbolic act but as a public identifier. I like having people know I'm married—it makes my life a lot simpler when men or women hit on me, and it indicates to other women that I'm no threat: *I've got mine, I don't want yours.* More than that, my relationship is an accomplishment in my eyes, an aspect of my life I'm proud of and like for people to know about. It is not easy to be married, and it is perhaps less easy to be married to someone who is transgendered. I'd like some props, as the kids say, for the work and patience and understanding and education I've gained as a result of being in this relationship. I want people to say "wow, how liberated," but often, instead, they say "well she must really be a lesbian," or "poor girl doesn't know her husband's really gay," or even "he's prettier than she is."

This is about when I start wondering why on earth I even bother. I want, sometimes, to insist that my husband just cut it out, so we can get on with our lives as a regular married couple. But he can't cut it out. If there is anything I'm sure of, it's that transgenderism is not a hobby, a lifestyle, or a choice. He can either be a happy, confident person who is transgendered, or a closeted, shamed transgendered person. Since closeted and shamed people do not turn me on emotionally, intellectually, or sexually, we're working on him being happy and confident instead.

Since he can't cut it out, my next option, I suppose, is to cut out— but that's just not an option for me, either. I love him and I take my marriage vows seriously. It is somehow liberating for me to realize I *can* go and that, if I left, I could stop being transgendered. Some days it's tempting, to leave this complicated and occasionally nightmarish theme park my husband and I like to call *GenderLand*, where a roller coaster may, in fact, be a Ferris wheel instead.

When a close friend's husband transitioned, she found herself divorced at thirty-two, but also found herself not transgendered anymore. She could date regular heterosexual guys again, expect not to share her closet with her partner, and expect to see boxer shorts or briefs, and not panties, when she took her new boyfriend's jeans off. I found myself desperately jealous of her because she was free of all this, free of online support groups and arguments about the difference between gender and sex, free of books about gender and being careful with pronouns. She could go back to living in a black-and-white world where men are men and women are women, except of course when she gets to an important date where she needs to explain her romantic past to a boyfriend.

"So, you're divorced," her new boyfriend might say. "What happened?"

"He became a woman," she says. "My former husband transitioned, because she was transgendered, a transsexual."

"Your husband had a sex change?" the uninformed new boyfriend might ask.

"Right. Exactly."

"Well why'd you marry a guy who wanted a sex change in the first place?" And so, for a while, she'd feel like the partner of a transgendered person again, explaining how there are transvestites and cross-dressers and how transgender is an umbrella term and how sometimes people who are CDs ("that's short for cross-dresser," she might explain) find out they are transsexual, and there's really no way of knowing. Her new boyfriend may sit with his jaw agape, or look at her a little differently, or realize that, even via a divorce, this woman is connected to some really weird people. He might think there was something about her that attracted a girly man, and question himself.

But despite that conversation, my friend is now untransgendered. She can't forget all the Kate Bornstein she's read, but she can think about it in more theoretical ways. My guess is she won't pick up a book about gender for a decade at least.

I'm aware that I could have that, too. I could decide to leave my husband and go back to being a more regular woman, one who complains about a man's inability to do anything but grunt when football is on. I could do that—but I don't. I can't really imagine that anymore. One of the big bonuses of being with a transgendered person is that your partner is effectively in a glass house when it comes to gender issues. I don't want to wear heels? I don't. I don't want to wear makeup? I won't. I don't want to wear formfitting clothes, or I don't want to pretend not to know the answer to a question so I don't look smarter than he is? To heck with it all. I get to do what I want. To me, transgenderism is the last tool in the feminist toolbox, the one that has potential for blowing our whole gender-driven culture wide open. I plan to take advantage of having a transgendered husband. Where previous boyfriends would unwillingly "let" me cut my hair short, my husband can't flinch in his acceptance of my presentation as less than traditionally feminine. That doesn't mean I'm going to start binding my breasts or wearing facial hair, but it does mean I might go a little longer between waxings. If I can sleep next to his clean-shaven legs, then he can sleep next to my hairy ones.

Surely, I could have found a man who would be tolerant of such gender variance even if I weren't married to someone who is transgendered. Of course, I could have. But the chief "trick" to being happily married to someone who is transgendered is finding and cherishing every single positive benefit there is. There aren't many. You see, my husband still grunts when he watches football, except he cracks beers with one manicured nail now, instead. Where is the advantage in that? The advantage, when it comes to our relationship, is knowing that I'm with someone who can fully be himself, someone who has the bravery, confidence, and self-acceptance to insist on being a whole person. He understands why I want the same thing and why feminism helps explain why I can't have it. Feminism gave me the language to explain to my husband that my breasts categorize me in ways I don't like: to me they mean I will never earn a man's dollar. It is difficult to love your female body unequivocally when that same body leaves you open to discrimination, harassment, and even violence. He understands why I'd prefer to be remembered as smart rather than pretty, because he knows that I don't have "a woman's brain" but just a brain. My bookishness, he knows, provided me with an escape hatch from being labeled "just a girl." He might wish I was the kind of woman who enjoyed shopping more, but he also knows he would never trade my ability to discuss Tolkien for my ability to discuss the sales at Talbot's. Our shared love of books is genderless, a bridge where we can meet. And he understands that feminism built that bridge, at least on my end. Transgenderedness might be the bridge that builds it from his.

So am I transgendered because my husband is? I don't know. What I do know is that my expectations, as the partner of a transgendered person, are always challenged by his need to express his complete self. I have days where I welcome the growth and liberation it takes to accept my husband's femininity, and days when I feel taken advantage of, as a woman by a man, in terms of compromising my own needs as a partner.

The growth and liberation are, in my opinion, worth the occasional self-doubt. My hope is that his femininity will foster the same sense of self-compromise in him that I was raised with so that our compromises, together, will lead to a fulfilling, challenging relationship for us both, one balanced however tentatively on the myriad disparate elements that make any relationship flourish.

A FULFILLING LIFE

Jane Ellen Fairfax

Like everyone else on this planet, I have within me the variant features that make humanity such an interesting species. Some of my background, personality traits, and world outlook are distinctly conventional, while some vary considerably from the norm. I am a heterosexual cross-dresser. By the grace of God, and considerable good luck, I have not had to carry a burden of guilt and shame. While my life has had its highs and lows, I have been fortunate enough to enjoy many fulfilling roles—servant of God, husband, father, healer, teacher, team worker, and leader. Within me masculinity and femininity live together in harmony, and I am content with my gender gift.

DECADE 1 (YEARS 0–10)

I was born the eldest son of a self-made man and woman. Both lost their parents early in life and knew the hardships of having to survive in a harsh world. My father worked his way up to becoming a prosperous merchant. His one regret was that he was unable to obtain the college education he desperately wanted, and he was determined that his children should achieve and be educated and successful. A hard-driving, type A personality, he had no use for softness, but rather, he prioritized competition and victory. One generation removed from the Old Country, he was very strict and conventional in his views on gender. My mother also was hardworking and very supportive of my father, but she had a phlegmatic way about her that balanced and complemented him.

We were Roman Catholics at a time when one went to "hear" Mass on Sunday and lived under fear of everlasting damnation from mortal sin. The Mass was in Latin, but I learned to understand that language at an early age. I was also fortunate enough to be assigned religious education teachers who opened the world of the Bible to me. There I learned that God was merciful and loving, as well as just, and that perception has colored my life through the years.

My earliest perception that I was different from other boys occurred at about the age of three or four. Early on I developed a love of music and expressed a desire for instrument or voice lessons. My father quickly squashed that idea on the ground that musicians "don't make any money." Around the same time, I told my mother that girls' names were prettier than boys' names and that I would like to be called a girl's name. She quickly dismissed my request on the ground that I was a boy.

At an early age, I became aware of a tendency to root for the underdog. My father and his friends always rooted for the best sports teams and for the fighter who seemed to be winning. A part of this pattern was a love for and a sensitivity toward animals. While my father thought it perfectly acceptable to settle arguments with one's fists, I totally recoiled from this approach. Perceiving these behavior patterns, my father told me, "You should have been born a girl." Perhaps because of his pejorative tone, or perhaps because I liked being a boy, I passed off his denunciation and considered it crazy.

At about the age of five, I was bombarded with a long series of illnesses. For a third of the year, my kindergarten teacher marked my report card "Not present enough for grades." There was some consideration of holding me back in kindergarten, because of my poor health, but my father insisted on my promotion. It turned out to be a wise decision. In first grade, prejudice from my kindergarten teacher caused my teacher to place me in the slow group. Within six weeks, I had been promoted to the "normal" group, and in another six weeks, I was in the accelerated group. My love affair with books and scholastics had started, and I was off! The following year my father took me to a football game at one of the most prestigious universities in America. I was entranced at the beautiful campus, with its interlacing oak trees, picturesque buildings, and the magnificent football game that packed a seventy-five-thousand-seat stadium. Wide-eyed, I told my father that this was the college I wanted to attend. "If you make the grades," he promised, "I will send you there."

That same year, I had my first little girlfriend, and another pattern started that lasted through high school. Every year I had a different girlfriend. While I had some male friends, including a couple of very close ones, I enjoyed the company of girls more than I did that of boys. In most areas I was not particularly athletic, except for baseball. Pitching, hitting, and fielding came easy to me, and I was one of the first boys selected on baseball teams. I threw left-handed and batted right-handed. Once I turned around and batted left. The coach said, "Aw, quit clowning! Turn around and bat right!" "Just put it in here," I said. He grooved me a fast one, and I knocked it over the right field fence. So in these early years, I enjoyed feminine company and feminine traits, but the masculine side was growing up healthy, too.

DECADE 2 (YEARS 11–20)

My adolescent years were a time of isolation, and I became increasingly uncomfortable with my lack of a social life. To some extent, this was unavoidable. My father's business opened early in the morning and closed late at night, six days a week. After school, I worked at the medical school and then walked back to my father's business, where I did my homework and waited for closing time. My grades continued to be high, and I almost always made the honor roll.

When I was in the eighth grade, I began to notice a startling change in the girls in my class. All of a sudden, their girlhood was being replaced by womanhood. They looked beautiful in the makeup with which they were experimenting, and their more grown-up dresses were beautiful. In fact, I found myself wishing I could exchange places with them. But that was as far as it went. I never experimented with feminine clothes or makeup, and I continued to have my Girlfriend of the Year.

Throughout high school my academic performance continued to gain momentum. In my last two years I received twenty-two academic awards, including highest-average awards in Latin, science, and combination math/science. Among the awards I received was the coveted Slide Rule. It all culminated when I received a letter stating that I had been admitted to the university of my dreams. I was in heaven! In the spring of my senior year occurred an event that freed me spiritually and gave me a lasting insight on guilt, shame, and condemnation. I tried hard to be a good Catholic boy, but it was not easy tripping through a maze of venial and mortal sins that were ravening to gobble up my hope of salvation. When I failed, it was sometimes hard to get up again.

It all changed at the Honor Society picnic. It was scheduled to be a wonderful day, excused from classes! We had a little party and then repaired to the beach for swimming, beach sports, and a cookout over driftwood fires. Unfortunately, the fare was only hot dogs and hamburgers, and the event was on a Friday, when Catholics were forbidden to eat meat under penalty of mortal sin. Hungrily eyeing the meat sizzling on the fire, the Catholic kids were a picture of misery. Finally, I could take it no longer, and I told them all, "I do not believe that Jesus Christ, who died on the cross for us, would condemn us to everlasting hell for eating a hamburger." We all enjoyed the feast. The insight I had gained would stand me in good stead later, for it would free me from the guilt others would later try to load onto me for cross-dressing.

The Honor Society picnic was a watershed event in my life, for it led to spiritual growth in several directions. First, it forced me to examine my relationship to the Catholic Church. Did I even want to remain a Catholic? Certainly, I had trouble with several of its teachings, including those on birth control, papal infallibility, and clerical celibacy. For several years I examined various denominations and "nondenominations." Ultimately, I decided to remain Catholic, because I was convinced that this was the church Christ founded and that all seventy-two books of the Catholic Bible were inspired by God. No longer, however, did I judge any religion, for I was convinced that the same God loves all His creation. Third, I ceased to condemn my fellow creatures because of who they are. As I encountered different cultures and lifestyles, I became more at peace with humankind in all its variations.

So I reached adulthood, ready to make my way in the wide world. My masculine identity was set and ready to take on all challenges. While I was aware that I had traits at variance with conventional expectations for males, I did not relate these characteristics to an inner femininity. During childhood and adolescence, I had had no cross-dressing episodes. I was too thoroughly socialized in the masculine stereotypes, and my parents controlled my life so rigidly that cross-dressing was unthinkable. The "trigger event" did not occur. My masculine side was in control, and my softer side slept, undeveloped and even undefined.

DECADE 3 (YEARS 21–30): FRANCES

In college I continued a successful academic career. Things rocked along until one September afternoon in my junior year, when I decided to attend a Newman Club mixer for the incoming freshman class. There I met a sweet, honey-blonde young lady and was instantly attracted to her beautiful smile and kind personality. The next Saturday we attended the football game and experienced one of our university's rare victories. Over the next four years we not only attended football games but also enjoyed movies, cook-ins, political rallies, the zoo, many long walks, and harvesting the blackberry brambles in the campus hedges. After going together for two years, we became engaged, but it was another two years before circumstances would allow us to marry.

Those early years were tough! I was the original starving student, and Frances worked at an office job to put food on the table. But we were poor together, and we were deeply in love. We supplemented our salaries with fish and crabs we caught, and we walked until we could afford a car. Things improved slightly when I graduated from medical school and went on to internship and residency. Finally, at the age of thirty, my training was over and I returned to Texas to open my practice, put down some roots, and start a family. During these years my feminine side slept. There were just too many other basic concerns. Frances and I were heavily burdened with college debts, and I had to be in first-class competitive shape to make it through my residency and the specialty board exams. Cross-dressing? Feminine expression? I never even thought of it.

Fortunately, my practice took off right away. For a few months we lived in a barely furnished apartment in a rabbit warren of other similar apartments. Within a year, however, we moved into a house, and within three years, all the debts were paid off. The years of having to compete to survive and to get ahead in circumstances where there was little margin for error had left their mark. Although I was successful, I had become the type of person one would not like to cross. My masculine aggressiveness had pulled me through, but there were many traits in my personality I did not like. Everything was "win at all costs, climb the next rung, become something more than you are." If I was on a team, everyone else knew they could relax and let me do all the work. I liked it that way, for I told myself "it would be done right." Unfortunately, I never seemed to be able to relax. Every little contretemps seemed to upset me. My wife must have felt she was living on the slopes of Mount Vesuvius. I was aggressive in all things. Or, as I would put it now, I was far out of balance. Soon, however, an event would occur that would put everything into perspective and change the course of my life.

DECADE 4 (YEARS 31–40):
THE EMERGENCE OF JANE

One Saturday morning after we had been married ten years, Frances went out to run some errands while I remained in bed, reading. Before going out, she had left on the bed a turquoise and white sweater and an elastic waist, pleated white skirt. Idly, I wondered what it would feel like to have on those clothes. So, I found some of my wife's underwear and put the skirt and sweater on over them. What a revelation! I felt so comfortable in those clothes, as if I somehow belonged in them. I felt a great sense of relaxation and peace. I went into the living room and read for about an hour. Finally, it was about time for Frances to come back home, so I took them off. The clothes slipped off easily, but a change had occurred that would never slip away!

"What had happened?" I wondered. What was behind my new-found affinity for feminine clothes? I knew I would have to tell Frances about it, for we both believe that honesty and trust are the bedrock of a marriage. But what could I tell her when I myself did not know the meaning of it? How would she react? Coming from a conservative background as she did, she would have no frame of reference with which to relate to cross-dressing. Would she be able to adjust to a husband who felt good in dresses? Our lives had been stressful enough, without this new factor. The questions were many; the answers, few.

The next stop was the medical library, where I did a thorough review of the sexological literature. There I found that the description of "heterosexual cross-dresser" fit me to a T. Actually, the description was fairly complimentary. I discovered that most cross-dressers were heterosexual family men, accomplished in school and successful in their careers. That there existed a population of men for whom cross-dressing was a form of self-expression was somehow very exciting. And I could easily relate to Virginia Prince's opinion that cross-dressing represented a way of escape from the pressures of stereotypical masculinity. That was me all over! The main problem cross-dressers seemed to experience was guilt and shame, based on societal stereotypes for masculine behavior. At the Honor Society picnic back in high school, I had determined for all time that I would never let an institution's stereotypes burden me with undeserved guilt and shame. Applying that determination, I saw no reason to feel guilty about cross-dressing. With time I would discover its fruits, and then I could determine what place it would have in my life.

Although most articles and books I read presented cross-dressing in a positive light, there were some disquieting features. At that time, psychiatry did offer a pathological diagnosis, albeit not a serious one, for cross-dressing. I could find nothing on the subject of telling wives or helping them adjust to cross-dressing. And on the subject of children, I found nothing but a deep, dark void. While on balance the literature seemed to suggest that I was "okay," it was clear that we would have some uncharted waters to navigate—provided, that is, Frances did not jump ship! So far, so good! I now understood that my desire to cross-dress had something to do with a feminine side that lived deep within me and that somehow it was connected to my aversion to macho behavior, my tendency to pull for the underdog, and my penchant for sharing feelings rather than "fighting it out." Now it was time to get in touch with those feelings. Who was I when I was en femme? Was "she" a separate personality? Was "she" "the real me"? Was I headed for a sex change? What was "her" relationship to the opposite sex? The easiest question to dispose of was that of transsexualism. The very idea was alien to my identity concept. One thing was certain; I was not a woman. I imagined myself dressed en femme in social situations with men. Would "she" like a gallant man to open a door for her? Of course "she" would! Would "she" like a suave gentleman to kiss her hand? Yes, indeed! Would "she" like to dance with a man? Oh, oh! Here discomfort started to creep in. And sex with a man? Unthinkable! And that was just fine, because it tallied with the concept of "heterosexual cross-dresser," with which I had identified based on my reading.

Gradually, I connected my feminine side with the "different" traits I had noted in myself from my earliest years. Included among these were an inclination to share my feelings, even if they made me vulnerable; a tendency to root for the underdog; a keen appreciation for art, music, and literature; a strong preference for female playmates; and an aptitude for peacemaking. My father considered all these things sissified. On several occasions, he groused, "You should have been a girl." At the time, I considered this a crazy notion, but now I understood that those traits fit into a pattern. While they did not mean I was a woman, I was a feminine, as well as a masculine, person. In my feminine presentation, these traits were natural, and I could express them to my heart's content.

Now it was time to share with Frances. I set aside a quiet time and spoke from the heart about the discovery of my affinity for feminine clothes and what I had read in the medical library. Two advantages I had from the outset were that I had never hidden the cross-dressing, nor did I feel any guilt about it. The first spared me having to deal with the most difficult issue wives face, that of deception. The second enabled me to take a matter-of-fact approach to telling Frances. Deemphasizing the clothes, I stressed the happiness I felt in my feminine expression and the relief it gave me from macho social expectations. I explained that, for me, cross-dressing was not a sexual thing and that I was not in love with anyone but her. Except for my newly discovered need for feminine expression, I was the same man she married. Later she was to tell me how much that reassurance meant to her.

Frances listened quietly, and said, "I've been married to you long enough so that I know you are not gay. Nor, knowing you, do I fear you will want to have it all cut off. But, where is all this going?" Over the next several weeks, we had long hours of discussions. She asked whether this meant that we would retire somewhere as a couple of little old ladies. I replied, "I honestly don't know, but I can give you my solemn promise that you will never lose your husband to cross-dressing. Our marriage vow to love, honor, and cherish comes before everything else." I believe that this reply was the key to the encouragement and acceptance Frances has shown me ever since.

Over the ensuing years, we were to discuss many other issues, such as security, considerations related to my profession, telling our children, and getting involved in support groups. Depending on our life circumstances, Frances would have her ups and downs about cross-dressing. In particular, she was put off by the sleaze, political conflicts, and selfishness in Genderland. But from that first sharing, she has been right by my side, and our marriage has become even more trusting and healthier than ever. At one point she asked, "Does your feminine side have a name?" I had looked up the meanings of various feminine names and was instantly attracted to "Jane," which means "God is gracious." This name was a perfect fit, for I have always regarded my feminine traits as a gift from God. Reading a book of heraldry, I found appealing the motto of the clan Fairfax: "I will accomplish while I live." It helped also that both "Jane" and "Fairfax" figured in my favorite novel, *Jane Eyre*. The name "Ellen" with its musical *l* goes well with "Jane." And so, Jane Ellen Fairfax was born!

DECADE 5 (YEARS 41–50): JANE GROWS AND DEVELOPS

As time went on, Frances solidified her strong support of Jane and told her, "We'll just make Jane the best lady she can be." It was not an easy process. At first, I went through a hyperfeminine stage that was partly fetishism and partly inexperience. After all, I did not have the advantage of a mother to help with my feminine development. One day I stood before the mirror in my white blouse, gold lamé miniskirt, and matching high-heeled sandals. I asked Frances whether I looked feminine. "No," she replied. "Why not?" I asked, my feelings hurt. "Well, Jane," she advised, "real women don't dress like that." From that point on, I decided to base my presentation on the way a professional lady of my age would dress.

It was a slow process, but an enjoyable and fulfilling one. I had my colors analyzed and was delighted to find out I was a "Winter" and that the jewel tones and black that I loved were indeed my colors. Little by little, Frances and I put together a wardrobe for Jane, complete with silver-toned accessories. It was most fortunate that I liked skirt-and-blouse ensembles. With only four skirts and four blouses, I could achieve twenty-four different looks! My male self has never enjoyed wearing "monkey suits," with their tight collars and neckties. From time to time, I found occasion to curse that sloppy French king who inspired a courtier to invent a triangular napkin, which evolved into the cravat! But how different was the feel of the lady's suit with its soft silken scarf, lacy blouse, and lined skirt! Dresses in floral prints and vivid solids, and a few pants that could be worn with blouses, completed the ensemble of the newly emerging professional lady.

Shopping for this wardrobe led to some interesting experiences. One evening my wife and I went dress shopping at a tall girls' shop. Since we had a good working relationship with the owner, we could browse in comfort, and I could even use the dressing room to try on clothes. Frances found a beautiful midnight blue damask gown and went to try it on. Independently, I had been attracted to the same outfit, and I asked the sales lady if I could try it on. This particular sales lady, however, had just started working at the shop, and the owner had not yet oriented her to her cross-dressing clientele. The sales lady must have turned two shades paler, wondering how to handle this request! Fortunately, the owner saw what was happening and explained the situation to her. All was well, and we both bought the dress we loved. Over the years we have enjoyed "twinning up" on special occasions.

Accessorizing provided opportunities for creative feminine expression. I really enjoy wearing my treble clef pin, which illustrates the musical part of me. My interest in horse racing is reflected in my riding scarf, and my elephant pendant might be regarded as an expression of my political identity. When I wear my butterfly hair ornament, I proclaim to the world the joy I feel in transforming into my feminine self. Perhaps the most interesting accessory is my "4 Kings" enamel pin. Not only does it indicate my love of bridge but it implies that my masculine self is present even when I am wearing feminine clothes. And of course, vice versa!

Even my office staff got into the act! Because of my leadership role in Tri-Ess, they have needed to know about Jane, and they have always accepted her. Knowing I do not wear neckties, and that I like to wear crosses as an expression of my Christianity, they gave me as a birthday present an ornate Greek cross and, later, an Easter cross with the shroud of the risen Christ draped around it. Over the years, many women have exclaimed, "How beautiful!" You can imagine how it makes me feel to hear this adjective when I am dressed en homme! It's a reminder that regardless of what I am wearing, my beautiful feminine side is always present.

Because society does not yet fully accept cross-dressing, I do not have the freedom to dress according to my gender mode. After all, I have a family to provide for, and I have a responsibility to maintain my livelihood. There are, however, ways to achieve feminine expression. My delicate feminine crosses are one, and my well-manicured nails, with their feminine arcs and clear nail polish, are another. On certain occasions, I can wear clear mascara and a nutmeg shade of lipstick that emphasizes ever so slightly my own lip color. Once I attended a Christmas party with my professional colleagues. Certainly this was not a place to cross-dress. So I came in my burgundy sweater and cross, along with the rest of my regular attire. Only my wife and I knew that the tag on the inside of my sweater read "Leslie Fay."

It must have been difficult for Frances when so much mental energy was spent developing Jane's presentation, rather than taking care of other aspects of our lives, or building Frances's wardrobe. Whenever we went shopping, I made sure we looked for nice things for Frances, too, so that there were several shopping trips, ostensibly for Jane, when Frances came back with the goods. Frances was able to understand that most of the clothing we bought during that time was for Jane, because we had to build her presentation from scratch. But this pattern was undoubtedly ameliorated by the fact that Frances's needs were being met, too.

Even while Jane's outer image was being established, a more important work was going on inside. Little by little, feminine traits were being integrated into the whole person who was me. The clothes served as a lens through which I could more readily focus on and express my feminine traits. Formerly, I had expressed almost all negative emotions as anger. Now I could express hurt, sorrow, even fear. I was able to cry at sad movies. No longer did I have to win at everything, but learned the value of networking, processing, and teamworking. I knew something wonderful had happened inside me when many of my female patients started to tell me variations of "I love coming to you, because you understand how I feel." This gift of empathy led me to be a peacemaker and a compromiser. Serving on many hospital committees, I found I was able to bring opposing viewpoints together and find win–win solutions. Thanks to Jane's presence in my life, I was becoming a better person.

In 1984 another life change occurred when I read in an advice column a letter from a cross-dresser. The columnist referred him to an organization called Tri-Ess. I wrote immediately, and my heart was thumping away when that special envelope came. I knew this was the perfect support organization for me, and I eagerly sought out my local chapter. I was most fortunate in my Big Sister, for she was an experienced cross-dresser with a background in psychology. Together we explored the question of Jane's sexuality. After a lot of thought, it occurred to me that the subject was moot. "Jane" was the name I gave to the feminine side of my personality. I was not two people, but one, and that one was a genetic male who was sexually attracted to women and who admired and respected their folkways. When I shared this insight with my Big Sister, she was ecstatic: "Yes! Yes! Yes! I do believe she's got it!"

What a breakthrough! Now I was able to separate my biologic self from my gender expression. I could accept my identity as a genetic male and reject society's macho stereotypes for masculine behavior. From here it was a steady process of identifying the masculine traits I did not like and replacing them with more constructive feminine behavior patterns. I was on the way to integrating both genders into the whole person who was me. Eventually, I no longer needed the cross-dressing to focus on my femininity and express it. Regardless of what I was wearing, I became able to utilize both my masculine and my feminine tools to cope with life's conundrums. For me, terms like "gender identity disorder" or "gender dysphoria" were irrelevant. I was integrated, whole, and happy!

Eventually, I had to work out Jane's relationship to my spirituality. The message of Deuteronomy 22:5 seemed clear enough. Men were not supposed to wear clothes that pertained to women. A little research and thought solved the problem. Studying the history of the Old Testament, I became aware that this law was God's way of protecting His people from the idolatry of the peoples surrounding them. Their fertility cults involved ritual cross-dressing and sexual relations with temple prostitutes (often cross-dressed men) as a means of worshipping the goddess Astarte.

I seriously doubt many cross-dress for that purpose today. Also, if we are still living under that law, we should be stoning unruly sons, observing various dietary restrictions, and following rituals related to "uncleanness." I realized that it was judgmental people who were hurling that verse at cross-dressers, trying to make them feel guilty for being who they are. Fortified by the lesson of the Honor Society picnic, it was easy for me to decide that I was not going to fall into that Slough of Despond. If people could not accept my feminine expression, I realized that it was they, not I, who had the problem. I understood that cross-dressing itself had no moral value, plus or minus. It was what I did with it that counted. So I resolved that I would use it for good, to replace despair with hope, ignorance with knowledge, judgment with love.

DECADE 6 (YEARS 51–60): TRI-ESS IS MY VINEYARD

At last I was in control of my life! While I no longer needed the clothes to express my femininity, I continued to cross-dress because I enjoyed the creative opportunities it provided. Yet so many others were suffering in isolation and fear! Once at an early Holiday En Femme, I watched horrified as a sister who had driven seven hundred miles entered the hotel, blurted out, "I can't do this!" and drove home. Many were afraid even to tell their spouses. Nor was the fear confined to cross-dressers. When I went to my first Holiday in New Orleans, my wife preferred to stay home to take my phone call from the Podunk Parish Jail. In Tri-Ess, I experienced the special relationship that is sisterhood. Attending my first Tri-Ess chapter meeting was harrowing. The meeting was in a beach house, and we had to cross on a ferry to get there. It was a real fishbowl atmosphere. With nothing else to do, people looked around at the scenery, and at each other. Having survived the crossing, we soon arrived at the meeting site. Now indecision set in. What kinds of people were going to be there? Was I really ready? At this point, my feminine presentation was far from developed. Would my sisters accept me? We must have driven around the place ten times before I got up the courage to go in. I need not have worried. My arrival was greeted with cries of welcome. Seeing I was uncomfortable with my hair in my eyes, a sister kindly pinned it back, all the while giving me tips on hair care and complimenting me on my outfit. What a wonderful feeling to know I belonged! I resolved to share that feeling with others.

Over the next two years I developed a vision for Tri-Ess as a cross-dresser- and family-focused organization, and circumstances made it possible for me to help others. In 1987 the avalanche of inquiries generated by the *Donahue Show*, and a hit-and-run driver, combined to make it impossible for Carol Beecroft to continue to operate Tri-Ess essentially by herself. She reached out for help from the membership, and I volunteered. The following year, Tri-Ess began to evolve toward a team approach, and I articulated the sixfold vision that was to become the core philosophy of Tri-Ess. The organization was to promote full personality expression, in both its masculine and feminine characteristics; integration of masculine and feminine traits; balance between masculine and feminine; education of cross-dressers and their families toward self-acceptance; education of society toward acceptance of cross-dressers; and relationship building in the context of cross-dressing. Cross-dressing with dignity and decency would be the hallmark of Tri-Ess. Frances made the commitment with me to devote our lives to making our world a better place for cross-dressers and their families, and to freeing them from guilt, shame, and fear. For the last fifteen years, we have worked as a team to that end.

Every year, we answer about five hundred inquiries. Many are from people who are so afraid that they include only the barest request for information and do not supply a location, or even a name. Our message to them is that they are not alone, and they can make many new friends among others like themselves. A few are so depressed that they are suicidal. For these, we supply peer support and refer them to knowledgeable professionals for the help they need. For those who feel ready to share with their wives or children, we provide advice based on our collective experience. There is nothing more fulfilling than seeing a sister once in need achieve inner peace and reach out to extend that peace to others.

Successful peer support requires a nurturing environment. That is why we enjoy developing local chapters. Working with a leader committed to bringing Tri-Ess support services to her area, we supply chapter formation kits, point out the reefs and shoals, share ideas for programs, teach leaders how to bring people together, and refer constantly to the lessons of history. Visiting our chapters and witnessing their accomplishments reassures us that our work is worthwhile.

In our work with Tri-Ess, Frances and I are partners in every sense of the word. She edits the *Mirror*, Tri-Ess's quarterly journal, whose message is victory over guilt and shame. We teach that there is no need to try to fool the public into believing we have two X chromosomes, and that "passing" is for footballs, counterfeit money, and bad bridge hands. So many cross-dressers have religious hang-ups, fostered by judgmental people telling them where they are going to spend eternity because of the clothes they wear. Having studied the Scriptures, we can put these fears to rest by sharing the love God has toward all His creatures, whoever they are.

For many years, wives were a footnote on the Genderland page. They could be seen but preferably not heard. Yet so many were struggling desperately to understand and accept the men they loved. Moved by their suffering, we brought them into Tri-Ess as full members and took the firestorm of criticism as it came. Soon wives were active at all levels of Tri-Ess, from the national leadership to the local chapters. At transgender conventions, programs for them were an afterthought, if they existed at all. After much discussion, we decided to establish for wives and couples a convention of their own, where they could deal with cross-dressing-related issues in a totally nonthreatening atmosphere. And so was born the highly successful Spouses' and Partners' International Conference for Education (SPICE). Over the years, we have seen relationships renewed and strengthened, and the light of hope rekindled in many lives. With our Tri-Ess colleagues, we are now approaching the latest frontier: establishing support for parents and children of cross-dressers. There is so much yet to be done, but we hope we are leaving the promise of brighter days to those who will work in this vineyard in the years ahead.

Today I can look back with happiness and contentment. Frances and I still share a beautiful love that has grown with each of its thirty-six years. Our sons are now fine young men. One is going into the healing professions, and the other is defending his country. I am still studying at the old university of life, gleaning nuggets of wisdom that will make me a better person, more worthy to help the sisters who come seeking a sisterly hand. While I have made many mistakes in life, I can say with St. Paul, "By the grace of God, I am who I am, and His grace in me has not been fruitless."

I LEAD TWO LIVES

Jennifer Stevens

I live my life in two genders. On one coast of the United States, I live as a man. On the other coast, I live as a woman. In many ways, I have the best of both worlds.

From childhood (as a boy) until my late forties, I had spent much of my waking time thinking about women. I loved girls and women, in any and every form. I loved the way they looked, the way they acted, the way they talked, moved, and especially the way they dressed. But my love of the feminine was different from that of the average heterosexual young man. I felt, and still feel, that I *am* a woman and a man.

There is now a name for people like me. I am *transgendered*. I have the physical characteristics of one gender but the inner feelings and psyche (much of the time) of the other gender. At various times in my life (and, I suspect, in the life of most transgendered people) I have been confused, both in my own mind and by observers, with being a transvestite (those who like to wear the clothes of the other gender) or a transsexual (those who have a wish to physically change their bodies). In some ways perhaps I have characteristics of both, but in more important ways, I am neither.

As far back as I can remember, I wanted to dress like a girl, act like a girl, *be* a girl. As a young boy I was actually jealous of girls. I would watch them at play and wish that I, too, could be as imaginative as to "play house" and "play nurse." As puberty began to manifest itself in my male body, my erotic fantasies featured me dressed as a girl. Sexual arousal came from viewing girls or women in many forms, then "projecting" myself into their bodies. Raids on my mother's closets became common-place. Indeed, as I grew older, I would actually sit on the floor of my mother's closet and put my head up her long dresses, content merely to experience (as closely as I could) the feeling of "being a woman."

I knew that behavior like this would be considered "sissy" by my friends. If they knew, they would make fun of me, probably branding me with the ever-popular homophobia term of the day, a *fruit*. There was no one I could talk to, for I believed I was the only person who felt that way. Although on occasion I would dress up in front of some of my childhood friends, the only relief I could get from the sexual tensions I was experiencing was to self-pleasure myself while wearing my mother's clothes.

In order to prove to the world, and to myself, that I was really not feminine, that there was nothing abnormal about me, I worked hard at becoming the virile person that society expected. Tall, naturally athletic, and encouraged by loving, supportive parents, I became a nationally recognized high school and college athlete, earning an athletic scholarship to a major university.

I believed it was expected of me to be a high school "stud," and I cut a swathe through the young ladies. From the physical standpoint, it never occurred to me that I might be anything but a normal, testosterone-driven young man. Yet, even in the midst of "proving I was a man," my daydreams, my fantasies, were always those of dressing, living, being a girl.

In college I continued to try to show the world that I was an all-American boy. I wanted to prove to the world (and to myself) that I was not abnormal. I craved the physical and emotional sensations involved in lovemaking and tried to exercise my newfound "talent" at every opportunity. Yet in those late teenage, early twenties years, my thoughts, dreams, and erotic desires centered on the feminine. I continued to fantasize about how women dressed, their makeup, their deportment. I would invariably picture myself in women's clothes.

Homosexuality had always been intriguing to me, but until almost a college graduate, I did not experiment in gay activity. In my senior year, one of my professors, in a gentle, caring way, introduced me to the gay world. The idea of making love to another man was fascinating, strangely enchanting. Yet having sex with another man made me feel guilty. The only way I could successfully perform was to envision myself as a woman making love to her man. Indeed, now in later life, after I became adept in actually living as a woman, I continue to picture myself as a woman when I am making love to a man.

All of the "normal" life span activities of an adult male (marriage, military service, and fatherhood) followed, and I have felt at least partially fulfilled, having done my "duties" as a man. Yet throughout my thirties and forties, my feminine fantasies grew more vivid. Eventually, at every opportunity (which seemed to come more and more often), I would dress in women's clothes, associate with others of the same persuasion, and even find sexual partners (both male and female) who would tolerate my dual nature. It took all these years for me to understand myself, to come to grips with the guilt that society places on those who don't fit the norm.

THE STRUGGLE FOR SELF

Some twenty years ago, I finally came face-to-face with the fact that I was unhappy *not* being able to express my femininity in other than an occasional weekend gathering of like-minded individuals. I discovered that when I could let the "woman within" escape her cage, I felt like an entirely different person. I felt free, complete, and relaxed. A week in the feminine persona turned me from a type A, hard-charging businessperson into a more gentle, loving, and, I like to think, more likable individual. The transition would last a few days or a week, but eventually I would revert back to my hard-charging male "self." The respite from him, provided by her, would soon wear off because of the day-to-day practical considerations of running a business (plus other social commitments) and having to do so appearing as male. I came to view my male clothing as "drag."

Even until today, there is a connection between my lifestyle and my health. My blood pressure, always a good indicator of health for me, goes down when I am living as a woman, back up when I go into the male mode. A failing marriage, frustrations in business causing a continuously heavy workload, and additional personal stress factors confronted me with my own vulnerability. The unhappiness in my life was amplified by what I came to understand later as a good old-fashioned case of depression.

On my fiftieth birthday I awakened to the fact that I was not spending enough time doing what I loved to do most: live as a woman. Perhaps a realization of my own mortality brought my life into focus. Somehow, for the first time, I understood that time was rapidly passing by, that to be happy in life I had to control my own destiny. In that deeply introspective moment, I made the decision that I would spend the rest of my life trying to find and express the woman within.

Luckily, my financial status allowed me to get professional help, and my education about transitioning into "womanhood" began. It took three tries before I found a psychologist who understood what is now called gender dysphoria. I always felt too embarrassed to tell my story to "another man," so I could never go to a male therapist. My new female therapist helped me come to grips with the fact that I was one of the lucky (or unlucky, depending on your point of view) people in the world who are transgendered. She and I agreed that attempting to subvert or "cure" my transgenderism would be impossible, akin to trying to dissuade a gay man or a lesbian from his or her sexual identity.

She knew I was blessed with the opportunity to travel extensively, to have relatively long periods of time for myself, and had the wherewithal to spend money on my search for gender tranquility. She wisely suggested that I try to find a balance in my life by living in two genders. I felt that I had been given permission to become closer to the person I felt I was. I experienced a tremendous sense of relief because at last I had a potential answer to my dilemma. I would get the best help I could find and afford to "become" closer to the woman I had always felt myself to be but, for business and family reasons, not have sexual reassignment (genital reconstruction) surgery. In my late fifties, the surgery, although still a prerogative, would have been more of a commitment to one gender than the other. I simply did not feel, and still don't, that what is between one's legs determines one's gender. I simply feel that the surgery is not necessary for my peace of mind. Thus I started on my move to live as a woman and as a man. The quest continues until now, with no end in sight.

THE TRANSITION

Over six feet tall and reasonably well built as a man, I, and those I would eventually enroll to help me, had our work cut out for us. It was and is essential to my peace of mind to be able to prove myself as someone clearly "belonging to" the gender represented. In retrospect, I didn't fully understand how I must have looked to the outside world in those early days of transitioning (perhaps it didn't matter). To me, there was and still is an inner glow when Ashe takes over.

With the help of friends, and with my own determination that nothing would stop me from becoming who I felt myself to be, I eventually developed the appearance of a reasonably attractive middle-aged woman. The first major step toward feminizing myself began with the removal of my beard and other bodily hair. Only those who are hugely motivated would go through complete electrolysis. The procedure is expensive, time consuming, and, yes, painful. But for a person undergoing transition from male to female, electrolysis is the only acceptable answer to a lifetime of five o'clock shadows. Just a few years ago laser hair removal was in its infancy, so my electrolysis was composed of more than fifteen sessions of pain, eight to ten hours per session. The key word for any genetic male who goes through complete electrolysis is *commitment*. An extensive wardrobe, initially partially chosen by women friends who better understood how to drape this size 22 frame, has gradually been built up over the years.

Voice lessons made a huge difference. A professional voice teacher taught me the values of timbre, pitch, and feminine vocabulary. For many transitioning male-to-females, voice is a major problem. Luckily, I've been able to develop a somewhat husky but apparently very acceptable speech capability. Friends tell me that my inner feelings and expression of my femininity also have a lot to do with the image I portray through my voice and my overall presentation as a woman. Perhaps they are right, but having lived so long in both genders, my masculinity and femininity is simply part of my nature, something I take for granted.

For a period of about six months, I took daily doses of estrogen. The psychological effects were noticeable almost immediately, with mood swings much more apparent (at least to me). I found it much more difficult to concentrate on my business dealings, perhaps because I was so aware of the developments going on within my body. But when my breasts began to grow, and it became obvious that I would either have to change my lifestyle to totally feminine or live my masculine life constantly hiding the upper part of my body, I stopped the hormones. So far as I can tell, there have been no ill effects on me, psychological or physical.

In the final analysis, however, what helped me most in transitioning was and is the fact that *this* is *who I am*. When I fully understood that I was *not* a man in a dress, but a woman with a deformity (male genitals), at least when I am in the feminine gender role, I no longer had any trouble "passing" as a woman. Yet there is no "passing"; there is complete acceptance of me in my feminine gender role because I am so comfortable with just being myself. I never think of myself as anything but the woman (or man) I appear to be.

Having lived for so many years both as a woman and as a man, I seldom, if ever, confuse the two in my deportment. It is difficult to claim that one "thinks like a woman" or "thinks like a man." No one knows how a woman or a man thinks. I do know, however, that as schizophrenic as it may sound, I conduct myself as two separate persons. One is more feminine than the other, one more masculine, but both have a mixture of gender characteristics that merge into a complete person.

My sexual identity is strictly heterosexual. As a woman, I like men. I've had lovers over the years (one relationship lasting for over fifteen years), but it is difficult without having had sexual reassignment surgery to find a man who can overlook my *handicap*. But I enjoy flirting, dancing, touching, and the other means of expressing my femininity. I'll have to live with that because of the lifestyle choice I have made. When I am living as the male person, my sexual drive has disappeared. I am no longer sexually attracted to women. This may partially be due to my age or to other physical limitations. Perhaps it is that way because of my latter-years move more toward the feminine side of my nature. I'll probably never know, nor do I care.

Now my life evolves around a working existence on both coasts. Many know me only as a man. Others know me only as a woman. A few know me in both genders, but for a variety of business-oriented reasons I keep the identities apart. And I must admit there is a certain amount of self-satisfaction, on one coast or the other, in thinking to myself: "If they only knew . . ."

I sometimes wish I could live peacefully and constantly "in" one or the other of the genders. But which of the genders would I want to give up, if I did have a choice? Upon reflection, I realize that we all live with limitations of one sort or another. Then I begin to appreciate the fact that, as a transgendered person, I truly am blessed to have the best of all worlds.

REPORTORIAL INSTINCTS

My background as a writer, a reporter, and an amateur but well-read psychologist has held me in good stead in my trip "into" (and remaining "in") both genders. Most people I know wouldn't envy my experience. For me, however, the trip through gender dysphoria (to use the latest PC definition) has been intriguing, fascinating, fun, and, most of all, a learning experience. I now believe wholeheartedly the old maxim that you must walk in a person's shoes before you understand him or her. Having walked in both, I have been able to understand each gender from a unique perspective.

The discoveries I have made along the way are probably the most flagrant violations of the old Voltaire saying, "All generalizations are false, including this one." But not to share what I have seen (and concluded) would be a waste of, well, a lot of seeing and concluding. As I have said, from earliest memory, I had always felt that I was as much a girl (woman) as I was a boy (man). Yet, until middle age, I was never able to fully express the feminine side of my psyche. Why did I wait so long? I knew, of course, that I was genetically a male. All I had to do was look down. I received constant validations of my own maleness. The word *disloyal* comes to mind. When I was reminded in so many ways that I was male, yet had yearnings for the feminine, the guilt of not being loyal to my genetic sex added to my psychological discomfort. My feminine self kept being pushed back when my masculine self kept getting pats on the head for his physical and social accomplishments. And yet in the back of my mind was the constant thought that I wanted, *needed*, to be something more. That constant thought over the years became a stronger discomfort than the betrayal of my assigned gender.

"If only" became my mantra. "If only I could sometimes dress as a woman." "If only I could have my own feminine wardrobe." "If only I could go out in public." "If only I could pass as a woman in public." Finally, "If only I could actually *live* as a woman." Those are but a few of the "if only" steps I took in my odyssey toward the "other" gender. As I took each step on my journey, I was only partially satisfied with my progress. "Pushing the envelope" toward more complete transitional experiences became the norm.

Now, after some years of successful living as a woman, I could, or can, go no further in my journey toward womanhood, other than by having genital reconstruction surgery (GRS). I have examined this issue deeply and have concluded that GRS is a step I neither need nor want. I would never criticize those transgendered individuals who elect to have GRS. I have friends who are completely happy in their physical transformation. On the other hand, I have a number of postoperative friends who are now questioning why they had the surgical procedure. For me, as opposed to what I used to feel as I looked down at my body, I now know that what is between my legs in no way determines who I am.

Now, rather than spend much of my waking hours learning or experiencing "how to be a woman," I face each day with the assurance that I am, indeed (at least in physical appearance and deportment), every bit as much of a woman as I could ask. I accept myself that way, and so does the world. When I am living as a woman, it is satisfying to be so sure of my gender that I no longer need to even think about that facet of my life. More of my time is spent as a man, but over the years I have learned to live "in the moment," not dwelling on the "other" gender role life.

These days the harsh light of reality shines, forcing me to ask that age-old question, whither? The years spent "becoming" now fade. The years ahead call for "being" a much different proposition. The time so taken up with learning experiences for "him" now becomes time that needs to be filled with meaningful, productive, and enjoyable activities for "her." She needs to be fulfilled, as a person and as a woman. This includes socializing with other women, contributing to society in a variety of ways, and otherwise leading an active retired woman's life. And that, I suspect, as many have found out before me, is the hardest part of it all.

CONCLUSION

If there is one overall lesson I've learned throughout my odyssey, it is that gender is a social construct. Behavior attributed to the genders has been constructed over the eons, to the point where certain conducts of demeanor "belong" to particular sexes. The question of how much of this behavior is genetic and how much is culturally developed remains open. At birth, or shortly thereafter, we begin to become conditioned to comport ourselves as do most others of our anatomical sex. Most of us go along with what society expects of us as a person of the sex into which we were born (males to masculine behavior, females to feminine gender behavior). But choice still exists for those of us who don't wish to, or cannot, conform to the indicated gender model. We still have the ability to behave otherwise. It is only when we realize that this choice of gender behavior exists that we understand just how gender brainwashed we have become.

Only within the past few years have psychologists understood that these gender constructs have created unrealistic expectations for many of us. Frustration, confusion, personal insecurity, a host of psychological problems, those are but a few of the manifestations of these artificially constructed gender expectations.

It was when I could answer the statement (boys are not supposed to act like that) with my own question, "Where is it written?" that I became a whole person. In the process I was, and am, able to construct my own gender expression.

AN ODYSSEY
IN QUEST OF SELF

Laura Quigley

Seven years ago, as a father of three and a tenured professor at a prestigious business school, after four decades of ambivalence, fear, and confusion, I made the decision to become a woman, knowing that, once the deed was done, I could never return to my former life again. This is the story of that odyssey and what I went through to arrive at such a decision, its impact on my life, and my thoughts on the reasons for my desire to be a woman.

Two circumstances impeded my ability to find clarity and understanding about my gender preference. One was my self-doubt and my failure to trust my feelings. And the other, the pressures to conform to what was expected from a male child during the period in which I grew up, monopolized my thinking in my quest for acceptance and love. Plagued by doubt and confusion over whether the desires I felt were possibly self-delusions, I refused to entertain the possibility that they were anything other than fantasies. During the more than four decades that they permeated my thoughts, I told no one, sought no help, and dressed secretly as a woman. Only after making the irrevocable decision to live my life as a woman; announcing it to my children, friends, and to my employer; and undergoing genital reconstruction surgery (GRS) could I really know. Only after living a "normal" life as a woman could I know that my decision was the correct one. If it was not, there would be no return.

For over four decades I played out a life in contradiction to how I felt. I had no revelation, no sign, and no clarity for most of the years of being a terribly fragmented person never comfortable playing the male role expected of me. Gradually and fitfully the idea of becoming a woman began to assert itself with increasing intensity and frequency until it became a constant obsession. This is the story of how I made sense of this experience. I have tried to find the most fitting language to best describe my feelings, thought process, and behavior, within the context of the fear that I would be discovered, that I would lose my job and my friends. To this end I outline the critical periods to break through the confusion over my gender. As it became gradually more apparent to me that dressing and playing the role of a woman in public was an essential part of my self-expression, I endured the persistent and suffocating fear that I would be discovered.

SETTING THE SCENE: SEEKING EXPLANATION

But before I begin this odyssey—for that is what best depicts this process, a wandering, without a consciously understood direction—I need to say something about my mental activity. The mind, the complex organ that it is, often allows us only vague glimpses of what we are about, often at moments that catch us off guard, especially when the recognition of those thoughts is abhorrent or unthinkable. And, of course, if being in denial and distracted by school, college, marriage, and the military, as I was, I would interpret my fantasies about being a woman as some sort of sexual perversion to be denied or withstood. These fantasies were relentless and, despite my efforts to rationalize them as meaningless sexual thoughts, mushroomed as time went on. It seems likely that the very denial of their significance gave them even greater power. In discussing my thinking with a friend, it struck me that I had two opposing personae who were always present, and where one would take over and ignore the other. One was a being that, because of the fear, shame, and guilt of her desire to be female, could not allow herself to be acknowledged as a legitimate woman. Given the period in the formation of my identity and the taboo about understanding myself, she could only surface in dreams and spontaneous fantasies. Outwardly the behavior was reflected in cross-dressing, which allowed me to live surreptitiously with my thoughts. Over time the inner self became more and more powerfully assertive, and the ever-stronger desires to live out these fantasies brought me to take greater and greater risks in public. Through most of these years, even after coming into contact with other gender diverse people, I saw myself as very different from all of them.

When I was dressed and out in public, I felt myself a woman, not a man. I even saw transsexuals as strange and more masculine in their behavior. In effect I did not fit any description, even though outwardly I participated in parties, meetings, and went to bars.

In attempting to understand my unwillingness to entertain the possibility that I may indeed be a "transsexual," that is, someone who actually is a woman, and not just playing acting "for fun," I offer three explanations.

First, that such fantasies or desires to act out the part of a woman are auto-gyna-eroticism. I saw this behavior strictly as sexual expression, narcissistically making love to myself as if I were a woman. This went on for years. As I picture it, it was sexual aberration that was okay, because I rationalized that I was not hurting anyone. Of course, the levels of testosterone made such experiences easier. Yet the desire to act out being a woman in *public* was so powerful that I could not be satisfied with a closet erotic experience. However, the public experience was not about eroticism since if I had any sexual contact with men, it was as a woman, at least that is how I felt. It gave me satisfaction to be able to drive, visit stores, and go to movies, as if I were an actual woman, like all the other woman around me.

A second explanation was my ignorance of transsexualism in the era in that I began to express gender confusion, which was as early as 1942. Little or nothing was known about transsexualism until the Christine Jorgensen story hit the headlines in 1952. Jokes abounded in the media and among friends. The people I knew considered her a freak. It wasn't until a decade later that I was expressing my preferred-gender self, secret at night in the basement. I had not entertained the idea that it was anything else but an erotic game. I did not really come into contact with transsexuals until the 1970s, and I tended to dismiss them as bizarre and misguided individuals who had severe emotional difficulties. A healthy introduction to such a world would have probably come as the result of being in the care of a knowing therapist or having a knowledgeable friend who could have provided a helpful direction or understanding. It turned out, that is exactly what happened when I finally made my decision in 1997.

The third explanation was my concern for living up to my responsibilities as a father and a husband. This served to restrain the frightening thought that I was really a woman after all. It is clear to me now that I sought the belonging and security of family. This became a priority, and anything that might jeopardize it could not be seriously considered. I wanted to become part of my future wife's family and what appeared to be the community of Estonians in America. I thought they had something very special, a sense of loyalty to each other and caring. My parents-in-law were entirely conventional, living the values and traditions of prewar Estonia, a bourgeois nationalistic culture that rigidly circumscribed individual and group behavior. One's social role was very narrow, indeed, and to be accepted by them and my wife, I was committed to learning the Estonian language, bringing up my children according to Estonian traditions. My priority was to have the security of a family that honored me and encouraged me to be a professional person. It was completely untenable for me to even contemplate anything more than playing the game that I had adopted, even perfected. I planned my secret life of dressing days and weeks, in advance, and for the rest lived the public life of a quasi-Estonian husband. I was playacting in both realms. I had no clue as to who I was. This way of behaving and thinking spanned more than thirty years. I was, to put it simply, in full denial of who I had become. I was acting out a part, a role that I had learned from social experiences in my family, school, and in social encounters. I became rather good at it. No one suspected, or so I thought. Inwardly I was hurting, in constant fear and torment. I played the role outwardly, but it was not comfortable for me. And I envied almost every woman I knew, because she did not have to act as a man in a man's world, which I saw as one of pissing contests, backslapping, bragging of sexual conquests, and vicious and humiliating (at least for me) taunting games.

And my desire to play the female was escalating. It became more frequent; the thoughts and the planning would consume much of my mental life. I was too ashamed to look at it any deeper, although part of me wanted to shout it from the hilltop. In my desperation to reveal it, I did risk divulging it to an Estonian couple once at a Christmas party, and a few evening later I came unannounced to their home to get their reaction. They never violated that trust.

What I have been able to do in recent months is to return to those periods in my life and try to recall my thoughts and feelings, and understand how they relate to my desire to be a woman. I have chosen several scenarios in my life that stand out. Let me now briefly outline the periods in which my awareness and thinking about my identity evolved.

DECADE 2 (1940–1951): BOYHOOD YEARS

One may ask why it took more than four decades to make the decision to become a woman. My condition as a male has to be understood within the context of the age in which I grew up. A life of denial began from the moment I put on my mother's dress and shoes at the age of nine. The feelings and urges that periodically burst forth terrified me. Putting on my mother's clothes was both exciting and frightening. I was always in fear of my mother, who had a propensity for inflicting bizarre and humiliating punishments on me. I was never able to anticipate or understand her reasons. I put her clothes away quickly and carefully lest she detect any change in their location with her "evil eye" (the one she convinced me that she watched my every move with). I now understand that it was experiences with my mother (I was not allowed to call her Mom or Mommy) and her insistence on obedience and control that conditioned me to be fearful. Fear has an enormous power to blot out anything that competes with it. The women teachers in grammar school also placed a premium on control, obedience, and intimidation. They were steeped in intimidation and humiliation lest any student dare any expression of independence. Boys were "snails and puppy dog tails," they proclaimed, while the girls were "spice and everything nice."

At this writing, it is still not altogether clear the extent of my mother's influence on my desire to be a female. I always knew somehow that she wanted a daughter and that her favorite picture of me at age two showed no evidence of gender. During the years following my parents' divorce (I was about two or three), I lived continuously with her, even when she lived with my aunt. I slept with her until I was seven, and she often remarked how warm my body was and how it kept her warm. It was a strange relationship: on one hand, I was convinced that she wanted a daughter and she treated me as if I was an extension of her personality. On the other hand, she was exceptionally cruel in devising bizarre punishments for minor mistakes. It is almost as if she resented the responsibility of brining up a boy.

She never made any effort to feminize me that I can recall. That I had no male role model may have been a much larger factor in my inability to understand how boys behave. My father would periodically take me for weekends and brief periods during the summer, but as a baker he worked nights and slept days so his rigid religious wife, Eleanor, would care for me during the day until he came home. My mother remarried when I was seven to a man, Bob, who avowedly disliked children. When he married my mother, I came with the territory. I was referred to, not affectionately, as "the kid" in my presence. Over the years I sought attention from him, but he showed little interest except to brag about his baseball-playing prowess in sandlot baseball. My image of him was as a whiner, complainer, unhappy with his job, inveterate gambler (he lost many thousands of dollars of his union's funds on the horses when he was treasurer), who gave me little reason to view him as a positive male or parental model. It was not until college that I began to admire my male professors, but never beyond their academic ability.

It seemed that I faced similar rambunctious behavior with boys my age whenever I would stray from the safety of my immediate neighborhood. I played only with boys several years younger for reasons that were not clear to me at the time. I shunned older boys because I feared them as being too aggressive. In the Cub Scouts, just prior to the safety of the organized meetings, the boys would play "capture the flag," which was for me a violent and scary practice that I avoided. One summer my parents enrolled me in a Boy Scout camp in the Boulder Creek area (near Santa Cruz) where for one month I lived a fairly solitary life after a round or two of name-calling and chastisement. I, of course, had no idea that life could be any different than the plight I faced as a boy. As long as the scout period was part of a carefully organized set of rules and tasks with an adult leader, such as getting merit badges or whatever, I was able to function well. Always, I chose the safe courses, joining a boys' chorus singing Christmas carols. I couldn't visualize any other options at the time.

Ultimately, the scouting venture ended abruptly when, after I got the courage to report that there was no toilet paper in Little Egypt—the outside tent toilet that I surreptitiously visited when there was no one else there—to the scout master, I was told (in front of the others no less!), "Hey kid, don't you know how to use your finger?" Exit scouting, permanently! Boyhood years were about avoidance and keeping everything inside. It never occurred to me that anything could be different. All the teachers were women, mostly cold, humorless spinsters who I was convinced were religiously anti-boy. From grammar school, through high school, already from the age of seven, I would look across the room in the first grade and envy the girls with their pink and blue dresses and curls, clean, sweet, and protected from the teacher's scorn and punishment. Oh, how I wish I could have escaped the struggle that awaited me at recess when I was released into the playground and the potential bullying. I unconsciously knew that I could neither be one of the girls nor one of the boys. Hence, I began a life of isolation from school activities, sports, and attempts at belonging. There was no group for me to belong to.

When my parents moved to the southern boundaries of San Francisco, I transferred from a predominately intellectual Jewish prep school environment to a principally blue-collar high school. In high school, I tried to escape the capricious male horseplay by joining the ROTC to avoid taking open showers with other boys after gym class. Boys who enrolled in ROTC were considered "fairies" and were often ridiculed by the gym crowd. Taunted to fight boy after boy, I finally decided to enroll in gym class and take my chances. Albeit unconsciously, I decided on a strategy of observing how boys behaved and copied their gestures, stories, and language in order to fit in. I discovered that by joining the track and cross-country team I could avoid physical contact. Although I knew somehow that I was different, I considered myself one of them. After all, was there a choice? This plan enabled me to avoid harassment, but I also found myself in the untenable position of having to go to the boys' locker room. Rather than take showers, I would hide behind the locker door when everyone was gone and wear my sweat-soaked clothes to class.

My efforts to fit in with other boys did pose problems. The topics of conversations were inevitably girls, sports, and cars. As I learned the entrance fee to belonging to the boys' group (I tried several) depended upon making up stories about how much I got from a girl on a date, I learned to fabricate stories piecing together bits and parts from listening to various conquests, or scoring. I thought I had pulled it off quite well until I recently discovered from my high school friend John, whom I told about myself two years ago, that the boys all thought I was gay. I did have a girlfriend, though, for a short time until her parents abruptly ended it for reasons that I was not able to figure out. She was the first woman whose demeanor affected my image of what a woman was other than my mother. Finally, I was able to identify with other boys who were less keen on female conquests. This was far safer for me. I do recall watching the girls playing basketball outside in their blue bloomers and fleeting fantasies had me playing along with them.

DECADE 3 (1951–1960): THE COLLEGE YEARS

College was a wonderful respite from all this. I could avoid the usual physical education courses by substituting ballroom dancing classes for them. There was no recess, sports were optional, and survival depended on getting passing grades. College was at first an escape to avoid being drafted and going to Korea. Then I began to discover that college was enjoyable. Free from the restricting atmosphere of school for the first time, I was able to take courses of my choice (to an extent) and realized that learning gave meaning to my life. The college's policy of accepting all graduates of the city's high schools without entrance examinations or requiring tuition payments was a timely opportunity. My parents refused to provide any financial help, and, in fact, at the end of my freshmen year, my mother confronted me one morning to demand that I pay her for room and board. I don't know whether it was the harsh way she approached me or the principle of paying them for board and room, but I decided to leave home immediately that same day. I packed all my belongings into my old Plymouth and went to class. I slept in the car on the hill above the college that night. The next day I found a boarding house and never returned home again. It was not the first run-in I had with her and my stepfather, but, as I saw it, it was a climax in my quest for becoming independent. I never returned except to visit or stay weekends when I was in the army. To the day she died, she never brought up the issue. In fact, my mother, in all the years I knew her, never expressed any regrets or mistakes and never talked about our differences. She always held others responsible for any arguments or problems. She burned all her bridges behind her throughout her life and almost succeeded with me.

I later found a boarding house near Nanny's Design Gallery, where I worked as a shipping clerk, and was able to survive financially. Two years later, after my matriculation, I moved to Berkeley and lived in a co-op for students. I cannot explain why I had no inclination during these years to dress or even fantasize about being a woman. It may have been denial or perhaps the distractions of going to college and working. It was a safer world for the student. The students I knew were not the macho types I had been exposed to in grammar and high school. They came from families who supported their children's education. My gay roommate, who revealed that he was in love with me, pursued me frequently even though I told him that I was straight. I was not appalled by his behavior. I just was not interested in sex with a man. Many years later I located him living in Oakland. He was married, although secretly having affairs with men from time to time. When I revealed to him my own "secret" life, he disclosed it to his wife, who forbade him ever to see me again.

THE MILITARY, LANGUAGE SCHOOL, AND MARRIAGE

Immediately after graduating from college in 1955, my life changed abruptly, and I gradually became acquainted with my feminine alter ego. Since college, among other things, had served as a deferment from the military, I knew that within a few months of graduation I would be drafted into the army, probably into the infantry. The thought of entering the infantry and the close contact with other men was untenable. I discovered that if I enlisted I could choose my own branch of the army. I chose the Army Security Agency (ASA) without knowing very much about it. Somehow I got through basic training at Fort Ord, California, finding various devious ways of avoiding contact with other soldiers. I would only take showers after lights were out; I hid under the bed with blankets drawn down to the floor, and I spent weekends in San Francisco or Berkeley with or without a pass. The physical parts of crawling on the ground in the muck, being teargassed, shooting a rifle, and all the other military shenanigans was less of a problem than life in the barracks with the men.

After basic training I was posted to Fort Devens, Massachusetts, the home of the ASA. There I discovered that I had not yet recovered from the mononucleosis I had contracted while at Fort Ord. I was so weak and demoralized by having a heavy schedule of KP and guard duty that I collapsed. This was a most fortuitous development, for the military physician mandated that I had to be on "light duty" for the duration. This meant that instead of KP and guard duty I worked in an office for the three months. It also provided me time to travel to Boston, where one afternoon on a very cold and wet day I met Kirsti at the International Institute of Boston where she worked as a social worker. This was January 1956. We married a little more than a year later when I graduated from the Army Language School in Monterey, California. I never realized at that time that I had any interest or concerns other than to be a good husband and part of her Estonian family. Shortly after our marriage, I was transferred to Fort Holabird (Baltimore) for training as an interrogator of prisoners of war. I became interested in her clothes and thus began a long and gradual process of decorating myself in the image of a woman. I had little opportunity to continue this practice in Germany during the succeeding year, for we were living together in a single room and had little time alone. Moreover, our first child was born during this period.

DECADE 3 AND THE YEARS OF EXPERIMENTATION (1958–1974)

As a twenty-five-year-old male, I was horribly ignorant about how I should conduct myself as a father or a husband. The role I assumed living with Kirsti's parents was as a student going to graduate school. Kirsti and her father assumed all the important responsibilities, while I focused essentially on going to school. I found myself in the downstairs study alone with my books and my fleeting thoughts about dressing up. I would purloin dresses from the Goodwill and hide behind walls seeing if I could really make these garments fit. Later, after I took my first teaching job in a small New Hampshire town, thirty miles from Kirsti's parents' apartment, I would squirrel selections of women's clothing and prance around the farm where we lived. It was exciting to think of myself as a woman. I was careful to transform myself back in time for her return from work in Concord. This practice became more and more frequent throughout the two years we lived there.

After we moved to Massachusetts, I got a job teaching in a suburban high school, and my forays into womanhood became more frequent. I would seclude myself in a basement storage room late in the evenings and venture out into the neighborhood. On the weekends I found excuses not to accompany Kirsti and the children to New Hampshire to visit her parents so that I could stay home and dress. It became my obsession. I plotted the times when I could be alone to dress up and go out to "transvestite" bars or events.

I constantly sought ways to transform myself into as attractive a woman as possible. I experimented with makeup, foam rubber padding, and even found a way to make latex silicone breast forms. I wanted to appear as authentic as I could. I was not interested in camp or drag. In the years when I was at home writing my dissertation, I would venture out in the car dressed and even pick up hitchhikers to perfect my poise and voice. It was a source of tremendous excitement and satisfaction to be able to bring it off. My greatest fear was that the police for some reason would stop me, and I would have to reveal my identity. But these fears were no match for my appetite for appearing and behaving as a credible woman. It was a risky business to be sure. The fear of being caught remained with me constantly. Still, I continued to dress and present myself in public as a woman. I never thought that perhaps it was more than a fantasy to be fulfilled, although I continually plotted my moments when I could live as long as possible as a woman. When I knew I was going to travel to Chicago for a professional political science convention, I mailed my woman's clothing weeks in advance to the hotel at which I was going to stay. At home, after everyone was in bed, I would dress up in the basement and go out for walks. During the day, while I was supposed to be writing my dissertation, I would dress up and go out shopping while Kirsti was at work, always careful to return home before my children came home from school.

DECADE 4 (1961–1970):
MARRIED AND PROFESSIONAL LIFE

Although I now realize more clearly the nature of these conflicting feelings, at the time they never came into sharp focus. They all seemed to
be dead ends, convincing me that there was no other choice except to
continue living the two lives that I had created. I lived a fragmented life
without attempting to understand it. I somehow disavowed any responsibility to look deeper into my behavior. I sought no help, although at
various times I tried to "kick the habit," to outwardly acknowledge that
I needed help to deal with my behavior, which was totally unacceptable
with the context of the Estonian culture. I knew that if I revealed myself,
I would be totally unacceptable. After many years, and after Kirsti and I
had a couple of drinks, I screwed up the courage to confide in her about
my behavior. Either because of her own wishful thinking or because I
failed to convince her of my unwillingness to want to change, she concluded that I hated this aspect of my life and wanted to get rid of this
"habit," just as if I was an alcoholic or drug addict.

I was totally unconscious of the toll my "obsession" was taking on
relations with my wife and children. I was simply escaping, increasingly,
into a life and persona that they could never share or understand. At least
this is what I believed. When the secret came out, I was relieved that I
was not banned to Siberia. In fact, I launched into my feminine life in
earnest. We moved into a new home, and when I set aside a closet for
my femme clothes, she began to realize that I had no intention of ridding myself of this behavior. Often at night I would take my clothing to
the dirt basement five feet high, get dressed, put on makeup, and in the
dark slink my way to the car, closing the door softly and driving quietly
out of the driveway. Inevitably, our marriage, what there was of it, began
to unravel. I attempted to get her to understand, even tried to get her to
visit meetings of cross-dressers that I had learned about. She resisted it
all the way. She never agreed to participate in the meetings or even
investigate the phenomenon of cross-dressing, all of which I found
rather curious since she was a psychiatric social worker.

Finally, one morning while the children were at school, Kirsti asked
to meet Laura, my feminine self. I dressed up and presented myself to
her. She looked me over, smiled, and said, "Is there any place you would
like to go?" I suggested a movie and lunch.

During the entire afternoon, it seemed to me that we were never
married, that we were strangers meeting for the first time. She was pleas-

antly formal toward me, treating me as if I were just another female acquaintance. I had the feeling then and now that if our situation had been different, we might have developed a friendship. She never asked to see Laura again, never discussed her feelings with me, nor did she ask questions about my desires or plans. When it became clear to her that I relished my feminine life and wanted to express it ever more frequently, our relationship became increasingly strained. Now that the secret was out, I became ever more assertive, informing her that if she did not want to come with me, I would go out alone. When I did so, she became silently resentful.

We would bicker whenever I announced that I was going out. Finally, as the semester ended, I decided to move out of the family home into a suite in one of the dorms being vacated by the students. I lived there until the fall, when I found a basement apartment in Newton, exchanging housecleaning chores for rent. Shortly thereafter, Kirsti asked for a divorce. I signed over the house to her, agreed to pay child support, and began a new phase in my double life.

I continued to pass as a traditional male at the college as well as with my children and friends, while appearing as a woman with people in the transgendered community and progressively in my private life as well.

Although I had ceased being interested in having a relationship with my ex-wife, I did not want my new life away from the family home to undermine my relationship with my children. There is much I could write on this, but suffice it to say that I was thrown into great uncertainty about what I should do about my two older children. My eldest son was already near high school graduation and was free to visit me whenever he wanted. He did not do so. He was involved with his own life and friends, and I suspect that he harbored anger toward me, not only because I left, but also because I did not support him emotionally for many years. My daughter was just entering high school and was consumed with her boyfriend. In recent months I have learned how upset she was with me, her feelings of abandonment, not only for having left the home, but for not addressing her feelings and needs. As a result, I spent more time with my younger son, listening to him and attending to him far more effectively than I did his siblings. My later work in therapy and self-understanding made it clear to me that I had a large unfinished agenda with my daughter and eldest son, and in the past decade I have encouraged them to express their feelings with me frankly. Eventually, both my daughter and son moved in with me.

My immediate concern at the time was to spend as much time with my five-year-old son as possible, and for that I had to battle Kirsti continuously. Living separately was liberating after so many years in the closet. I no longer had to plan for the moments when I could dress and go out, but I was nonetheless determined to be a good single parent. Throughout my marriage I had surrendered my authority and responsibility as a parent and acquiesced to Kirsti's decisions. As I write this, it is clear that I was repeating the same role I lived with my mother. I had really abandoned my children. My stifled and denied feelings served to neglect them emotionally. I was not really present in terms of being sensitive to their feelings and emotional needs. As a parent I went through the motions, so to speak. The thoughts and fantasies of being a woman consumed much of my consciousness almost every day, sometimes almost every hour. Every morning in the shower my thoughts regularly gravitated to trying to figure how I could extricate myself from this dilemma. I failed to take full responsibility for myself as a father and did not intercede on behalf of my children in their conflicts with their mother based on my inner values. I am certain that my two oldest children still resent that behavior. Still, I have now tried if not to rectify those mistakes, certainly to be more present for them and seek them out. And this continues today.

It is a credit to Kirsti in retrospect that after the divorce she never used the "cross-dressing" card against me as I exercised my visitation rights. Perhaps she knew I would have fought very hard to be able to see my son. The two older children were free to visit whenever they wanted. By the time they came to live with me, although I did not know it, they had found out about my secret life, but they ever said anything to me.

I always knew that I needed to understand my behavior. I certainly wanted help, but, given the clandestineness of my nature and the guilt associated with it, I would not openly seek professional help. I was long convinced that they would say that I had an illness and have me go through frequent therapy to rid myself of this disgusting practice. Given that the psychiatric profession at the time considered being gay a mental illness and had classified my condition as gender dysphoric, I felt that I could come to no other conclusion.

After my divorce and the move from the family home I fortuitously came upon information about a Gestalt therapy–training program to be held in the summer. I signed up for the program, hoping that it would enable me to understand myself. I knew that help was important and that I was not in very good condition. As the program progressed, I realized how much pain I had been denying. I was not able to see my children every day, my mother officially disowned me, and I felt compelled to dress as a woman. Unfortunately, despite the Gestalt program and subsequent therapies I tried, I gained no clarity about who I was, why I was behaving the way I was, let alone what I should do about it. Therapists at that time knew little about "gender dysphoria" or how to treat it. Still my fellow trainees and therapists were quite understanding and accepting when I showed up later in the summer all dressed to the nines in my first venture into normal society. It was wonderful. I did come to the conclusion that I was not crazy, but I still did not know who I was or where I was headed. The year was 1975.

Living alone, I felt free to explore my womanness, traveling, doing workshops, going out to clubs, deliberately placing myself in harm's way with the police. One Thanksgiving Day in Newton, the upper-income area where I lived, I was out for an early evening stroll when two police cruisers stopped me and accused me of being a hooker. After demanding to see my driver's license, they informed me that being dressed as a woman was a violation of the law and they would have to take me in. Thinking quickly, I told them I was in therapy for transsexuals and was required to be dressed. They still would not let me continue my walk but insisted on driving me home. The next week the college newspaper had a thinly disguised reference to a "Dr. Larry in drag," but no one seemed to have caught it as referring to me. I continued, over the years, to have unhappy experiences with hostile and cruel policeman and even spent a night in jail on false charges. In that case, I hired a very competent gay lawyer and, after several court appearances, I was acquitted. It was these experiences that strengthened my resolve to find a way to be legally protected from such harassment. I needed legitimate identification as a woman. I can only empathize with the drag queens prior to the Stonewall riots. The gays could seclude themselves somehow, but the queens had high visibility and were not about to succumb to being harassed by homophobic cops. I learned a great deal about how dishonest some policemen are and how much they enjoyed ridiculing me.

The source of much of my anxiety was the discrepancy between what my official documents indicated and how I felt about myself. This played no small part in my determination to press on to become free from such fears and restraints on my behavior. I was determined to find a way to become "legitimate" at least in the eyes of the authorities. I was also fearful of undergoing surgery because I thought it would mean losing my job, perhaps even my children and my friends. It is instructive that of all the fears I entertained over the decades, not one came true. I wonder if I had known at that time twenty years ago that none of my worst fears would be realized whether I would have taken the surgical next step.

DECADE 5–6: THE FORMATIVE YEARS IN MY FEMME PERSONA

Even though I continued to keep my extracurricular activities secret, I was always on the lookout for sympathetic people who would be open to my female persona. During a party sponsored by a cross-dressing organization, I met a lesbian and her lover who became my lifelong friends. Throughout the years I knew them, they always regarded me as a woman, even during the times when I was dressed as a man. This was the acceptance that I was looking for. Their support over the years had a profound effect on my self-confidence as a woman.

What I did not realize until many years later was that, in seeking the affirmation of others and in living my fragmented life of self-denial, I would never be free of anxiety until I had come to accept and love myself more. Beneath my awareness, I always considered myself somehow illegitimate, that there was something wrong with me. I carried this shame with me constantly.

My father, in fact, some twenty years ago revealed to me that I was probably not even his child, that my mother had taken on lovers during their marriage, and that I had been actually given to a family with the option to adopt me. I learned from a cousin that my mother actually had attempted to abort me by falling down stairs, and then, when I was born, she somehow made it known that she wanted a girl. All this evidence was consistent with my parents' behavior toward me: my mother's impatience with me and absence of nurturing; my father's lack of interest in my life and his tacit acceptance of my mother's decision to (illegally) change my name to that of my stepfather. I recall now with sadness and guilt how much I blamed myself for his disinterest.

Throughout several decades, I faced continuously the mystery of whether how I felt about myself as a woman corresponded to how women felt about themselves. Was I a man who was just pretending to be a woman? How could I really know? Physical similarities and simply appearance alone would never satisfy my yearning. I lacked the experience of girlhood and female adolescence. I studied women intensely, while not mimicking them. I worked assiduously at perfecting my feminine presence to look as passable as I could in order to gain access to discussions and meetings of women. Given my looks, especially my height (five feet ten inches) and some male features, particularly my prominent nose, this was difficult and often frustrating. Later, after rhinoplasty, this became much easier. Fortunately, I did not have a prominent forehead and chin bones common to most men.

DECIDING AT LAST (1981–1990)

During a leave of absence spent in Denmark in 1987, I decided that I could no longer live two roles. Living and teaching in Denmark, I no longer feared the authorities. I could travel to Hamburg and Berlin to visit friends and be open to them (even traveling across the Danish frontier with a male passport). These were liberating experiences. Denmark has a well-deserved reputation of tolerance toward minorities of all kinds. I was able to confide in several colleagues and students during that period who respected my lifestyle and encouraged me to pursue my dream of becoming a woman. Except for the times I was teaching, I lived as a woman. Reluctant to return to the States, I feared that I could not feel safe there. It was shortly after my return that I decided to begin the regimen on the path to surgery. It was clear to me that I could not really return to the fragmented life I had before. For reasons that are still not clear to me, I did not feel conflicted anymore. There was no ambivalence. I would do whatever it took.

I launched into a self-taught program to find out everything I needed in respect to name change, hormone replacement treatments, the necessary procedure in preparation for surgery, and planning how to come out at the college I taught in. I was no longer worried about my children, who had resigned themselves to accept the strange ways of their parent. They were, however, certainly not ready to give me permission. I had to do what I had to do for me, and then hope for the best.

DECADE 7 (1991–2000): TOWARD MY FULL EXPRESSION AS A WOMAN

Never before had I experienced such clarity. Now in my sixties, it was easy to imagine how I would live my remaining years. Growing old as a man was completely out of the question. I met a Dutch "woman," Ari-anne, one night in a bar who was also in the process of making the same transition to womanhood. We became friends within a short time. Sharing our knowledge of transsexualism, surgery, and therapists, she and I ventured forth exploring our new personae. We traveled this road together for about a year until her visa had expired and she had to return to the Netherlands. I have since lost contact with her, but traveling the same road together for a short period was helpful to both of us. Now patience was called for. I focused on getting the proper medical and psychological help. There were always obstacles but also solutions. My health provider of many years had a clause in the contract that specifically disallowed any medical services or pharmaceutical insurance for "transsexuals." I discovered that simply informing the provider by phone of my name change solved the problem; I was officially classed as a woman.

With a court order for name change, I was able to get a driver's license, passport (albeit temporary until after surgery), and began to draft a letter to the president of the college. It is a strange twist of fate that the rules which the gay students whom I had supported as the faculty advisor many years before had pressed the faculty to adopt regarding gender identity and sexual expression had come to benefit me. The various procedures and steps from that point on were for the most part pro forma. I realized that at my age hormones or surgery couldn't alter some bodily characteristics. The ordeal of electrolysis tests the resolve and determination of any male-to-female transsexual. The biweekly, weekly, and then monthly visits to the electrologist to remove unwanted facial or body hair can be very painful, can last up to five years, and can cost upward of four thousand dollars a year. Results come slowly and require considerable patience. I estimate that electrolysis constitutes about half of the total costs of transformation. After a year of living as a woman, including teaching at the college, I was ready for surgery. The related plastic and genital reconsctruction surgery (GRS) went as I had hoped, and, finally, I was free to be the person who I had visualized for almost forty years.

Of course, there were uncertain and anxious moments during my transformation, such as teaching my first class as a woman in a college where I had taught as a man for thirty years. I had decided to go directly to the president of the college with my plans and ask for his support. He announced to the staff, faculty, and students that they should respect and honor my decision. With that kind of support, there would be no open ridicule. When the moment arrived, when I had to meet my colleagues as a woman for the first time at a faculty meeting, I entered the room in a new navy blue tailored suit and took my seat avoiding eye contact with everyone. One faculty member, my dear colleague Janet, came over and said, "You look just great." I was relieved.

DECADE 8 (2001–PRESENT): LIFE AS A WOMAN IN POSTMODERN SOCIETY

Today we live in a universe of change, and we can never be certain about outcomes of experiences and desires in our lives. Yes, the fantasies and wishes had been there for years, but how could I know that after surgery this was the chosen role for me? Daily dressing or acting the role of a woman may provide some clue, but it still may not be an accurate or reliable portrait of what it would be like after surgery. As my neighbor asked recently when I told her of my attempt to understand this odyssey for this book, " What, Laura, does it mean for you to be a woman now?"

Now that I have completed the process, what has been my experience as a woman? Did I make the right decision? Has it enabled me to find fulfillment in my life? What were the reactions of students and colleagues? How did it affect my relationship with my children? My relationships with other women, whether or not they knew about my past? My relationships with men? My ability to have satisfactory sexual relations? What would be my sexual preference?

I discovered that students for the most part had little concern with what I looked like, although some used the anonymous student questionnaire to criticize my sudden change. They were more disgruntled over grades than over how I appeared. In the following semester I never really knew who knew about my past life. I assumed that it was common knowledge, for the student newspaper conducted an interview with me and the president sent a campuswide e-mail requesting the college community to respect my decision. As the semester progressed, several girls came to me for personal advice, regarding me as their surrogate mother. Another woman student, as part of a sorority tradition, invited me to be her sorority "mother" for the annual awards ceremonies. Some have even invited me out to dances at local pubs or for lunch and dinner. Never did the issue of my gender or past come up. This was true of the boys/men as much as the girls. Some of them would bring little gifts to thank me for my counsel. Others would confide in me about their romantic concerns. I never expected any of this. Some of the gay male students felt more comfortable talking to me in private, for at the college the fear of homophobia was prevalent.

I should note that the response of students to my teaching and counseling had become better than at any previous period. At first, I credited this to my improved teaching style and my new approaches to my courses. I doubt if any of that made a difference. My son recently told me how different I had been in recent years. When I asked what he meant, he said: "You used to be upset most of the time, nervous, quick to anger. You were a walking anxiety. Now you are easy to talk to and fun to be with." It was not my pedagogical techniques at all, but rather it was the comfort I felt with whom I had become. A colleague told me earlier this year at a retirement luncheon that he remembered that he and his wife sat with me at a soiree for the international students many years ago. When he and his wife returned home, she told him that I "was a man trying to get out of his body."

During the few years I remained at the college (I retired in May 2002), I did not experience a single negative or derogatory comment, at least to my face. A few male faculty members had difficulty looking at me when I passed. I realized that this was about them, not me. I looked good as a woman and felt good. It was more about them.

Although it was difficult for my three children (now in their thirties and forties), eventually they came to be accepting and understanding. They were concerned over losing a parent, and because I liked myself more and had more self-confidence as a woman, the more I could attend to them, their lives, and their feelings. The best indicator that I was fully accepted by my son was when he asked me to speak at his wedding two years ago. I was delighted. They had made efforts to read books and understand the nature of those who change gender. At first I was impatient trying to get them to understand. It did not work. I eventually realized that all I could do was to try being a quality parent and be patient, and that required loving them as much as I could. Actually, I am doing a much better job at that than ever before.

All of this was new territory, for I could not have known or anticipated how others would react. One of the most unexpected and most welcomed gifts was how it is to be in a world of other women. As I mentioned earlier, as a man I could never know how women related to and treated each other without men around, how they talked with each other, for women behave differently when men are not present. I noticed this sitting at lunch with a table of women, that when a man sat down, the conversation changed. Men and women converse differently. In my male life I often felt so frustrated in faculty committees with men, where the discussions were intensely competitive and marked with constant interruptions and little listening, that I wanted to walk out of the room and cry. In order to speak at all, one would have to interrupt and speak louder. Recently at a conference at the college where I was the only woman in the room, I raised my hand frequently to speak but was ignored by both the moderator and other participants, while men had no compunction of interrupting others. They often seemed to try to outdo each other. I did not feel that I should have to struggle to say something. Several times at other professional meetings I heard male speakers make disparaging remarks about women. I suspect that if men really were privy to some of the conversations women had about men, they might be very surprised at their perceptions and learn a great deal more about how to relate to their wives. Frequently, as I listened to my female students, I realized how women tended to be reactive rather than proactive toward their fathers and boyfriends. So much of the time they complained that these men do not listen to them.

Although I cannot define it or explain it, I find the conversations I have with other women are more satisfactory than those I had previously with men, as a male. What a boon this has brought to my life! Today my relationships with other women bring more fulfillment and satisfaction than I could ever have imagined. In some cases, because I am a woman, other women have told me that they are able to open up to me and be more intimate, even those who knew me before. In several cases I have maintained friendships with women I knew as a man. Our way of relating to each other has taken on an entirely new dimension. They are more likely to call me or ask me to go to dinner, a movie, or shopping, something they never would have done before.

My relationships with men who I knew professionally before have also changed. Although most of them are cordial, I suspect that they are not quite comfortable with the new me. Some colleagues have chosen simply to ignore me altogether. Others have been very polite and respectful. But the vocabulary has changed and the buddy-buddy, so-called male bonding mannerisms no longer define how we relate. However, most men who were Larry's friends (my former name) no longer contact me. One friend expressed profound anger at me for making such a decision and insisted that I fight it.

Now men in a social context always treat me as a woman, even those who knew me or knew about me before. I have been to dances and bars and been confronted with the usual male come-ons that I have heard women talk about. I do not encourage them as a rule, but there have been exceptions. It has taken several years for me to return to the social and community groups to which I formerly belonged. With few exceptions, I have been welcomed back by members of both sexes.

I had no idea whether I would be able to have satisfactory sexual relations after the surgery. Frankly, I had not given it much thought, for it was not a priority. Afterward, I discovered that my body functioned quite well, an unexpected gift.

One of the most difficult issues has been to whom I should disclose my past. The problem arises when I get to know someone well and we have personal discussions of our relationships and experience. They may assume that I have given birth and that I had a husband. This is very awkward. I have an aversion to lying or even to engaging in simulation or dissimilation. Recently, I rented an apartment I own to a woman who I came to like and respect. It developed into a friendship, so I told her. It was the right decision. I am also in a relationship with another woman who I told some months after we had been lovers. Although she was understanding, she was upset because I waited so long. I do not have an easy formula to deal with this. I have begun to realize that in all these encounters, it is really about trusting myself. When I can do that, then trusting others is not a problem.

I have referred several times to myself as having been fragmented, split into different parts without being able to resolve differences between them. To some extent this is still the case. Given the age in which I grew up and the social forces at home and in society, it is understandable that I had developed considerable self-doubt and could not listen to the voices inside. I heard them, of course, but refused to honor or acknowledge their significance. Again it was about trusting myself, difficult to do because so much of my life had been about repressing or denying them. As one friend suggested, it was like two separate parts, one male and one female, who could not coexist. One had to win out eventually if there was to be inner peace. This interpretation seems to make sense given the contrast between the anguish of hopelessly wishing to be accepted as a woman over many years and the mental and emotional peace I feel today. Although I do not miss Larry or being a male whatsoever, he is still there with his humor, spontaneity, mechanical skills, and his insatiable and intellectual curiosity. In a curious way, many of those traits have come to greater fruition in my femme persona. In some ways I am very fortunate. I have the mannerisms, expressions, and voice that are natural to me and the average woman, although I am very critical of my body because it does not have the curves I would prefer.

EPILOGUE: TOWARD AN ETIOLOGY OF GENDER AND IDENTITY

We are still a long way from understanding the cause or causes of transgendered people. Is it biological deriving from the brain or DNA or do we focus on psychological factors and the process of childbearing? In my case, I can only speculate that much of my personality formation and my development as a woman have come from my relationship with my mother. I concluded this from reflecting on my dreams and fantasies from the Jungian perspective to what is called *individuation*. Jung taught that the anima is the personification of the feminine psychological tendencies in a man's psyche, such as vague feelings and moods, hunches, and the relation to the unconscious. He saw this as strongly shaped by the mother who could have a negative influence on the son. As Maria Louise von Franz put it, in such a case "his anima will often express itself in irritable, depressed moods, uncertainty, and touchiness." She concludes that

> within the soul of such a man the negative mother-anima figure will endlessly repeat this theme: "I am nothing. Nothing makes any sense. With others it's different, but for me I enjoy nothing." The whole of life takes on a sad and oppressive aspect. Such dark moods can even lure a man to suicide, in which case the anima becomes the death demon.[1]

Such negative death wishes and feelings of nothingness were untenable for me. I wanted to live, to get the fullness of life. I chose to become the good anima by being the woman herself.

I believe the following story explains something about my individuation process. Less than two years before my mother died, I bought a round-trip ticket to San Francisco, ostensibly to visit with her in the San Leandro trailer park where she lived. After a very difficult day or so with her in her trailer, I felt such anguish and sadness that I was even uncomfortable sitting in the same room with her. I decided not to stay with her but rented a hotel room. I had my suitcase of women's clothing with me, and the next day, without really planning or thinking about what I was going to do, I dressed, put on my makeup carefully, rented a car, and drove to San Francisco. I parked in the same underground garage where my mother used to park her car, walked down Market Street where she would take me shopping to buy her clothes, went into the Emporium which we had frequented, and then I went directly to the women's restroom where I used to wait outside for her as a child. This time, however, I went into the restroom, came out, left the Emporium, and walked back to the car. As I walked on the sidewalk of Market Street, it struck me, "I am the good mother." I had done what I had to do and went home.

NOTE

1. Mary Louise von Franz, part three, in *The Process of Individuation*, C. G. Jung et al. (New York: Dell, 1970), p. 157.

FROM THE SHADOWS
TO GIVING BACK

Linda Wade

Growing up itself has some difficulties. Along with that I was also transgendered, which added even more challenges. I was reared in Southern California, but in the 1950s in my adolescent years it was not the "liberal" place it is now. My parents were decent people and did their best to raise their only child. This often-described transplanted New England town I grew up in wasn't into shades of gray yet. If you were male, you played with trucks, and if female, dolls were your choice. Let no one put asunder what was male and female, and never the twain shall meet.

When I was about five or six years old, my eyes were already focusing on women's clothes. I for whatever reason first fixed my ogling on slips. One day when I was about seven, I was being babysat by my grandmother. She was taking care of me while my folks were away for the day. I noticed the slip that was showing under my grandmother's dress, and I was drawn to it. At that age I was oblivious to the "wrongness" of it. I wanted to wear it; it was that simple. I was supposed to be taking a nap in her bedroom but just had to look for slips. I, of course, found one and put it on. I don't remember my grandmother (doting type) saying much of anything, and she let me continue to wear the slip. So I pranced around the house and I was in slip heaven. The next-door teenage neighbor boy who was mowing her lawn came in for a drink. Then came the first negative response to being in female attire. He said, "Boys don't wear girls' clothes and you will be called a sissy." I had experienced the joy of wearing that slip, but now those good feelings were stifled. Was it an erotic experience? I don't think my hormones were raging at seven.

I didn't as I remember indulge again in dressing until I was about ten. Then I got the courage to don my mother's slips and wished I could try on other attire as well, but the risk was to great. My folks actually were pretty liberal people when it came to social injustice. The overall "sex" topic, though, was pretty much taboo. My enigma was gender not sex, but I didn't know that until later. Not that it would have made any difference in being talked about. When topics such as this are in your own family, then it is often a different ball of wax.

When it came to homosexuality (not really termed *gay* back then), lesbianism, or transvestism (term used then), people reacted differently. Even people in the more liberal homes would at that time laugh at it or give a quizzing look. To actually come out was just not done because of the fear of being ostracized from one's peer group. Today, for some that is still a problem. Accepting someone who wanted to dress or act like the opposite gender was on any barometer used, negligible.

When speaking of the opposite sex in those days, the word *gender* wasn't part of the lexicon used. Now the word *gender* is used more appropriately when transgenderism is discussed. I point this out again because the public needs to understand the difference. Whether being transgendered is due to chemistry, brain wiring, or whatever doesn't mean much to me in the way I conduct my life. I am curious to know but only on a scientific basis.

I understand that we need labels in order to help us learn, but I personally don't care for them. In fact, many labels in our society take on different meanings. Take the term *transgender* as a good example. Originally this word was coined by Virginia Prince (whom we will visit later) as describing a male who lived full time in the opposite sex without surgical reassignment. Now the word is used to encompass all those who personify themselves as the opposite gender for whatever reason. I don't agree or disagree with these label changes, only believing that we should keep in mind that they do change. Even if labels don't change, they mean different things to different people.

Am I a transgenderist, transvestite, transsexual, or a cross-dresser? I could add even more, but you get the idea. What I saw on one transgendered person's (I have to use some label) license plate sums it up for me: I AM WHAT I AM.

In elementary school I was infatuated with girls, since this was my "natural" inclination. This was amplified, however, with my feelings of wanting to be like one. Except for a couple of Halloween chances to dress, nothing else much happened in the dressing department in elementary school. There were a few stolen moments with my mom's clothes, but all the times this happened I was fearful I would get caught.

Before I get to my adolescent years, I need to share this. I had some athletic ability and was really into sports. I say this not to show how masculine I could be but to show that I loved sports then and still do. One doesn't change likes and dislikes when one puts on a dress. I didn't like sweet potatoes then and still don't.

In dealing with my suppressed energy to dress, sports was a healthy outlet for me, as was school politics, and creative arts. Being busy with these activities gave me some relief from my fantasies. I say relief as if my fantasies were the wrong ones to have, but whether or not they were or not, I was fearful of being found out. My desires, though, in one form or another, whether it was wishing, plotting, or thinking about it, were pretty much with me 24/7 (twenty-four hours a day, seven days a week). Just one of many examples of this was during a basketball game. I had just received a pass from a teammate and I muffed it. My coach yelled, "Quit daydreaming and concentrate." I said, "Yes, coach," but I didn't tell him that my eyes strayed a little too long on the cheerleaders' outfits.

In junior high I took a few more chances, plus the hormones were kicking in (alas not estrogen), so masturbation became an outlet for me. Wearing girls' clothes, looking at girls in magazines, along with a lot of imaginative thinking, was the order of the day. We go with what turns us on. The magazines were not *Playboy, Penthouse,* and all the others, because we didn't have them yet. Don't get me wrong, though, we didn't read from stone tablets either. I don't want to age myself any more than I am. The ogling of *National Geographic, Vogue,* and others did the trick. What was lacking was information about me and hopefully others like me. Although as I got older, I pretty much realized I couldn't be the one in a billion to be selected for this adventure. I just had to find others.

All I had for a definition of people who dressed in the opposite gender was the word *transvestism* (the term used back then). All I got from it was that they probably didn't have just me in mind for a dictionary word. We did have in our town, and way out on the outskirts of it, a store to purchase magazines you wouldn't find lying about at home. We had the *Police Gazette, True Love,* and a couple of others. That was pretty racy for us. I did find some reference to men dressing as women, but it was fiction, or taken out of context and sensationalized.

Two major things happened in the 1950s as far as reading material. One was the appearance of the magazine called *Transvestia.* The person who put this magazine together was Virginia Prince. *Transvestia* was about people who did what I did. I (in high school) traveled fifty some miles to downtown Los Angeles to get it. As I have stated, I didn't think I was alone in this, but it was wonderful to have it authenticated. The pictures and stories were real and for the first time gave me a sense of belonging. Virginia was a real pioneer for the transgendered movement, and still is at it today in her nineties. I had the honor of meeting Virginia through the Alpha Chapter of Tri-Ess in Southern California. She has become a good friend.

This next source of reading material appeared in most of America's newspapers; in magazines such as *Time* and *Life*; on television and radio; and everywhere. It was in 1952 that the Christine Jorgensen story broke. George Jorgensen was an ex-GI who went to Denmark and changed his gender and genitalia with hormones and surgery. I could of course not get enough of it.

There was now purpose and longing for me to find out about my feminine self. My feelings now were well beyond a single garment of women's clothing; I wanted to dress totally.

The peer pressure to conform, however, grew ever greater as I got older. In the eighth grade I did manage to go to a Halloween dance as a gypsy girl. I played it as silliness and laughs, so as to keep my macho image. It was a wonderful feeling, though, to walk around in those clothes.

I, of course, realized later what was happening to me. I was beginning to find my true identity. I can't describe how fearful this all was. Fearful as I was, I still felt impelled to act on my feelings in spite of the risks.

During this time I had not discussed my desires with anyone, which was a lot to carry around by myself. There were also just a few other things that needed attention—like schoolwork, and family and peer boy-girl relationships, just some of the things a teenager starting high school deals with.

I finally found ways to dress and go outside, as I entered high school. When my folks would go to their bridge club once a week, I felt I could seize the opportunity to do some exploration. I labored over it quite awhile. I wanted to dress so much that I would have to give it a try even with the fear and guilt I felt.

I visualized and took copious notes on how I would hopefully pull it off. I got up the nerve to at least try a dry run. After they left, I quickly dressed in my mom's clothes from head to toe. She was quite small, but then so was I. I didn't have a wig so I wore a scarf and put on a little makeup. I thought I looked pretty okay, much better than when I was a young adult. The main reasons were that at fifteen I had soft smooth skin and hair.

I tried to time everything just right. When I would dress, go out, come back, and put everything back just the way I found it. On a dry run, I dressed quickly, peeked out the front door, turned around, and took everything off as fast as I could. I did learn from this brief experience that I had a lot of time to do more before they would return. The next time I walked out the door to the lawn in my mother's clothing, and the next time to the sidewalk and even walked a little. Finally, I went out and walked around the block not looking from side to side. I was really out and able to express my feminine side. This may not seem much to the reader, but for me it was like conquering space.

I repeated the procedure a few more times and did other things. While trying on my mom's nightgown, I broke a strap. I pondered what to do. I was taught that the truth up front was in the long run the best thing to do. So I told her some of the truth. I said I had been bored and, for a lark, I had tried on her nightgown and broken the strap. She bought this or maybe she didn't want to probe further. We never did discuss it again.

My dressing episodes came to an end with this episode and I dared not try again. There were complicating factors. We moved to a new home in the same town for the rest of my high school career, and my folks lived there until my father passed away. Where we moved was an area literally rampant with social friends of my parents. Our home was also a place where a lot of my peer group liked to hang out. The going outside dressed was over, at least for a while.

My high school years were ones of intense activity in sports, campus politics, and what have you, in order to keep my mind occupied. However, even though I used my energy for those activities and it did help, I was still consumed with thoughts of dressing. The feeling is always there. You can purge and stay away from acting on these feelings, but you still think about it *a lot*. Every time I saw a girl or a female teacher at school, at the movies, or at a restaurant, I was looking to see what she was wearing. I fantasized about being made to dress, not only because I would be dressed, but also because then I had an alibi. I would sit in study hall pretending to be studying, but actually sketching clothes on my not-so-well-drawn models.

Like most of my fellow students, I had a high school sweetheart and I was definitely in love. We were planning to marry after her senior year in high school and my freshman year in college. To make a long story short, we broke up. There were many reasons for the breakup, but a significant one was what I called my secret, my cross-dressing. The secret remained just that, since I still hadn't shared it with anyone. There are more stories to tell about high school adventures, fantasizing, thoughts, and dreams, but if I put them all down, this autobiography would challenge *War and Peace* for length.

My senior year ended with the traditional talent show in which some senior boys impersonated girls in the show. I was one of the eleven chosen to impersonate girls. Without going into all of it, I was (probably because I was small) the lead femme impersonator. Can you say *tutu*? We played it with straight faces and it got a lot of laughter from the audience. As for me, you take what you can get.

Following high school, I was off to college in the east to earn a degree and drink beer. College was to give me an escape from my secret. Actually, though, the thoughts of feminism were there when I got up in the morning, bigger than ever. My envy of girls never wavered. I want to stress here that my feelings and actions were still not shared with others. It was not that I was afraid of what I was, but of what other people would think.

I contemplated getting married a couple more times in college. I know that part of my decision not to do so was based on my parents wishes, as well as my own, that I would graduate. But it was also fear of someone discovering my secret. Living in a sorority house (oops, fraternity house) didn't afford me the freedom I thought it would to dress. I was disappointed that being about a thousand miles from home didn't open up all kinds of opportunities for me. It probably did, but fear again was a huge stumbling block. I did manage a couple of dressing gigs all in the same mode of playing the clown.

After I finished college, since the draft was still going even though the United States was not involved in anything, I enlisted in the Army National Guard to avoid being called up. I did six months active duty and five and a half years of active reserve. I was discharged (honorably) in 1966, just before fighting in Vietnam intensified. My basic training was not a great time for dressing. I don't think I would have been appreciated if the sergeants found women's garments in my footlocker or duffel bag. I coped whenever I had short leaves. I would buy some women's clothing, go to a motel, dress up, and when I left dispose of the clothes. I didn't venture out, but simply dressing was of solace to me.

After my six months active duty, while living at home, I worked in a business office where I quickly decided this was not for me. I went back to college locally in Southern California to get a teacher's credential, while working in a department store part time.

Before I go on with the rest of my story, I need to reiterate that the urge to be feminine was forever with me, and it was very lonely. My social life tended to deteriorate as my fear of being found out increased. Finally, when I started teaching, I found my own apartment. Finally, I should have been free to come and go as I pleased, *but I was not!* Fear again raised its ugly head and I was literally trapped in my apartment. Gradually I began to venture out in the late evenings and walk around. I looked about as feminine as Ma Kettle (by the way Marjorie Main who played Ma Kettle was a stylish looking woman), and for those of you not familiar with the character Ma Kettle, I think you still get the idea. I had a horrible wig, my makeup needed overhauling, and my clothes were ugly retro.

I was pretty sure that teaching was for me, and that was proven to me quickly in my first year. While teaching really kept me hopping, I also threw myself into a lot of extracurricular activities with the students. I thought this would help me bury my feelings. But my feelings were part of me, and trying to shut them out only made things worse.

After about four years of teaching, I found myself not coping with life around me very well. The teaching was fine and I relied on it for escape, but my personal problems mounted. Finally, I went to a psychiatrist who turned out to be strictly Freudian. He didn't say much and neither did I. But I spent three years with him. He did, however, start me using Valium. I'm not blaming anyone, but these kinds of sessions were not for me. I quit, but kept up the Valium. A few years later I came off the Valium on my own and started to really feel again.

My real problem, however, was my overwhelming feeling of loneliness. I don't want to beat a dead horse, but I needed to share with *somebody.* I needed to share with someone I knew, someone who would understand. Finally, I got up enough nerve to tell about four people. They listened politely, then either shrugged it off or said it must be a phase. Some phase. In other words they didn't want to deal with it. That was their prerogative of course, but I needed somebody to *listen.* A huge problem was that I couldn't explain my feelings very well at the time. Simply hearing I liked to dress was not enough for my friends, and the fact that I did not delve into it further with them didn't help matters. The most important thing for me was to really look at myself and find out who I was. Later I would understand this and come to terms with it.

I was dating a nice woman for a couple of years, and again matrimony seemed plausible. We, in fact, went to a Halloween party, each of us in the opposite gender. I had to really do some manipulating to have this work out. Under the guise of laughingly saying a couple I knew had switched roles for Halloween, I got the response I wanted since she thought it would be funny. I then said I was just kidding, although I wasn't kidding at all. Neither was she. My woman friend and her roommate took over and we were under way. They both made me up in the afternoon for the party that Halloween night. For the first time I saw a pretty respectable feminine person. My partner looked pretty good as a male as well. I had a glorious time. After the party we went back to her apartment, and I did not want to go home and burst the bubble.

We later decided to go on our separate ways. We remained good friends. I called her one night and asked her to come by because I had something I wanted to share with her. When she came over I was dressed. The party experience I thought would soften the blow. I told her my story as best as I could, and she was a good listener. It felt so good to have told somebody whom I respected and who would keep it to herself. I'm sure she told a couple of people that she knew someone who . . . yada, yada, yada. We are still friends to this day although we have never discussed my secret again.

The years went by with secret outings until I finally did get married. I thought I could really purge, throw away the clothes, and settle into marital bliss. I was wrong. We divorced after a fairly short marriage. My wife was a nice woman and we parted without much fanfare. There were not any children involved or any financial things of note, so it was fairly easy in that respect. Divorce, though, no matter how it happens, is still not an easy thing to go through. My wife never knew about my feminine side, but I knew that I felt cornered and wanted to move on. I was ready to do something about letting myself out.

About a year later I talked to a lesbian friend of mine and confided in her. She told me about an acupuncturist who she went to who was a good listener and would be interested in me. I went to this woman and she began the process of acupuncture. This in itself turned out to be quite relaxing. I will call her Lynda, and why not, that's her name. I, after a while, started talking about my feminine feelings and she listened and bolstered my confidence. A couple of times I brought clothes and put them on in the waiting room. This seems light-years away now, as I now just walk out my front door and do what I please. Lynda wanted me to seek a therapist and gave me some names. I chose a woman therapist who was one of Lynda's two favorites. This was a great choice, since Toni the therapist would be my rock for the next few years. I refer to her as Toni because that is her name. I haven't mentioned my name yet; it is

Linda with an *i*. I picked this name long before I met Lynda with a *y*; it felt good though that I had her name, except for the *y* and *i* thing.

I will try to capsulate my years in therapy, even though I haven't been successful in doing that so far. So here goes. I was cured. Well, that is too short. *Cured* isn't really the word, either. I learned so much about myself— not only about my transgenderism but about other issues as well. Toni was such a super therapist and wonderful human being. Toni was not versed in transgender issues, but she was a quick learner. She was, moreover, very well versed about issues that affect all of our lives. It was those issues that I needed clarification on in order to find out and to feel who I was. Later in therapy, I started coming dressed and from then on always came as Linda. My confidence was definitely growing.

The main thing in therapy is that you and the therapist must work hard together, and we did. The bottom line is that I came to who I was and that I was one person. I wasn't a fragmented Humpty Dumpty put back together again. One of the hardest things that I ever did in my life was to say good-bye to Toni. I had found a support group and got up the courage to call. The national group is called Tri-Ess and the local group, Alpha Tri-Ess, is located in Southern California. The person I called was Virginia Prince (small world), and after she checked me out, she encouraged me to come to Alpha.

Although my confidence had grown a lot, I still had a ways to go. On my first trip to Alpha I was sure that all the people in other cars were staring at me. I thought that the transgender police were out in force. I was welcomed at Alpha and met nice people from all walks of life. Many of those people I met that first night and met again later are still friends today. I also found another support group in Orange County, PPOC (Powder Puffs of Orange County), and met more people. I started going out to restaurants, movies, malls, San Francisco, Las Vegas, and so on, and all the time my confidence was growing.

There comes with most of us transgender individuals, especially if it has taken us years to get out, a rush period. Many of us now that we feel good about going out want to do it all in a short period of time. We want to try all the fashions, to try various cosmetics, nail polish, nail lengths, wig styles, to get makeovers, breast enhancers, and shoes from six inch heels to flats. This isn't a bad thing; in fact, it is a natural thing to want to do. We essentially are going from girlhood to womanhood in a short period of time. We need to try out everything. I wore heels for a while a lot, but after some time I chose to wear flats or sandals. I now wear heels but only when the outfit or a special occasion calls for it. I get out a lot though; if you don't go out much, then heels might be your choice a lot more. There are some transgender "girls" who start thinking about more then fashion choices—hormones to make the body more feminine, implants, and maybe surgically changing your genitalia. If you are a candidate for some of that or all of it, great. If you have doubts, take it slow; these are life-altering changes.

The first step out of the front door is sooo difficult. I now feel comfortable going clothes shopping, grocery shopping, and to movies, church, restaurants, and what have you. As a male, being short and small boned could be a detriment; as a woman, it has been a plus. Passing as a woman, though, isn't really about adorning these bones and muscles; these bodies of ours will someday be dust. It is the acceptance of one's self that is important. This is the real passing, the passing of one's soul. If you don't pass inside, then it will be a difficult road to travel. The more one goes out in public en femme, the more confidence one attains.

In one of my early visits to Alpha meetings, I remember saying to a friend how much I appreciated the acceptance the group gave me. She said that one day I would give back. She was right. I later became a board member and then president of Alpha. This has afforded me the opportunity to give back to others just like me who were so fearful to take that first step. All our members give back and make new people welcome.

I have been able to meet a lot of other people throughout the community no matter how they "label" themselves. We in the whole transgender community give back because we have all been there. We are educating our families, friends, and strangers that we meet along the way. I have met nontransgender persons who have given so much to our community: professors, psychiatrists, owners, and workers in public places. Every time we (in the transgender community) are in public *we* are all ambassadors. People see us actually eat food with forks. *We* want people to get to know *us* not just as another man in a dress.

The community has made progress educationally, legislatively, and *we* are more accepted in society today. Still, there is a lot to be done. No matter what label we use in the whole spectrum of the transgendered community, we must recognize the importance of all of us. I do not know what the future holds for me, but I do know this journey will always continue. I gained a wonderful social life and met great friends. I am so thankful that at this point in my life, I am thoroughly enjoying it. Hopefully many who read this will also take that first step and will be able to enjoy being themselves.

PILGRIMAGE

Lynda Frank

This year (2006), as I turn seventy-four (eighth decade), I feel a little bit like Don Q, old and decrepit. My quest is to find out what my life is all about. The men in my family are not known for longevity, so I certainly did not expect to be living in the twenty-first century. But here I am and being asked to tell a little about a part of my journey. I asked my three children to each comment on that part of my journey and how it impacted them. What I got back was somewhat expected and certainly an important part of my story. I had asked them to write something as an afterthought to my story. Reading them now, I think a better place for them is in the beginning.

MY FATHER IS A LESBIAN!

I am currently forty-nine years old, and I did not learn about my father's affinity for cross-dressing until about twenty years ago. At the time, my wife and I happened to be a young couple on the fast track! I had a great job at a major financial institution, we lived in a beautiful spacious home, our incredibly cute baby boy was about to turn one year old, and our little Shetland sheepdog rounded out our new suburban family—perfectly!

My mother and I were alone in her bedroom one afternoon. (I was up for a visit to celebrate my niece's first birthday.) She said she had something to tell me about my dad. She never had said anything like that before, and my immediate thoughts drift to the devilish *C* word

(*Cancer*—a major illness, a drastic health issue—assuming the worst!). Reading my face, as only a mother can, she immediately said there was nothing wrong with Dad's health but just that he was "a cross-dresser— he likes to wear women's clothes [we didn't use "transgender lifestyle" in those days]—he is not gay." She explained how she found out about fifteen years prior and explained how she learned more about it through the years, that other people did this—that Dad wears ladies clothes and sometimes even wears ladies undergarments under his regular clothes. She was telling us (the children) now since both my parents had became active in helping others learn more about "cross-dressing" and there was a chance someone we knew might detect my parents from an interview or talk show on radio or TV and say something to us.

I have always been a liberal thinker. Therefore, I probably didn't react like the average individual. I had two top issues that my mind was racing with. First, how the hell did he hide it from me?! How could I not see it? As a kid growing up, my parents were frugal and they didn't have a lot of clothes. I had been through all his stuff, hundreds of times! I used to go through all his drawers to borrow clothes throughout the seventeen years I grew up at home. I guess I must have just made the assumption if I came across any that they were my mom's if, in fact, I saw anything, but even to this date, I can't recall ever seeing any women's garments among his clothes. (And as I found out at that moment they were there!)

The second issue brought a big smile and a resounding *yes*, from the spirit deep inside me that says things don't have to be, as they seem—yes, turn the world, turn the conventional thinking, turn so-called reality upside down and shake it around! (That is the world I so enjoy being a part of!) Here was my father after all—nothing less than a cross between John Wayne and Archie Bunker! Dad was a man whose physical presence alone was intimidating from a distance. Then you heard that booming deep, nasty, aggressive voice no matter where you were. Hopefully it wasn't directed at you. (You could easily observe his strength when you saw him up close—when he would lift and carry huge amounts of dead weight up flights of steps when he was running his local trucking business. I'm still not sure how he did it!) I knew him as a proud Korean War veteran who threatened my very existence if I demonstrated against the Vietnam War when I was in high school. His definition of "tolerance" then was you had to agree and see everything his way. Then he was tolerant!

And now I found out that the father of steel who terrorized me when he was angry (fortunately not often) liked to wear ladies' clothes! What a hoot! I can think of no better example or positive confirmation that life doesn't have to be a set way—that you can open your mind and Live!

I am also fortunate to have the most important women in my life, my mother and my wife, play major roles in supporting my dad, which made it easier for me. I told my wife the same day I found out. She has always been fond of my parents, and even though she is more conservative than I am, she didn't even bat an eye. Again, I believe her own personal self-confidence makes it easier for her to accept new ideas about people. Over the past few years my father and some of his friends have even consulted her on makeup, accessories, and she has hemmed my dad's dresses more than once. If I didn't have a supportive spouse myself, I could have had additional problems, I suspect. My mother is probably the only person I know who truly understands and believes in "unconditional love." She has always loved my father and went to incredible lengths of personal sacrifice and humiliation to support his cross-dressing, as well as taking a great interest to understand it and help others who have experienced the same "shock" themselves when they discovered their "Man" who likes to wear "Women's" clothes. I am so proud of my mother! What an incredible woman—still old school in so many ways about traditional values and thought, yet she is now one of the most progressive individuals I know involved in this area. I am sure I love her even more as a result of how she has responded to Dad's cross-dressing.

I have also come to a couple of interesting conclusions. First, I found out at the right time of my life! I was very secure about my sexuality and my overall being at age twenty-seven. Had I been a teenager learning this "shocking" news, I am not sure I would have taken it as well. We all have such insecurities, especially as teenagers. We are not exposed or taught enough in school to accept and be tolerant of such nonconforming lifestyles. I am also sure it could have had an impact in my personal development as well. (Would I have experimented? Probably not, but I can't say for sure, although I have never felt any inkling.)

The other conclusion is consistent with most things in life. Ignorance is dangerous! We are so afraid of things we don't understand—I also believe most people are insecure about themselves and they don't want to be even exposed to something that doesn't fit into their "box." I am amazed at how outraged most people are to even know this might be happening. Men dressed as women—oh my God?! I am not sure if anyone died from wearing pantyhose but I just can't see the harm. (And if that helped mellow my old man out, even better I say!)

The best example of this I remember is a few years back when we were both working a fund-raising event in the village, in New York City. We had both signed up as volunteers separately. Dad turned a few heads when he showed up as Lynda, but he was serious about working. Although the organizers of the event were not sure how to best use Lynda, Dad suggested that if they needed a coat check, he could do that. (My parents worked one together for a year or two when they first got married, so he had experience in how to work the job.) Once people were coming in, it became apparent that they had found the right "person" for the job! It was a long fun night. I was working the crowd (probably doing odds-and-ends stuff like selling raffle tickets). I checked on Dad a few times throughout the night—but he was working hard and smiling and doing his job to the point where the organizers were *glad* he was there. During the evening, while I was working the crowd, I remember coming across this attractive woman about my age. She was engaging me in regular conversation, and I was certainly interested in learning more about her. She caught my interest being attractive, intelligent, and vibrant. As we grew closer to the end of the night, we were taking and sharing a few drinks. She gave me her business card and said I should give her a call. Well, the night was ending and she had to leave. While I was working the crowd, she went and picked up her coat and returned.

"Did you see the coat check?" she asked with surprise. Not thinking, I immediately smiled and answered, "The coat check? Yea, that's my dad!" And then I got the *look!*

Here was an intelligent individual who literally lost it! I could see fear, anger, disgust, and almost hatred—toward *me!* (What changed? I wasn't wearing pantyhose.) Without saying anything else, she bolted to the exit as fast as she could. Keep in mind that many gay and lesbian individuals who lived in the area attended this fund-raising event. Therefore, I had also assumed that the crowd would be receptive to "alternate lifestyles," but this single incident represented how much of a hurdle "cross-dressing" had to overcome. *Huge!*

I doubt I will be able to comprehend it all—I try at times, but I know I can probably only "get it" to a certain point. The real question is, just because we cannot understand something, does that make it wrong? Unlike most of the family, I'd go public in a heartbeat! I am probably even more proud of my father because I think it takes some serious guts to walk the streets like a Mrs. Doubtfire. It can't be easy to hear the comments and get the nasty looks from people who have no idea who he is. I love him and actually admire him even more for trying to educate people who are so narrowly focused as well as to help similar individuals like himself come to a better understanding of what they are doing. Without support groups, many cross-dressers would be lost and even more depressed about their situation of feeling the urge to cross-dress. He is not looking to change people nor does he feel compelled to fight the "normal" world!

Which brings me to the title—"My Father Is a Lesbian!" Well, in my mind, I sometimes find it the easiest way to explain the phenomenon. You have to think outside the box—maybe way out—and that opening line of mine clearly allows my audience to take that first step.

And there is an additional irony to a lesbian comparison. Since Dad is not a drag queen, many gays are not even comfortable with his lifestyle. My parents are comfortable going to lesbian bars because there seems to be a better acceptance among the ladies! (Go figure.) I remember my dad and another cross-dressing friend were at this one lesbian bar a few years ago and I was working late in the city. I stopped by to pick them up. (My first time in a lesbian bar.) I walked in toward the bar in the back, and it took me about ten seconds to hear Dad's voice coming from a bar stool. There he was joining the other ladies, talking day-to-day stuff and complaining about the "women" in their lives!

HAPPY READING. MINE IS SHORT & SWEET. LOVE SIS

How I feel about my father's cross-dressing. I don't like it. I don't care to see it. I don't care to be involved in it in any way. We have discussed it, and I think it is bull. These people think it feels good to be a woman. I don't like pantyhose, and I don't like cramps every month. (And hot flashes really stink!) Real women are too busy being moms and wives to have so much spare time on their hands. I could never find enough time to have a second life. I live in a real word, which means I will see Lynda only on Halloween.

Impact on my life? This has no impact on my life since I didn't learn of it until I was an adult. It helps that Lynda respects my not wanting to be a part of it.

HALLY

It was 1984; I was twenty-one and home on break from college. Alone, lying in my parents' bed, I was browsing the titles of the books on an adjacent bookshelf. *The Transvestite and His Wife* was a title that caught my eye and resonated in my thoughts. When my mother entered the room, she answered "Yes" to my dire question, "Is Dad a transvestite?" This newly learned piece of information was incredibly humorous and totally unbelievable. My dad was the epitome of manliness, even manlier than John Wayne! So gruff, my friends feared him: so rigid and clean cut, I thought of him as militant. This was just too funny! Not wanting to discuss this with *my mother*, and never really good at keeping secrets, I knew I had a challenge ahead of me.

How do I feel about my dad being a cross-dresser? It doesn't really matter to me. It has zero impact on my feelings toward him. In my eyes, being a cross-dresser is no different than being tall, old, a teacher, or what have you. These "characteristics" shape you because of the experiences you encounter as a result of people's reactions to you because of them. These "characteristics" make people unique and interesting. If he were not my dad, I know I'd enjoy his friendship: being he is my dad makes it a *little* different, and I prefer not to meet Lynda. For the first twenty-one years of my life, I had a perception of who my dad is. For twenty-one years this perception influenced and shaped who I am. I love my dad, and my childhood memories are of him as Len. So, again, not meeting Lynda is merely a preference because I really like being with the Dad I've grown up with: the Dad who taught me to ride my bike; the Dad who I had long talks with; the Dad who taught me so much in life. I love my dad, and if it were *really* important to him that I am around Lynda, I would do it.

How has it impacted my life? It keeps me carrying around a secret. Sometimes I'd love to just burst out and tell people but, having young children and not knowing how the repercussions of people knowing might affect them, I keep it quiet. I did tell one person, however—it was the day after I found out. It was rush hour and I was meeting my (Wall Street) boyfriend (who is now my husband of eighteen years) on a train platform in Penn Station. We met, kissed, and boarded the crowded train with the huddled masses. Standing pressed against strangers, in the noisy car, unable to hold my secret any longer, I blurted out, "My father's a transvestite." And so ensued just your standard subway conversation, shared with many inquiring ears.

LYNDA FRANK

My story starts in 1930 at a time when the world was a much different place than it is today. My earliest memories go back to the time the first Superman comic book came out. My father was part owner of a live poultry market in the Midwood section of Brooklyn. We were not poor, even in those days (early thirties), so I do not recall knowing of any money problems. I have a sister one year older than I am, who I remember being very active and getting into trouble from time to time. I remember having talks with and cuddling with my loving mother. My father, although a compulsive gambler, worked hard and always had good jobs. Mother died of some sort of heart condition when I was ten, but she was ill for a few years prior so between the ages of eight and ten I lived temporarily on and off with a few families. Our family moved around a lot when I was young, and my sister was able to make friends much easier than I. So it was easier for me to play with the girls than to make friends with the boys, who generally gave the new kid on the block a hard time.

Interestingly enough, when I was about twelve years old (1942), I remember being in the living room of one of my aunts' homes and listening to a heated discussion between four of my aunts. My Aunt Edith, nineteen years old at the time, being about twenty years younger than her youngest sister, was extolling the virtues of the new style in women's clothing, pants. She talked about the comfort and freedom of leg movement it offered. Her older sisters were shocked at the thought of wearing pants, "men's clothing out in the street." I remember at that time not understanding what all the fuss was about. Even in men's pants, she sure didn't look like a man.

I knew that the girls were different from the boys, but I never even thought about sex till I was about thirteen years old when a cousin of mine showed me this new thing he had learned from his friends. Masturbation started then, and it was a great new thing (sex) to be experienced, when alone of course. So the bathroom turned out to be the place to have a good time, because back in the early forties few children had their own room. And if you could get ahold of an *Esquire* magazine, you could masturbate looking at the naked girls, more fun. The next step was rummaging through the hamper for women's underwear for an even more heightened arousal. Working under the assumption that if some is good, more is better, whatever girls' things that were in the hamper were fair game. Having sexual intercourse, being inside a girl, was the great fantasy. Next to being inside a girl came having the girl body parts, and that was really erotic and exciting. Now I knew all the other guys were also masturbating, but it was now a private thing, so, although I thought all the other guys were doing what I was, I kind of kept it to myself because maybe they weren't and nobody wants to be made fun of.

The next great event that took place in my midteens was Christine Jorgensen, and *wham* being a girl—the greatest sexual experience ever. But this just seemed like a lot of fun and was great nourishment for daydreams. The next few years till I turned eighteen I would put on whatever girl things I could find, masturbate, then take them off and feel a little foolish.

At eighteen (1948), after graduating from high school and not wanting to go on to college, I joined the air force on a three-year enlistment. Along came the Korean War, and I was away for four years. In all that time, two years stateside, no privacy, no masturbation, no girls' clothes, and no more than thoughts of sex. Then two years in Japan, where there was more sex than even a twenty-year-old could possibly use. But still no thought of girls' clothes. Once back home, sex again became hard to get and privacy was available again, so it was back to masturbating and gals' clothes as before. Two years later, 1954, I married the greatest little gal from across the street, and a new era began. Even with regular sex, I found I still had the desire to put on girls' clothes. Whenever Marilyn was away from the apartment for a while, I would get all dressed up in her clothes and masturbate, making sure to return everything back exactly as it was. This was usually on Saturdays when she would be gone to the hairdresser or if she was out for an evening with her friends.

This behavior went on for about the next ten years. Along the way I had managed to acquire a black bra, garter belt, and stockings, which I hid in the back of a drawer that was rarely used. Then ten years into the marriage and three children later, around 1964 (I was thirty-four), Marilyn found my hidden clothes and all hell broke loose. For the next week it was a real war zone till things quieted down a little and we seriously started looking into my feelings. We spent days and days discussing her feelings and mine, and we finally arrived at a compromise of sorts. She would buy me my own women's underwear, and we would go out with it on under my men's clothes. We would do this every couple of weeks, usually going to the movies and out to dinner. Although she was very uncomfortable with this arrangement in the beginning, we went along this way for about the next ten years.

Here, again, there were other very important things going on: starting a business, supporting the five of us, and that most demanding job of raising children. And, in addition, there was building and repairing things around the house. When there was no Boy Scout troop in our neighborhood, I started a troop so my son could have some of the great experiences I had had as a youngster. And then, as had always been my wish, I adjusted my schedule so we could all eat dinner as a family. I guess I did not have much free time to even think about dressing.

Around 1974, after a very bad year financially, things turned around, and there was more then enough of everything. Marilyn, always grateful when things went well, looked for volunteer work as a way to give back some of our good fortune. She got involved with a crisis intervention hotline, and as part of her excellent training she went to a "conscious raising" program. This opened up a whole new feeling of self-assurance for her and helped her become more comfortable and understanding with my cross-dressing.

In 1977, when I was forty-seven and she was the director of the hotline, we started to do some research into the gender-variant community under the guise of enhancing the resources of the hotline.

It was sometime around then that I first visited Lee's bookstore on Tenth Avenue in New York City. I had found its advertisement on the back page of the *Village Voice*, and I sneaked into the city to check it out. It was there that I found out someone had written an entire book about cross-dressing. It was by Virginia Prince and it explained to me that I was not the only one who felt the way I did about women's clothing. From that point on, she has been the object of my gratitude and love for giving me back a feeling of normalcy and helping me to understand I was not crazy after all. I will forever be in her debt. (In 2002, in her ninetieth year [tenth decade], I escorted her for three days at the IFGE convention in Philadelphia and was still overwhelmed with her enthusiasm, intelligence, and willingness to help anyone who sought her out.)

When I had first read her book *The Transvestite and His Wife* in secret and found it to be so wonderful, I gave it to my wife, Marilyn, to read. Her response was to throw it back at me with the comment that " I have enough of my own books to read when I find time to read anything." Raising three children did not leave much time for reading books. Years later she told me she had secretly read it when I was at work, always putting it back on the shelf so I would not know.

In questioning the psychologists who did the hotline training, Marilyn got the name of a doctor in Brooklyn named Leo Wollman who had written a number of papers and was currently doing research with transsexuals. She sent him a letter requesting information about his work and received some interesting literature from him. She put it on file, and about a year later I made a secret visit to Dr. Wollman's office to pay him a visit in my search for information about my cross-dressing feelings. His diagnosis was that I was a transvestite and not a transsexual, and he gave me a referral for a transgender group run by a Garrett Oppenheim in Tappan, New York. Getting up enough courage to actually visit a group was another very long process. It was hard to visualize a group of cross-dressers and not think it might be something like a sex orgy, which definitely was not what I was looking for. I must have called at least a half dozen times, always hanging up when someone answered the phone. I finally got up enough courage to speak to someone. Years later when I was doing interviews for the Tri-Ess meetings and people would tell me how hard it was for them to speak to me the first time, I was able to understand just how they felt.

The group consisted of about a dozen people of which about three-quarters would show up at any of the bimonthly meetings. There were transsexuals, male-to-females and female-to-males, and a few transvestites, one was Roger Peo, with whom we became very close and who later did his doctoral dissertation, with considerable input from Marilyn, on the wives of cross-dressers. It took Marilyn some time to get over his untimely death at a young age. We were with this group about two years. For the first six months I attended by myself, during which time Garrett's wife, Fay, took me into New York City to Muriel Olive's boutique to buy a padded girdle and a bra. Then we went to a tall-girl dress store for a couple of outfits and then on to a shoe store in midtown Manhattan where they let me try on women's shoes in the back room. After purchasing my shoes, I was now completely outfitted in women's clothes, and for the first time in my life I felt this great weight was lifted off my shoulders. There was and still is this feeling of well-being, peace, and real comfort when I am fully cross-dressed. However, at this point another problem developed. Marilyn got very angry and expressed a feeling of betrayal because she had always gone shopping for Lynda's undergarments (with Len) and took offense that another woman was shopping with me for intimate apparel. Who was this Muriel? Where did she live? Was she some young, slim, good-looking woman looking to take advantage of some unsuspecting man in need? Her thoughts ran wild. A couple of years later when she met Muriel, they both had a good laugh about the incident, and she and Marilyn developed a nice friendship. Interestingly, Marilyn never liked the dresses we picked out, and it was a happy day for her when several years later we gave them to Goodwill. After that Marilyn would go shopping with Len for Lynda's outer garments as well. Generally we went to large department stores. She even went with me to pick up wigs for "Aunt Sarah" so no one would know they were for me.

I continued to go to Garrett's house every other week, getting fully dressed in one of the bedrooms upstairs and then going downstairs to the basement for our meeting. After the meeting, I'd go back upstairs to change back to my men's clothing to go home. After coaxing Marilyn for many months, she agreed to attend the meeting if I did not dress the night she attended. I told her I would only dress when she became comfortable with the group and would not be upset at seeing me fully dressed and in front of strangers. Well she attended the next half dozen meetings, each time saying she was not ready yet to see me dressed. Finally, Garrett came down on her for stalling so long, and it would have been a bad scene except that Roger came to her defense and she was able to save some face. I think it was a turning point for her, and a closeness developed between her and Roger. Garrett's was an excellent learning experience, except for the fact that no one was allowed to talk about any other groups or meetings. Then one night someone mentioned Fantasia Fair, and I got the information before Garrett could stop him.

So in 1981 I talked Marilyn into giving Fantasia Fair a try. She agreed to go for three days and took a couple of books to occupy herself, but she never got to open even one. We were assigned a beautiful apartment on the bay with a magnificent view and very nice neighbors. In fact, one year I had to interrupt my stay with a short business trip to the West Coast in the middle of the week. Marilyn agreed to spend the time there by herself until I returned. Only the day I was to leave, she became very ill, with dizziness and an upset stomach, and we went into a panic. When I spoke to Ari, she told me to speak to my next-door neighbor and he could help me. It turns out he was a gynecologist and had a wonderful couple of days making house calls en femme.

What we saw when we got there was eighty or ninety men crossdressed and walking in the street, going into restaurants and attending lectures. Nobody we saw in town seemed to be concerned or even interested in the men running around in women's clothing. We were both overwhelmed by the experience, and before we left we signed up for the entire week for the following year. We did, in fact, attend the next ten Fairs, and in one instance we arrived early so I was able to stay dressed for ten days. For years the Fair was the highlight of my year. I once told Ariadne that Virginia took me out of the closet and into the living room, and Ariadne took me from the living room into the street. So my first experiences being out and about cross-dressed were very pleasant ones; thank you, Ari.

In 1982, our second year there and in the midst of my reading everything I could find on the subject and talking to as many gender variant people as I could find, Ariadne introduced me to Virginia Prince. What a wonderful experience to finally meet the person who had such a huge impact on my life. I need to say the quality of the presenters at the Fair was always of the very highest.

Realizing that I had started out many years ago with just a pair of panties and having now progressed to the point that I was now fully dressing a week at a time, I needed to know where this was going. Marilyn had been asking me that same question, and I felt unable to give her an honest answer. So I went to speak to Virginia about it—the one whose book had brought Lynda to life. Her answer was immediate, direct, and exactly to the point. She told me at that time that if there were other things in my life that were important to me, *that* would make the difference. Yes, my wife, my children, my family, and my profession were all of paramount importance in my life, and so to be able to accommodate for all those things, I would adjust my cross-dressing activities accordingly. Her answer was right on in my case because that's exactly the way it actually went. And to this day I will put off dressing for an important family event. Virginia also informed me at that time of the existence of an organization called Tri-Ess, the Society for the Second Self, which she had cofounded. It was in essence a self-help group for heterosexual cross-dressers. At that time and to some degree even today people think that if you like women's clothes you must be gay, which in most cases is not true. It was making that point and the one that says I am not a transsexual that would help make our wives a little more comfortable. After all, some of us had lied in not making our feelings known to our wives before we got married, and it would take some doing to reestablish their trust.

In our second year at the Fair, a writer named Darryl Rist came up to do a piece about the attendees. Darryl, an accomplished feature writer for some of the best magazines in the country who also happened to be gay, did not believe there was such a thing as a heterosexual cross-dresser. He was sure that they were just another bunch of gay men in denial, and he was coming up here to investigate and write the true story. *Wow* did he get a shock; there really was such a thing as a heterosexual cross-dresser. I don't know how many people he interviewed, but he spent a whole day with me and two days talking to my wife.

Since I had been interviewed many times not only in regard to my gender activities but in my business ventures and as chairmen of the planning board at home, I had learned to be weary of interviewers because there are some who tend to be less than honest in their reporting. This guy Darryl, though, was a new experience; he would ask me a question, and when I was finished answering, he would give me input on his feelings about the topic. I was learning as much about him as he was learning about me.

Now at around fifty years of age I had never personally known any gay people, at least not that I was aware of. I have to admit that I did believe that gay people were different—wasn't sure how, but different. Lo and behold, this gay guy really isn't any different from any of the other nice people who I have known all my life. Not only that but he had a lot of the very same feelings growing up as I had. He may have been con-cealing a different secret, but we both had secrets. A real feeling of kinship developed. Then I felt not only anger at my past ignorance but terribly sad that I had lived half my life separated from a group of people I could learn from and share experiences with. Darryl and his partner went on to become very close personal friends and spent time with our family and us during Passover and Christmas gatherings. It made me feel good to know my children and grandchildren would not grow up as ignorant as I had been! In fact, one of my fondest memories was at the formal sweet sixteen party of my oldest granddaughter. The band played the anniversary waltz for my wife's cousin who was married for forty-five years and I had Darryl and his partner join them on the dance floor to celebrate their fifteen years together. It made my heart burst with pride to see the two couples dancing alone on the dance floor and me just daring anyone to say any-thing short of congratulations. Darryl passed away at a young age, and I lost a true friend I had grown to love very much.

A new group had just started at that time in northern New Jersey, about an hour from my home. It was a small group of about eight or so with most coming from Poughkeepsie in New York. There were three IBM engineers, a schoolteacher, and a retired Eastern Airline pilot. The group was meeting in a hotel room on the second Saturday of every month.

After two years in-group with Garrett and a couple of trips to Fan-tasia Fair, we felt comfortable enough to switch to Tri-Ess. We joined in 1982. Marilyn started a wives' group, and I got some of the guys together for some rap sessions. I also became treasurer for the next two years and then president for the next eight. The group grew to the forties, going up and down over the years. Many of the guys would come for as long as it took them to get comfortable and then go on to other places. When our numbers went down, I would put an ad in the *Village Voice* in New York, and the membership would go back up. This system worked well right up to the time the computer took over and started sending us a continuing supply of new members. It opened up a new world for anyone who had any feelings about trying on women's clothing. They could just type in a few keywords and get a heck of an education and a listing of groups in a very short time.

Tri-Ess was a limited group strictly for heterosexuals, perhaps because such a limitation was necessary to help us convince our wives that we were not gay or transsexual. I have over the years been a strong supporter of that concept, and especially so after joining an open group and seeing how different the needs of the transsexuals are. We have since become members of not only Tri-Ess but also the IFGE, which is an open group. Marilyn, having been instrumental in establishing a wives' group at Fantasia Fair, also set up the programming for the first IFGE convention, where I was an alternate board member.

Getting back to 1982, when my youngest daughter went off to college, our two older children already married and living on their own, we took her teen phone and started listing it as a gender information center. For the next twenty years or so we were helping cross-dressers and wives and even some parents with where to find information and where to get help for any problems they may have.

Hurdles still had to be overcome. After the children left, for example, the question was whether Lynda would dress in the house before going out to meetings or other engagements. Since we lived in a small town, about seven thousand residents, in northwestern New Jersey, I was concerned about how the local police might handle a driver that was cross-dressed—a real fear since I had heard or read numerous times about police officers harassing cross-dressers. We also worried about something happening to us when I was out dressed and that our children would find out at what might be an inappropriate way or time. So we decided to tell them about Lynda and educate them about the gender community.

That job fell to Marilyn, since Mom always had a closer relationship with the children than Dad. As it turned out, Lynda and Marilyn were coming home from a formal affair one Saturday night around midnight when the flashing red lights of a police car pulled us over. Even though

the road was empty, I was driving in the left lane, the reason being that
it was a deer area and my wife had already totaled one car in the area by
hitting a deer. When the officer came up to the car to ask to see my
license and registration, my evening purse and gown were in plain sight.
He asked if I had been drinking, and when I said no and there obviously
was no smell of alcohol coming from the car, he very politely said thank
you and went back to his car. I wasn't sure if I should be glad he didn't
comment or upset he didn't ask me to get out of the car to see my
gown. Anyway, it was time to tell the children about Dad's big secret.

Bruce, my oldest, at twenty-eight, married and living in south
Jersey, thought it was just great. He was always a rebel growing up, and
it fell on me to keep him in check. Being young myself and not knowing
much about parenthood, I think I may have been a bit more stern than
necessary. He was very smart and aggressive, always trying something
new, and like most children always pushing the boundaries. I had always
been the conservative, trying to control him enough to keep him from
getting into trouble. He thought it wonderful that I was able to express
my inner feelings, and I think that secretly he was glad I wasn't the mean
old man who didn't understand the freedom he wanted. His only comment was to wonder how in his seventeen years of living at home he had
never found out about it. His wife also thought it was okay until a
couple of years later when she found out her favorite cousin was also a
cross-dresser, then she really got into thinking it was great.

Sis, my middle daughter, twenty-six, also married and with a little
one, thought it was crazy, but if it was okay with her mother, then it
would be okay with her.

Hally, my youngest, just twenty-two, thought it was cool, but her
boyfriend (later to be husband) had a few doubts. I had to go skiing with
him, taking him down some expert ski slopes to reestablish my manhood, and he was okay with it after that. They are both very careful to
shield their young children from it.

Apparently we made the right decision in having Marilyn tell them,
because she came across with a positive attitude and they all picked that
up. All making about the same comment, "If it's okay with you, Mom,
it's okay with us. You have to live with him." The following year, Mariette Pathy Allen, who was compiling her book called *Transformations*, was
looking for some stories with children. Bruce and Michelle, his wife,
allowed us to do a shooting in their house with my two-year-old
grandson. We really had a good time, and it was a lot of fun. She also got
some great photos for her book.

I do not dress as Lynda in front of my children, except maybe for Halloween, but they do see pictures, and we like to tell amusing stories about Lynda's adventures. Marilyn always likes to tell stories about the meetings and conventions with a little touch of humor, which most of the time is easy to find. We did have a breakthrough two years ago when Sis said Lynda could come to her Halloween party. Marilyn said I had better not look too good or someone might get suspicious, so she had me use my own hair, which she did up a bit, and that made me look a little older and not too convincing. It had Sis's friends, who always saw me as a strict disciplinarian redneck, shaking their heads and wondering what the hell was going on. In fact, one of her friends insisted I looked just like one of her aunts.

In the late eighties we traveled all over the country attending gender events, going to all the Tri-Ess conventions and also many of the IFGE conventions, and meetings in Biloxi, San Francisco, Port Angeles, Texas, and quite a few others.

It was at a Texas Tea weekend in the late eighties that I first met Phyllis Frye. She gave a seminar on legal issues in relation to the transgender individual. She was doing a tremendous amount of work on their behalf, with lots of energy and dedication. She exhibited a sincerity and honesty that I found very impressive, and when in the early nineties she called for volunteers to go to Washington on a lobby mission, I immediately signed on.

The mission was to visit every senator on Capitol Hill to explain our position on inserting the term "gender" into the existing Employment Non-Discrimination Act (ENDA) bill that was being brought up for a vote every year. I left my apartment in Manhattan, took a cab to Penn Station, and bought a first-class round-trip ticket to Washington. I was wearing and carrying a suitcase with only clothes for Lynda and had the most wonderful feeling in the world. I was sure to pack very conservatively with comfortable one-inch heels. It was the most exciting thing I had ever done. Lynda was out alone in the world doing her thing. The cab ride to the train station, the train ride to Washington, and the cab in Washington to the motel where Phyllis had set up her headquarters all went beautifully.

The ENDA bill had been up a number of times and always defeated, but by a smaller amount each time. We were to inquire from each senator who had voted for the bill whether adding the term "gender" to the bill would have any effect on his or her vote. The volunteers were set up into three-person teams and each given a list of senators to visit. We walked around the Senate office building (my heals clicking on the marble floors) for three days, meeting to compare notes at lunch and again each evening. We did not, of course, meet any of the senators but rather their aides who were handling the ENDA bill for them. They all stated unquestionably that they would still vote for the bill. All told, it was a very pleasurable and rewarding experience. The trip back to New York went equally as well, and it was an experience I still think of fondly today.

Also in the late 1980s Virginia Prince and Carol Beecroft decided to form a board of directors to direct the future course of the Tri-Ess organization. Virginia called me with a request for me to join the board. I told her I would be honored, and in November 1988 we held our first meeting at a Tri-Ess convention in Chicago. The meeting gave me a chance to meet some of the movers and shakers of the gender community from around the country, an exceptional bunch of ladies. It was and still is an interesting experience that I have always enjoyed.

The following years Marilyn and I involved ourselves in speaking at colleges and to professional groups in the Greater New York area. Prof. Ron Moglia, who teaches graduate students at New York University, had us speak to each of his classes. Amy Altenhaus, PhD, who lectures to psychology interns and clinical staff members for the Department of Human Services for the state of New Jersey, had us speak as part of her program once or twice a year. We have also given programs to undergraduates at Caldwell College and Livingston College (Rutgers University). There are a couple of very interesting differences I have found between speaking to professionals and graduate students as compared to undergraduates. One difference is the level of trust. In an effort to make sure everyone knows exactly what I mean when I use specific terms, in the first few minutes of my talk I give my definition of the two terms: *sex* and *gender*. I say that when I speak of sex I am talking about a person's physical characteristics, having a penis or a vagina, and when I speak about gender I am talking about a *social role* that society has set up for the behavior of a person of that sex. Although trans people themselves do not always conform to such definitions, graduate students and professionals will accept these definitions on face value without comment, whereas in a class of undergraduates there will usually be at least a handful of students who will challenge these definitions. When I stated in one class that I was heterosexual and that most cross-dressers also were heterosexual, one student insisted I was not telling the truth and that I was hiding the fact that I was really gay, even though my wife was there presenting also. We did finally convince him that there was such a thing as a heterosexual cross-dresser, and it was a great learning experience for everyone.

There was an incident at one Tri-Ess meeting that I would like to tell you about. At our meetings we generally keep the door open and if people come by and look in, we invite them in to learn all about us. Sometimes they say "no thanks" and sometimes some inquisitive person comes in and has a great experience. This one Saturday night there was a large group of teenagers staying at the hotel who were involved in some tournament in the area. When any of them would pass our meeting room, they would stick their head in, giggle, and run away telling all their friends to go past us and look in. Knowing teenagers, we just laughed at them. Later that evening when Marilyn and I were leaving, we happened to pass a few of them on an elevator getting ready to go upstairs when one of the boys said to the others in a stage whisper, "Hey, there goes one of those women that looks like a man." You can guess the great laugh Marilyn and I had with that.

Then there came the time when we felt the need to change our chapter meeting place. The hotel we were meeting in, in Westchester, was taking in welfare families and there were a lot of children running around—besides we were now getting around thirty members to the meetings and more were coming from the central and southern parts of the state. Looking for a different meeting place was no small undertaking. There were certain criteria we needed to meet. First, we needed a room that could hold at least fifty people comfortably, in a location next to regular sleeping rooms that we could rent to use as changing rooms (we used two, a smoking and a nonsmoking), because many of the new members were uncomfortable with walking in the halls when dressed. We did not want to be located near a bar since some of the gals came already dressed and wanted to avoid people who had been drinking. We wanted a separate entrance and a room with its own bathroom, if possible. I found I had to look at older hotels because the new ones all had meeting rooms together and away from the sleeping rooms. I finally found a place on Route 4, a few miles south of where we were, that met all our requirements. The group had decided that wherever we moved the management would know about us and would be approving of us as a renter. In getting ready for my meeting with the manager and signing a contract for the next year, I spent a week going over ways of presenting us in a favorable light. Things like we were mostly professional people who would not make a lot of noise, would pay every month in advance, and would even clean up a bit before we left. Feeling confident with my presentation, Len went to sign the contract. The manager was a middle-aged woman and seemed to be quite friendly. Everything went smoothly until I asked her if she would like to know something about our group and she politely said that that really wasn't necessary. So I just as politely said that I would like her to know something about the group anyway. When she agreed, I started off with "We are a group of heterosexual transvestites." At this she put her pen down, turned to face me with a questioning stare, and after a few seconds very softly said to me, "What's a heterosexual?" Now all my preparation on explaining transvestism went down the drain and I sat fumbling for a simple nonsexual way to explain what a heterosexual was. Anyway, after I fumbled around for a few minutes, she said no matter and finished signing the contract.

The main newspaper in that part of New Jersey is the *Bergen Record*, and a little while after we moved down from Westchester a reporter and photographer asked to do a feature story about us. We were delighted and invited them down to a meeting. Their intention was to come down for about an hour, talk to some people, get some photos, and be on their way. Once they met us, we couldn't get rid of them; they stayed the entire meeting and finally left when we all started to go home. They gave us a beautiful spread in the Sunday Living section of the newspaper. Strangely enough, the same thing—different reporter, same newspaper—happened almost exactly twenty years later. And we got another great Sunday spread. These were both really great experiences. Teaching people who have a real interest in gender-variant behavior and getting people to understand and accept the feelings of others I have always found to be unbelievably rewarding and enjoyable.

In the following years I chaired two Tri-Ess conventions in the New York area, and another cross-dresser and I started to run a yearly open-weekend event in Manhattan. We called it Moonlight in Manhattan, attracting seventy or eighty people for each event, but lasting only two years. I also set up two cross-dressing weekends a year at a gay resort in the Poconos that they are still successfully running.

Currently, I am trying to track down some of the other seniors to see how their bi-gender feelings are evolving. I know that my feelings have not only been cyclical over the years but have gone through changes, and I am interested in learning how other seniors are handling any changes they may be experiencing. The most outstanding of my changes is that the great feeling of anticipation I used to get when I knew I would be Lynda is gone. When I knew I would be going to Fantasia

Fair, I would start getting excited a week in advance of our leaving for Provincetown. Currently, although my feelings when dressed are as wonderful as ever, I just do not get excited at the prospect of getting dressed.

Now, I got out of bed at eight o'clock this morning, same as every other morning. Taking off my nightgown, I put on my panties (size 6 nylon) and my bra (36A) and a cotton "Haynes for Her" sweat suit. Since my retirement a few years ago, sweat suits in and around the house have been my favorite choice of outerwear. I don't give a second thought to the panties—they being just another form of shorts—but the bra does invoke thoughts. I know that after the first few minutes and an occasional adjustment throughout the day I may not think about it for the rest of the day. I wonder, then, why do I feel that I want to wear it every day? But getting back to my current situation, is putting on the bra daily, or questioning putting on the bra every day, the issue? Anyway, my wife calls me half a woman because there are a lot of things women do that I have no interest in doing: getting dressed up and going out, yes; housecleaning, no. But I do really try to be more understanding and nurturing and to carry some of the gentleness over to my male role.

We have over the years developed two sets of friends. Local people, business associates, and some friends from our childhood know nothing of Lynda. Then, having met some very nice people at our gender group meetings and others from events around the country, we have put together another group of good friends. Also included in this group are the wonderful people we have met at the gay bar we know in the West Village and the gay synagogue we attend most Fridays. We have on rare occasions brought some of the people in the "know" category to functions with the "not know" friends and family, but not often. We kind of go along with the "need to know" concept, because you can never tell in advance just how any individual will handle this information.

Ever since I first realized I had mixed gender feelings, over sixty years ago, I have read almost everything published on the subject and spoken with a great many professionals and hundreds of people with various gender feelings. I learned a long time ago that no one knows the cause, which is no doubt buried somewhere in the nature verses nurture controversy. So I gave up my search and just accepted and enjoyed my feelings.

As I enter my senior years and knowing there are a great many others like myself out there, I have been seeking them out to learn how and if their feelings are changing. My curiosity has again been aroused as to how others in my age category are managing what gender-variant feelings they may still have. I now put myself in the category of "recreational cross-dresser." However, given the free choice every morning, I probably would enjoy dressing en femme more than in my male role. Unfortunately, with male facial features and a large body (5'11"/190 lbs.), it is quite difficult to pass unnoticed, and I am *not* always ready and willing to defend my presentation. Then there is the discomfort of my loved ones with my presentation not being generally acceptable with our social environment. I am not yet ready to sacrifice their comfort for my own. Basically, I am not far from where I have always been when it comes to my cross-dressing. The main change being that since it is just my wife and me at home, and I get to spend a lot more time at home, I do get to dress more then ever. No wig or makeup, though, too much trouble for me now.

Now we go out as Marilyn and Lynda every Friday into New York, visiting our favorite girl bar, going to a restaurant for dinner, and then to the gay and lesbian synagogue—Lynda's night out. Every other Thursday Lynda goes to a movie and to dinner in a local restaurant with a transsexual friend. I believe that the more time Lynda is out in public and the more people see her, the more familiar and less unknown transgender people become. I think people fear the unknown, so the more people who see us and get to know us will generally lead to less fear and more acceptance. My story would not be complete or my life half as enjoyable as it has been without the companionship and understanding of the woman I love, who has always loved me. Her journey has been as big if not bigger than my own. Her path through the years, starting with complete ignorance of my cross-dressing feelings to total acceptance, is nothing short of a small miracle to me. Her unconditional love, intelligence, honesty, and sincere willingness to understand have made our fifty-year marriage something to be envied. She has educated herself to the point where for the last twenty years she has, as a peer counselor, been able to help countless other wives. I can't imagine how many couples there are whose lives she has helped. To this day, her story leaves people in awe. This was her reply to my children writing about me:

> I just read what my children wrote about their father being a cross-dresser and am proud of our family. Since this biography is not about me, I will be brief about my journey with Lynda. Looking back over the past fifty years, I must say it was a good journey since we were best friends before we were lovers and still are best friends.
>   When I think back there were tumultuous times, but my goal was

to learn as much as I could about cross-dressing and gender issues and to try to accept it as best as I could.

I keep hearing on the news that sex and finances are the top causes for divorce, but neither of these was ever an issue for us. Over the years we received excellent advice from many professional therapists in the gender community, who also taught us how to communicate better. To name a few, Roger Peo, Sandra Cole, Niela Miller, Ariadne Kane, Richard Docter, and I couldn't leave out Virginia Prince. We learned early in our marriage to communicate, negotiate, and have a sense of humor. This seemed to work for us on almost all problems that had come up in our marriage—the cross-dressing was a small part of the large picture, since I had my parents, children, and extended family to keep me busy (they didn't know about the cross-dressing).

There are still challenges for me and bridges to cross, but I am certain I will meet them all. I believe that my experiences over the years at various group meetings and conventions have made me a better and more objective person where other people's values are concerned.

LIFE GOES ON

Marlene Liston

Looking back, my childhood seems quite normal in most ways. I had a circle of friends (all boys) and was born and raised in a very Catholic household. My mother was forty and my father fifty-six at the time of my birth. I had two slightly older sisters who were both beautiful and talented. We lived well in a house over three thousand square feet on a half-acre lot. My father had been quite wealthy, and while we were still well off in the Depression, we are not as rich as we once were.

When I was seven years old, I was confirmed into the Catholic Church, and on the same day I was confirmed I decided that its teachings were utter nonsense—largely owing to actions of a single blockheaded nun. Still the pervasive culture of Catholicism continues to have an effect on me to this day.

Secretly, I began to cross-dress when I was ten years old—borrowing some of my sister's old clothes, making them into my own with needle and thread. Fortunately, I had access to a large house and garage and a huge cellar where I could disappear for hours on end. I got very good at hiding things. At first, I focused on skirts, because they seemed the most important in cross-dressing since my shirts could be more easily neutralized. I got so good that I even attended school en femme at two Halloween parties in the fourth and fifth grades, and I recall that I "passed" easily.

At age twelve, I developed a fascination with astronomy (which I have to this day), and I spent hours grinding telescope mirrors in my cellar lab—usually dressed en femme. My mother seemed to ignore me there. Among my friends, however, I was social, and we played a lot of games together: chess, basketball, Ping-Pong, pool (billiards). I was also a good student, and my grades were good (except for Latin, perhaps because my mother wanted me to consider the priesthood). Physically, I grew rapidly in junior high school and was fairly apheretic. In the ninth grade finals for physical education, I came in fifth in the three-mile run, high jumped five feet seven inches, chinned myself twenty-two consecutive times, and did sixty-four consecutive push-ups. At five feet eleven inches, I held my own easily in school yard fights. The only thought that really worried me was that my habit of cross-dressing would be discovered. (I did not even have a word for it then.)

In high school, I discovered motorcycles—still a passion of mine. In spite of my secret cross-dressing, I seemed to have done the normal high school things. My friends and I group dated, although I was rather shy with girls. Still, I went to the senior prom. I was active in the drama club, was on the school newspaper staff, and directed some public radio programs. I also started earning money—shoveling snow and delivering newspapers. At home and by myself I also became quite skillful with sewing my growing hoard of feminine clothing, which I hid in secret panels I built in the basement. When I knew my parents would be out for a night and would be late coming home, I would sneak into their bedroom and try on my mom's nightgown and some of her clothes. I became expert at putting them back in their right places since my mother never made any comments.

On an academic level, I read Plato and became quite interested in philosophy. I was, however, much more interested in physics. I completed my ten-inch Newtonian telescope and got an article about my accomplishment published in the local newspaper.

My early college years, however, did not go well. I flunked out of a rather nice Ivy League college, found work as a lab tech for General Electric, and was more or less at loose ends. I did join the National Guard, which I regard as one of the smarter moves in my life. The Korean War was going strong and I knew I would be drafted at age twenty, so I joined the National Guard to get a head start. My Guard experience I think made a world of difference in my military career. After basic training I was sent to leadership school for two months and then on to Fort Benning for officer candidate school. Unfortunately, I was dropped after three months when it became apparent I had no leadership capacity.

Reassigned to the West Coast, I hitchhiked from Fort Benning to

San Francisco in three days. After that things went very well. Within six months, I was a corporal with a great job at division level, owned my own car, was living in my own room, and carried a pass in my pocket.

I gave lectures on astronomy to the local astronomy club and had my own lab at a local college where I worked on a large telescope project. Of course, I managed to store my dresses and other fem clothing in my new lab, and I did a lot of work while cross-dressed. I also lost my long-preserved virginity to a USO girl who was doing her best to support the troops. I even got credit for a year in college by taking an exam at the end of my two-year enlistment. After that I headed south with five hundred dollars in pay in my 1947 Chevrolet.

Arriving in Los Angeles in February 1955, I put on a dress and a wig and headed out in public. Looking back on this period, I must admit that the Old Catholic doctrine of guardian angels gains a certain credibility since I got by without any serious problems. I soon decided, however, that I needed to work on my femme image.

Up to this point in time, I was unaware that there was anyone else in the world who was also a cross-dresser. In an obscure Hollywood bookstore, I discovered a copy of *Bazaire* magazine, which had photos and stories of men in dresses. There were others like me.

Still, I had to get on with my life. Going back east to my family did not seem a good idea. I was sure they would find out my big secret, and I felt I could not stand the potential embarrassment. After a few weeks working at unpleasant jobs, I applied to Cal Poly in San Luis Obispo, passed the entrance exam, and moved into a dorm, all of this financed by the GI Bill.

I declared physics as my major, although I did not think I would do well since, after all, I had flunked out of college only three years before. Still things went well. My roommate turned out to be from my hometown, so we had something in common. I got a part-time job as a lifeguard and started dating. After two quarters, I had a B+ average.

Living in a dorm limited my opportunities to cross-dress. Furthermore, there was a serious shortage of women at what was then an all-male school. I decided to transfer to Fresno State College. To make a long story short, I graduated three years later with a degree in philosophy/psychology and minors in math, physics, and education. In all of the psychology classes, there was not a word about cross-dressing, transsexuality, or even homosexual behavior.

Going on to a graduate year, I fell in love and married, received my general secondary teaching credential, and went job hunting and became a high school teacher. I was certain that marriage would end my cross-dressing, but all it did was lead to a series of purges—that is, I tended to destroy all of my feminine clothes, and I became increasingly frustrated.

Outwardly I led a normal life. My wife was a teacher, valedictorian of her college class, spoke five languages, and was an accomplished pianist. During the next twelve years while I taught high school science and math, she taught elementary grades. We both loved our work. Every summer I would travel back to the East Coast to visit my family. My sisters had graduated from college, married, but continued to look after my now aging parents.

Together in California we took up little theater—I acted in twenty plays over the next twenty years, but she only acted in three plays and dropped out of theater work after a few years. We played a lot of tennis, and I found myself captain of the local men's B team for a decade. I took up jogging early in the 1960s. Later I ran a lot of ten-kilometer races, a few half marathons, two full twenty-six-mile marathons (too damn far), and finally even triathelons. I ran my last race at age fifty-eight in 1991. On top of that, there was soccer and downhill skiing and backpacking all over the High Sierra. Every winter I would take vanloads of high school boys to local ski resorts for a weekend of Kamikaze-style downhill. Every summer from 1961 to 1967 we would drive to the University of Colorado where I finally received a master's degree in chemistry in 1967.

While all of this was going on, I continued to secretly cross-dress. I never told anyone. I built secret panels in the attic to hold my stash of dresses.

At the end of twelve years of marriage, we divorced. I do not blame anyone but myself. I am sure she had found out about my second self. I still do not know for sure, but it's more likely that I spent too much time on sports and science (and cross-dressing) and not enough with her.

Though my divorce in 1969 emotionally devastated me and I thought she had discovered my cross-dressing, I was still so embarrassed that I could not even broach the subject. For the next three years I concentrated on work and sports. My school was an excellent one with small classes and good kids, and I enjoyed being the science teacher.

In 1973 I met Susan. She taught in a local elementary school and was fourteen years younger than I. She was attractive, played good tennis, and liked to ride on the back of my motorcycle in the nearby High Sierra mountains. I invited her to live with me, and she moved in. (I did not tell her about my cross-dressing but rather purged most of my femme clothes, and hid the rest.)

Finally in 1978, after attending an eight-day seminar on personal development at the University of Santa Cruz, I got enough courage to tell Susan I was a cross-dresser. She did not like the idea, but she accepted it. She even bought me dresses for Christmas presents and taught me how to sew skirts for myself. I started electrolysis. I also ran a twenty-six-mile marathon in exactly four hours at age forty-five.

The next year Amber moved in with us. A close friend of Susan, she was a member of the same Transcendental Meditation Group. Amber was brilliant, beautiful, and working hard to become a rock singer. On occasion she sang with a traveling nightclub band. Often the three of us would play Scrabble for hours in the evening with Amber usually winning. Though a few of my friends accused me of running a harem, my relationship always remained platonic.

Susan also joined me in the community theater. In 1981 I did my last play, Arthur Miller's *The Crucible*, which meant that over the years I had played twenty roles in twenty plays. I even won a trophy for best support in one of them.

To this point, the only individuals who knew I cross-dressed were Susan and Amber (unless my ex-wife knew). I continued to cross-dress and, wherever I could, I read about it. In one article, the post office box of Tri-Ess (Society for the Second Self), a national heterosexual cross-dressing group, was listed. I was very much surprised and delighted to learn that the headquarters was only ten miles from my home in rural California. We exchanged letters, and I sent her two tickets to a little theater production in which I was acting at the time. Carol and her wife, Norma, introduced themselves to me after the final curtain. I was very cautious. As a schoolteacher in a very conservative community, I felt that any hint of such activity would immediately result in my being fired.

Tri-Ess at this period of time was fairly small: chapters in New York, Chicago, Los Angeles, and Tulare, with perhaps three or four hundred members scattered all over the country. Carol was doing almost all the work, which included publishing a magazine, the *Femme Mirror*; maintaining a directory of members; letter forwarding (people did not directly communicate with each other but for security reasons used a forwarding service that Carol ran); being interviewed on television and radio; answering anguished letters of inquiry; plus the simple business of billing and mailing. In addition, Carol was president of the Alpha chapter in Los Angeles, 180 miles away. And she also ran several more public business ventures.

My life took on a whole new direction. I started helping out in her office—answering mail, forwarding letters, and going out in public in a dress with Carol and her wife, Norma. At first, I did not pass too well, which led to a number of somewhat amusing incidents, but gradually I got better. I did have a few advantages at five feet eleven inches and 145 pounds with no visible Adam's apple, small hands, and feminine prescription glasses, and I soon passed into the woodwork. Gradually Tri-Ess became a major part of my life. Together, Susan and I attended Carol's local Tri-Ess group as well as the Alpha chapter in Los Angeles. The girls of the Alpha chapter really helped me develop my femme image. I found one wig that really seemed to work, and by the early eighties, Susan, Amber, and Marlene (my femme name) would drive to Fresno for dinner and a show on an occasional weekend. My femme voice seemed to get me by well; I think theater work helped here.

In 1984 Susan left me for a job teaching at a college in the Midwest while Amber stayed with me (still a platonic relationship). I began attending numerous cross-dresser get-togethers. I attended my first Holiday en femme in San Francisco with Carol and Norma and spent five days en femme in the big city. We hit all the tourist spots, went to seminars, and I finally met Virginia Prince.

Next year Karen moved in with me, and Amber headed for Texas. Karen was twenty-seven years younger than I. She invited me out on our first date. Karen has her master's from Stanford and taught a couple of years at my school before moving to teach at the local college. On our second date I gave her a Tri-Ess brochure and explained that I was a cross-dresser. As a card-carrying feminist, this did not seem to bother Karen at all. Most important, she was a good tennis player.

I became ever more daring, attending a Femme Fling at Lake Tahoe, a four-day weekend get-together at Pajaro Dunes near Santa Cruz, and gambling en femme in Reno and cruising around Santa Cruz.

In 1992 Karen, who had taken a job teaching at a college in the Bay Area, moved out, although we did visit often over the next few years. On the local scene I met several other cross-dressers who remain good friends. Finally, when I retired from teaching after thirty-six years, I began to lecture publicly in college classes about cross-dressing. My transgendered social life expanded with a Cotillion in San Francisco, Hearts of Gender in Burbank, and various projects for Tri-Ess on what is called the Big Sister program and the library project.

I became more daring. The tennis club that I belonged to holds an annual Halloween costume party and tennis match, and in 1997 I showed up wearing a gold miniskirt instead of shorts. The following year I dressed fully en femme—wig, padding, jewelry, makeup.

After the match I pulled on a long skirt and explained to my friends that I was going to do a little shopping downtown before going home and that a miniskirt was not appropriate. The women in the club were surprised and full of questions, and I finally explained that I was a part-time cross-dresser. Everyone seemed to accept it. I should not have been surprised since by 1998 the TV talk shows and the movies had educated the public well.

I have often been kidded by some of the members through the years, and some of the women ask me about what I will wear next year. Since they are all aware that I frequently appear elsewhere in public en femme, they just seem to accept that this is me.

In 1998 I drove to Los Angeles, and Virginia Prince and I flew to Miami en femme. This was my first flying trip as a woman. We took a four-day cruise with Peggy Rudd's group, then rented a cab the next day to tour Miami with two other cross-dressers. I wasn't out of a dress for a solid week. Knowing that I can go out in public, en femme, virtually anywhere is astonishing to me. If I look in a mirror, I still see a guy in a dress, but when I go out in public, no one seems to notice.

I am now in my seventies, and I live en femme about half of the time. My social life revolves around transgender friends and activities. I still play a lot of tennis. I have also gone car camping in Sequoia Park with transgendered friends. Our local transgender group has about twenty persons, with a large group of them young female-to-male trans-sexuals. Over the last five years I have had several young transgenders live in the back room. One of my best friends is a transgender, who is eighty-two and in a wheelchair most of the time. On Tuesday night, however, he and Marlene always go out to dinner.

Though the Salvation Army probably benefited from the frequent purges I went through in my earlier years, each time I was motivated by a decision to never cross-dress again. It is sort of like the old joke about smoking. "It's easy to quit," one man said, "I did it seven times last year alone." Finally, I could accept myself and enjoy life. I wish I had not been so fearful about discovery for so long, but times change, and my lifestyle has changed with them.

RUN BEFORE THE WIND

Marty M. Hagglund

I see that it's time to own up to the disaster as well as the heavenly joy. I suppose I had it better than most, at least for a while. My spouse of twenty years is married to someone else. My home on Annabessacook Lake now belongs to someone else as well. My career is finished, and my mental health has more twists and turns than a Stephen King novel. Am I bitter? Angry? You bet I am. Along with that feeling is also soaring joy. My spirit has come home to my body. Granted it's a wounded spirit, but nevertheless I am whole, finally for the first time in my life.

I guess I should start in the beginning. For the sake of clarity, I will use a decade approach. The first ten years of my life saw what appeared to be a male child born into the world. My family consisted of Mom, Dad, and one brother four years my elder. I have found many milestones in my life that pointed to the fact that I was a girl child and not a boy child. The first one was when I was about four or five years old. We lived in an apartment in Long Island, New York. My next-door neighbors were of Chinese decent. There were three daughters. I used to play house with the youngest daughter. I remember one summer's day Betty and I were deciding who would be the mommy and daddy for our game. She looked at me with her big beautiful eyes and said, "You can't be the mommy because you're a boy." I remember being very sad and not really understanding why she said that to me. I know I felt numb and ashamed of myself. I carried that hurt around with me for some time. We continued to play house, but it never was the same to me after that. The next milestone of my journey occurred in the playground at the elementary school I attended. I will never forget that day. Our kindergarten teacher came out to call us all in to class. She had an old-fashioned school bell she rang. "Attention," she said. "All boys line up on my right and all girls on my left." Well, I think you know where I went. I lined up at the end of the line on her left, since I am a tall person. My teacher looked down each line as she examined each student. As she came to me, she smiled a big smile and said the most devastating words I have ever heard. "Marty, you are a little boy, you belong on the other line." The whole class laughed. I went over to the other line and just cried. I cannot tell you what that short moment did to me. It was then that I realized the nightmare was true. Through that week I was devastated. In fact, the school called my mother in to tell her that I was immature and just cried all the time. Little did they know the true reason for my tears. It must have been one year later that I ran across the issue of anatomical differences between girls and boys. Again, it was with my Chinese neighbors. I had stopped in to their store to pick up some laundry. My neighbors ran a laundry and did a very brisk business that supported the family. I was waiting for my change when out of the corner of my eye I saw my friend come out of the bathroom, with Mom close behind, with no clothes on. It was in that short minute that I saw that she did not possess the same anatomy as I did. I remember running home and straight into the bathroom where there was a long mirror. I took a long look at myself and saw that I was different indeed. I guess there comes a time when your brain puts all the pieces together. It was then that I knew that there was something terribly wrong with me. Confusion set in, and for a few years I just kept my feelings and fear to myself. Secrets are difficult to keep. I think back now and realize that this knowledge was something I couldn't tell anyone about. The time frame was the 1950s. Men still wore large-brimmed hats, and women stayed at home to mind the children. There was no blending of gender in those days. You either were a boy or a girl. In my mind I knew and felt enough to shut up and keep my feelings to myself. These first ten years set the stage for how I would deal with my dysphoric feelings.

My family decided we were to move to a new town. This meant I would no longer be around my Chinese friends anymore. I started in a new school, a Catholic school with nuns as teachers. The classes were for most of the next year separated into boys' classes and girls' classes. Gender or sexuality was not taught in any form. We were taught that "good boys and girls" never thought about their bodies in any fashion.

There were school clubs to drive home the thought that purity of mind and body was paramount.

DECADE 2 (YEARS 11–20)

It was during this decade that I found my secret would bring me to be hospitalized for trying to get "rid" of my anatomy. Let me begin a bit earlier. The first two years progressed until we were told that the school would now have both girls and boys in the same classes. My schoolwork took a turn for the worse. I spent most of my time observing the girls nearest me. I watched how they carried themselves and especially how they were so much softer than the boys were. I watched as they grew into the ladies they would become. Many nights I cried myself to sleep praying that I would wake up as the girl that I knew I was. It was during the last week of classes that year that I remember the teacher discussing with the girls that they were allowed to wear nylons and some makeup to class the next year. Puberty had struck. During that summer I remember thinking that I would be able to wear, act, and be the girl that I knew when school resumed. I suppose I lived more in my mind than in reality. That next school year brought major changes to the girls and I wanted so much to be just like them. Puberty had blessed the girls with varying degrees of breast growth and the typical widening of their hips. I watched in the school yard as they learned social skills and started to look at boys in a different way. The best I could do was to live in a fantasy. My own puberty was very late in coming. I was made fun of by the boys and told I was a fairy. I just retreated back into myself even more. I can remember looking at my anatomy and hating it. I thought if I could just get rid of it, I would feel better. It was then I tried what is now called "tucking." It's not something I learned from anyone, only my feeble attempt to rid myself of this anatomy. At such a young age and considering the force with which I pushed body parts where they didn't belong, its no wonder I finally hurt myself. I remember passing out one night at a school meeting. When I awoke, I was in the emergency room of the local hospital. I was in agonizing pain. My scrotum started to swell up. It reached the size of a grapefruit. I was told I had damaged a testicle. I was put in a private room, and what is called a Bellevue Bridge was erected under my scrotum. It is a way to keep the testicles elevated to reduce swelling. To my horror, they left no covering over my body parts and packed me with ice. Nurses would come in and ask how I felt.

Naturally, they were all very pretty young women. Here I am with my anatomy packed in ice for the entire world to see. I became very depressed and nontalkative. I remember a doctor coming in my room and shutting the door. He began by telling me he was a psychiatrist. He told me he knew that this was no accident as I had told everyone. He said, "I know you did this to yourself." I just looked at him and would not speak. He asked me if I liked being a boy. I just looked at his eyes and cried. I wished I had the ability to tell him the truth. He already knew the truth. It must have been 11 PM that night when the shift changed. A very friendly nurse came in and sat at my bedside. She looked at me and said, "What's wrong? You can tell me." I looked at her and said for the first time in my life, "I am a girl not a boy." She came in to talk to me every night until I was discharged home. It was after that experience that I made my mind up I would be the girl I should have been all along.

It was at this time I started to cross-dress. I found that the place we lived in had this cool attic. It was here that my sense of self started to take shape. My mother and I were about the same size in clothing. She always stored clothing upstairs. It wasn't hard to find complete outfits to wear. I think the first time I put on one of my mother's dresses I cried so hard I had to dry the dress out before I put it away. The attic was up two flights of stairs from our apartment, so the rest of the family hardly ever came up. I used every excuse to spend time up there. As I look back now, I see this time as very special to me. It was at this time that I became aware of transsexualism.

The sixties brought about many changes and a chance to slightly change my appearance. I was in high school now. I had found that my love for music would give me opportunities that most persons would see as only a passing fad. I grew my hair very long. I was seen as just another hippie. Keeping my secret started to have some serious consequences. I started to use pot on a regular basis. It took almost twenty more years before I gave the habit up. In later years I came to understand that pot does decrease serum testosterone in the bloodstream. It was during those high times I felt the calm I so desperately needed. I fully committed into playing music. I have some wonderful memories to look back on playing music in these turbulent times. I know that music saved my life during those difficult years. When my body finally did go through puberty, I had all I could do to not commit suicide. My deep faith and my music prevailed to help me get through it all.

DECADE 3 (YEARS 21–30)

These years between the ages of twenty-one and thirty found me making a last attempt to conform to my birth gender. I had graduated from high school and decided to pursue music as a full-time occupation. It was during one of my "gigs" that I found the person who I would fall in love with. It seemed impossible to me that anyone would love me. What took almost another thirty years to realize is that, to other people, I looked and sounded like any "normal" man. It was only after reassignment surgery and divorce that I was able to see the man I had been. This statement is not easy for me to write down. The dynamics of gender identity disorder are quite insidious. It took until my soul, spirit, and body were in alignment to understand and accept myself with all the many changes. I tried to tell her that I am not what you see. It was a halfhearted attempt because I wanted to spend the rest of my life with this person. I had to try to make this "gender bender" idea just go away. I returned to college and decided that nursing would be a good career to pursue. I certainly would feel right at home with all the women in nursing. It took many years to succeed, but I have found with most transsexual people that the drive to persevere is incredibly strong. I give a lot of the credit, for keeping me on track, to my ex-spouse. She provided the support, the love, and the reason to go on. Without her support, I might never have finished college. All through school I was so severely affected by dysphoria that I had difficulty concentrating. She gave me the focus, and my love of people brought me the rest of the way. After being married one year, my dysphoria resurfaced. I decided to seek counseling in the hope of ridding myself of these feelings. Now I had reason to just forget all this girl stuff. I walked into a meeting with a psychologist. I discussed my history with him. He looked at me and said this is an abomination to God. I stayed for months listening to his indoctrination of me. I became so frightened that it took me another ten years to finally face myself. I returned to my studies and music.

DECADE 4 (YEARS 31–40)

We decided that a move to Maine would benefit us both, since living in New York was becoming too busy. We found a year-round house on Annabessacook Lake in Maine to call home. My soul started to find peace there listening to the loons in summer and watching the seasons go by. My wife and I grew closer and closer as years went on. I had found the solace I needed to get up each morning. After some time, I began to grow very ill. Doctors couldn't find anything wrong, but I continued to grow weaker and more ill by the day. My work started to be affected by this strange illness. I finally had to leave nursing for a time and work with my wife cleaning buildings. Although I had told her that I did cross-dress, I never could admit to her or myself the depths of my feelings. As my condition grew worse, my family grew more and more concerned. Finally, one Sunday she came to me with tears in her eyes and asked me to tell her what was bothering me; that nothing would tear us apart. She told me she felt as if I would die if something were not done soon to help me. I looked at her and thought, and said, "I am a woman not a man." She looked at me and said, "Is that all?" I startled myself telling the one person who had accepted me, as I am, that I had felt this way all my life. She asked me what could I do about it. I told her I needed to explore my feminine side. We agreed to continue talking about this together. I felt a great relief, but at the same time I felt fear, fear for us about how this would work out. I think she felt it, too, but she never said anything to indicate her feelings.

DECADE 5 (YEARS 41–50)

This decade proved to be the defining years in my life. Since this encompasses the remainder of my story, it will be very detailed. Since I am fifty-three years old, as I write this, the details are still fresh in my mind.

The time is 1991. I am just forty years old now. Up until now, I only could dream and imagine what my life would look like as a woman. I made a decision to find out more information about transgendered people. At the time, I did not have a computer. I did it the old-fashioned way. The relevance this has to my story is to put in perspective finding any material on the subject and my elation over that "find." I think that manic describes the first time I read a copy of *Tapestry*, a transgender periodical. I stayed up until 3 AM looking at the articles in complete awe and wonder. After so many years have passed now, I still see persons coming to their own realizations, having the same sense of wonder. The more material I found, the more excited I became. In an article I recently published, I described the feeling as an "obsession." I looked for an experienced therapist who had understanding of these issues. I distinctly remembered the fiasco with the psychologist and didn't wish to repeat that experience. As I began working with a therapist, I found that transgendered persons could come in various types. Relevant to me, I found immediately that there were cross-dressers and transsexual people. It was at this time that I decided to look for a support group here in Maine. I assumed that the chances of finding such a group in Maine were slim. To my surprise, there was a group meeting not far from my home. I wrote to the address I was given and then I had to wait. It felt like an eternity, but finally a letter came. The president of the support group wrote to me saying to call her to schedule an appointment for an interview. All during this period I spent many hours talking with my spouse. I think the shock of it failed to reach us both, especially the realization of what the future might hold for us.

It was a Sunday afternoon when Catherine came from *Transsupport* to our home. She had a friend with her, another transsexual person. We sat in the living room with the two of them talking. At first, the conversation was light. We talked about the support group, when it met, and details of the group. I remember the look on Catherine's face when she spoke of marriage. She was trying to be as gentle as possible. All I remember was the one word spoken and the deadly silence that followed. She had said that if you are indeed transsexual, that we, meaning my spouse and I, would have to *divorce*. Divorce? Us? Never! I felt numb, shocked. We escorted the two girls out and came back into the house. My spouse looked at me and cried. All I could do was to comfort her and tell her that I was not sure what I had to do yet. That was why I needed to be with a support group. I also made my mind up that I would look into this idea that two married people had to divorce if one of them was to obtain reassignment surgery. The pain that this information had caused to my small family made me say "forget it" to the whole idea. I had no intention of divorcing just to please others. I felt that was up to the two of us and not anyone else. I remember that the thinking of this time period was that some surgeons required the person to produce a writ of divorce before they would schedule you for reassignment surgery. The surgeons had experience with being sued by the spouses of transsexuals. I contacted a lawyer who had a great deal of experience with these matters. I felt a huge relief when I was told that idea was old fashioned. The attorney said that some surgeons may require that, however it was my choice which surgeon I used. My spouse was relieved. I felt I had won another battle, that I was indeed closer to my lifelong dream. I began to make inroads with the transgendered community. I started to understand more about the process and just what it would take for this to become reality. I had not made my mind up that I needed intervention on this level. I was still in denial. I have been called stubborn, but I felt that when it comes to rearranging your genitals, I have to be absolutely sure. One day after surgery is not the time to think whoops! I goofed.

An opportunity came up that I couldn't refuse. A friend had told me about Provincetown, Massachusetts. I looked into the possibility of spending some time in that community confirming if I was indeed a cross-dresser or a transsexual. I had never been away from my spouse for any period of time before. I knew that I needed to do this alone. If I had taken my family along, I am sure I would have spent more time concerned with them than myself. I had to be sure. All through this process, milestones had arisen. These are moments that define the next part of the journey. Decisions made at this time are critical. I had made arrangements to spend a week in Provincetown with a close friend. My spouse must have felt lost at that moment. Here I am excited, completely euphoric over the prospect of spending time as the woman I know I am. What could my spouse feel? The dichotomy is so difficult to cope with that it's a wonder anyone can realize the full impact of what they are doing to their family.

I was unsure of what the Provincetown experience was all about. I wanted to fit in. I decided for the most part to forego the heels, fancy dresses, and such. I did bring some of the fancier clothes; after all, how could I pass up this opportunity? My hair is naturally very curly, so I really had no trouble with that aspect of my presentation. Most days sauntering around the town were spent in jeans and a light top. I had only started electrolysis, so I had to cover facial hair carefully. Another blessing is my heritage as a Swede. Most Swedes are fair skinned and have light color eyes and hair. Although my hips are typically male, that can be rectified easily. For the most part, I felt completely comfortable and was surprised at how I fit in. I realized much later in my journey that its "attitude" that either makes you or breaks you. One experience I had is especially momentous to a person just coming out. I was seated on "the benches" in midtown. This is an area that is well known to most transgendered persons. The locals or townsfolk usually take up their positions early in the day on the benches. They certainly get a good show most days with the sheer numbers of transgendered folks that pass by. I had a container of coffee in my hand and found a shady spot to watch the crowds. After a few minutes an older gentleman sat down and commented on the nice weather. I had been practicing my feminine voice, so I responded to him. I thought all is well so far. I didn't think he knew that I was one of the transgendered persons visiting town. We struck up a conversation, and I really did very well. He began commentating on some of the cross-dressers passing by. "She looks good," he would comment. Occasionally I would put in my "two cents'" worth. After an hour or so, he got up and said he must be off to home. He said to me, "It's a pleasure to spend some time with a nice girl like you!" You could have peeled me off of the clouds passing by. I had done it! The rest of that day went superbly, mostly because of my attitude. I felt very comfortable and accepted. I learned that day that I didn't need to be dressed up fancy; I just needed to be real.

It's probably the best day I had, for the next day would prove to be one of those milestones in my marriage that I spoke of before. I had been in the habit of calling home each evening since my arrival. I sensed no problems except those any couple would face being away from each other. This evening when I placed my call, there was no answer. She hadn't said she was going out. I guessed that something special had come up and she just went out. I decided to wait until later, knowing she would be home then. I called and still no answer. Now I worried. We lived out on a lake in Maine. The area is very rural. The surroundings are all wooded. I felt something had happened for sure. Sleep eluded me most of the night. I woke early and got dressed quickly. I called home again, sure this time she would answer. There was no answer. By now even my friend who knew us both well was worried. I tried to keep busy, but my mind just couldn't stop from worrying. We decided to go out to lunch. When I arrived back at the hotel where we were staying, there was a message from a friend in Maine. I immediately called. My friend told me my spouse was admitted to a psychiatric hospital the night before. I was in shock. A million questions came to mind. None quite expressing what I felt inside. It turned out that my spouse couldn't bear being away from me. Instead of bringing up red flags to me, it just worried me about her safety. I spoke on the phone to her in the hospital. She managed to calm my fears and told me to stay the rest of the two days I had left. The decision I was making was so fierce in nature that I couldn't see the writing on the wall. Gender dysphoria can be totally encompassing. I was not able to see that this journey would probably not include my beloved wife. Hindsight is always 20/20. Now I see clearly the signs of impending divorce, but at that time I could not. It's not that I made a conscious decision to ignore these signs. It is more that I found myself for the first time, in Provincetown, as the woman I am, I could not see anything else. When I arrived home, I went to pick up my wife from the hospital. It seemed that nothing else mattered to us. We just wanted to be together. Although the time I spent in Provincetown was cut short, I did accomplish what I set out to do. I realized the day we left that I indeed was transsexual. It hit me like a ton of bricks. The motel we stayed at hosted a support group of mainly cross-dressers. They all showed up early in the morning ready to depart. They all appeared in their birth genders. I couldn't tell to whom I was speaking. One person seeing me that morning said to me questioning, "Are you having difficulty returning to being a man?" He told me that it was normal for a first-timer. I looked into his eyes and simply said that this is the way I look all the time. I told him I was a transsexual not a cross-dresser. He said, "I thought you looked rather serious, most cross-dressers are much more lighthearted." He was right. It was then I knew where I had to go. I knew I needed reassignment surgery. Perhaps my wife felt that across the hundreds of miles. They say two people feel things about each other.

I had decided that, if I were to have reassignment surgery, I would need a lot of money. After researching expenses of electrolysis, psychotherapy, and hormones, I realized it was more expensive than I thought. I had not even looked at the surgery itself. I began looking for a better job, one that would possibly pay for some medical expenses. I was lucky to be a registered nurse. The field I am in is always looking for nurses, especially psychiatric nurses. I found a good position with a home health agency. The benefits were superb. I was able to use the group insurance to pay for psychotherapy and hormones when the time was right. I contacted a friend who is a doctor. She had completed reassignment surgery that year. She was able to point me toward a competent doctor in my area who might prescribe hormones for me. After the required time frame with my therapist, she did a referral to this doctor for me. Many issues needed to be addressed: transitioning at work, informing family members of the change, clothing, and electrolysis. My head was swimming with the future, and I really started to believe that I might just accomplish my life's dream. It was time to look toward how to ask my employer about transition. I conferred with my therapist and members of the transgendered community in general. I found the courage to ask my immediate supervisor if I could transition on my job. Her response was very positive. I went about my business for a few days until she called me into her office. She told me after consulting with her supervisor that she would not approve me for transition. She further explained that she felt what I was doing was against God's will. She told me that the staff was her responsibility and that they were Christian people. I left her office devastated. The next few months found me battling with a serious depression. I knew that it was a result of the conversation I had with her. I used therapy and sheer willpower to continue. I was told my work was not up to their expectations. I was on a thin line of probation now. I found strength with my family and my therapist. I pulled my work quality up to expected standards. All I could do now was to wait. I used the time for electrolysis and other matters.

At home my wife and I grew closer than ever. We talked about what changes to expect. I recommended that she see a therapist, especially now. She began counseling. We both saw a chance for us to remain together. She began to involve herself more with the transgendered community. She became a beacon to other couples looking for answers. They all looked up to us as role models of how this transition could be. We took vacations together to Provincetown. My spirits soared. I found success after success at work. Our home was nearly finished. We had become a magnet to other transgendered persons. Our home saw many Christmas parties and gatherings for our community. I felt blessed and nervous all at once. We decided that another support group was needed to deal with serious issues of transition. My spouse was instrumental in forming the group. We had monthly meetings now at our home. It was time for us to find a therapist to act as a moderator. Again, my wife came to the rescue. She had been working with a therapist cleaning his home. I knew him and thought it a good idea to ask him. She wound up asking him, and he said yes. We now had come almost full circle. I was positive now that she would stay with me forever. I cannot explain the joy I felt. I was looking at how to start transition at work. The word came down that the boss who refused me transition would be resigning. The day she left I was in my office. I looked out on the parking lot. I saw her packing boxes in her car and finally leaving the building. I went down to my immediate boss's office and looked at her. She knew what I had come for. We talked for a while. She was supportive but cautious of how my clients would fare with a person changing gender on them. I thought it was a fair statement and worthy of study. I waited for several days. Finally, I received a notice that my employers would indeed work with me. Again, my spirits soared. I would have to work with the staff psychiatrist to assure that the clients would continue to be served. A notice went out to all employees that I would be transitioning to a *female* role on May 1, 1996. I think I broke my face smiling so much.

I still am not sure how there can be such incredible joy and at the same time, worry. Therapy was going well, and my work was very accepting. I received many letters from upper management and other staff. I was well liked, and all seemed well. I have heard of the nightmares people go through during their transitions. None of this was reality for me. It was time for me to schedule my reassignment surgery. Just as everything I had accomplished before, I did the same with surgery. I asked about surgeons and techniques. I wanted to know if I would maintain sensation. I wanted to know who the best surgeon was. After exhaustive research, I learned the best was not necessarily the most expensive. The surgeon I chose had improved the technique used worldwide. His name was Yvon Menard. I had the fortune of speaking to my friend, the doctor, who had her surgery several years before in Montreal with Dr. Menard. I was convinced that having Dr. Menard as my surgeon was the correct choice. I had to have one more conversation before I made the appointment for surgery. My wife and I sat together in our living room looking at the lake. The loons were singing the haunting melody they are known for. I asked her with tears in my eyes, "Are you sure you will stay with me? If I continue any more with my plans there will be no turning back." I told her I would stop now if you tell me to. She responded quickly. "You must do this for you. I will stay with you. I love you." I believed her with all my heart. From that day until my surgery I no longer looked for signs of impending doom. I realized I needed the time now to prepare myself. I began to look over my transition. I started adding up all the positive effects I saw. I looked at the side effects and consequences. I saw no need to worry. My clients at work all wished me well. They were and still are the most supportive people I have ever met. Remember that they are all affected with very serious mental illnesses. Without exception, they accepted me. They knew in their hearts what I had to do was right. The transgendered community all wished me well. No one had any doubts about the validity of my decision. My date for reassignment surgery was set for May 5, 1998.

DECADE 6 (YEARS 51–60)

That winter went along slowly. All I could think of was how wonderful I would feel finally completing my journey. Spring arrived. I busied myself with last-minute preparations. Strenuous housework was out of the question when I returned from Montreal. I prepared as best I was

able. I would be the first male-to-female in our support group to complete surgery. Everyone was nervous for and with me.

My surgery was scheduled for 8 AM, Monday, May 5. I was to arrive
on the preceding Thursday. My friend had agreed to drive me up to
Montreal. She was scheduling her surgery for later that year. She wanted
to see the residence where you are cared for after your surgery. We left
my home early that Thursday morning. My spouse had left for her walk.
As we passed her on the road, we beeped the car horn. She looked up,
and I could see tears in her eyes. For a split second I hesitated, then I
drove off to Canada. The trip was uneventful, but as my friend told me,
"You are a basket case. Let me drive." We arrived in Montreal in the late
afternoon. We were given the tour of the residence. The residence is Dr.
Menard's home to recover after the surgery. The setting is specially
suited for postoperative people. There were at least eight bedrooms, most
with private balconies and set to accommodate at least two persons.
There was an outdoor heated pool. Since it was early May, the pool was
just being prepared for summer use. The staff were all postoperative persons themselves. They knew what to expect and how best to assist you.
The evening was busy with new persons coming in from the airport. I
met my roommate for the first time. I knew we would hit it off well.
Friday morning arrived, and my friend had to be off for a long ride back
to Maine. I remember saying to her, "Don't leave me . . . stay." She
laughed and said, "You need to be with your roommate now." I watched
as my red Saturn moved off down the road. I was alone, in Canada,
waiting to have the most invasive surgery a person can have. I went back
into the house and sat with my roommate. We hit it off very well. We
spent this first day wandering around Montreal seeing the underground
stores and the old city. I was in total shock. When we returned, we found
the house was buzzing with fresh postoperative people. The good doctor
Menard scheduled them to come home the day after new patients
arrive. We were excited and scared to see the extreme discomfort they
were in. One girl called me to her room and showed me the result of
the surgery. I was in awe. The miracle of seeing such delicate work pre-
formed was overwhelming. We were given very explicit instructions for
preparation for our own surgery. The two following days passed, as Jenny
and I talked. We formed a bond that will last forever. Even now, four
years later, we still keep in contact. Sunday was the day to start preparations for Monday's surgery. We were told to shave our pubic region. I
quickly realized that some areas were rather difficult to see. Jenny and I
agreed to help each other with this task. I will never forget the scene sit-

ting in a bathtub spread-eagle with Jenny's head in my pubic region saying, "I found one more hair." We laughed so hard we both cried. The next task came that evening. A staff member called me into the office and gave me some papers to sign. For the first time, I saw the words printed: vaginaplasty, castration, and orchiedectomy. I read the warning for complications, irreversible, vaginorectoseal. If that is not enough to give you pause, I don't know what is. Jenny and I discussed some serious issues late into the day. We both looked at our lives and how we got to this point. Jenny said something to me that has served to get me through some difficult times ahead. She simply said to me, "Remember, Marty, what it took for us to get here, remember." I have never forgotten that simple statement. At 7 PM Sunday night we were called by a staff member, "Jenny, Marty, it's time to go." We held on to each other for what seemed like an eternity. The trip to the hospital was very short. I remember standing outside for a moment just to try to pull all of this together. The nurses were very professional and knew what we were feeling like. A small snack, a sleeping pill, and we were out like a light. I awoke to a very pretty nurse holding two pills for me to put under my tongue. She walked me to the elevator and up to the operating suites. I remember looking up into three very large round lights. I was thinking of the Saturn Five booster rockets. I remember nothing else.

I awoke and I felt a pain that I cannot describe. I also pulled the covers up and saw a large dressing and an ice pack. I slept for the next twenty-four hours, and I was smiling, I know I was. Jenny and I woke the next day. We both looked at each other and laughed; that hurt! The days are fuzzy from here. I remember one call from my spouse. She asked me if it was okay for her to quit her job. I told her she could quit three jobs for all I cared. She didn't know the nurses had given us both morphine for two days. Frankly, I didn't care what they did to me! Slowly we started to heal. First drinking, then moving. All told, we spent three days flat on our backs. The fourth day we were allowed to get out of bed. On Friday we went back to the residence. I can assure you the trip back was not as comfortable as the trip over. They had given us rubber donuts to sit on. Mine is hung on my wall now. Just as we had experienced, we were the *postoperative girls* now. Saturday and Sunday went slowly amid requests for pain pills and another pillow. We hardly ate because of the pain. Finally, Monday morning a smiling Dr. Menard came to take the stent out of us. This is a device to hold the new vagina open. We were finally able to take a bath. We learned the routine for dilating, five- to thirty-five-minute sessions daily at two-hour intervals.

We had tub baths in between the dilating. Meals were very quick. We were unable to sit for more than ten minutes.

I expected my wife on Tuesday. We were scheduled to leave for home on Thursday. I was able to move around quite well by now. The pain was minimal. I remember sitting outside my room early Tuesday morning. The trees were just blooming. Jenny was still asleep. I was just peaceful. I felt a hand on my shoulder. I turned to see no one there. Very suddenly a feeling came over me. A feeling of peace encompassed me. I sensed a circle forming around me. I saw at a distance my home, my wife, and my work. I felt good, but these visions seemed distant. It was as if they didn't exist anymore. After two days of morphine, I put it off to a delusion. Late that day my wife came with a friend. The feeling I had was so good and I was so happy to see her. I felt the love and contentment to be in her arms again. Thursday was very difficult. To say good-bye to these new friends. My Jenny and I cried buckets of tears. When you go through an experience like that, you never forget the people you went through it with. We said our good-byes, and we were off to home. The trip home was brutal. The pain and sitting for seven hours was more than I could stand. Coming home to my lakefront house was wonderful. I received many visitors and well-wishers. My routine remained similar to the one I had in Montreal. I found strength returning to me. My wife had been there with me through it all. I now looked forward to returning to work and my new life. If my story ended here, I would be happy. Life isn't always so simple. Within one week of arriving home, my supervisor called me. She said she needed time cards signed so I could get paid. I managed to get to my office and fill out the paperwork she needed. She asked me to come in her office. I was told the job I had been doing was being cut. I would have to make a decision where I wanted to go. I was given several options. I told her frankly I was in no shape to make a decision like that right now. She needed me in a different job but remaining in the same office. I accepted the change and went home. When I finally returned to work I was still very weak. My body had a difficult time adjusting to the hormonal changes from testosterone to an estrogen base. I found out that many nurses within the agency were disheartened. My yearly evaluation was due in October. My supervisor told me all was perfect. We would just wait until then to sign it. My recovery continued and work was going okay. I had realized that I returned to work too soon. Since my work was not physical, I just put my mind to it.

September in Maine brings the cool evenings and the mark of fall.

The fall season had come to Maine. My wife had been a little nervous lately. We hadn't spent much time in deep discussion. It was September 8. We just finished dinner and she got up from the table and started to scream at me. "You are just like my mother. I don't want another mother." I just looked at her dumbfounded. She started for the door. I stopped her, asking where she was going? She answered, "I can't live with you anymore. I need time to think." I looked at her and said, "Are you leaving me?" she just cried and said yes. She left me that night. I was frantic all day at work the next day, not knowing where she was. I assumed she would stay here in Maine. I was wrong. I finally called my neighbor, who my wife was very good friends with. She told me she put her on a plane to Virginia that day. The depression was immediate and very severe. I took some time off from work, but it really did not help. I couldn't eat. I wasn't sleeping. My family and friends drew close to me. I felt like a bomb had dropped. My recovery from surgery suffered. I made every effort to continue dilations and the regular routine. I returned to work probably more for support than anything. The day I returned from a leave of absence I was called into my supervisor's office. I was handed a memo telling me that I was given two weeks to "pull out of it." I couldn't react to anything now. Working as a nurse makes it difficult to seek help for you when it is needed. I pleaded with them to give me some help. My answer came in another two weeks. Again, I am called to the office. This time the division manager is on a conference call with my supervisor and me. I am told that I need to resign my position. If I do not, I will be fired in another two weeks' time. I am beyond controlling my feelings now. I just sat there and stared into space. This person who has been so supportive and kind to me looks at me and says, "We don't know who you are anymore. We want the old Marty back." I left on that day, Friday, for the weekend. After consulting with my attorney, I was advised to tend my resignation.

It is less than five months since my surgery. I now have had my wife of twenty years walk out on me. My workplace has told me to leave. I have no way to support myself anymore. I begin to pull together whatever finances I can find. I realize that I do have a retirement fund from work. I contact them to inquire about using some of the funds for the near future. I am informed that my wife's attorney has frozen the funds and they are not available to me. My family is able to help with expenses, so I can keep paying the mortgage. Divorce papers are served and the lines are drawn. I am told because I am transsexual that this issue will be used to support my wife's claim to property, retirement income, and

alimony payments. Court hearings and arbitration meetings are set up. I
have to list all belongings we have together. This battle goes on for
another year—draining my family resources and my mental health as
well. I ask that she return long enough to settle household items with
me. I want to try to make this divorce as pain free for the both of us as
possible. She refuses.

I am continuing with my therapist now. I need her more than ever.
We schedule two meetings a week. I arrive for one meeting and no one
is there. Several weeks go by and no answer on her phone. I finally contact the other therapist she shares the office with. She returns a call to
me, and with a shaky voice she informs me that my therapist is very ill.
No other information is available. Weeks go by amid hearings and legal
battles. My strength from obtaining a life goal is leaving me. I am drained
and broken. I make a conscious decision to continue my work with the
transgendered community. I have always found strength with them
before. I schedule some other members going for their reassignment
surgery to recover in my home. On a Sunday afternoon my therapist
finally calls me. Her voice is shaky and she is crying. She tells me she has
been diagnosed with brain cancer. I cry with her. We have been together
for ten years. After Christmas I receive a message from a close friend. My
therapist has just passed away. I have now lost everyone in my immediate
life who I can rely on.

My first postop friend comes to stay with me before the holidays.
I am looking forward to concentrating my efforts on someone else for a
while. We get along well, and I am able to provide the care and attention the person needs to recover. I remember all the details of my
recovery, so helping is easy for me. I find over the next year that a total
of seven male-to-female post-ops will come through my home. In spite
of all that has happened, I hope that I will be able to hold on to my
home. It has provided support, and the caring that "my girls" need.
During one of my dilations, I notice that there is a thin stretch of tissue,
very hard and sore. This is something new. I watch it for several weeks,
and it continues to impede on dilations. The area becomes so sore that
I contact my physician, locally. She suggests that I call Dr. Menard and
ask his opinion. He states he is not sure what is happening to me. I will
need to make an appointment to see him. I find now another one of
"my girls" needs a follow-up also. We schedule an appointment for May
5, 2000. It is my second anniversary of GRS. It is good to see Dr. Menard
again. He examines me and says it looks like a nerve that has not healed.
He is unsure if he can fix the problem. He kindly tells me it may have

to stay that way. We schedule an office surgery appointment for two weeks from that date. Since I am not working, I do have the time to travel to Montreal a few times. Money issues become a major problem. It's time for me to use the old credit card. Luckily for me, my friend has to have a minor adjustment at the same time. Again, we travel up to Montreal. I am beginning to know this wonderful city as well as my own. Dr. Menard prepares me for the surgery. As he goes to put me to sleep, he does a quick exam. He looks at me and says he cannot operate. My vagina had closed up around the opening. He sees what I have been telling him. We have no choice now but to schedule surgery under anesthesia. We schedule it for one month, on June 5, 2000. This will mean another trip, the third trip in two months. My situation at home is getting critical. Lawyers are trying to remove me from my home. They say that it is a marital home and needs to be sold and the money split. After so much time has passed since my original surgery and my marriage breaking up, some friends are growing weary of my plight. I know this to be normal, but it doesn't help me to cope. I contact my attorney and put all hearings on hold for the next month. I will be in Montreal for at least one week, possibly two. A friend drives me up to Montreal again. I meet Dr. Menard on Monday morning. He brings me to the hospital. We discuss the fact that I will need a skin graft. He tells me it will be a very small site no more than one inch by one inch. This time I am scared. One time through is enough. Facing this surgery twice is a nightmare. I am put under anesthesia. I wake several hours later. This time I have the same stent inside me and a large dressing on my leg to boot. I am told to get out of bed right away. Dr. Menard is taking me out of the hospital. I am puzzled now and still sedated from anesthesia. A nurse comes in and helps me to use the toilet. She speaks to the doctor in French. The tone is very serious. Dr. Menard takes me in his car and tells me that I have not paid for aftercare at the residence. I am in no condition to argue with him. He leaves me at a bed and breakfast in Montreal. I am told I will need to find a place to stay after today. I frantically call my brother to ask him to wire and transfer the money needed to Dr. Menard's office. The dressing on my leg starts to bleed profusely. I am in a strange country and without the aftercare I thought I would be receiving. Dr. Menard says I can now come to the residence, that he has received the money. I have never been so glad to see the residence in my life. The nurses are concerned, asking, "Where have you been?" I avoid the questions and settle in for the rest of the week. After a day or two, I realize that the one-inch-by-one-inch graft site has turned into a four-inch-by-four-inch site. I begin to wonder what else has happened to me. I also begin to realize that the stent that was so painful the first time is now very comfortable. This should not be, I think. My questions are answered at the end of that week. Dr. Menard comes in to my room and closes the door. He sits near my bed and looks at me quite lovingly. "Marty," he says, "you have lost considerable depth to your vagina." I start to cry. He explains that he needed much more tissue to replace than he realized. He had to pull the needed skin from the graft site and inside the vagina. He tells me I can recover some of the lost depth but not all. Maybe the depression that was affecting me is a blessing in disguise. I just am thankful that I am all right and going home.

The trip home is more brutal than the first trip. I pass in and out of consciousness. When I arrive home, there is no one to help me or assist me in recovery. On Sunday morning I receive a call from an angel of a friend. She comes over and brings me to her home. The next week is just as difficult as the first time. I am supposed to start the dilation procedure all over again. The graft site is in the front of my left leg. It is very painful and difficult to heal. After the week with my friend, I finally am able to go home. Now I am faced with all the divorce issues again. My attorney informs me that I will have to get my wife's name off of the mortgage. I go to the bank and speak to the loan officer I have known for close to twenty years. He tells me that this is a family bank and we do not want to assist you anymore. I find out my wife's attorney has contacted the bank and expressed her opinion to them. They will not redo the deed to remove my wife's name from it. I am forced to find a way to refinance the house. With the fact that I haven't worked since fall 1998, I have no basis for asking to refinance. My wife's attorney knows that and she now pursues getting me out of the house.

December of the year 2000 brings the divorce to a close. My wife never shows up for her own divorce. I am given eight months to either refinance the home or it will be sold from under me. My home has always been my sanctuary—the one place I can go and feel safe. I must sell it now or lose it altogether. I find a wonderful couple who fall in love with the home quickly. It breaks my heart to have to sell, but the lawyers are screaming for money. I finally put the key in the door on October 3. I leave the home on a warm fall day. I have had to go through twenty years of belongings alone. I had to call people to come and pick up things I have loved and used most of my adult life. I give my boat and motor away to a good friend on the lake. I stand on the shoreline and say good-bye to Annabessacook Lake. My belongings that I will need for an apartment are all put in storage. I move into a room a friend rents me in northern Maine. I continue to find my depression escalating. I now am having panic attacks. Up in northern Maine services for depression are difficult to find. In the spring of 2001, I run out of money for my room. I return to the capital area of Maine where I worked and lived for twenty years. I am now homeless. I am staying with friends and in my car when no other place is available.

As I write this story down, I am now in subsidized housing and receiving assistance for food and medical care. My family is still helping me. I have begun the process of healing. I am still reminded of the losses I have faced. Now at night when all is quiet, I am thankful for the roof over my heard and food to eat. Perhaps I was cocky to think I would be the one transsexual to beat the odds and keep my family and my home. I wish to thank Ari Kane for friendship and making this opportunity for me to tell you about my journey.

ANOTHER PATH

Paula J. Coffer

All of us want to be happy. We want to have a really great relationship and we want to have the opportunity to love and be loved. Truthfully, nothing else really matters. What goes into building a great relationship? Isn't self-acceptance the first ingredient? For most of us that degree of self-acceptance necessary for a desired relationship with someone is pretty much a given. We just "are" and therefore don't think about it. Okay, so an obese person or a person with scars from an accident or a person with some sort of physical deformity has to overcome a lot of self-hatred that has been learned from others before self-acceptance is a reality. But, if you basically look "normal" on the outside and for all intents and purposes are a normal everyday person, what if within you there is such a raging storm that self-acceptance is far from being a given. What if that storm never really calms completely and having that successful relationship is just a dream?

Mine is a story about facing the raging storm within and how I've attempted to calm the waves enough to enjoy a relationship; a relationship with myself as much as with another.

DECADE 1 (YEARS 0–10)

Growing up in the desert Southwest had its unique qualities. Grass, for an example, was a luxury that most of us didn't have because the water bills would have been too high. So that meant playing in the dirt or in some other makeshift play area. For example, we had this large tractor tire lying in the backyard. It was filled with sand in the middle and we could sit on the tire and wiggle our toes down into the cool damp sand. What a wonderful place to sit and share tea and conversation. We'd look at magazines and just know what we would wear and do. We were so big! Even if we were only three.

Pricilla, Chris, and I would play for hours in the backyard together. We were okay with playing house together. We had that portion of the yard with the tire set aside where our brothers weren't allowed because they kept stepping on the tablecloth or messing up the rocks we used for room dividers. Pricilla and I were only three years old and really had no cares in the world. We just played with our dolls and tea sets and enjoyed life together. Suddenly, the neighbor put a fence up. Not just any fence, but a privacy fence. Now Chris couldn't come over any time he wanted. We all cried when Chris's mother told us that Chris had to play in their own yard and couldn't come over anymore. We could still look through the cracks in the fence, though, and talk with each other. Chris's mother began to dress him in the cutest dresses and shoes. Oh how I wished my parents could afford to buy me dresses and shoes like his. So for the next year and a half or so, Pricilla, Chris, and I would play apart and talk through the fence. This period of my life was pure innocence, joy, and a pure love of life. No responsibilities, no worries, no concerns, just the love of a friend, family, and of myself.

A turning point for me was when my father accepted a job in Utah and we had to move. Oh the truth of a relationship. It was moving day, and we were all packed up and ready to get in the car for the ride away from all I knew. I was almost five and I was leaving my best friend and everything I knew behind. We were all saying our good-byes when all of a sudden my brother was fighting Pricilla's brother. Pricilla and I were holding on to each other not understanding why they were hurting each other when my brother broke off the fight, looked at me, and told Pricilla's brother that even if I was a sissy, he couldn't call me that. Then my brother just pushed past me and told me not to ever talk to him again. I didn't dare ask what a sissy was, and we loaded up in the car and drove away. So this is what leaving a friend behind was all about. Crying, fighting, and having my brother tell me not to talk to him. During this journey to Utah, I learned that I wasn't supposed to be such a good friend to girls who only wanted to play "girlie" things. I struggled with this change in my environment. If I wasn't supposed to play like I always had, how was I supposed to play?

I still held on to too much of my innocence. I learned that boys were expected to play in the dirt and get all grungy. I learned that boys were expected to be tough, to not cry, to want to push others around, to play rough and tough. I learned those things and kind of did some of them. But I didn't enjoy being the best at everything. I didn't enjoy making someone feel bad because he or she couldn't do something as well as someone else. It was this spirit of aggressive competitiveness that I disliked most about being a boy.

Most important, I learned to be secretive and for the first time I learned what rejection was. Unfortunately, the lesson was from my own family. But I also learned that I could overcome this rejection, and I could overcome my sense of loneliness. Within me I had the strength to endure the silence. Within me I had the strength to keep my innermost feelings to myself, but I so wanted to be able to talk to someone. There were just so many questions, so many things I wanted to know. Like why am I this way, my two brothers aren't, nor any male figure in my life. There's something wrong with me.

What was it about me that kept me gravitating toward beautiful girls who wanted to be my friend? Gloria Jean was just such a person. We would play and talk and walk together. We even started the first grade together. I even kissed her! She was everything that I saw myself as being. Really, it took a little while before I realized that she and I were very different people. My mother would give us three boys a burr haircut each summer and then let it grow some during the school year. Gloria Jean didn't get the haircut; her hair was allowed to be long and flowing. How I wanted hair like hers! She got to wear the most beautiful dresses and Mary Jane shoes to school; I had to wear pants and button-down shirts.

I really don't recall many issues during the first decade of life that would contribute to early gender experiences. My mother and father had some very angry talks about me on the subject that indicated I was to be this little boy and do little-boy things. It wasn't difficult for me to repress the feelings I had about being a little girl; my mother told me that I felt this way because I liked girls so much and that I would soon begin to feel more like a little boy.

Being named "Jr." was a curse for me because my father felt I should be just as macho as he. He absolutely abhorred my behavior. Is it any wonder, then, that I ended my first decade living two distinct lives? I feared my father. He would pull the belt off of his pants and use it with very little provocation. The net result of this was to learn to adapt. In one life I lived in a world of fantasy of what could or should be, and on the other side, I lived a life of harsh reality. This made me pretty much of a loner, but it also allowed me to adopt a personal resolve to face the most challenging of issues and manage to overcome them.

DECADE 2 (YEARS 11–20)

Ah, the sounds of the gymnasium locker room, the smell of all the boys getting ready to shower and dress for the next class come rushing back to me. I was a year younger than most of the boys in my class. I admired how some of them always seemed in control. They could rally folks around them, have others follow their lead in everything they did. They could tell jokes, get good grades, as well as do some of the meanest things to their peers. The locker room, for me, was okay. Sid was one of those "special leader" types who protected me when any of the others began to pick on me. It could be because my body hair wasn't growing like it did on everyone else or if I had some difficulty with some of the physical exercises, things that others could do. He told the other boys that it was due to my being a year younger. When my hair did start coming in, no one noticed that I shaved it off. I didn't want to look like the other boys. I wanted to look like the girls—smooth, fresh, lovely, cute. Even though I knew that I couldn't, I made a sincere effort to look more like them. I wanted to fit in the world that I was thrust into, no matter what personal discomfort at being with boys rather than girls, and to measure up to the physical demands expected of a boy my age. I relied on the lessons from the first decade. I could deceive these boys and my teachers into believing that I was a boy. I could adapt myself to be on the outside what I thought they wanted me to be. This is how I was surviving my everyday life at home, so it was easy to expand it here at the school.

I still had a special separate life where I could be me. I wasn't sure what me was. I felt that I wasn't quite like everyone else. The magazines and TV shows of the day (early to mid-1960s) really glamorized smoking. Leaving a ring of red lipstick on a cigarette butt, or holding that cigarette up with red painted nails and slender hands. Ah, that was glamorous and sexy. I would go into the garage and smoke my mother's cigarettes, Tareton. The commercial was of this beautiful woman with a blackened eye stating that she would rather fight than switch brands. Now, that was a nice combination of manliness and femininity. I would feel very feminine when holding up that cigarette, sensuously blowing out the smoke, imagining the red lips and nails.

Life changed drastically when my father broke his back. We were forced to move into the country where new responsibilities and demands were placed on each of us. The arduous task of rebuilding the home, irrigating the desert to grow alfalfa, digging fence posts, working the cattle and horses—all developed my body into what a thirteen- to fourteen-year-old boy was supposed look like. I became lean, and tall, not exceptionally muscular, but I had a lot of strength. That first summer I had a job as a lifeguard for a swimming pool. Jerry and I would ride our bikes the four or five miles to the pool and clean the pool prior to opening. He was a year behind me in school but the same age. He was very well developed, while I was this lean young man. I remember a swimmer named Woody, who shaved his legs to allow for faster swimming. It prompted me to learn to swim, for then I, too, could shave my legs. I could now appear in public without fear or humiliation from this practice. I had to look more feminine. It was exhilarating not to hide or live in a secret world. What pure joy it was to do daily things without shame. Alas, the workload became too strenuous at home and I had to give up the swimming pool job.

I went back into hiding. Somehow, I knew that I was doing something wrong. I struggled incessantly with *why* I felt that way. Why am I doing this when no one else my age wants to do it? I didn't see any other boy in school having the same desires, or were they hiding like me, living a secret life? Are there other people like me? I didn't think so because I would surely have heard any rumors to that effect in this small Southwestern desert town. One day I heard about a soldier who had a sex change operation and was now living his life as a woman. Christine Jorgensen became a part of my imagination and lifelong dream. What if I could become a woman? Could I do it now, while in my teens, and stop the male development of my body? I began having this recurring dream. I dreamed of having breasts like other young girls were developing. When I awoke from dreams, I would feel down my chest; oh no, another dream and no breasts. Those dreams were so real! There were times when I would run to the bathroom and look in the mirror to make sure. The disappointment and realization that I could never be like the other girls in my class made for withdrawal into a private secret world. My other recurring dream was in the form of prayer. Dear God, I would ask, please make me whole, make me into a girl or into a boy, but make me whole.

I found myself attracted to girls but not physically. I wanted to be like them, look like them, be able to act like them—heck, I wanted to *be* one of them! I dated a few times. There were some beautiful girls who really wanted to be with me, and I wanted to be with them, but only to just hang out. I wanted to learn all I could about them, live my life through them, and to know what it was really like to be girl. My fantasy world only provided me with so much input before the harsh reality hit me and it made me look at who I was. I felt tremendous rejection within myself at this time. I didn't think I was good enough for anyone. I felt that I was "damaged" property. I just didn't have anything to offer. My family didn't have much money, and I was neither a scholar nor an athlete.

One clear memory occurred during my teenage years. It is an incident related to gender presentation. I would put on mom's bra when I went to the bathroom. I was taking a bath and had forgotten to lock the door. So, when it opened, I threw the bra over my shoulder and it landed behind the old eagle claw bathtub. My mother found it later. She looked at me squarely when she asked how it might have gotten there. I, of course, maintained a deafening silence. Adolescence was difficult for me. Whether it was the verbal and physical abuse from my father or an inner desire to be someone different, I just don't recall much during this decade.

At seventeen I enlisted in the navy. As soon as high school graduation was complete, I was off to San Diego, California. I was convinced that by getting away from home I could "be the man" I was destined to be. Furthermore, it was a great opportunity to escape from my family and start a new life.

After a few months in the navy, I realized that I couldn't be the man I wanted to be. Something inside prevented me from acting like other men. I wanted so much to have these femme feelings go away. As I mentioned before, I wanted to be like other guys. At the age of eighteen I volunteered for Vietnam. I found myself wishing for combat duty that would allow me to die without shaming my family. I thought that the insurance money, provided by the navy, would benefit my parents and they would never know about my gender struggles. I did two combat tours in Vietnam. My feelings vacillated from one gender to the other. Sometimes, I would feminize my body as much as possible, while at other times I would be as macho as I could. It was a regular tug-of-war. Who was I? What did I really want to be? I was still plagued with the why. What did I ever do to God to make this happen to me? What could I do differently to make it all go away and be "normal"? Why can't I die instead of getting these medals? Why me, what have I done to deserve this?

After my first tour of duty, I thought I'd look for others like me. My ship was home based out of Alameda, California, and we were allowed to have a locker on base where I kept civilian clothes. I had a wig and makeup hidden away there. I visited San Francisco and found a gay newspaper. The thought occurred to me that maybe I was gay! I looked through the paper hoping to find a personal ad that seemed appropriate. Mind you, I didn't know what appropriate was. I was looking for someone to talk with. I found an ad with a phone number and got up the nerve to call. I called and spoke with a man who said he would see me. I rode the trolley, the bus, and then walked the several blocks to where this man lived. I had my wig and makeup kit in a paper bag. Oh, what an adventure I was on. When I got into his house, he offered me a drink and a chance to talk. Nervously, I asked if I could use his bathroom to get "ready." He said yes, and after more than a half hour, he got worried because I hadn't come out yet. Finally I came out, wig and makeup on for the first time where someone else could see me. He smiled and asked me to sit. He said that if this is what I desired, then I wasn't gay. I didn't want to be rejected again, and I begged him to let me do anything that would allow our meeting to be a gay encounter. He said he appreciated that. However, since I wasn't gay, he wasn't going to do anything with me and that I should leave. Crying, I cleaned the makeup from my face, ran down the street, and got public transportation back to the ship. I disposed of my bag with the wig and makeup and vowed *never* to do anything that foolish again. That was the first of many purges. It is common for cross-gender folks to "purge" as a way of cleansing the closet and the mind.

DECADE 3 (YEARS 21–30)

At age twenty-one I was assigned to an aircraft carrier that was moored in the Gulf of Aden during the Middle East crisis of 1973. At that time I had a girlfriend back home. It was during the stage of life when appearances were everything. Becky was her name, and she considered me a hometown hero. She wrote me letters, and, more important, she indirectly validated my masculinity to the men I served with. I had a poster-size photo of her hanging in my workspace. All who saw it thought I must be in love with her. I suppose I was in love with the idea of being in love. Becky was, and I think still is, a beautiful girl. Whenever I could I would emulate her looks, her eyebrows, and her makeup. I would dream that I was her, waiting for my sailor to come home.

During my time aboard ship, I was very discreet with my femme/masculine presentations. I would shave off all my body hair, trim my eyebrows, and sometimes use clear polish for my nails. As a macho man, I would sometimes grow a beard or a mustache. I truly thought I was living in my own world, unknown to anyone else. A second-class petty officer told me one day to call him when I've had my sex change. That came as a complete surprise. To me, that meant that people knew about me and they just didn't care. I had spent most of my time alone and away from others, and that comment may not have been necessary.

Upon my return home from the navy tour of duty, I married Becky. I regret that I couldn't muster enough courage to tell her about my innermost feelings. I wanted to break off the wedding plans, even though I had pushed for her to marry me. I didn't know how to stop the whole process without embarrassing me, her, and our families. A few weeks after taking our marriage vows, I had all these feelings, desires to feminize again. I couldn't stop them and perhaps, more important, I didn't want to. One day my mother came to the house unexpectedly. While Becky was at work, I had just polished my nails. I almost died when she knocked on the door. For the whole time that she was there I kept my nails hidden. She looked at me quizzically, but didn't say anything. The experience was both a frightening and an exhilarating moment, of nearly getting "caught." What if I had been caught and my gender conflict had been out in the open, in what ways would my life have changed? Would such exposure have allowed me to live openly that which I had kept secret all my life? Or would I become a victim of humiliation to all?

One time, my wife did her own nails and she offered to paint nail lacquer on one of my hands, too. It was a pivotal point in my life. Later that night I awoke, took a shower, shaved all my body hair, and applied makeup before going back to bed. Becky woke up and asked me where I had been. Crying, I told her I took a shower and feminized my body. It was then that we talked about the inner me for the first time; about how I felt inside. Finally, I was able to share my secret with someone close, and it opened many doors. I went to the university library and looked for anything related to what I was feeling, but I was not successful. I had no idea what the terminology was or how to search for anything about the subject. I knew for certain that I wasn't gay.

During college I enrolled in Army ROTC and, upon graduation, accepted a commission in the Finance Corps of the army. The Finance Officer Basic Course was a tremendous experience. I got instant recognition as a second lieutenant and was given my own private sleeping quarters. This enabled me to feminize without fear of discovery. To ensure to my peers that I "was a man," I would act more macho than most of them. However, I still couldn't be a man. I could look, walk, and talk like a man, but I definitely felt that I was not like other men. Knowing within myself that I could never change being a man, I tried time and time again to "be a man" and couldn't. Now that I was back in the military, I had to work much harder at disguising this inner me. I had developed tricks to hide my femme side. I had to conform to what all those around me considered a man to be: an army officer, a father, a husband. I couldn't shake my desire to be feminine. It was like an obsessive-compulsive thing. My innermost feelings would begin, much like the beating of a drum, and it would be intense, and overwhelming. All was quiet within my mind when the "drum beating" stopped. Only by feminizing myself, even partially, would these intense feelings stop. At its peak, I would finally give in to this emotion and "take action." This evoked a new set of emotions that would take over. I felt guilt, fear, and shame. In the quiet of my mind I would doubt my sanity, reasons for living, and an inability to control my inner feelings. I felt terribly inadequate and inferior. I asked God, the "why me?" routine. This led to redoubling my efforts to be "right" and "normal." During these periods I was highly productive. I could focus on any task and do it well. However, the drums of my feminity returned, would reach a crescendo, and the cycle would begin again.

DECADE 4 (YEARS 31–40)

Having been married twice by the age of thirty, I was about to marry for a third time. This time I went to several psychiatrists to get help with my gender conflict. Each of them had their own idea of what I should be. One suggested that I was fundamentally gay. Another believed that the conflict was due to an "abused childhood." Still another said that my grandmother's "sweetness" during childhood was a cause of my gender troubles.

By this time, I had read a few books on my own and had even visited with a physician who performed the sex change operation. I was living in Germany at the time, and all I had to do to meet his criteria was to be on hormones for the next six months and he would schedule the surgery. I would return to the States as the woman I've always wanted to be. I feared making that quantum leap without a clear means of knowing how I would support myself. I feared how the army and my family would react. I decided not to choose this option. Instead, I married again in an effort to put an end to all my struggles with gender, for-

ever. I told her about me, and the gender conflict. I guess I didn't communicate it effectively enough. Even though she said she understood,
years later I found that she really didn't. She said that the thirteen years
we were married were stolen years. She felt betrayed and could not
accept my transition toward full womanhood. This decade was the
hardest for me. I decided to make the military a career now. I had been
offered an opportunity to attend graduate school and wanted to have a
secure life. I looked into the process of becoming an army officer on the
outside while allowing for my inner self to grow. While in graduate
school, I did not have to dress in military uniform and was free from
much of the military protocols. I even grew a beard to prove that I was
a man. I went back to the desert Southwest to visit my two sons in the
hope that I could be a convincing enough man to gain contact and
parental rights. I wasn't successful, and I was kept from seeing or having
contact with them for the next fourteen years. Again I called upon my
inner strength to cope with the issues in my life. I got the message that
I was a bad person and as such could not let my children know all about
me. I'm such a bad person that I can't share my true self with my parents. I did share with my older sister. Her only comment was "I didn't
sit and walk like a woman." Hence, the gender shift and presentation was
a reaction to blaming our parents for my conflict. On reflection, I think
that her response was due to her own failed marriage and not about me.

In the early years of this decade I was getting hormone treatments.
These were illegally obtained because I feared that if the military found
out I would be dishonorably discharged. The hormones over the last ten
years of my career definitely affected my ability to meet the military
physical fitness standards. I almost didn't make it a couple of times. I had
to stoop a little and pull my shoulders in so that my breasts would not
show. Daily life was a challenge to physically be a man and an army
officer. There was always present the constant fear of discovery. If people
suspected anything about my feminization, they never mentioned it
directly. My home life was becoming very hard. My wife found me
physically repulsive and asked that I sleep in pajamas to keep her from
seeing my body. While we slept in the same bed, we didn't touch.

It was during this time that I made some key decisions. I would
retire and leave my wonderful family. I would live alone and learn how
to be me. I had achieved a degree of success in the military, became a
field-grade officer, and was being considered for a promotion, transfer to
another part of the country, and would have a new set of responsibilities. I decided not accept promotion and transfer. I preferred to stay with

the transgender friends and acquaintances that I had met in Indianapolis, and so I retired.

DECADE 5 (YEARS 41–50)

This was the decade of awakening, the decade of experiencing life. Upon retirement from the military, I moved out of my family home and began to live life alone. I was lonely and occasionally prone to some serious crying jags. However, this was a period of positive growth. I slept alone, and there was no one to find me repulsive and unlovable. I no longer lived in a constant state of rejection. The decision to give up everything I had was overwhelming and brought with it major consequences. I gave up my home, my family, and my career. I was starting off fresh. A clean slate. I had no money, no job, no support network, and only a few friends. This is when I found out what being alone truly meant.

Even before my retirement, I experienced the first phase of my gender reassignment, an *orchiectomy*. I remember that it was Mother's Day and this was a gift to myself. I had finally stopped the source of the "bad hormones" that had been coursing through my body. Now I would see the real me develop over the course of the next several months. I wished that I could've afforded to have the complete *sexual reassignment surgery* then. The recurring dream of just knowing I was a woman was still with me. All my life I had dreamed that I was a female, and upon awakening I would run my hand down my body. First the hand would pass over my budding breast and I would smile and know it was true, but then my hand would continue to the genital area and discover that I was just deluding myself. I wasn't really a woman. I was just a velveteen rabbit. I was a "wannabe." When I awoke, I would sit up and say "Oh shit" and begin my day.

I began my transition with Tiffany. We both retired from the military at the same time and lived together for a short period while attempting to get a business started. I was overdosing on hormones, and she was experiencing the loss of a dear friend. Both of us were too depressed to get the business off the ground. I moved on, without clear purpose, but I did cut back on the hormonal intake so at least I wasn't suicidal and totally depressed anymore.

Transition in the normal sense wasn't for me. As I saw it, it was a big lie to present myself as a woman when I wasn't. I didn't get a big thrill out of wearing feminine clothing. Rather I wanted to *be*. I wanted to be the woman I knew I was. This was a physical desire, not a desire to pretend I am a woman. My outer presentation was less important than to be true to myself; then I could dress appropriately. In effect, I did the transition in reverse: have the surgery first, then dress and live accordingly. If I couldn't get a job and live as Paula, I would work as Paul. Who cares what is between my legs except me? I had a forty-one-year history of being a male. I can't turn that away and create a false past. I decided that I am neither a man nor a woman. I am me. If I must label myself, I am a transsexual woman, a spiritual being having a human experience.

I focused on creating a business as a way to deal with all the stresses of my life. I took the concept to several states in the Southwest. I tried to forget that I was neither gender and just worked at the survival skills. I needed to eat, sleep, and make enough money to support my estranged family. I was honest with myself during this two-year period, though. I was in a disguise for the express purpose of creating work or at least a life where I could support myself while going through transition. I just nearly didn't make it. Once again, I couldn't make a success of the business venture. I was considered too passionate, too focused. I didn't bother to tell anyone that this was my life for the moment, that there was nothing else for me, that I had to make this work or die. One person during this time told his girlfriend that I was on the edge and a person to be wary of. His making that comment brought me to a realization that I was on the edge and had no idea of how to move away from it. I returned home and asked to live in the guest room until I could find employment and support myself again. The children were ecstatic. They had always given me unconditional love and valued me being in the house again. Of course I presented as Paul, and that meant my wife didn't have to face the embarrassment of having others know and be aware of me or my transition.

I found a job as a traveling consultant, which suited me just fine. My spouse even fronted me the funds to do what needed to be done. My life was on track again, but as a man and not as the woman I had wanted to be. The consulting firm went out of business while I was on a job site in Tennessee. I stayed there and took over as general manager on a temporary basis. After four months in this position it became apparent that I would not remain there, so I began a search for another job. I had met a gentleman who helped me to formulate some of my strengths into a meditation program. I spent the next several months writing a book for meditation. It was a "how-to guide" showing others how to survive the struggles within and succeed. During this period my spouse made the decision that we should get divorced. That would allow her to move forward with her life. I allowed myself to be taken advantage of during the proceedings. I felt I owed her because I had caused her to lose the most valuable years of her life. My daughters still provided me with unconditional love and are unafraid of showing me affection. Two days after the divorce was final, I had a penectomy and altered how I went to the restroom. After healing from the surgery, I had the final episode of the recurring dream. The one of waking as a woman and running my hand down my body and just knowing that I was real and not the velveteen rabbit after all. Finally, I was the woman I wanted to be for most of my life.

The next year was a struggle for me. I had my surgery and without the experience of the Real Life Test. I refused to live my life in masculine presentation again. I lived in fear of being caught in a women's restroom or of being labeled a pervert by someone with no knowledge or education concerning gender conflict. So I transitioned after surgery, and I stayed with a friend who was very supportive. She even had romantic desires toward me both before and after the transition. It meant that I could still have a relationship. But that isn't where I wanted to be. I didn't want to share my life, with her, at this point in time. I just didn't love her in a romantic way. Now, I was working in my chosen role as Paula. I was open as a transsexual and giving lectures at several Midwestern universities. I had accomplished all I set out to do. I was a professional woman working at a big-ten university as a financial analyst. My dream became a reality, at last.

While giving a lecture at an Indiana University class, I was asked if there were any differences between being a male manager and a female manager. I responded, yes, there are many differences. Men tell, demand, or require; women ask, request, or suggest. Women work within a work group; men work outside of the work group and bring back to the group the suggestions of others. What a turnaround. One of the most positive things to come out of these talks to students is that they would remark afterward on how positive I spoke about my experience. Other transsexual people they heard were always talking about what an unhappy life they had before transition and how they are still unhappy. I have been fortunate that I've never experienced any derogatory aspects to transition. I remember a regional gender gathering in Pittsburgh called the "Be All" where the folks in the bar were looking at us. We all decided that we would boldly go where no trannie had gone before. We went and sat with the folks all around the room and introduced ourselves and began conversations. It was amazing! There was one woman whose brother was transgendered, and she was seeking help in how to deal with it but couldn't talk to him about it. How very rewarding that event was.

I'm no longer fearful or apprehensive about life, but I wonder which position I want to accept, where do I want to go next, or what do I really want to do. I have about given up on a relationship. Lesbian women tend to want a real woman, and I don't want to involve myself with a man. I suppose I'll continue to look for that one special person, male, female, third gender, or no gender, who will allow me to love them or at least share with them life's daily routines and events—the happiness, the sadness, the joy, and the tribulation. Life for me during this decade has been exceptionally rewarding. If nothing else, I have learned to live with myself and have worked toward being of benefit to others.

I'm at the fifty-year mark, and I reflect on what I would like to have said at my memorial service. I would want people to know that I made a positive impact on others; that they have the strength within to succeed, not just survive; that I once had a kind word for some people at just the right instant when it was needed; that I was a good influence on how they behaved toward others. I could only dream that members of my family would stand and say they were proud of me, that I lived by my convictions, and that I brought about a positive glow and direction to them.

Most important, I want to be remembered for being a person, one who would smile at you on the street. A person who would not turn away from her fellow man during a time of need. Just a spiritual being having a human experience. As a friend of mine is wont to say, "Warm Flo."

THE LIFE JOURNEY

Phyllis Randolph Frye[1]

As I reflect upon life, thus far, I recognize that mine has been shaped by a variety of social values and psychological forces, some in concert and others in opposition. Listed in no particular order, the major ones are loyalty, tenacity, optimism, honesty, and basic happiness mixed with intense bitterness, hypocrisy, and ostracism.

Add to the above that I am transgendered. This has been the filter through which most of my life experiences have been poured. Being intensely transgendered, while not understanding my inner self and at the same time being afraid to admit being transgendered, intermittently affected much of my closeted life from my earliest remembrances until I began to transition during the period of twenty-four through twenty-eight.

As I will be well past fifty-five years of age when this is published, the second half of my life has been while living totally out of the closet. As harsh as some of it has been at times, I have enjoyed it more being *out*—much more.

DECADE 1 (YEARS 0–10)

My first ten years were boringly ideal. I say that because the television talk shows that use us as freak show spectacles—as well as the stereotypes—place us with either clinging mothers or with a brood of sisters or in reaction to an absent father or an abusive father. I had devoted parents who remained married until death at old age, and I had an older brother and a younger sister. All four of my grandparents lived in town, and we visited them each week. I had lots of aunts and uncles and cousins, most living in town, and of those in town, I saw them frequently. We were closely knit, at least I thought we were closely knit.

I did not grow up in a liberal atmosphere of either the East Coast or the West Coast but instead was in conservative San Antonio. I was very familiar with the inside of the local Methodist church, and I went to Sunday school and vacation Bible school from way back.

We were not rich, but we were not poor, either. The food selection variety left a bit to be desired, but I never went to bed hungry. And I never went to bed without a kiss from both parents. Our neighborhood streets were safe, well paved, and with good sidewalks so that I could walk to school. The teachers and equipment and books were good. I was well dressed for school, I was not a discipline problem (although I did get conduct marks for talking in class), and around the fourth grade I began to excel both academically and athletically.

The first toy I remember was a truck that my Nonnie gave me for my fourth birthday. I loved that truck, and I played with it and cap pistols and even jumped off of the picnic table wearing a kitchen towel around my neck as I raced around the backyard "flying" like Superman. My favorite toy (and I have it even today in a box in the attic and got it out for my first grandchild to put around the Christmas tree) was my electric train.

Sorry, but there is nothing to "blame" my being transgendered on. Actually, "blame" implies that something is wrong with my being transgendered, which I strongly reject. During those years, I remember that I really preferred, if left alone, to play with my sister's toys and with my girl cousins and their toys. I always felt dorky in boys' clothes, especially my Sunday suit, and was jealous of the way the girls were dressed. I remember vaguely that when it became apparent that I was drifting too far over the gender line, I would get a correction. We all do, no big deal. Except it was a big deal.

The correction I most remember was the underwear war. This was after I hinted to my brother that I really liked wearing my mother's shoes. After that, my parents and my brother embarked on a campaign to ensure that I wore my underwear below my navel instead of above my navel. It lasted for months with shaming, mild spankings, and other recriminations. So after that, I learned to keep my gender self to myself and my cross-dressing a secret.

And so I did church softball every summer (right field when I was eight), and I was in the Cub Scouts where I did the Bobcat, Wolf, Bear, Lion, plus Gold and Silver Achievement Points, and even Webolos when I was ten. And I crossed-dressed in something almost every day, even if for a few moments. And I dreamed of being a girl.

DECADE 2 (YEARS 11–20)

This would be from the fourth grade through the first years of college. Although it sounds like bragging, this was a time of great achievement. I became aware that I had a real talent for math and sciences, made good grades through all of my school years, and went to college on four scholarships.

I continued in scouting and became Senior Patrol Leader, Eagle Scout, God & Country Award winner, and Junior Assistance Scoutmaster. I enjoyed camping and was very adept in outdoor skills including cooking over a campfire. In a similar vein, my father took me hunting, and I shot and skinned a few deer during those years. My mother's parents had a thousand acres near Harwood, and we would go there several times a year for branding and driving cattle. Frequently, when other duties were not pressing, I would take my .22 rifle and leave the ranch house on a Saturday morning and roam until dark. I was a good shot with a rifle and lettered on my high school rifle team. That team beat every team in a four-state area at one competition.

I was small, but I was learning to be tough. As the summers progressed, I went from right field to center field to left field and could catch anything. I was no longer the last to be chosen. In junior high I tried football, but I got creamed since I was small. I was picked on a lot until my ninth grade year when I grew. During that year I went from four feet eight to five feet five and from 85 pounds to 130. My shoe size went from a 6½ to a 10 (so I could no longer wear my mother's shoes). In gym I would climb the rope without using my feet or legs (all upper-arm strength), and when boxing class came around, I would openly challenge, and whip, the thugs who had made me miserable in years past at junior high.

In high school I was in ROTC, and my senior year I was the Cadet Colonel, Commanding. I did the high school yearbook, a cappella choir, and senior play. I went on to Texas A&M and was in the Corps of Cadets and studied civil engineering. I was in the Singing Cadets. Hey, I was very, very, very good at acting out the guy that they wanted. Meanwhile,

I cross-dressed almost every day, sometimes twice if I had the chance, and I dreamed of being a woman.

I dated a lot, and I fell in love many times. Yes, I liked the girls. Not only did I want to be one, I liked them—a lot! I remember being horny back when I was seven. I was grabbed and kissed in the cloakroom by Cheryl in the first grade, and had a crush on Billie in the fourth, and Janet in the sixth. In junior high it was Carolyn and then Kay. In high school, I had use of the family car and it was Paula, Karen, Jan, and Sandy. In college it was still Sandy, then another Karen, and then Jeanne, who I married while a college junior. Meanwhile, I cross-dressed almost every day, sometimes twice if I had the chance, and I dreamed of being a woman.

During that decade I also became aware of various values as I mentioned in the beginning of this writing. I was extremely loyal, and I had the tenacity to see things through. I was full of optimism and, basically, very happy. I tried to be honest in all things except my being transgendered. Of course, at that time, I was still unaware that other people felt the same gender desires that I did.

I had not yet experienced bitterness, hypocrisy, or ostracism, but I had a good taste of all three during a week when I was caught. I was beginning my senior year in high school when my mother found some of her clothes hidden in the bottom of one of my dresser drawers. The short description is that I knew what answers they wanted to hear. The body language and voice inflections of my parents during the questioning allowed for only one outcome. I knew that if I gave the honest answers, I would be ostracized and put out onto the street. Homophobia (and racism and sexism) was palpable in my home. So the answers were "Yes, this is just a fling, an experiment of youth" and "no, I will never do that again." And I was cross-dressing within a week of this scare, but I was even more secretive than before.

DECADE 3 (YEARS 21–30)

How do I write this? My third decade was topsy-turvy. I began my third decade as a loyal, tenacious, optimistic, happy, mostly honest (except as to my inner self), horny, racist, sexist, homophobic, soon to be married, college man, and I ended my third decade as a loyal, tenacious, optimistic, happy, honest, much less horny (female hormones are wonderful things), divorced but remarried, unemployed, transgendered woman who was learning to deal with bitterness, hypocrisy, and ostracism.

While a sophomore at A&M, I told Jeanne that I loved her, but I did not to tell her about my gender desires. She put off her college, and we were married and lived in a duplex off campus. I had scholarship money and worked part time at school, while she took on a full-time job. We were a typical college couple, except I was learning that frequent sexual intimacy was not in any way affecting my desire to cross-dress and to be a woman.

I had taken, and was taking, so many credit hours that I realized I could finish my engineering degree in a mere three and one-half years. When I graduated, I was commissioned as a second lieutenant in the Regular Army. (That is an important distinction, because other than the military academies, most ROTC folks were commissioned with Reserve rank. Being a US Army scholarship student, I was commissioned Regular.) My military orders were to stay in school and get a master of engineering degree. This was fine with me because Vietnam was really fueling up.

By that time, we were very pregnant, and I was blasting through graduate school in record time. (I was also secretly cross-dressing whenever I could and dreaming of being a woman.) About that time, we were visiting the in-laws (very nice people, by the way), and one evening as I was drifting to sleep in the next room, I heard my wife and her mother laughing and ridiculing Christine Jorgensen on some late-night talk show. I had never heard her name, but listening to the discussion and the ridicule, I became aware that I was NOT the only such person. It was also reinforced in my mind, just as it had been years before by my parents, that it would not be accepted by my wife.

What a pickle I was in. Actually, that is not fair because we were BOTH in a pickle, except she did not know it yet. I had married her dishonestly, not understanding what this gender need was and figuring it would go away with maturity and sexual intimacy. Unplanned, yes. Unintentional, for sure. And yet, while it was very hard on her down the line, the result was a wonderful child who has since become a fine adult with a good wife and has two lovely children of his own.

And it is here, where I must write, as it happens in other places in our lives, that I would not change a thing if I could go back. If I had been honest with my parents back in high school, I would have been a homeless and out-on-the-street teen. If I had been honest to my wife, I would not have known this wonderful child. And if things had not gone on as they did, I would never have met my second spouse, my Trish, who became and remains my best friend.

And so, while pregnant, my wife learned about who I was inside. She rejected the idea, ridiculed me a lot, and I went back into my secret life, promising to her that I would never do it again. I cross-dressed the next day.

Our son was born. We finished graduate school, and I went on active duty. I got orders to go to Vietnam, but through luck while in officer training I found an honorable way to get my orders changed to go to Germany. The three of us went to Germany and had a mostly good time. I was twenty-three, and I was not handling my secret very well. She caught me and left. As she left, the knowledge came out to the military, and they began to process me out for being queer. Being Regular Army and army scholarship, I threatened a media stink if I did not get an Honorable Discharge.

Before I left Germany, I took leave and went cross-dressed to Denmark. It was there that I learned that I was not sexually stimulated by men. It was while crossing the border that the German police threatened to confiscate my passport. And on my return, I learned that my bottle of fingernail polish remover had leaked, so that the next day, in August, I went on post wearing gloves until I could get another bottle at the PX and wipe my nails clean in the restroom. One day before I left Germany to come back to the States, I slit my wrist.

All said, I was pretty screwed up and filled with a boatload of guilt. When I arrived back in the States, my wife divorced me, and I moved up to College Station. My graduate sponsor had agreed to employ me as a research engineer at A&M. That was interesting work: we were designing improvements in artificial limbs. In order to reduce the weight, we were using fiberglass. Covering the artificial support was done with polyurethane foam. We could not get the "skin" texture right, but my knowledge of pantyhose brought me to suggest lining the mold with hose so that when the hose were peeled away from the cured foam, the texture was cellular and dull like skin, rather than slick and shiny. So the recipients of our newly designed legs could thank a cross-dresser for having the experience to make that suggestion. But I was back in the closet.

I was a mess for several months. I was cross-dressing, working, feeling guilty, dealing with the stitches coming out of my wrist, and the healing of the scars. I went to a local Methodist church to meet people and to sing in the choir. While there I attended a group that was heavy into subjugating women using the writings of Paul. I got interested in the Bible and decided to read it through, from cover to cover, for the first time. As I read, I began to see that I had been fed a load of bullshit most of the time that I grew up and went to church and Sunday school.

What emerged were two things. One was a loving God, and two was the hypocrisy of the Church. I read a lot of really neat stuff that filled me and made me feel okay about who I was, gender confusion and all. And I noticed that most of the *bad* stuff that I had heard being preached so often was secondary and frequently away from all the main themes.

I must spend some time here, because this revelation saved me. The Jesus that I read about never said anything about homosexuality. Neither did the Ten Commandments. But mixed into the Bible were a very few verses, subject to misinterpretation, about homosexuality, which did exist. On the other hand, there was a whole truckload of lines, paragraphs, and whole chapters about heterosexual problems that were and are mostly ignored to this day by the great heterosexual majority of the churches.

I found the greatest New Testament story about God's forgiveness in the Old Testament telling of the story of David and Bath Sheba. You see, while they were punished by the death of their firstborn, they were not to separate, but continued to live together, and were later blessed with the birth of Solomon.

I read the Woman's Bible,[2] which was written by early feminists in the nineteenth century. The theme of this book was to demonstrate that a just and loving God would not have put into the Bible some of the things that are found therein. The argument is essentially that the Jerry Falwells and Pat Robertsons of millenniums past had their own sexist, homophobic, controlling axes to grind back then and inserted, omitted, or edited the texts to suit their bias.

Several years later, I read self-help books, and two gave me the most help. One taught me how to take risks in a consciously competent manner,[3] and the other taught me how to deal with the supposed authority of others and then how to claim my own authority.[4]

During this same time, I was meeting with a Jewish psychotherapist named Burns Dubose. After hearing me go on and on for several months, he said that while he was not Christian, if I was, he would have asked why I would not accept the sacrifice of Jesus' life to take care of my guilt. Why did I require Jesus to suffer more for me than he already had suffered? The short story is that with those thoughts, and those readings, over time, I began to heal and my self-esteem began to reemerge.

Another significant thing happened at about this time. I met Trish. Actually, since we are soon to celebrate our thirtieth anniversary, twenty-seven of those years with me being a woman, I must more correctly say that this was the most significant thing to happen in my life. Trish and I became friends, we fell in love, and we remain both best friends and lovers.

Earlier I had written about how I would not have changed anything because the ripple effect would change outcomes. Our meeting was either fated or with God's blessing or both. During those horrible last months in Germany, I met an American schoolteacher who taught the children of military families. She and Trish had taught together in their beginning years of teaching. This person saw my Texas A&M sticker on my car and learned that I would be going back there to work. She knew that Trish was from the area, so she suggested that I meet Trish when I got there.

I had been working at the school for several months when I decided to try and find her. I did not know it at the time, but she had been off teaching in Houston and then at an American school in Mexico and had only returned to this area the year before. She and her dad both had the same gender-neutral first name, so when I first called her, I got her mother on the phone. Bette was a sweetheart, but her phone voice was off-putting, so I hung up. I tried again a week later, made it through Bette, and learned how to find Trish. We agreed to meet for a drink.

We both admit that our first meeting was not that great. I was newly divorced, stitches recently out of my wrist, carrying a lot of guilt, and looking like an animal caught in the headlights of an oncoming truck. Trish was almost thirty, had been on her own for a long time, had her own car (a blue Mustang, and she looked good driving it), as well as money in the bank. She had not been overly impressed with the men she had met over the past twelve years since high school, and there was no family pressure for her to marry. So over the coming months we met once a week or every two weeks and then once or twice a week and then more often. We became friends.

In a fit of guilt, I told her about my cross-dressing. She said she had never heard of such a thing, but wasn't particularly put off. We decided that I would see Burns Dubose. I told Trish of everything that he and I discussed. I shared what I was learning from reading for myself instead of being spoon-fed my beliefs as had been done in the past. One weekend we drove to Houston and I spent a day at the medical library digging out articles (back when there were not many, and those that existed were not always favorable) from the professional journals. We had several rolls of coins, and as I found articles, I stacked them up and she would photocopy them. Yes, she was a good friend.

We fell in love. I need to pause here for another lesson. The best person to love is your best friend. And if you already are in love, make that person into your best friend. Cultivate the friendship. As I have observed, people who are in love find that the love ebbs and flows in varying cycles and frequencies. If there is no best-friendship component, then the ebbs can be dangerous times for the relationship.

While this was going on, I was not making an overly secretive thing about my cross-dressing, although I never cross-dressed at work. My boss found out and fired me. The hypocrisy was that, it came out later, he was married but sleeping with his secretary, who was also married. My supervisor was angry that I had been fired because I did good work. He put in a good word at a firm where he had previously worked in Pittsburgh, Pennsylvania. I got the job, and Trish and I then had to decide what to do about our love and our friendship. Her words were "If this is all that is wrong with you, I think I have a good deal, and I am willing to take a chance." So we agreed that I would go to Pittsburgh and she would finish the school year. Then I would come back for the wedding, and we would pack up and move north.

We enjoyed the people in Pittsburgh. My job was a grind but good experience, and I took the test to become licensed as an engineer. Unfortunately, she could not find a job. I shaved off the beard I wore at our wedding, then grew another, and then shaved it off again as I dealt with the gender needs that I had. She showed a lot of patience and friendship. We agreed on a way to handle both of our needs. When I came home from work, I was free to cross-dress—unless she told me that she could not cope with it that night. Unless, in rebuttal, I told her that on that particular night, I really had to cross-dress. And it worked pretty well.

While in Pittsburgh, I became aware of Virginia Prince and obtained some of her earliest newsletters. Through those, I learned of a gender symposium to be held at Slippery Rock State College. I took a day from work and went, fully cross-dressed. Gawd, I was a sight. Heavy makeup to cover the shaved face, horrible taste in clothes, overdressed. But I was there, and I met Zelda Suplee of the Janis Society and Paul Walker of Johns Hopkins Medical Center. That day was very validating. I came out to my bosses but did not cross-dress at work, although some of the unisex stuff I wore did raise some eyebrows. About that time, the so-called Nixon recession hit the aircraft industry and engineers flooded the market. I was asked to leave. Not a problem; I had connections in Texas and so did Trish, and we were ready to come home.

I got a job immediately in the oil and gas industry via a former college professor. Trish met her former principal and was assured a teaching job the following August. So we bought a house that was thought to be our starter. And we rocked along, pretty much as we did in Pittsburgh. I cross-dressed, I read, we lived and loved, and our friendship grew. I grew another beard, trying to be a guy, but shaved it off again after several months when I could not stand not being able to leave the house cross-dressed.

I finally began to decide on a name, and it was Phyllis. I simply changed an *i* to a *y* and a *p* to an *s*. Two years later, when I legally changed my name, I decided that my middle name was a good strong family name, so I saw no need to change that.

I found some university professors who were interested in me lecturing to their classes on this little known subject. I came out to my boss, but did not cross-dress at work. I went to a newly organized Metropolitan Community Church (MCC) and stood before an altar and a cross. I felt clean and safe and whole. The guilt was gone. As a result, when talk of religion would occur at work, I would talk of my MCC where a lot of gay people went. Interestingly, it was okay to talk about religion at work, as long as it was heterosexual and Christian. Kind of like the continual push for school prayer. I often wonder what these same people would say if Monday was Buddhist day, Tuesday was Jewish day, and so on. Oh, well. What day do the Hari Krishnas get their turn?

My boss threatened to fire me because the word was out that I cross-dressed at home and the men did not want to use the same restroom as me. That was a twist in the old panties. Here I was still dressing like a guy, but because they knew I was some kind of queer, the men did not want to unzip in the same room. As I write, I am beginning to feel the sarcasm starting to flow. And, I was told, I could not cross over and use the women's either. So I was fired because I could not use either restroom at work.[5]

June 23, 1976, was my third anniversary with Trish and the date that my firing took effect. At the time, I was not really worried. I had two degrees from A&M in a geographical area and in a profession where A&M degrees were highly valued. I was a veteran at a time when that meant something, and I had professional licenses from Pennsylvania, Texas, and Virginia. I had been fired in the past after people learned of my cross-dressing, so I would simply be upfront at application time that I cross-dressed at home (never at work), and eventually I would find the right employer. Besides, my resume showed that during my last job I had successfully managed almost thirty projects, valued at over six million dollars (a lot of money then), all at the same time. There were no complaints about my work.

Two hundred resumes and two dozen interviews later it was the same story. Real interest until I became honest about what I did at home. No callbacks. After three months, Trish was furious, but not with me. She told me that if they were not going to hire me because of whom they thought I might be, then I may as well be myself. And so I became

Phyllis, full time, but without hormones or a legal name change (so that I could go back if it did not suit me to be full time).

Oh, there was one time several months later when I had to dress as a guy. It is a sad story but a funny one also. The sad part was that this person was also a cross-dresser who had run into the same discrimination, had gone full time, and had been arrested. At the time, the law was that cross-dressing was illegal. She called me and asked if I could help. So I showed up at the courthouse in guy clothes looking really weird with long hair, plucked eyebrows, and long fingernails. When it came time for my friend, I opened my briefcase to get a newspaper that showed advertisements for a "men's wear" line of women's clothing. As I whipped open the briefcase, the judge ducked behind his desk and the bailiffs came at me with guns drawn. They thought I had a weapon, but all I had was a fiction novel, a newspaper, and a sandwich. My friend's charge was dismissed, but even if she had been found guilty, she would have gotten out because the fine equaled a night in jail. In short, even if you beat the rap, you completed the ride (to jail) first.

As Phyllis, I took every job interview I could find. I even interviewed to sell kitchen knife sets door to door, but was told I could not cross-dress. I could not even get hired to do telephone work. We were going through our savings account fast. Trish had a good job, but in a so-called women's profession, so it did not pay much back them. Our combined income was reduced by 67 percent. We were struggling to keep up our mortgage and child support and car payments. We started cutting back severely. I started to become depressed. A year later, I started becoming very bitter. The bitterness grew in intensity and lasted for almost ten years.

During my twenty-ninth year, I had my name legally changed. I continued to send out resumes, being very honest about who I was. No jobs came my way. Collecting unemployment became a nightmare. Even though my former employer did not protest my claim, an unemployment referee wrote up my case in such a way that I could not get unemployment. Back then it was forty-three dollars per week. I fought with them for two years before the logjam was broken. I remember when the approximately one hundred weeks' worth of checks came in the mail. They were all forty-three-dollar checks, each in its own envelope. One day we got two, the next a dozen, the next one, the next four, and so one for almost three weeks.

Although friends and in love, this was a testy time for Trish and me. Not only were most of the neighbors going nuts (graffiti sprayed on the driveway, slashed tires, verbal taunts and jeers from outside at night, and lots of obscene phone calls concentrated around Christmas and Easter),[6] but my family ostracized me as I thought they would back in high school, and Trish's family put the big pressure on her to leave me. In her words, this was a time "when the pressure was so intense that a couple will either split or bond." We bonded. She kept telling her family "Phyllis has done nothing except be true to who she is." For the most part, we were alone. And she was afraid of losing her job as well. Those were crazy, fear–filled times.

We agreed that to keep us together, I would continue to transition, but that would go slowly, and that I would stop short of genital surgery. So, if I was patient, I could be all I could be and still keep my best friend. Such a great deal. And no one could force us to divorce.[7]

As I ended my third decade, I began a low dose of hormones.

And during the last Christmas of that decade, our church brought us all the canned goods that had been placed under the altar for the poor families.[8] We tithed 10 percent of the food to our friend who I had gotten out of jail. She was hungry and homeless at the time. Because we did not have to spend money on food, we were able to buy some warm shoes for winter.

DECADE 4 (YEARS 31–40)

Although I made a lot of inroads and had many good times, I also spent much of this decade dealing with bitterness. I could not get work. I could not get work because I was being truthful about who I was. There is more to work than a paycheck, although that is important. Without work, the feelings of self-worth become very fragile. The neighbors were hostile, there was a law that made me illegal, my family divorced me, and Trish's family continued to pressure her to leave me. So what got me through this time? Obviously, my anchor in Trish. But I would say that it was my MCC family, politics, Amway, and softball that got me through that decade.

The MCC family was vital. Not only did it teach us about the value and dignity of lesbian, gay, and bisexual people, but it also provided us with family. We both sang in the choir. (I often joke that with singing tenor in high school, and singing baritone just before my transition, and then singing alto and second soprano at different times, I am the only person I know who has publicly performed Handel's "Hallelujah

Chorus" in all four parts. Now when it comes on, I just sing whatever part I choose and change parts as it goes along.) We had Bible study. We had potluck suppers. We had various projects. They were family.

Politics took many forms.[9] The first was the overturn of the city ordinance that made me illegal. This was a three-year project that was mostly a solo effort with lots of mentoring along the way. It is discussed in several endnoted articles. I guess what was the worst part of this ordeal was that every single day, when Trish went to work and she knew I was going out to lobby for the repeal or go to a church daytime activity, or to guest lecture on being TG at a university, or to interview for a job, or to deliver Amway products, she never knew if she would come home to learn that I was in jail. That burden took a heavy emotional toll on her. It was so unfair because all she had done was stay true to her wedding vow.

I became very active in the feminist movement in Houston. I was there when we stormed the city council after it fired Nikki Van Hightower as the city's women's advocate. And I was there as a volunteer to the International Year of the Women where I was able to meet firsthand Bella Abzug, Betty Friedan, and Gloria Steinham. One of my good neighbors got me involved in the League of Women Voters. I attended state league conventions, learned how to lobby in Austin, and contributed both my engineering knowledge and later my law knowledge in the process of study of the various issues that the league voted to support. A decade later I was elected to be one of their vice presidents.

While on the subject of good neighbors, there were two other sets. In the first set, her name was Lynn and her husband was Bill and they had two young boys. They lived diagonally behind us and were good to us. After I transitioned and Bill explained to the boys as best he could for kids that age, the youngest ripped out some of his mother's flowers to give to me. He lovingly called me "momma-daddy" for a while. During the workday, if I was depressed and bitter to tears, I could always go over to visit Lynn and just talk about nothing while she folded clothes or ironed or did her chores with the television going on with something noisy but mindless. And there was also Martin and Marsh, who lived directly behind us. They were dealing with a gay son and were receptive. Although they have moved to a newer neighborhood, we still see them over dinner six or eight times a year.

Politics also involved the Democratic Party. Although Trish and I considered ourselves Republican-leaning independents when I transitioned (we had both voted for Nixon), we learned quickly that there was no place for us at the Republican table. Mostly, the friends that left were

"Rs" while the people who stuck with us were "Ds." At that time the LGBT community was trying to make inroads to the Democratic Party. For a number of years, I was elected to the county and then the state Democratic Party conventions. At that time, the party platform was just as hateful of LGBT folks as the Republican platform still is. I was involved in getting that changed. A friend, Jerry Mayes, had printed up some buttons for some previous event that read "I'm straight, but I support gay rights!" I had a few and took them with me to the next state convention. People just snapped them up, and I told Jerry to go home and get the box that he had not been able to unload at the previous event. By the evening of the second day, nearly 60 percent of the delegates were wearing our button. So the next day they joined us to vote out that plank.

I went to law school during that time and did a lot of important work and made a lot of important inroads, which I have written about in other places. It was not a fun time or a fun place. I struggled academically and nearly flunked out the first year. When I graduated, I had climbed up to the very top of the bottom third. Some of the students, and the Christian Legal Society in particular, were so mean that there were many times I stayed at home on class days and simply cried. My greatest satisfaction was proving and having them placed on a campuswide probation for discrimination. As part of the proof process, most of the students learned how badly I had been treated and gave me an outpouring of love during my final weeks and at subsequent reunions.

I had tried the Amway business while in college, but my wife then was really negative about it, and I had other fish to fry, so I gave it up. In my third decade, unemployed and in law school while drawing money on the GI Bill, I decided to give the Amway business another chance. Trish was excited that I had something to do to bring in some cash (we were so broke that we did not run our air conditioner for eleven summers) and to keep me from dwelling on the pain and hurt that were my frequent companions. The three things I got from the Amway business were some good steady income, not a lot, but enough, plus a sense of and experience in running a retail business, and the tremendous amount of self-improvement books and tapes that we both studied as motivational tools. As I was active in the MCC and in lobbying to repeal the ordinance and in local LGBT politics in general, I went to the gay bars and established commercial accounts. Every week, I took stock and delivered cleaning products. If Amway did not sell it, I would find another supplier of whatever it was the bar managers wanted.

I should say that another income stream developed through a very nice gay architect named Thom Roark. He knew that he could get his drawings approved with a professional engineer's stamp faster and cheaper if he gave me the work. So every two months, I would spend about four days going over all he had done during that time and get a nice check. That and the Amway business died out in 1986, near the end of my fourth decade, when the so-called Reagan recession finally made it to Houston. Although I had graduated as an attorney in 1981, no one would hire me and my self-esteem was too beat up to hang out my shingle back then. By 1986, with my income streams dying out, I hung out my shingle and began practicing law.

But the real joy of my fourth decade was women's league, slow-pitch softball. As I wrote above, I played church softball every year from the time I was eight. I played through the time I left for Germany. By then I had learned to hit with power, and I was either playing second base, pitcher, or catcher. I was a great pitcher with an arc so high on the ball that it would cross the plate at a forty-degree angle unless the umpire ruled it illegally too steep. My favorite position was catcher. Simply put, the catcher controls the speed of the game. And there were usually two or three plays at the plate each season that could be replayed in my mind or over a beer during the cold months and during the following season.

I had not played since I had left for Germany, and I knew I would never be allowed to play as a woman. But when I was thirty-four, on an out-of-town Democratic women's political trip, I visited with Annise Parker, who later became my coach. She had a lesbian team in a lesbian league. When I mentioned how I missed the softball of my youth, she asked me if I was good and what position I played. She was short a reliable catcher. I agreed to her invitation but suggested that I was not going to put up with any prejudice. The hormones had been going through me for six years by then, and the reduction of my shoulder girth was obvious. As I told her, if I hit the ball hard and true, it was from playing since I was eight. As it turned out, in our league there were two teams with some big women, bigger than I was, who could also hit further than I could. So it became no problem.

I played every summer league and every winter league until I was thirty-nine, the spring that I contracted the shingles. I remember hitting the ball far enough to run all the bases, only to see that after a few seasons they had learned and were out so far for my at bat that I could barely make a three-bagger. To make the other team pitch to our best hitter, we placed her as number three with me as number four. If she did not clean the bases, I would. And the plays at home came. I was a rock at guarding the plate. Several slid around me, but in eleven seasons no one made it through me or knocked the ball out of my glove. My teammates were the best. I still have their picture on my wall. But after the shingles, I was not able to fully recover for two seasons. By then I was forty and decided that I would not be able to get back into shape to play head-to-head with twenty-year-olds.

DECADE 5 (YEARS 41–50)

My forties were the years that I practiced law and made decent money. By then Trish was making much better money. Trish and I had learned that we could never trust my income stream, so we never changed our standard of living from living off of her check alone. Instead, we took my income to pay off the mortgage, to put braces on my teeth, to pay off our cars and other bills, and then socked it away. As it turned out, it was a good decision since four years ago when the Republicans took over *all* of the judgeships, my court appointments went to nil. It was sad, but we had never learned to live off of my income, and we were debt free with new-model cars paid for with cash.

It was also the decade that I created the International Conference on Transgender Law and Employment Policy (ICTLEP) and personally trained many of the activists (or those who trained their own group of activists) that are currently around the nation doing the grassroots politics and changing the laws.[10] It was the decade when we began the push for transgender reintegration (after all, we were at Stonewall) in all things lesbian, gay, and bisexual. All of this is documented in many other writings found in the endnotes.

This was also the decade that I experienced my son, Randy. I had only seen him once since he was five. When he was twenty and in college, he contacted me. We had a great decade. He was cautious at first but soon became proud of the many obstacles that Trish and I had overcome. He asked lots of questions and was satisfied. He knew I was non-op. Trish and I were invited to his wedding and to his graduation. We held his firstborn and did lots of neat things together. It was our first real taste of blood-family activities. Trish still had her family, but she did not visit them very much because I was not welcome (that resolved about three years ago). A few years ago, Randy and I had a spat, and it suddenly became escalated. No contact in three years, but I still feel that decade with him was very healing. I waited for him once: I guess I will have to wait on him again.

This was also the decade when Trish and I resolved the issue of my having genital surgery. We had a sweet gay queen of a neighbor who, as he grew old, kind of adopted us. His name was Sam. Actually he was the one who first got the neighborhood Democrats to elect me to go to my second state convention. As he grew older and more feeble, he asked if I would watch over his business and such. I managed him through his last three years and ensured that when he was buried he had his pink triangle in the lid of his coffin (much to the chagrin of his family members who wanted him buried in the closet). During Sam's last months in the nursing home, I commented to Trish that when we die, I hope I go first. She asked what I meant, and I said that they would have a field day with me, being nonsurgical, at a nursing home.

I thought nothing more about the conversation, but I learned that she stewed on it for several days. Later that week, she told me how that comment had profoundly affected her. She said that when I turned fifty, then as far as she was concerned, I had fulfilled my end of our bargain, that she would support my having genital surgery, and that she would stay with me. So I had the green light from her, and I knew that we already had the money to do it. So I thought long and hard about something that I had not considered before—the chance to have genital surgery and still keep my Trish with me.

After months of thought, I decided that I had already lived full time as a woman, complete with legal change of name and hormone therapy for almost twenty years. I was a woman, fully and completely, and a surgery that no one would see except Trish and me and a doctor was just not a big deal to me. But, I did very much want an orchiectomy. While I had never felt uncomfortable with what I had come to call my large clitoris (which by the way shrank after decades of hormones), I had never been comfortable with its two little friends hanging on down there. So I had them removed. Best thing I ever did. Not only was I rid of what I never liked, but the female hormones really took over, even more than the eighteen years prior. (Oh, how I hate dry skin!)

When I tell people this, a lot of postoperative folks get mad and say that I am not a real woman and that I am antisurgery. Well, whatever floats their boat. I do know that I had a true choice and I made it without coercion. And as a result, I began to see that if legal status of gender becomes the primary goal rather than complete surgery, then a true and uncoerced choice can be made. After all, many people have surgery as the last step toward getting all of the legal bona fides. But since we say that our gender is in our brains, then why cannot we seek the legal bona fides based on our feelings before we have to decide on or have the final surgeries?

DECADE 6 (YEARS 51–57)

As I write this I will soon be fifty-five. Next summer Trish and I will celebrate our thirtieth anniversary. What have I experienced during these five years?

Proudly, I have become a true authority. Not only have I taught law but I am now published, as you will see in the endnotes. Another law article is being printed, and some friends and I have submitted my fifth article for consideration. I have been flown to numerous out-of-state law schools and universities, with expenses paid for both Trish and me, to relate the ideas that I have developed and written about in the area of transgender politics and law. I have keynoted several large transgender conferences, at their expense. I have the Phyllabuster e-mail list that is into its eighth year. Now what I write (or what I feel is worthy of being repeated) is sent around the world on my personal list and is echoed many times over in other people's lists and subsequently printed in local newsletters. Estimates are that I reach over five hundred thousand people. I have been honored with numerous awards, and one was even named after me. It is becoming very humbling, but I must say that after a decade in the desert of bitterness, this is much better.

I have become active in the State Bar of Texas. I was one of the founders of an openly LGBT section[11] and served as its third Section Chair. Since that time I have attended many annual bar conventions and am meeting lots of folks. I began by wearing my TG MENACE shirt, just in case they did not know I was there. After the Littleton decision,[12] I handed out hundreds of flyers (printed on appropriately pink paper) that ridiculed the decision at the following convention. During the next year, with help from the past chair and the chair-elect, I moved the Bar Board to accept an employment policy for its own staff, which included sexual orientation protections that were inclusive of transgenders. At the last convention, I wore some nice dresses just like all the other women. Several friends commented that they did not recognize me without my advocate uniform. I told them that there was nothing to fight about at that convention. I ran last year for a position on the Bar Board and got 32 percent of the vote. Not bad for a mostly retired, solo practitioner, and out-queer transgender. I am running again this year. If I win, they get a great director for three years. If I lose, they get educated another year. Either way it is a win-win. And besides, this year several prominent lawyers are going to take me around to the big firms and introduce me. Who would have ever thunk that!

My music has become very important. I have always been a singer in church and school choirs since I was about ten. My best opportunity was with the elite Singing Cadets, men's choral group, of Texas A&M. And yet, I have never been able to sing without other people providing accompaniment. I tried the guitar as a youth, but the klutz teacher would not put the music in my vocal range, and I lost interest. I tried to pick it up several other times, but, as you have read above, other things were happening. But when I turned fifty, I picked up my guitar, and I have not put it down. Two tips if you wish to start out. One is get nylon strings while you build the calluses on your fingertips. You are less likely to quit if your fingers are not overly sore. And, two, learn how to read and transpose sheet music. Determine your vocal range and move the song up or down so that the notes on the page are within that range. Transpose the chords respectively. You will stay with it if you can sing what you play. Most folks who tell me they cannot sing, find that they can sing when the music is in their vocal range.

I self-taught for about a year. This included the lumbering process of learning how to transpose. Then I took lessons. Lessons are more meaningful if you already know how to form about eight basic chords and already have the calluses. I took beginner lessons, advanced lessons, and blues lessons. Then I joined a guitar circle of a dozen folks who gather once a week to play and sing as the spotlight moves around the circle. The feeling of satisfaction at being able to "capture" the songs that I have always enjoyed is a completion for me.

And the neighborhood has come back. Now, all the previously jerk neighbors have either gotten over themselves, moved, or died. As it turns out, with me being mostly retired—for the health reasons of a stress-related anemia and because of having only Republican judges and, of course, because we planned and saved everything for this eventuality—I walk the neighborhood daily with my dogs, and most days Trish joins us. It had become a mess with loose dogs, junk cars, heavy trash violators, and people using their homes for a variety of construction, car repair, and resale shop businesses. Essentially, I got other neighbors active, and in two years we have turned it around. I laugh when I relate that "most folks don't care that I am queer, if I am fixing their neighborhood." I have been asked by the civic club for each of the last two years to accept an at-large board position, which I have thus far declined. Even so, I am honored to be asked.

Imagine that. Queer, old, unemployable, and unliked Phyllis, now financially stable and sought out for advice in her field and by her neighbors.

Making lemonade out of lemons by being OUT! And happy!

NOTES

1. See "Friday Profile: In-Your-Face Advocate," State Bar of Texas Home Page, http://www.texasbar.com/frontpage/frye.asp.

2. See Elizabeth Cady Stanton and the Revising Committee, *The Woman's Bible* (Seattle: Coalition Task Force on Women and Religion, 1974).

3. See David Viscott, MD, *Risking* (New York: Simon & Schuster, 1977).

4. See Wayne Dyer, *The Sky Is the Limit* (New York: Simon & Schuster, 1980), especially chapters 2 and 3 about authority.

5. See Phyllis Randolph Frye, "The International Bill of Gender Rights vs. the Cider House Rules: Transgenders Struggle over What Clothing They Are Allowed to Wear on the Job, Which Restroom They Are Allowed to Use on the Job, Their Right to Marry, and the Very Definition of Their Sex," *William and Mary Journal of Women and the Law* 7 (2000): 133, also available at http://transgenderlegal.com.

6. See Lisa Gray, "The Transgender Menace Next Door," *Houston Press*, June 28, 2001, also available at http://www.houstonpress.com/issues/2001-06-28/feature2.html/1/index.html.

7. See Phyllis Randolph Frye and Alyson Dodi Meiselman, "Same-Sex Marriages Have Existed Legally in the United States For a Long Time Now," *Albany Law Review* 64 (2001): 1031, also available at http://transgenderlegal.com.

8. See Phyllis Randolph Frye, *The War Stories*, seven short stories written by her in the mid-1990s and published in whole or in part by numerous transgender publications. Available upon request from prfrye@aol.com. *The War Stories* are: #1 "The White Christmas"; #2 "NAWBO (Nat'l Ass'n of Women Business Owners)"; #3 "My Son"; #4 "Law School"; #5 "League of Women Voters"; #6 "Hormones—One Person's Experience"; and #7 "The Repeal of City of Houston Ordinance 28-442-4."

9. See Phyllis Randolph Frye, "Facing Discrimination, Organizing for Freedom: The Transgender Community," in *Creating Change: Public Policy, Sexuality, and Civil Rights*, ed. John D'Emilio et al. (New York: St. Martin's, 2000), also available at http://transgenderlegal.com.

10. See http://transgenderlaw.org for a list of the various jurisdictions. For Proceedings of the ICTLEP Conferences, some are being loaded onto my Web site at http://transgenderlegal.com. Frye still has the masters and can make sets for libraries or for your personal use upon request to her at prfrye@aol.com.

11. The Sexual Orientation and Gender Identification Issues (SOGII) Section of the State Bar of Texas, http://sogiitx.org.

12. For details on this tragic and bigoted court decision, go to http://christielee.net.

THE HAJ

Shiloh Nan

S ome years ago, as I prepared my autobiography (which remains to this day still a manuscript), I came across a small passage from James Michener's *Chesapeake*. It succinctly tells the story of the journey encountered by most transgendered persons.

Michener wrote:

> Each soul on earth faces an Armageddon, when all the forces are arranged pro and con. Now comes the one great battle; if thee runs away or fails to fight with vigor, thy life is forever diminished. Armageddon is even more compelling when it is a battle of the spirit.

While Michener had other Armageddons in mind, there is no doubt in my mind that each person facing the journey to find gendered peace faces his/her own "Armageddon of the spirit." And, if he/she fails to meet this challenge, that person will be diminished.

In July of 1980—two years after completing the male-to-female gender odyssey—I wrote:

> [T]here is a cave of the mind, a cruel and dark place to be. To emerge from that dank world of shadows is breathtaking. I have just been freed from this cave. My checkered life history is filled with strange incongruities. I pretzeled my way through *grand mal* seizures of mental, emotional, and physical gyrations. I desperately tried to extricate myself from this suffocating place. The Roman Catholic priesthood, marriage, public positions, degrees, honors, awards—all helped to

deaden the impending "Armageddon," yet none sufficed. I played the *pagliacco* role until I could neither laugh nor cry at the Sartre "no exit" I had reached.

A transsexual once wrote: "There are those who say that we do this (i.e., gender change) for money or for glory but I say that our eyes could see no other way." And so it is. The highways and byways of our lives are filled with contradictions and finally, for many of us, there is euphoric peace. Gender dysphoria is a long and lonely journey.

In the same manuscript noted earlier, I composed the following: "I cry and shout of contradiction. I am and will never be all I want to be. But, at great price, I am given a new lease to careen happily into an uncharted future. For this I am grateful." That was written in decade 5. Now, entering decade 8 it is time to reprise this lifetime and share some thoughts about the first seven decades.

I entered this blue marble planet in a typical turn-of-the-century, ethnic, and Slovenian/Slovak neighborhood in Ohio. Aunts, uncles, grandparents, and even one set of great-grandparents literally surrounded our home nestled in the shadow of a huge woolen mill factory. And, due to the cultural heritage, it was a Roman Catholic enclave. Church steeples literally dotted the immediate landscape (some for Hungarians, others for Poles, Germans, Italians, and, of course, Slovaks). My earliest memories—probably age four or five—were about the constant agony of being left-handed.

In the cultural tradition of my parents and their parents, to be left-handed was a sure passport to evil. (In fact, the Latin word *sinister* means "left," and, like many other languages, the simple word *left* connoted idiocy, craziness, or extreme clumsiness.) My father—a semipro ballplayer (and professional printer by trade)—was adamant that I must be retrained to become a right-hander. Mealtimes were tragedies. Holding a baseball bat right-handed was agony. Learning to write was a complete fiasco.

Yet my father persisted—indeed, he persisted. All relatives and primary grade teachers (nuns) were given strict instructions to work toward right-handedness. It was, of course, a losing battle on their part. But he—and they—persisted. Except for one person: my great-grandfather Matthew. He, his wife, and my maternal grandmother lived next door to us. Great Grandpa did not speak English. (I imagine, like many of the old timers, he understood more than he let on!) He ignored my father's instructions. Each day he ate his lunch of veal and rice sitting on a wooden bench by the side door of his house. He would wave for me to come over and sit with him. Gladly I came through the low hedge dividing our properties and sat next to him as he ate and drank from his beer bucket (from the neighborhood saloon down the street). Then, wiping the foam from his big mustache, he would motion for me to accompany him to his "secret" shed wherein he kept all of his treasured tools.

The only word I remember him saying to me was *Billichki* (little Billy). He would allow me to enter his private domain, take a hammer from his workbench, put it in my *left* hand (on purpose), and direct me to straighten bent nails that he kept in untold numbers of old coffee cans. I would sit on the floor of his shed and, with a paving brick for my anvil, I would spend hours straightening bent nails. I was in seventh heaven. Great Grandpa Matthew was my hero. I clearly remember the twinkle in his eyes as we both defied those who were insisting on making me into a right-hander. When he died, a part of me died, too. My hero was gone. I had no one who would honor what I was. His funeral cortege to the church (one block from home to church) was one of the most awesome events in my memory bank: his old cronies lined up, some with huge horns (tubas and bass horns), playing so mournfully. Old bubbas, their heads covered by their ever-present babushkas, sobbed. As I did. I was so very small and, without my "buddy," I felt even more dismal. A chapter had ended. I was now at the complete mercy of those intent on making me a right-hander.

At age six we moved from this ethnic city neighborhood to a small town in central Ohio. Gone was the dusty old shed (which was like a palace to me), and matters continued to go downhill. I was never able, in my father's eyes, to do things correctly. Whether it was using a tool, catching a baseball, or writing in school, the agony of correction continued. My younger sister became the object of my envy. No one hassled *her*! She went about her business of being my kid sister. Somewhere in the labyrinth of childhood confusion, I remember thinking how nice it would be to become just like my little sister. It never occurred to me that she, being right-handed, would never be badgered. I thought it was that girls were immune from harassment. And so the thoughts of "becoming like my sister" persisted and enlarged as the years went by. She and I were the best of friends and would play for hours at some imaginary game scenarios. But, as each meal or event occurred—and she was left peacefully alone—I yearned to be also at peace. Inside of me was building the foundation for realignment.

As decade 2 dawned, I was allowed to become an acolyte (assisting the priest at Mass). One of my psychiatrists later in life opined that perhaps I simply relished the lacy surplices and dresslike cassocks we wore around the altar. I would not venture that as a definitive part of it all. I relished being in the quiet of the church and bustling about assisting the priest. And, being left-handed was not an impediment to the task. It was not long before the thought of becoming a priest became a viable option—on two counts. One, I would be doing something "godly," and I would leave for the seminary after the eighth grade. I would not have my father daily insisting on right-handedness. I hope the former thought was the predominant one, but I would be less than honest if I did not mention that leaving home for the minor seminary was a very workable option!

For the next thirteen years (decades 2 and 3) studying for the priesthood was all consuming. Sexual expression was, of course, not an option, and this suited me because I was in great conflict. I can remember so very well—in the eighth grade—going on a "retreat" (a spiritual exercise) in which the priest railed against sexual actions and "impure thoughts." I was baffled, but I interpreted him to also mean imaginings about *being* a girl. I was sure this was also a perversion. With great trepidation, I entered the confessional to "recite my sins." I noted that I had had "impure thoughts." I never got another word out (such as, "thoughts about being a girl"). The priest on the other side of the confessional screen exploded. He raged and yelled at me. So, mistakenly, I assumed he knew what I *really* meant. I was doomed. Every confession after that for a number of years entailed the admission of these "impure thoughts" (not about girls, but about *being* one). It was not until I was well into the seminary that the issue became clarified.

Studies came easily, and I was slowly being groomed to teach after ordination. The major issue was my growing feeling that I might be in the proverbial "wrong locker room." At least four times—with four different priest counselors—I brought up my dilemma. Each time my feelings were dismissed as either inappropriate or the temptation of the devil. One counselor priest reminded me that if I looked between my legs it would solve the dilemma! Another, a crusty old German priest, pounded his fist on the desk and reminded me that if God had meant me to be a girl, he would have made me such. I was admonished not to raise the issue again.

I moved inextricably toward the Roman priesthood. May 31, 1959 (decade 3), I can honestly say was one of the saddest, most agonizing days of my life. It was Ordination Day. I was to become a priest. In the ceremony there is a long period of time when the priests-to-be (the *ordi-*

nandi) lie on the sanctuary floor with their heads in their arms while the choir wends through a very long litany of prayers. I remember—as clearly as on that day—that I wanted to run. But I did not. I think I knew deep down that the final Armageddon was yet to be fought.

Decade 3 came to a whimpering end as I worked on my final degree and was assigned to be the athletic director of a large, metropolitan Catholic high school. Teaching, coaching, counting money from sock hops, and arguing with unruly parents of athletes became the stuff of my existence. Coaching brought me squarely in conflict with my inner yearnings. What was a girl like me doing in a boys' locker room?! Patting backsides at football games was not exactly what I had in mind. But, dutifully, I served as best I could; preached as well as I could; ran a successful athletic program; and, most of all, I regularly spent some twenty hours a day in frenetic diverting activities (games, dances, going to the university, teaching in the high school, directing the glee club, saying Mass, etc.).

This whirlwind existence kept me from having to endure the one, constant nightmare that I had since I was a small boy: running through a dark cave with someone chasing me. Every night, always the same mantric dream. I never knew who was chasing me (and to this day I do not know unless it was the personification of my genderal confusion). Many a morning I would wake up in my office chair, having dozed off for a few hours.

My life took another strange twist. After President Kennedy's assassination, the war in Vietnam escalated. President Johnson was caught between the proverbial rock and hard place. The war was unpopular and the draft was still in place. Young men were being shipped overseas and many began to come home in body bags. My scholastic grooming process was almost over and it was expected that I would begin teaching. Instead, one evening at dinner, a military chaplain was present and lamented that no one wanted to volunteer as a chaplain. I sat transfixed. Not that I identified with the war or even liked it, but I saw a chance (much like leaving home years earlier) to finalize my life. My agonies were looming larger and larger each passing day. It would be a perfect plan! I would volunteer to become a chaplain, go to Vietnam, and get killed! (Talk of flights of fancy.) That way no one would ever need to know of my deep-seated gender dysphoric problem. I would get killed and hailed as a hero.

My parents, friends, colleagues—all would sorrowfully lament that I had laid down my life for my country. The next day, before the priest left the rectory, I asked him how I would go about becoming a chaplain. He explained the simple process, and I informed my superiors of my decision. After apoplectic seizures were over (and the vision of apple pie and motherhood came to the fore), my superiors reluctantly gave permission for me to volunteer for the military chaplaincy. In short order, "Billichki" was off to war. (I shall pass over the inane, grueling training and boredom, which, mercifully, was over in nine weeks.) The sixty-three-day wonders were assigned. Not everyone in our "class" was assigned to Nam. Fortunately I was. I am not sure what I would have done had I been assigned stateside. So, off to war and getting killed. A hero was about to be made. I would not have to endure life in my "discombobulated" state. I had come to believe—along with the help of a therapist where I had been athletic director—that much more therapy would be needed to "cure" me of this dysphoria. Now it would not matter.

I was assigned to a frontline unit. I joined a ragtag group of tired, bored, and angry American GIs who wanted to be anywhere but where they were. Fighting an elusive enemy and knowing, deep in their guts that the cause was lost did not allow for much esprit de corps. Day after day the Hueys came in and left with body bags. Day after day we had to drag body parts back to base camp. These young men would forever remain twenty-one, twenty-two, twenty-three years old. Day after day I heard confessions, became soaked with stinking jungle sweat, and prayed for deliverance by way of an enemy bullet or mortar. But none came my way. A whistling whine here and there; a young man moving through the camp would suddenly drop, having been shot in the head by a sniper—life was frightening and boring. War may be hell, as someone once said but, in fact, it is sloggingly boring.

But, most of all, I could not get killed. The weeks and months dragged on. One day I celebrated a hurried Mass on the hood of a Jeep. My altar boy (man) was a quiet, reflective lad from Massachusetts. He had been drafted, interrupting his college and marriage to a childhood colleen from Boston. In the middle of the Mass, there was the sickening thud of a sniper's bullet just as he arose to go to Communion. I watched in horror as he crumpled before me. Oh Lord, why could it not be me? I was destined to remain alive, complete my tour, and come back to the States. The war had revolted me, and I had no stomach to teach. The drab decade was coming to an end. I was assigned to travel about the country preaching. I became the roving, preaching "troubadour" during decade 4. Much like the years in Detroit, I worked constantly. I preached to small groups and large crowds, young and old, from coast to coast.

The assignments now blur into a collage of sermons, suitcases, and coping. Preaching was easy; living out of a suitcase became a way of life.

But coping with the nightmares, uneasiness, and dread exacerbated. Recently, I located two interesting items: a poem I wrote, titled "Suicide," and a sermon I delivered in a prestigious seminary on the East Coast. Both reflect the strange yin and yang of my life.

Bear with me as I review this plaintive verse:

SUICIDE

Between the mountains of pain and nowhere,
There is a time to obliterate the pages of life.
A chimera of hope has finally eluded me.
Time now to wrench the pounding blood-line.
No spirit left to fight; no breath worth drawing.
A good night to life and a hope for new-found peace.
If God you are—wherever—a hand of welcome please.

This tragic piece of writing is not presented as worthy of a Pulitzer. By no means. In fact, I suspect some of my literature professors of yore would cringe at the makeup of this piece. But it shows more clearly than anything else the depths to which I was sinking. Some years later I actually attempted to leave this plane but was "accidentally" thwarted in that attempt.

Ordinarily, when preaching, I spoke from jottings, not prepared scripts. I had boxes of notes, quotations, phrases, and isolated words. But I did save one sermon: the one I delivered to a chapel filled with seminarians and faculty members. The chapel was huge and ornate. Preaching in it was a public speaking triumph. Words echoed and rang from nave to apse.

The evening sermon was the major presentation of the day. Faculty—at the directive of the cardinal—were mandated to attend. I sensed rebukes as priestly prayer books were opened and tight-lipped silence cascaded from sullen, priestly faces. The seminarians, on the other hand, seemed eager to listen to the message of the Living Water instead of the stagnant pools of quasi-religious pap they were given as a daily diet.

The sermon was titled "A Man Named John" in honor of the little, roly-poly Pope John XXIII who had died earlier in the decade. It is not my intent to share the entire sermon but to point out that, even in my agony and spiritual dark night of the soul, I was trying to live and believe in the Good News. Pope John had opened the windows to let the "fresh air" of change permeate the Church. He had disrupted the creaking barque. Some did not like it. John's major theme was that Christ had come to teach us Good News, not tepid news, not bad news, not terrible news—but Good News. He had reminded seminarians that they must "come alive with a philosophy of wisdom and love, a theology of truth and charity, and live in a rule, rite and creed which could be believed with the heart and mind." Dear Pope John had reminded us that we did not need prophets of gloom. He once asked a papal audience: "[T]he question of our judgment will be: did you try to form community; did you work for it; were you willing to suffer for it; love for it?" The chapel had become eerily quiet. Young seminarian eyes were aglow with challenge. I will now share with you, the reader, the poignant ending to that sermon. It contained the kernel of my faith belief (and, hidden in one sentence, the fact that one could be in agony and still live the Good News). I was begging this Joshua ben Joseph to help me find the ultimate Good News for myself. "Gentlemen, our task is to form community—to love in good will, forgiving one another. This is our only task. 'I am for you' is the command of Jesus. Nothing else matters or comes close. Not our daily office, our tests, our sports, even our Mass. Even when we are entwined in the agony of the spirit we must hear and follow the passionate plea of Jesus. 'This is the New Law.'" The breviaries were closed. This was the only Good News I could proclaim. Even in those days of being all mixed up, I could still be at home with the proclamation of this breathtaking message. The seminarians rose as one and applauded. But, as I left the chapel, a moral theology professor stopped me in the vestibule. He whispered a one-liner that, to this day, still haunts me: "My dear Father, it will never work." He turned and walked away. How sad that he was teaching these young men such a message of gloom. In a nutshell, it is the great battle of the spirit: either Jesus will work or He won't.

Following on the previous theme, I recall with sadness and pain working in the civil rights movement. We always think of Selma and Little Rock but, perhaps as part of my death wish at that time, I became involved (courtesy of some friends of mine at Marquette) in a civil rights march in Milwaukee. It was a heady time in an era that consumed our national attention. I met a priest named Jim. He had accepted the challenge to strive for change. Much like the prophets of old, he was doomed to failure (eventually leaving the priesthood a bit tattered and bruised).

The task for the day was to march across a bridge in South Milwaukee. It seemed simple enough. I had been cajoled and challenged to put my words into action. In those days South Milwaukee was an enclave of racial hatred. Looking across the bridge, I could see a huge throng of people. It suddenly dawned on me that it would have been much nicer and relaxing in a rectory talking theology. Or dozing in front of a television set with a baseball game on. But here I was in clerical black, ready to engage in my first real confrontation on behalf of the black minority. We were instructed about nonviolence and how to protect ourselves from flying objects. I had not counted on *that*! There was no time to debate the issue. Some waved placards; some joined hands; and all of us were singing. People like myself nervously squinted into the afternoon sun wondering what was to come.

The area across the bridge was, at that time, a bastion of white, eastern European Catholicism. It was a hardworking, blue-collar section of the city. In the distance we could see numerous church spires dotting the landscape. As we neared the other side, we saw a sea of white faces—angry, white faces. For the first time in my life I saw venomous hatred stamped on the faces and in the eyes of Americans. Spittle began to fly. People came up to us and screamed profanities. Only later did I realize that my Roman collar was a symbol of contradiction and hatred to them. I could not believe what I was witnessing. Here were thousands of people who, I am sure, had recently come from the 10:00 or 11:00 AM parish Mass. They had probably listened to a beautifully worded sermon on some sweet subject. Surely their priests had proclaimed the Good News of the gospel. Surely. Until I saw two priests in the mob spitting and throwing rocks like everyone else! Sadly I realized that both sides were calling on Jesus Christ to bless their cause. It reminded me of parochial high school football games some years earlier in Detroit. Both huddles were praying to their beloved parish patron saint for victory. To whom would God listen? The saint with the greatest "pull"? The saint closest to Him? If so, any parish named after the Virgin Mary was a sure winner! Unless, of course, that parish played a parish named in honor of the Holy Spirit, Holy Redeemer, or, zounds, the Holy Trinity! But since life is not magic, it did not work out that way. Yet here I was watching two sets of "Christians" colliding under the banner of Jesus Christ. A brick sailed by my head; a rock thudded against my shoulder. Spit was splattered all over my black suit coat. Someone struck me with a placard and uttered some obscenity about being a Judas priest. At the far end of the bridge the police moved in to set up a human barricade. The march stopped and Father Jim preached a brief message on racial freedom. The residents of South Milwaukee jeered and threw garbage. Finally, with a call to freedom and justice, and the song "We Shall Overcome," we snaked our way back across the bridge. At last it was over. I was emotionally drained. My clothes were a shambles. My psyche was even more tattered. I found out that this was not my cup of tea. We also found out that the majority of superiors and bishops were not especially receptive to clerics on the front lines. And the "new" theology was becoming a bone of contention. Some of my colleagues and I found ourselves spending undue amounts of time fending off ignorant, episcopal attacks about our preaching. Between spittle and theological ignorance, the spittle was easier to take. At least spit could be cleaned off a coat. Pseudotheological expertise was harder to erase or wipe clean.

The gray twilight of the seventies lay ahead. Theological turmoil and inner *angst* was the tandem of my being. Both took their toll. My entire being was in severe shock. One day, while preaching, I collapsed and was rushed to the hospital. An ultimate diagnosis of multiple sclerosis became the label of my life. The neurological specialists were skeptical and valiantly tried to encourage me to surface the inner Armageddon. But I was not yet ready to acknowledge the duality within me. Surely I was smart enough to "beat" the odds. It would take one more decade before I would be honest enough to wave the flag of truce and face the real ordeal of my life.

In the meantime, in quick succession, I left the Roman priesthood and, at the suggestion of one psychiatrist, got married. I entered the mental health arena as a psychologist, conducting research on state hospital recidivism. I soon found myself gaining expertise in the up-and-coming field of alcohol and drug abuse treatment. (Not as a client but as an administrator!) And, not to leave any stone unturned, I became deeply involved in operating a suicide prevention center. Little did I realize how very close to the deepest core of my Being this subject would become. Along the way, I survived a plane crash in the Colorado mountains; a car crash in Indiana; and spent two days staring into the barrel of a .38 wielded by a distraught, suicidal client. Looking back, there were ample "opportunities" to punch my ticket to the "beyond," but nothing seemed to work. I dutifully plodded on. Finally, after almost a decade away from the priesthood, I married a woman who tried her best to keep me sane, and assisting in the "war on drugs" (itself a sad story of ineptitude on the part of both federal and state governments), I could not bear myself any longer. Decade 4 ended with the decision that

"Billichki" had to give way to the real me. The genderal agony had reached the point of making that Armageddon decision. After an ill-fated suicide attempt, it was time to move on.

Tearfully, I bade good-bye to my ever-patient wife, Dee; quietly departed from my role as drug "czar"; packed my belongings; and moved west. I wanted to make a new start. Shiloh would begin her life, go through the preoperative stage, and, like the chrysalis, emerge as the *papillon* I had always dreamed I should be.

Decade 5 was a watershed part of my life: *SRS (sex reassignment surgery)* was a heady experience, performed in a little mountain town and hospital in Colorado (labeled the "sex change capital of the world"). Friends rallied (those that remained from the previous "incarnation"); my own need for permanent hair removal (a beard is not very becoming on a woman) led to becoming an electrologist. I was awarded a research grant on reincarnation and transsexualism, demanding a move to California. There, after pages of newsprint on the "priest who traded a cassock for skirts" appeared, life became unbearable from another angle: the crackpots of the world emerged. From threatening phone calls, to getting shot at, to my car being bombed—I beat a hasty exit (after two years) from the glitzy glamour of Hollywood to the serenity of the Colorado Rockies. I had hardly settled into my new home when I was introduced to Jackie, who was to become the second love of my life. She honored me as the woman I wished to be. Jackie openly proclaimed her love for me and I, in awe, responded to this new relationship. My worth did not depend on being left-handed nor on my MENSA status. She accepted me as the woman I had become. My odyssey had taken another marvelous turn. I owe Jackie my deepest thanks and respect. We remain friends to this day (even though we each found other partners).

There was no doubt that I felt much more comfortable in the feminine role. Gone were the daily nightmares about being chased by an unknown but persistent pursuer. The heady world of learning how to use makeup, wear heels and skirts, and entering the world of females (e.g., the first ob-gyn examination complete with stirrups, pap smear, mammogram) had settled into the routine of finally living as fully as possible. Being comfortable with my identity had finally occurred. It was a feeling too marvelous to describe! Peace, contentment, congruence—all were part of this new world, this new persona, this genderal euphoria. Finally!

There have been, indeed, blips and bumps along the way. Decade 5 gave way to decade 6 almost without notice. Teaching electrology and becoming involved on the national scene of that profession were elixirs.

Being "read" was not an issue. Being accepted by most people was a marvelous feeling. Facing bankruptcy was terrible reality, occasioned by the belief that a private, technical school company I had joined was honest and aboveboard. But the company "bellied up" owing me (and others) thousands and thousands of dollars. But even that, while discouraging and embarrassing, was not daunting—much like the old saying: you pick yourself up, dust yourself off, and get on with living. Even in that disaster, marvelous, new friends emerged as well as unique opportunities. At the insistence of a dear friend, I moved into a gorgeous 1844 cabin nestled in the hills of North Carolina. The serenity and solitude were needed tonics after the humiliation of the bankruptcy.

At one point during decade 6, I received some very distressing news: a series of tests had revealed that I had lymphoblastic leukemia. I saw my dreams shattering into a million pieces. The prognosis was dire. After all the agony, stress, and inner pain, I was going to die. Fortunately, the goddesses of good fortune always come through! I had been invited to deliver a keynote address at a New Woman's conference on the East Coast. I did not look forward to the long trip. I was ever so tired. But, to honor a friend, I agreed to go. While there, as we shared some preliminary thoughts, I noted that I had leukemia. From the back of the room a voice emerged: "You need healing!" When I traced the voice to the person, it turned out to be that of Rena S., a shamanka of the Apache tribe. To this day I am not sure of all that transpired, but I do know that after her fireside healing later that day (eagle feather, sweet grass, hot coals in her mouth, etc.), I emerged a revitalized person. I felt as if I had been shot out of a cannon!

Rena and I had a chance to share thoughts, views, and, eventually, a relationship. Looking back, it is breathtaking to note that I was "cured." (By whatever word, the leukemia was gone and the medical community which had been preparing my obituary could not explain it.)

However, later in the decade Rena developed Hepatitis C with jaundice, fatigue, two liver transplants, and very much pain. She died peacefully, and I was permitted to move forward in the company of the great-grandmothers and grandfathers of the universe. Rena, may your great shaman gifts be greater than ever! Aho.

Friends abounded; enemies receded (even the Roman Church, as the years went on, found itself becoming immersed more and more in its own ineptitudes, scandals, and failing systems). I was given the great opportunity to become a Native American pipe carrier and eagerly participated in sweats, all-nighters, ceremonies, and sun dances. I had the good fortune to participate in many psychic events, and I relish those marvelous times that allowed me to face myself more deeply and bask in the greatness of being an awesome entity indeed.

The clock of time is winding down. Decade 7 finds the joints creaking a bit more. But the peace and tranquillity of being the "real" me remains constant. I faced my Armageddon of the spirit and prevailed. I am sure I could have done more and could have been better, but my eyes could see no other way. I relish my friends and now, as a crone, I watch the world career by. The crusading days are over; the days of sheer enjoyment at the grandeur of this Blue Marble are as immense as the state of Texas in which I now live.

I am still interested in good theology; appalled at cretinism, whether in churches, politics, or business. *Retirement* is a word I am not sure I truly comprehend. I think, as in my case, *retirement* enables me to pick and choose times I want to teach, lecture, or just relax. My latest life gift has been the entry into my home of two marvelous felines. Their youthful vitality has invigorated me. Retirement allows me the luxury of allowing the cats to come up on my desk and "chill out," and, if an hour later they still want to be petted, cuddled, or noticed, there is no stopwatch on my time. They also allow me to continue my indoor pipe ceremonies, looking at me with that mixture of quizzical wonder and feline intuition. And, although they do not know it, 2003 brought me to the quarter century mark in the gender lifestyle I so desperately sought for years.

Mortality, however, has become ever more apparent. Fortunately, I believe we live more than once. If gods are there (and I believe *They* are), we are more than the sum of our parts. We are not just a passing blip on the horizon, nor just a collection of protoplasmic "Star Stuff." We are all, in the words of Fritjof Capra (*The Hidden Connections*, Doubleday, 2003), members of "oikos," the earth household. We each have responsibilities. And, while we yearn for the stars, we also have untold opportunities. St. Jerome (340–420 CE) noted that we are all wayfarers on many journeys through many lives. He concludes: "We visit the womb and the tomb many times." The point is well taken. In that light, a genderal change or shift is really no "big deal." Whether Billichki or Nancy, whether priest or woman, whether twenty or seventy, the Armageddons we sometimes dread become the footpaths into the present and the future. I am now in my third decade as a changeling. It has been a heady adventure. I would not alter one day of this new "lease on life."

Appendix 1A

MALE-TO-FEMALE GENITAL RECONSTRUCTION SURGERY

Ariadne Kane, EdD, and Yvon Menard, MD

Male-to-female transsexual surgery has radically changed over the years. When Christine Jorgensen had her surgery, it involved a penectomy and castration. Initially, there was no attempt to establish a vagina, although later surgery involved attempts to do so using part of the intestine. It was a very unsatisfactory solution. A radical change was initiated by Dr. Georges Bourou, a physician who lived in Casablanca, Morocco. He developed a technique known as *penile inversion*, the aim of which is to create a vagina with a minimum depth of five inches and preferably six. His procedure was widely copied and used during the last part of the twentieth century.

There are many surgeons worldwide who perform transsexual surgery. Almost all reputable doctors and clinics are in compliance with the Harry Benjamin International Gender Dysphoria Association (HBIGDA) *Standards of Care*. These standards have been modified and updated over the years. The latest version (2003) for preoperative candidates includes the following protocols:

- A one-year continuous hormonal program with selected monitoring analysis for each third of that period.
- A real-life experience in the femme gender role and presentation. It must be continuous and satisfactorily functional for a minimum of one full year.
- Two letters of recommendation from a health provider with a specialty in gender and transgender issues and a psychiatrist.

For male-to-females (M2Fs) the reconstructive surgery used is known as the *penile skin inversion* technique. It is done under a general or spinal anesthesia and typically lasts about two and a half hours.

The space for the *vaginaplast* is created by dissecting behind the meatus (urinary tube), between the bladder and the rectum. The penis is eviscerated and its skin is inverted and used to form the lining of the new vaginal opening.

The scrotal skin is removed along with the testes. Some thinned scrotal skin may be used to extend the vaginal lining. It is grafted onto the lining and provides the necessary covering for the entire length of the *neo-vagina*.

The *neo-clitoris* is formed by attaching the neurovascular island of the glans to the dorsal nerves and blood vessels of the eviscerated penis. This provides for the sensate activity of the *neo-clitoris*. The *labia minorae* are formed using the mucosa of the urethra and some of the penile skin. The *labia majorae* are formed with some of the penis skin. To maintain postoperative urinary function, a catheter is placed in the urinary bladder. The prostate gland of the patient is not removed. Occasionally, skin grafts are necessary, and these are typically obtained from the inner posterior thigh. These procedures are all part of the single-stage technique to create the basic elements of the *neo-vulva*.

The intended result of this surgical technique is a naturally appearing external female genitalia (*vulva and vagina*) with adequate depth (greater than five inches) for intercourse and clitoral sensation.

There are specific risks associated with this surgery, and these are discussed with the patient prior to performing the surgery. Complete healing and recovery from this surgery may take from six months to one year. The success of this technique depends on the maintenance of the length and girth of the *neo-vagina*.

Two important postoperative protocols that must be followed during this period are *dilation* and *douching*. *Dilation* involves inserting a stent into the *neo-vagina* and holding it in place for periods of from five to twenty minutes. There is a set of five dilators of graduated diameters, all of about five to eight inches long. It is recommended that this process be done five times a day over the course of a year and gradually be reduced to once a week for the rest of the lifespan of the client.

Douching of the *neo-vagina* should be done in the morning and the evening. It helps to remove sloughed off tissue and keeps the *neo-vulva* clean and septic. This protocol is recommended for the first two months after the surgery.[1]

Cosmetically, the resulting perineum, for male-to-female patients appears nearly identical to that of a typical female. Postsurgical treatment involves keeping the vagina open during the healing process, which is described by Marty Hagglund in this book.

Additional cosmetic surgeries are sometimes done if the patient wishes them. These include rhinoplasty (nose surgery), a tracheal shave (reducing the prominence of the Adam's apple), breast augmentation, eyelid surgery, brow lift, and face-lift.

During the presurgical phase of the gender shift process, the transsexual will be on an HRT (hormonal replacement treatment) program, under the care of a physician with a sound knowledge of the endo crinology of the gonads.

For male-to-female patients some breast development occurs, after a period of time, while on an HRT program. For female-to-male patients, the menstrual cycle stops and there is some elongation of the clitoris and increased growth of both facial and body hair. There is also a lowering of the frequency of the voice.

For removal of unwanted facial hair, electrolysis is usually recommended and done prior to genital reconstruction surgery (GRS). This procedure can take one to two years, depending on the nature and amount of beard growth.

NOTE

1. This information was provided by the Institute de Chirugie Cosmetique of Montreal, Quebec, Canada. For further details, please consult its Web site, http://www.grsmontreal.com.

Appendix 1B

FEMALE-TO-MALE GENITAL RECONSTRUCTION SURGERY

Vern Bullough, PhD, and Ariadne Kane, EdD

Before gender reconstruction surgery (GRS), the patient should have had a complete hysterectomy/ovariectomy and many would have had breast removal operations. They also would have been taking male hormones for a year or more before any GRS procedures and would have had a psychiatric evaluation. The operation is technically known as a *phalloplasty*, which uses a radial forearm flap. This description is based on the surgical procedure now being used in Ghent, Belgium, by Dr. Stan Monstrey and his team.

In layperson's terms, the Belgian group use tissues from the non-dominant forearm to make a phallus. The skin, tissues, two nerves, some veins, and one artery are harvested down to the muscle and formed into a tube within a tube. The inner tube has the skin surface on the inside to form the urethra; the outer tube has the skin on the outside to form the corona of the penis. The veins, nerves, and artery are all redundant systems in the arm, and, typically, the arm should heal with no lasting effects. The skin removed from the arm will be covered by skin removed from the leg.

The *penis* itself is formed on the arm with the blood supply kept intact until it is transferred to the genital area. The genital area is prepared, the vagina is removed, and the pelvic floor muscles are sewn together.

The *scrotum* is formed from the outer labia and brought forward. Artificial testes are placed in the newly formed scrotal sac. The penis is then transferred to the genital area. The artery end is attached to the common femoralis artery and the vein to the greater sphenoid vein. Two nerves of the flap are also connected—the first to one of the dorsal clitoral nerves for erogenous sensation; the second to an ilea-inguinal nerve for protective sensation. The *clitoris* is denuded, directed up, and buried under the base of the shaft of the penis for additional erogenous sensation. The radial forearm flap consists of an inner tube for continuation of the urethra and an external tube for coverage of the penis itself. Construction of the *glans* and *corona* of the penis are also performed. The donor arm is then covered with partial-thickness skin grafts taken from the thigh area. The operation requires four to six surgeons and lasts from six to ten hours. Cosmetic touches are then done to enhance the final form of the *phalloplast*.

When the patient becomes conscious, he will have many connections on his torso to monitor the vital signs; the donor site of the "thigh" leg is bandaged, thoroughly; and there is a small bandage by the lower ankle where a short artery was harvested. There is a subabdominal catheter (basically a tube coming out of the belly area between the bellybutton and the penis). A metal "cagelike" structure surrounds the lower genital area during the postoperative phase of recovery. Its function is to protect the *neo-phallus*. Hot air is pumped under the covers to keep the new penis warm. There are temperature gauges on the abdomen and on the penis, and the temperatures are routinely checked. The new penis and scrotum are not bandaged. The new penis is resting on a "penis pillow" taped to the thighs. A catheter is placed in the *neo-phallus*, which serves to keep the *urethra* open.

During the second week of recovery, the subabdominal catheter is clamped, and the process of training the bladder to void itself starts, via the new urethra. This is done by opening the valve of the urethral catheter, periodically, and attempting to urinate via the new penis. To make certain the bladder is empty, the subabdominal catheter is unclamped.

As the patient adjusts to the new direction of urinary flow, this catheter can be removed.

It is important to note that many of the current procedural steps of this surgery are continually being improved and modified. Today's common surgical practice might not necessarily be the same in the future.

Two references relevant to the male-to-female and female-to-male transgender process and GRS are the following:

K. K. Wilson, "Clashing Views on Issues in Sex and Gender," in *Proceedings of the ICTLEP Conference* (Guilford, CT: McGraw-Hill, 2000), pp. 31–38.

A. Vitale, "Implications of Being Gender Dysphoric," *Gender & Psychoanalysis* 6, no. 2 (Spring 2001).

Appendix 2A

THE ISOSTACY MODEL OF GENDER DIVERSITY

J. Ari Kane-DeMaios, EdD

G ender has always been an important component of the human experience and has played a major role in guiding social behavior in different cultures. Its main function is to differentiate patterns of growth between males and females over the lifespan. It also creates norms for social role behaviors and allows for cultural stability over time.

When cultural change occurs, it is reflected in the role patterns of males and females. These roles give rise to a spectrum of behaviors known collectively as *gender diversity*.

In the twenty-first century, many cultural changes and behavioral shifts have occurred and with great rapidity. As a result, new tools and concepts are needed to help us understand both conventional and aconventional gender behaviors. One of the new concepts that can clarify and provide new insight about these changes is known as the *principle of dynamic equilibrium* (or *isostacy*). Applying this concept, we have developed a potentially useful schema or model for understanding and demystifying the complexities of *gender diversity*.

In our work with the transgender population, we have identified three basic gender variables. These are:

PERCEPTION (P): defined as a recognition and interpretation of sensory stimuli based chiefly on memory; a neurologic process by which recognition and interpretation are effected. (*American Heritage Dictionary of English Language*, 3rd ed., 1992).

ROLE (R): the characteristics and expected social behavior of an individual; a set of social behaviors that defines a gender form. (Ibid.)

PRESENTATION (Pr): a state of being presented; the process of offering for consideration or display. (Ibid.)

Using the *isostacy principle,* one can create a model that illustrates the relationship of these variables to each other (see the diagram below). By quantifying (where possible) these variables over specific time intervals, one can attain a realizable model of the gender (not sex) of a person. It is known as the *isostacy model for gender diversity (IMGD).*

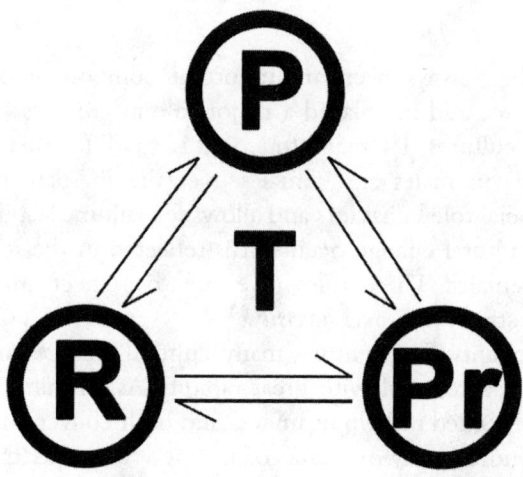

IMPORTANT NOTE: The choice of time interval (T) is an important factor in applications of the IMGD model (e.g., single years, decades, quarter century, etc.).

Below are some applications of the IMGD model:

- To study gender diversity patterns for different cultures
- To study gender diversity patterns of historic cultures (Egypt, ancient Greece, Rome, etc.)
- To study and map the gender diversity pattern of an individual over the lifespan
- To use in a variety of clinical settings for clarification and resolution of gender conflict issues

The IMGD model is a *sociological* model for understanding gender diversity. It is neither etiologic nor rigidly biologic.

This is an abstract from a presentation given at the National Meeting of the Society for the Scientific Study of Sexuality (SSSS), Montreal, Quebec, Canada, in 2002.

Appendix 2B

THE FLOWCHART FOR TRANSGENDER CATEGORIES

J. Ari Kane-DeMaios, EdD

To help the reader unfamiliar with labeling and identifying the transgender (TG) individual, the following chart is presented.

The TG phenomenon can be grouped into three broad categories.

GROUP A all relate to *gender role* behaviors that cross traditional boundaries.

GROUP B focuses principally on the *presentation of gender*, in public or in private settings.

GROUP C refers to individuals whose role behavior and presentation mode are associated with some biologic modification(s) in achieving congruence with self-image and *perception.*

CORRELATES and COMMENTARY

All categories represented by the flowchart apply to females and males.

There are always possibilities for "shifts" from one group or category to another.

For all the groups and categories, *time (T)* is an important factor.

Individual gender/sexuality choices are always interactive between the person and (her/his) primary culture.

The *isostacy model (ISGD)* can be applied to all categories on the flowchart.

This flowchart is taken from the Gender Attitude Reassessment Workbook, *page 67.*

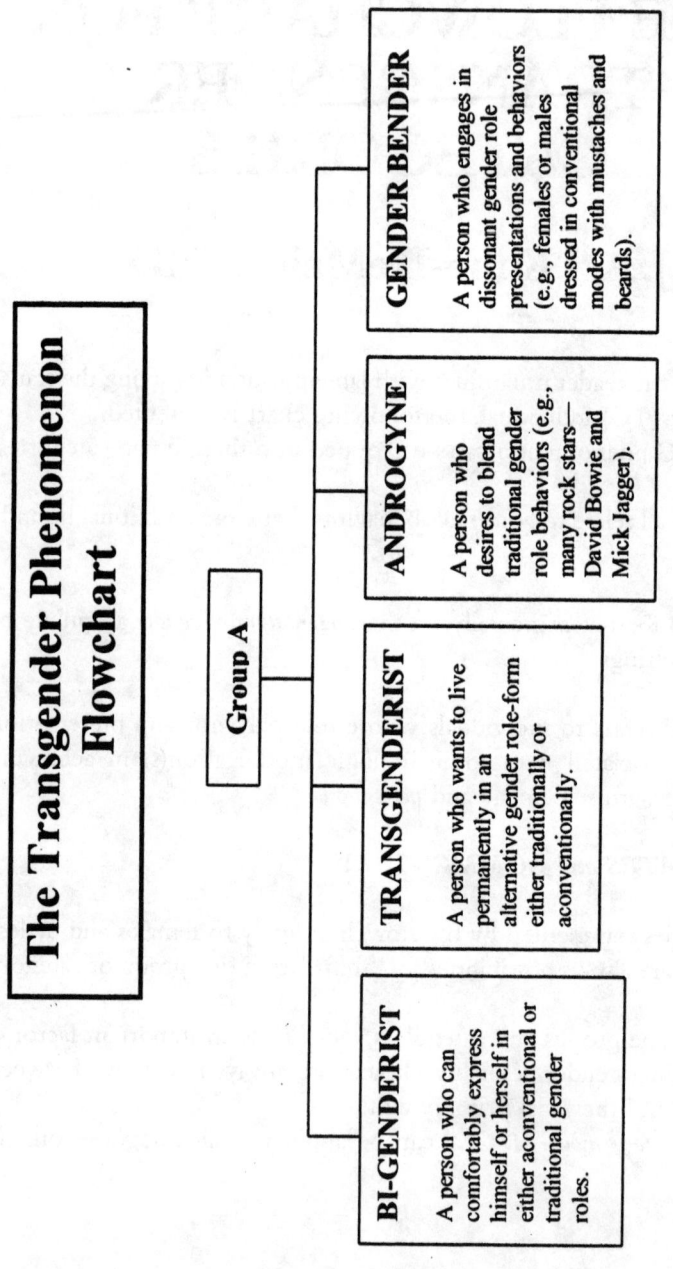

The Transgender Phenomenon Flowchart

Group A

BI-GENDERIST

A person who can comfortably express himself or herself in either aconventional or traditional gender roles.

TRANSGENDERIST

A person who wants to live permanently in an alternative gender role-form either traditionally or aconventionally.

ANDROGYNE

A person who desires to blend traditional gender role behaviors (e.g., many rock stars—David Bowie and Mick Jagger).

GENDER BENDER

A person who engages in dissonant gender role presentations and behaviors (e.g., females or males dressed in conventional modes with mustaches and beards).

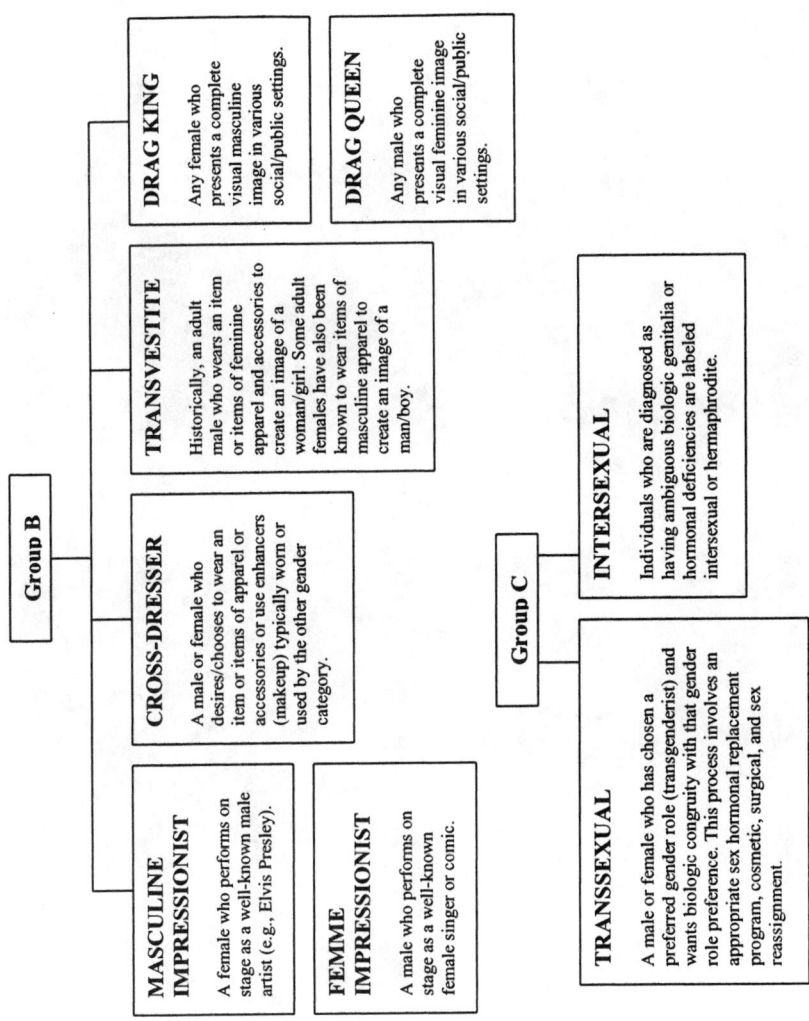

Group B

MASCULINE IMPRESSIONIST

A female who performs on stage as a well-known male artist (e.g., Elvis Presley).

FEMME IMPRESSIONIST

A male who performs on stage as a well-known female singer or comic.

CROSS-DRESSER

A male or female who desires/chooses to wear an item or items of apparel or accessories or use enhancers (makeup) typically worn or used by the other gender category.

TRANSVESTITE

Historically, an adult male who wears an item or items of feminine apparel and accessories to create an image of a woman/girl. Some adult females have also been known to wear items of masculine apparel to create an image of a man/boy.

DRAG KING

Any female who presents a complete visual masculine image in various social/public settings.

DRAG QUEEN

Any male who presents a complete visual feminine image in various social/public settings.

Group C

TRANSSEXUAL

A male or female who has chosen a preferred gender role (transgenderist) and wants biologic congruity with that gender role preference. This process involves an appropriate sex hormonal replacement program, cosmetic, surgical, and sex reassignment.

INTERSEXUAL

Individuals who are diagnosed as having ambiguous biologic genitalia or hormonal deficiencies are labeled intersexual or hermaphrodite.

Appendix 3

A SELECT LIST OF BIOGRAPHIES AND AUTOBIOGRAPHIES IN ENGLISH OF TRANSGENDERED INDIVIDUALS, PLUS SOME IMPORTANT NEW WORKS ON GENDER DIVERSITY IN 2005

Allen, J. J. *The Man in the Red Velvet Dress.* New York: Carol, 1996.

Almas, Elsa, Esben Esther, and Pirelli Benestad. *Kjonn I Bevegelse.* Universietsforlaget, 2001.

Boenke, M. *Transforming Families.* Imperial Beach, CA: Walter Trook, 1999.

Bogdan, Robert. *Being Different: The Autobiography of Jane Fry.* New York: John Wiley & Sons, 1974.

Bornstein, Kate. *Gender Outlaw.* New York: Routledge, 1994.

Boyd, Helen. *My Husband Betty.* New York: Thunder's Mouth, 2003.

Boylan, J. F. *She's Not There: A Life in Two Genders.* New York: Broadway Books, 2003.

Califia, Pat. *Sex Changes.* 2nd ed. San Francisco: Cleis, 2003.

Choisy, Abbé de. *Memoires de l'Abbé de Choisy habille en femme.* Translated into English as *The Transvestite Memoirs of the Abbé de Choisy* by R. H. F. Scott. London: Peter Owen, 1973.

County, Jayne, and Rupert Smith. *Man Enough to Be a Woman.* London: Serpent's Tail, 1995.

Cowell, Roberta. *Roberta Cowell's Story.* London: William Heinemann, 1954.

Cummings, Katherine. *Katherine's Diary.* Melbourne, Australia: William Heinemann, 1992.

Docter, Richard F. *From Man to Woman: The Transgender Journey of Virginia Prince.* Northridge, CA: Docter Press, 2004.

Everage, Dame Edna. *My Gorgeous Life.* London: MacMillan Limited, 1989.

Fitzmaurice-Kelly, James. *The Nun Ensign.* London: T. Fisher Unwin, n.d.

Green, Jamison. *Becoming a Visible Man.* Nashville, TN: Vanderbilt University Press, 2004.

Hodgkinson, Liz. *Michael, Nee Laura.* London: Columbus Books, 1989.

Hoyer, Niels. *Man into Woman.* New York: E. P. Dutton, 1933.

Hunt, Nancy. *Mirror Image*. New York: Holt, Rinehart and Winston, 1978.

Jorgensen, Christine. *Christine Jorgensen*. New York: Paul S. Eriksson, 1967.

Kando, Thomas. *Sex Change*. Springfield, IL: Charles C. Thomas, 1973.

Kates, Gary. *Monsieur d'Eon Is a Woman*. New York: Basic Books, 1995.

Lev, Arlene I. *Transgender Emergence*. New York: Hayworth Press, 2004.

Martino, Mario, with Harriett Martino. *Emergence*. New York: Crown, 1977.

McCloskey, Deirdre. *Crossing: A Memoir*. Chicago: University of Chicago Press, 1999.

Middlebrook, Diane Wood. *Suits Me*. New York: Houghton Mifflin, 1998.

Morris, Jan. *Conundrum*. New York: Harcourt Brace Jovanovich, 1974.

———. *Pleasure of a Tangled Life*. New York: Random House, 1989.

Munroe, Carolyne Jayne. *A Tale of Two Sexes*. Torquay, England: Bonden Publications, 1993.

Pepper, John. *A Man's Tale*. London: Quarter Books, 1982.

Richards, Renee, and John Ames. *Second Serve*. New York: Stein and Day, 1983.

Rodi, Robert. *Drag Queen*. New York: Dutton, 1995.

Stanford, Peter. *The Legend of Pope Joan*. New York: Henry Holt and Company, 1998.

Sullivan, Louis. *From Female to Male*. Boston: Alyson, 1990.

GLOSSARY

Androgyne. A person who blends traditional masculine and feminine gender roles, traits, and presentations (e.g., many rock stars—David Bowie, Mick Jagger).

Bi-genderist. A person who can comfortably express him/herself in either a nonconventional or a traditional gender role.

Cross-dresser (CD). A person who wears apparel usually associated with the other biologic sex, as defined by socially acceptable norms. It is descriptive of behavior. It is synonymous with the term transvestite (TV).

Drag kings and queens (DK and DQ). Individuals who cross-dress and entertain on stage. Those who perform using their own voice and natural attributes are known as impressionists.

Eonism. A term used by Havelock Ellis to describe the phenomenon of cross-dressing. It was derived from the name of an eighteenth-century French cross-dresser, the Chevalier D'Eon.

Femme impressionists. Males who perform on stage as well-known women.

Fetish. A fixation about an unusual idea or object. It has been used in a sexual context to describe an attraction to inanimate objects such as women's shoes or underclothes.

FTM or F2M. Refers to transition state from female to male.

Gender bender. A person who engages in dissonant gender role presentations and behaviors such as a male wearing a dress while also having a beard or a female wearing traditional male clothing but also wearing makeup.

Gender dysphoria. A severe discomfort characterized by a feeling of incongruity between biologic sex and gender identity assigned at birth.

Gender positives. Individuals who are positive about their gender role(s) and presentation.

Gender specialist. Refers to an active healthcare practitioner (counselor, coach, educator, or therapist) who devotes much of her/his work toward gender diversity issues.

GRS. Abbreviation for genital reconstruction surgery. It replaces the old term, SRS, or sexual reassignment surgery.

GLBT. Abbreviation for gay/lesbian/bisexual/transgender.

Hir. A pronoun used by some people who identify outside the traditional male-female spectrum, in place of his or her.

Intersexual. Individuals with medically established physical or hormonal anomalies or attributes of both male and female body types. They are also known as hermaphrodites.

LGBT. Abbreviation for lesbian/gay/bisexual/transgender.

Masculine impressionists. Females who perform on stage as well-known male artists.

Metagender. Individuals who do not identify as either male or female.

MTF or M2F. Refers to a transition state from male to female.

Queer. Individuals having a sexual/gender variant identity or who engage in unconventional sexual practices.

Sex positive. Individuals who are positive about their sex and their sexuality.

Shemales. Individuals who are biologic males and choose a feminine gender role and presentation mode. They present as sex-variant persons.

Transgender (TG). Refers to a person who identifies as a member of his or her biologic-birth sex but through use of appropriate hormones and surgery presents in the gender of the preferred alternative sex. It is also used as an umbrella term to describe the entire trans community.

Transmen/transwomen. Individuals who live in a bi-genderal mode different from their original gender role and presentation.

Transsexuals (TS). Individuals who identify as gender dysphorics and who want congruity between their preferred gender role and their biologic anatomy.

Transvestite (TV). Historically, an adult male who wears an item or items of feminine apparel and accessories to create an image of a woman/girl. Some adult females have also been known to wear items of masculine apparel.

NOTE: This glossary has been compiled to assist the reader in understanding specific terms and abbreviations. Its basis is derived from the traditional binary model of sex and gender. As such, some terms may be limiting in their application to a specific person or behavioral context.